Camille Claudel & Rodin

Fateful Encounter

Camille Claudel & Rodin

Fateful Encounter

musée
ministère de la Culture
RODIN

HAZAN

Musée
national des beaux-arts
du Québec
Québec

This catalogue is published in conjunction with the exhibition *Camille Claudel and Rodin: Fateful Encounter* organized by the Musée national des beaux-arts du Québec and the Musée Rodin, Paris, in collaboration with the Detroit Institute of Arts and the Fondation Pierre Gianadda in Martigny.

Musée national des beaux-arts du Québec, Quebec. May 26–September 11, 2005
Detroit Institute of Arts, Detroit. October 2, 2005–February 5, 2006
Fondation Pierre Gianadda, Martigny. March 3, 2006–June 15, 2006

MUSÉE NATIONAL DES BEAUX-ARTS DU QUÉBEC
John R. Porter, General Director
Yves Lacasse, Director of Collections and Research
Line Ouellet, Director of Exhibitions and Education
Marc Delaunay, Director of Administration and Communications

MUSÉE RODIN
Jacques Vilain. Director
Antoinette Le Normand-Romain, General Curator

DETROIT INSTITUTE OF ARTS
Graham W. J. Beal, Director
Alan Phipps Darr, Walter B. Ford II Family Curator of European Sculpture & Decorative Arts

FONDATION PIERRE GIANADDA
Léonard Gianadda, President

CURATORS
Yves Lacasse, Director of Collections and Research,
Musée national des beaux-arts du Québec, Quebec
Antoinette Le Normand-Romain, Curator of Sculpture,
Musée Rodin, Paris

PROJECT DIRECTOR
Line Ouellet, Director of Exhibitions and Education,
Musée national des beaux-arts du Québec, Quebec

PROJECT COORDINATION
Claire Desmeules, Exhibitions Coordinator,
Musée national des beaux-arts du Québec, Quebec

EXHIBITION DESIGN, QUEBEC
Denis Allison, Head Designer,
Musée national des beaux-arts du Québec, Quebec

ÉDITIONS HAZAN
Designed by Sylvie Milliet
Front cover designed by Jean-Marc Barrier
Edited by Bernard Wooding
Copy-edited by Jane Jackel and Louise Gauthier
Production management by Claire Hostalier

TRANSLATION BY DAVID WHARRY

COVER: Camille Claudel, *Vertumnus and Pomona* (cat. 93)

© 2005 Hazan / Musée national des beaux-arts du Québec / Musée Rodin
© ADAGP (Paris 2005)

ISBN (Hazan / Musée national des beaux-arts du Québec / Musée Rodin)
English hardback version: 2 85025 999 3
English paperback version: 2 7541 0001 6
Dépôt légal: July 2005

Photoengraving by Lithoart, Turin, Italy
Printed in Italy by Graphicom, Vicenza

AUTHORS
ODILE AYRAL-CLAUSE
Author of the biography *Camille Claudel: A Life* (2002)
CATHERINE CHEVILLOT
Head of Research, Documentation and Library Services,
Musée d'Orsay, Paris
BRUNO GAUDICHON
Chief Curator, La Piscine – Musée d'Art et d'Industrie
André-Diligent, Roubaix
VÉRONIQUE GAUTHERIN
Formerly Assistant Curator, Musée Bourdelle, Paris
YVES LACASSE
Director of Collections and Research,
Musée national des beaux-arts du Québec, Quebec
Co-curator of the exhibition
ANTONETTE LE NORMAND-ROMAIN
Curator of Sculpture, Musée Rodin, Paris
Co-curator of the exhibition
LAURE DE MARGERIE
Researcher, Musée d'Orsay, Paris
RAPHAËL MASSON
Curator of the Archives and Library Services, Musée Rodin, Paris
MARIE-VICTOIRE NANTET
Lecturer, Reims University, comparatist,
editor of the *Bulletin de la Société Paul Claudel*
JEAN-MICHEL NECTOUX
Scientific advisor, Institut National d'Histoire de l'Art, Paris
LINE OUELLET
Director of Exhibitions and Education,
Musée national des beaux-arts du Québec, Quebec
Project Director
JOHN R. PORTER
Executive Director,
Musée national des beaux-arts du Québec, Quebec
Initiator of the exhibition
ANNE RIVIÈRE
Art Historian
JACQUES VILAIN
Director, Musée Rodin, Paris

ABBREVIATIONS
AMB Archives du Musée Bourdelle, Paris
AMR Archives du Musée Rodin, Paris
ANF Archives Nationales de France, Paris
BLJD Bibliothèque Littéraire Jacques-Doucet, Paris
BMD Bibliothèque Marguerite-Durand, Paris
BNF Bibliothèque Nationale de France, Paris
HSL Handwritten signed letter
SMAF Société des Manuscrits des Assureurs Français, Paris

LENDERS

CANADA
Montreal, Montreal Museum of Fine Arts
Quebec, Musée national des beaux-arts du Québec

UNITED STATES
Boston, Museum of Fine Arts
Chicago, The Art Institute of Chicago
Detroit, The Detroit Institute of Arts
Norfolk, The Chrysler Museum of Art
Philadelphia, Philadelphia Museum of Art
Philadelphia, Rodin Museum

FRANCE
Abbeville, Musée Boucher-de-Perthes
Avignon, Musée Calvet
Bar-le-Duc, Musée Barrois
Beaufort-en-Vallée, Musée Joseph-Denais
Calais, Musée des Beaux-Arts et de la Dentelle
Cambrai, Musée des Beaux-Arts
Château-Gontier, Musée du Pays de Château-Gontier
Château-Thierry, Musée Jean-de-La Fontaine
Châteauroux, Musée Bertrand
Clermont-Ferrand, Musée d'Art Roger-Quilliot
Dijon, Musée des Beaux-Arts
Honfleur, Musée Eugène-Boudin
Lille, Palais des Beaux-Arts
Martigues, Musée Ziem
Montauban, Musée Ingres
Nogent-sur-Seine, Musée Paul-Dubois – Alfred-Boucher
Orléans, Musée des Beaux-Arts
Parçay-les-Pins, Musée Jules-Desbois
Paris, Archives Nationales de France
Paris, Assurances Générales de France
Paris, Bibliothèque Marguerite-Durand
Paris, Bibliothèque Nationale de France
Paris, Musée Bourdelle
Paris, Musée d'Orsay
Paris, Musée du Petit-Palais
Paris, Musée Rodin
Paris, Société des Manuscrits des Assureurs Français
Paris, Société Paul Claudel
Poitiers, Musée Sainte-Croix
Reims, Musée des Beaux-Arts
Roubaix, La Piscine – Musée d'Art et d'Industrie André-Diligent

NORWAY
Oslo, Galleri Kaare Berntsen

SWITZERLAND
Martigny, Fondation Pierre Gianadda

PRIVATE COLLECTIONS
Paris, Alain Beausire
Paris, Jean-Michel Nectoux
And all those who have wished to remain anonymous

ACKNOWLEDGMENTS
Camille Claudel and Rodin: Fateful Encounter, the culmination of
a project first discussed in 2001, has benefited from the generous
support of numerous colleagues. We would like to express our
heartfelt gratitude to all who have helped us prepare this
exhibition and the accompanying catalogue:

Denis Allison, Isabelle Arizzoli, Mireille Arsenault, Odile Ayral-
Clause, Anne-Marie Barrère, Bernard Barryte, Philippe Bata,
Charlotte Beare, Alain Beausire, Geneviève Becquart, Michel
Bélanger, Ioana Beldiman, Claude Belleau, Anne-Marie Bergeret,
Mauricette Berne, Claude Bilodeau, Isabelle Bissière, Didier Blin,
Marie-Claude Boisly, Nathalie Bondil, Violaine Bonzon Claudel,
Marie Bouchard, Bruce Boucher, Gilbert Boucher, Dominique
Brisset, Christina Buley-Uribe, Véronique Burnod, Ruth Butler,
Marietta Cambareri, Agnes Cascio, Rémy Charest, Muriel Chatelais,
Blandine Chavanne, Catherine Chevillot, Henri Claudel,
Marie Claudel, Philippe Cressent, Alan Phipps Darr,
Dominique De Coninck, Marie-Pierre Delclaux, Pantxika
De Paepe, Claire Desmeules, Lise Drolet, Louise Dubois,
Roland Dumas, Marie-Josèphe Dunaway, Sir Robert and Lady
Vivian Eborne, Sylvester Engbrox, Gérard Fabre, Régis Fabre,
Christiane Faucher, Amy Foley, Nadine Gastaldi, Bruno
Gaudichon, Véronique Gautherin, Sophie Gauthier, Louis
Gauvin, Brittany Gersh, Léonard Gianadda, Agnès Granoux,
Catherine Gras, Florence Harnay, Jefferson C. Harrison,
Emmanuelle Héran, Hugues Herpin, Patricia Hoeppe, Louise
Jobin, Ina Johannesen, Nancy Jones, Claudie Judin, Pascal
Kowal, Juliette Laffon, Sophie Lafortune, Pierre Landry, Rosine
Lapresle-Tavera, Monique Le Pelley Fonteny, Eli Lesser, Juliette
Levy, Emmanuel Lhermitte, David Liot, Iva Lisikewycz, Michèle
Maier Claudel, Count and Countess Christian and Albane
de Maigret, Count and Countess Yves de Maigret, Jérôme
Manoukian, Laure de Margerie, Linda Margolin, Hélène Marraud,
Guylaine Mary, François de Massary, Raphaël Masson, Véronique
Mattiussi, Annie Metz, Marie-Hélène Moitier, Jérôme Montchal,
Michel Nadeau, Marie-Victoire Nantet, Renée Nantet Claudel,
Michèle Naturel, Jean-Michel Nectoux, Lire Ouellet, Christine
Parent, Reine-Marie Paris, Catherine Ferron, Jacques Piette,
Hélène Pinet, Anne Pingeot, Donald Pistolesi, John R. Porter,
Pierre Provoyeur, Chantal Quirot, Maryse Redien, Syân Reynolds,
Joseph J. Rishel, Anne Rivière, Philippe Romain, Anne Schaefer,
the late Mr. and Mrs. Gilbert Schil, Annie Scottez-De
Wambrechies, Jean-Michel Seguin, Amélie Simier, Christiane
Sinnig-Haas, Phyllis Smith, André Sylvain, Vincent Teissier,
Roxana Theodorescu, François Thomazeau, Diane Tytgat,
Anne-Isabelle Vannier, Florence Viguier, Jacques Vilain,
Sophie Weygand, Eric Wronko, John Zarobell

Y. L.
A. L.N.-R.

CONTENTS

PREFACE

The major Camille Claudel retrospective inaugurated in 1984 at the Musée Rodin in Paris, and subsequently shown at the Musée Sainte-Croix in Poitiers, was a revelation for the French public. Soon after, the artist's life and work were being enthusiastically discovered in Europe, Asia and North America. In literature, film, theater, dance and music there was the same fascination with Camille and her tragic destiny. And of course her story was distorted by the media, with, more often than not, Rodin coming out the worse in these Manichaean interpretations, with Camille cast in the role of the poor woman unjustly exploited by an unscrupulous boor.

With the benefit of a certain distance vis-à-vis the Claudel/Rodin "case," the time is right to take a more nuanced and more objective look at the art of Camille Claudel, to examine her critical fortunes and, above all, shed new light on the personal and professional bonds that marked both her and Rodin's destiny. Following on from the research by Reine-Marie Paris, Anne Rivière and Bruno Gaudichon and, more recently, Antoinette Le Normand-Romain, *Camille Claudel and Rodin: Fateful Encounter* has exceptionally brought together all of Camille Claudel's important works, including the most fragile. Not since the exhibition in 1988 at the National Museum of Women in the Arts in Washington has there been such a dazzling exhibition of Camille's works in North America. These works are being displayed alongside several masterpieces by Rodin, thereby enabling their objective and exhaustive study in context.

Camille Claudel and Rodin: Fateful Encounter is firstly the fruit of the friendship, generous complicity and passionate commitment of our two museums devoted to late-nineteenth- and early-twentieth-century French sculpture. In the wake of the major *Rodin in Quebec* exhibition, which in the summer of 1998 attracted over half a million visitors to Quebec City, the project for this exhibition first saw the light of day in autumn 2001, at a lunch during which we quickly agreed on the initial idea for a major Camille Claudel exhibition in Quebec. This was later developed and enriched into a comparative exhibition examining the mutual influences of Camille and Rodin, with the help of two remarkable curators, Antoinette Le Normand-Romain, General Curator at the Musée Rodin, and Yves Lacasse, Director of Collections and Research at the Musée national des beaux-arts du Québec. They threw themselves heart and soul into the task of putting together an exhibition and catalogue that would meet the expectations of both the general public and specialists.

Over the ensuing months and years, the two curators rallied some fifteen specialists to their cause and convinced some fifty institutions and private collectors to give the aid essential to a museum event of this magnitude. At its three venues—Quebec (Canada), Detroit (U S.A.) and Martigny (Switzerland)—the exhibition brings together one hundred and seventy-seven works and eighty-five archive documents, half from the Musée Rodin and the other half from fifty-three collectors in France, the United States, Switzerland, Great Britain, Norway and Canada. We would like to express our heartfelt thanks to all these lenders, especially as they have often consented, whether private collectors or institutions, to part with their works for the full duration of this traveling exhibition.

Among the many archive documents is the extremely moving letter Rodin wrote to Octave Mirbeau in 1895, in which the great sculptor discusses the talent of his protégée Camille Claudel and the constant support he was trying to give her work. Offered to the Musée Rodin by the Musée national des beaux-arts du Québec, this exceptional testimony to the two artists' relationship is a symbol of the unique bond between our two institutions.

In order to increase the influence and scope of *Camille Claudel and Rodin: Fateful Encounter*, successive agreements were made with the Detroit Institute of Arts and the Fondation Pierre Gianadda in Martigny, enabling the integration of complementary pieces to the American and Swiss venues. In this respect, we would particularly like to thank our colleagues Graham W. J. Beal and Alan P. Darr in Detroit, and our old friend Léonard Gianadda in Martigny.

The work done by all is echoed in this catalogue, which is published in French and English. More than an update, this book has been treated as a unique opportunity to overhaul the body of knowledge concerning the art of Camille and Rodin, by shedding precise and nuanced light on the complex dynamics of their personal and professional relations, as the exhibition's subtitle clearly states.

Without wishing to duplicate the content of this book, it is worthwhile trying to put it in context, at least from the perspective of their critical fortunes. Camille was committed to an asylum in 1913, and sank into oblivion at the very time Rodin was at the height of his glory, a glory that would continue unabated after his death in 1917, fueled notably by the opening of his museum in rue de Varenne in 1919. In 1951, the Musée Rodin, at the instigation of its curator Cécile Goldscheider, organized the first solo exhibition devoted to Camille, who died in 1943 aged seventy-eight. In his admirable preface to the 1951 catalogue, Paul Claudel glorifies the memory of his sister with "magnificent eyes, of that dark blue so rarely found elsewhere than in novels," in phrases only a poet could write. In many respects, this text and his gift of four of his sister's sculptures were a means for him of appeasing the demons of family guilt.

More recently, after the sometimes erratic turbulence of the years of rediscovery, the time had come for a reexamination with a new exhibition which, for the second time, following the exhibition at the Kunstmuseum in Berne in 1985, would bring together as exhaustively as possible the works by Camille Claudel and Rodin that bear witness to their intermingling destinies. An entirely new light has been shed by these works and, more specifically, the interrelationships of certain closely linked pieces. One of course immediately notices that Rodin was a towering sculptor, whose prolific output— over a thousand sculptures—contrasts strikingly with Camille's ninety or so pieces. The latter's ultimately rather small legacy cannot be entirely attributed to her deliberate destruction of her work during the years preceding her incarceration. Setting aside the imbalance between their oeuvres and their differing ambitions, notably regarding format, it becomes clear that Camille

Claudel was a peerless artist at a time when the status of the woman sculptor was far from attained. Her works using marble-onyx, *Les Causeuses* and *The Wave*, are high points of the Art Nouveau style which, when they were created, had spread throughout Europe. Profoundly original and unique, they could never be classified as mere multiples.

Camille Claudel and Rodin: Fateful Encounter is in fact a fine opportunity to do justice to two artists while avoiding the gross distortions whereby Rodin has to be diminished to the benefit of Camille. As an example, one should recall Louis Vauxcelles's beautiful comparison in his preface to the catalogue of the first exhibition of Camille Claudel's works at the Galerie Eugène Blot in 1905, where he notes that Camille Claudel was to Rodin what Berthe Morisot was to Manet.

This exhibition and the accompanying catalogue also have the merit of bringing out the complexity of the relationship between Camille and Rodin, between pupil and teacher and between lovers. They clarify and enrich the corpus of knowledge, correcting here and adding there so that the works presented can be interpreted with the fullest knowledge of their context. Both the exhibition and this publication are peopled by an impressive gallery of figures, including, of course, the great writer and diplomat Paul Claudel, for whom 2005 is the fiftieth anniversary of his death. It is a great pleasure to see the three busts Camille sculpted of him reunited again, along with his *Journal* and some of his letters to the artist, and of course his famous article published in *L'Art décoratif* in 1913, the year his sister was committed.

We would like to express our gratitude to the Claudel family for their generous support. Whether via the intermediaries of the Société Paul Claudel, the Association Camille Claudel and the Association Camille et Paul Claudel en Tardenois, or privately, Claudel's descendants—Mesdames Rénée Nantet Claudel, Violaine Bonzon Claudel, Marie Claudel, Michèle Maier Claudel, Marie-Victoire Nantet, Reine-Marie Paris and Messrs. Henri Claudel and François de Massary—gave us their unwavering support.

The two co-curators, Antoinette Le Normand-Romain and Yves Lacasse, united by the friendship they struck up during the preparation of the *Rodin in Quebec* exhibition in 1998, worked closely together to define the concept of the exhibition and the catalogue, the choice of works, the negotiation of loans, the choice of authors, and the scientific validation of the texts in the catalogue and of the educational material and exhibition design. They were aided in this work by Line Ouellet, Director of Exhibitions and Education at the Musée national des beaux-arts du Québec, who supervised the entire project. She also insisted on giving it a genuinely international dimension, on the one hand by organizing the exhibition's traveling to two other venues, and on the other, by securing the collaboration of Éditions Hazan and the museums to make this catalogue an accessible and widely distributed work, both in Europe and North America.

This catalogue contains essays by fourteen authors. They draw on the fruits of an ambitious research effort whose daily coordination was carried out with efficiency and dedication by Claire Desmeules at the Musée national des beaux-arts du Québec. Véronique Mattiussi went over the documents in the Musée Rodin with a fine-tooth comb. In parallel, Jean-François Barrielle and his colleagues Pierre-Emmanuel Halimi and Anne-Isabelle Vannier at Éditions Hazan have worked wonders.

In Quebec, *Camille Claudel and Rodin: Fateful Encounter* has benefited from a superb exhibition design by the museum's head designer, Denis Allison, which focuses first and foremost on the enhancement of the works and documents on display. The Quebec exhibition benefited from the support of the Quebec Ministry of Culture and Communications, the National Bank of Canada, the Bureau de la Capitale-Nationale, the Office du Tourisme et des Congrès de Québec and the French Consulate General in Quebec.

In a broader context, we would like to pay tribute to the enthusiastic help of all the staff of both institutions. The staff of the Musée Rodin in Paris spared no effort to ensure that this major exhibition, which will not be presented at the Hôtel Biron, is a complete success, in keeping with the friendship between the two organizing institutions. At the Musée national des beaux-arts du Québec, the entire staff has at one moment or another over the last two years been involved, either in the General Office, in the Exhibitions and Education Department, in the curatorial and research departments, or in the administration and communications departments. Our warmest thanks to all.

The combined efforts of various people and the unconditional support of others have ensured that this meeting of two destinies, of two geniuses of French sculpture, will be a memorable success. This is a unique opportunity to celebrate both the greatness of Camille Claudel and her often tragic destiny, irrespective of the actual course of her life and the level of recognition she enjoyed both during her lifetime and after her death. Both the visitor and the reader can measure the weight of different times and of Time itself beyond the singularity of the artists' individual careers. The recognition of genius goes above and beyond the ephemera of every-day life. Discussing Camille Claudel's and Rodin's destinies, the generous Eugène Blot was undoubtedly being prophetic when he wrote this famous phrase in 1932: "Time will put everything in place."

We are delighted that this meeting of two museums, with the exceptional exchanges that have taken place on both sides of the Atlantic, has given us a fresh opportunity to develop the priceless friendship enjoyed by both institutions over the last ten years—a friendship extended this time, to our excellent colleagues in Detroit and Marigny.

JOHN R. PORTER
General Director of the Musée national
des beaux-arts du Québec, Quebec

JACQUES VILAIN
Director of the Musée Rodin, Paris

INTRODUCTION

This catalogue and the accompanying exhibition follow the mingling paths of two sculptors, Auguste Rodin (1840–1917) and Camille Claudel (1864–1943), focusing on the works that bear witness to their artistic and personal relations. It is therefore a genuine comparative exhibition of the work of both artists, comprising sixty-one works by Rodin and seventy-three works by Camille Claudel. It focuses in particular on the relationship between the two artists, spanning a period lasting from the early 1880s until the late 1890s. This period is divided into two sections, "Happy Times (1882–1892)" and "Stormy Times (1892–1899)." The artists are also presented "Before the Encounter," when Camille was still training and Rodin was already at the height of his powers and on the brink of success. Counterbalancing this first section, which naturally focuses on Rodin's genius, is an entire section devoted to "The Freeing of Camille Claudel (1895–1905)." The conclusion, "He Never Loved Anyone but You," analyzes Camille Claudel's last works in relation to similar works of Rodin's and outlines Rodin's glorious late career and Camille's exile and descent into oblivion.

The catalogue includes a series of complementary studies enabling one to better situate Camille Claudel in her time: Camille Claudel's relationship with Claude Debussy, Camille Claudel and the women sculptors of the period, and finally, an investigation of the notion of "genius" frequently used in the nineteenth century and particularly with regard to Camille Claudel.

To compare the work of Rodin and Camille Claudel is a daunting undertaking. Rodin, whose career spanned almost sixty years (1860–1917), produced an enormous body of work, while Camille Claudel produced very few pieces over a relatively short period (1880–1907). Rodin systematically kept all his works, which enabled him to donate the extraordinary collection of works and archives that would become the Musée Rodin. Camille Claudel, on the other hand, destroyed most of the works in her studio in the last years of her life. Furthermore, her exile and oblivion had a disastrous effect on her artistic heritage, which was scattered among members of her family and in several provincial museums. The two catalogues raisonnés of her work (Reine-Marie Paris, 2000; Anne Rivière, Bruno Gaudichon and Danielle Ghanassia, 2001), the publication of her correspondence (Anne Rivière, Bruno Gaudichon, 2003), a detailed biography (Odile Ayral-Clause, 2002) and the in-depth research carried out by the Musée Rodin, which possesses a large portion of Camille Claudel's work, have enabled a fuller picture of this artist's tormented work, career and life. As a result, the pieces selected for this comparative exhibition cover almost all of Camille Claudel's oeuvre, and include her masterpieces, notably *Sakuntala*, *The Waltz*, *The Age of Maturity*, and *The Wave*. For Rodin, the works selected—*Saint John the Baptist*, pieces relating to *The Gates of Hell*, *Pierre de Wissant*, *Balzac*, and *Thought*—although representing high points in his career, are only a very small portion of his production.

The works—their formal analysis, the context of their creation and their critical reception—have been at the heart of the research undertaken, and have inevitably drawn on the relevant archival sources (correspondence, notebooks, photographs, invoices) and primary sources from the artists' lifetimes (articles, exhibition catalogues, books). A large part of the exhibition and catalogue is devoted to these documents. notably the correspondence between Camille Claudel and Rodin (ten letters), Paul Claudel's journal, Camille Claudel's album of confessions, her "contract" with Rodin, the famous photograph of Camille taken by Carjat, some of the correspondence with the state, which gives an idea of the complexity of a public sculpture commission, the review *L'Art*, which supported Camille, and the discussions with Rodin published by Paul Gsell in 1911. These documents give us an intimate but fragmented daily portrait not just of relations between the two artists, but also of the life of a sculptor in the nineteenth century: the costs of materials, models and marble carvers, access to the Salons, the power of the critics and the vagaries of public and private commissions.

The approach adopted for this exhibition is above all based on the research tools of art history. It deliberately avoids a psychoanalytical dimension that would emphasize family background, or even a feminist angle that would focus primarily on the condition of the female artist at that time. From the outset Camille Claudel had to fight for a foothold in the man's world of sculpture, and would continue to do so uncompromisingly throughout her career.

As in all research in sculpture, the question of bronze editions was central, and we have deliberately sought, for Camille Claudel in particular, to compare various versions of her works (*The Waltz*, for example), thereby showing that the work of a sculptor continues with the edition itself, with variations, modified dimensions and different patinas. Hence the importance given to the selection of pieces produced during the artist's lifetime and more particularly, under her supervision before she was committed to an asylum.

Running through this book, which focuses essentially on the intermingling of the work of Camille and Rodin, is the bliss and then gradually the tragedy for both Camille and Rodin of their intimate artistic and romantic relationship. Rodin's refusal to marry Camille, depriving her of the social status that went with marriage, and the importance of her artistic emancipation from the burden of her teacher's influence, combined with her deteriorating mental health, paved the way for her tragic predicament, leading eventually to the asylum. For Rodin, it represented the painful loss of someone he loved passionately, of someone who, for the first time, he felt understood him completely, the lover and the artist in him finding their echo in the same sublime female genius. We have for the most part chosen works that tell the story of two artists resolutely searching for their respective, unique and uncompromising paths. If Rodin succeeded, through the raw power of such works as *Balzac*, in opening up the way to modern sculpture, Camille, with such pieces as *The Wave*, was also one of modernism's precursors, but in a more decorative vein.

An analytical comparison of the works lies at the heart of this catalogue, and to this end we have tried to track down studies, plasters and a variety of editions in an attempt to compare compositions by both artists. Examples include *Young Girl with a Sheaf* (Claudel, c.1886) and *Galatea* (Rodin, c.1887–88), *The Eternal Idol* (Rodin, before 1891) and *Sakuntala* (Claudel, 1888), *She Who Was Once the Helmet-Maker's Beautiful Wife* (Rodin, 1889) and *Clotho* (Claudel, 1893), *The Psalm* (Claudel, 1889) and *Thought* (Rodin, 1895). These works show the profound influence the artists exerted on one another, their constant experimentation along similar lines and even—as with *Inner Voice* and *Meditation*, large model (Rodin, 1896) and *Wounded Niobid* (Claudel, 1906)—of the parting of their ways. This focus on the works has also permitted the compilation of a list of works in the catalogue in the light of new information. Attribution, dating and provenance have all been reassessed, leading to advances in research. For example, Camille Claudel's drawing *The Old Lady of the Pont Notre-Dame* (c.1885) and a letter from Camille Claudel to Madame Léon Lhermitte (1891) are being exhibited and published for the first time.

Several specialists have contributed to this catalogue, notably Antoinette Le Normand-Romain, author of the most recent publication on Camille Claudel and Rodin (*Camille Claudel & Rodin: Time Will Heal Everything*, Musée Rodin, 2003), who not only co-curated the exhibition but also wrote nine of the catalogue's twenty-two texts. Her deep knowledge of the vast corpus in the Musée Rodin, which includes works by both Rodin and Camille Claudel, as well as yielding highly enlightening analyses, has also set the tone for the entire catalogue, which weaves the life and work of both artists with the same thread. We have also benefited from the invaluable collaboration of Bruno Gaudichon and Anne Rivière, co-authors of a catalogue raisonné of Camille Claudel's oeuvre, and Odile Ayral-Clause, author of a major biography of Camille Claudel (*Camille Claudel: A Life*, Harry N. Abrams, 2002). The Musée Rodin and the Musée national des beaux-arts du Québec have also contributed their respective directors, Jacques Vilain and John R. Porter, and members of their scientific staff: at the Musée Rodin, Antoinette Le Normand-Romain, mentioned above, and Raphaël Masson; and at the Musée national des beaux-arts du Québec, Yves Lacasse, co-curator of the exhibition, and myself. Also in the team of authors are Catherine Chevillot and Laure de Margerie, both specialists in nineteenth-century sculpture, Véronique Gautherin, a specialist in the work of Bourdelle, Marie-Victoire Nantet, editor of the *Bulletin de la Société Paul Claudel*, and Jean-Michel Nectoux, author of a soon-to-be-published biography of Debussy.

In all, fourteen authors have examined various aspects of the two artists' works and relations. The aim has been to paint a more accurate portrait of the complex trajectories, full of stops and starts, fusion and rejection, experimentation and passion, of two artists totally dedicated to their art.

LINE OUELLET
Director of Exhibitions and Education
Musée national des beaux-arts du Québec

ANONYMOUS
*Paul Claudel with
the bust of Camille
by Auguste Rodin*
1951
Photograph
Private collection

I

CATALOGUE

I

BEFORE THE ENCOUNTER

CAMILLE CLAUDEL: THE EARLY WORKS Yves Lacasse

CHILDHOOD IN THE TARDENOIS

"Laughter, whining and sniveling, never-ending stories whose details get all muddled up with one another! it's so boring being surrounded by all this, I'd give 100,000 francs if I had them to get out of here straightaway. I don't belong here in the midst of all this, I must be removed from this environment: after fourteen years now of such a life I am crying out for freedom. My dream would be to go straight back to Villeneuve and never leave . . . how happy I would be to be back at Villeneuve! Beautiful Villeneuve ike nowhere else on earth!"[1]

Writing to her famous brother, the author and diplomat Paul Claudel, in 1927, Camille Claudel, confined in the Montdevergues asylum since 1914, expresses her longing to return to where they spent their vacations as children. This unique reference by Camille to her childhood and early years spent in the Tardenois does not accord with Paul's more somber verdict on this region on the borders of Picardy, Champagne and the Île-de-France, to which he too

remained greatly attached. Writing late in life, he described it as "an extremely austere land, a land of continual winds, where it rains far more often . . . than in any other region of France." For this fervent Christian, there was "nothing severer, bitterer and also more religious . . . in the strictest sense of the word, than the village of Villeneuve-sur-Fère."[2]

Thanks to the comfortable family situation of their mother, Louise-Athénaïse Cerveaux, the Claudel family spent every summer at Villeneuve-sur-Fère in the 1870s and 1880s. Camille Claudel was born five miles away, on December 8, 1864, in the county town of Fère. Her father, Louis-Prosper, had been appointed receiver of registry fees and stamp duties at Fère in 1860, and it was here, in an as yet unidentified house, that Louise was born in February 1866. Paul, the youngest, was born at Villeneuve in August 1868,[3] two years before the family moved to Bar-le-Duc, where the earliest known photograph of Camille Claudel was taken: around six years old, holding a doll, she is standing to the left of her father, who has his hand affectionately on Louise's shoulder and Paul sitting comfortably on his knees (fig. 1).

Yet Paul would later refute this idyllic image (from which the mother is curiously absent), recalling that "everybody in the family quarreled: my father and mother, and the children with their parents and among themselves." Added to this, the Claudels were "a very unusual and withdrawn family, living largely among themselves, with a kind of fierce, cantankerous pride." They behaved like "a small clan" that considered itself "immensely superior to everyone else."[4] It was against this backdrop that Camille Claudel's to say the least singular character developed. A very headstrong girl, she seems to have shown an interest in sculpture at a remarkably early age. The journalist Mathias Morhardt, who in 1898 pub-

lished the most important monograph on the artist during her lifetime and who saw her frequently in the 1880s and 1890s, must certainly have been told by Camille herself that "from her childhood," sculpture was "an all-devouring passion, one which she despotically imposed on family, neighbors and servants alike."[5] Nor did Paul ever forget, despite he and his sister's enduring affection for one another, "the often cruel ascendancy she exercised over his young years."[6]

THE EARLY WORKS AND THE MEETING WITH ALFRED BOUCHER

As Morhardt notes, "It would be invaluable for anyone intending to study the young artist's character and oeuvre from the works themselves, to see the clay studies she modeled as a young girl and which depicted the illustrious or cruel figures who peopled her childhood dreams, Napoleon I and Bismarck, for example." Having deplored that the "initial evidence" of the young Camille Claudel's "prodigious imaginative power" should have "crumbled to dust," the journalist points out that there in fact remains only "a single fragment of this so recent past": a "sketch" of *David and Goliath* which the artist "modeled in her twelfth or thirteenth year."[7] The Claudels had then only recently moved to Nogent-sur-Seine, around sixty miles from Paris, where Louis-Prosper Claudel had been appointed registrar of mortgages and where the family lived from the autumn of 1876 until the autumn of 1879.

Although the young Camille's clay *David and Goliath* had already "suffered the effects of time" when Morhardt examined it, in his view the "small biblical group" nonetheless had an "incontestably noble allure." Goliath having "become an uncertain mass" except for the "right leg . . . whose movement and modeling are indicated with surprising energy," Morhardt focuses instead on the young David, with his "knotted and robust" muscles "triumphing in a superb surge of enthusiasm and victory."[8] To emphasize the precociousness of Camille Claudel's talent, he takes pains to insist that this study, which "from the point of view of movement as well as the modeling" reveals an "indomitable passion," was executed at a time when the artist "had not yet had a single lesson either in drawing or modeling," and had "no notions of anatomy other than those she had got from *écorchés* and a few engravings in old books."[9]

While they lived at Nogent-sur-Seine, the three Claudel children were fortunate to benefit from "the teaching of an excellent schoolmaster" by the name of Colin. According to Paul Claudel, "He had good methods, took a special interest in us and found a way of making schoolwork interesting."[10] It was also at Nogent-sur-Seine that, according to Mathias Morhardt, "the sculptor Alfred Boucher occasionally visited the young artist's studio. Interested by the studies that the fervent young girl fashioned so intrepidly, he gave her the first advice she received."[11] Born in 1850 in Bouy-sur-Orvin, a village near Nogent-sur-Seine, where his family moved nine years later, Boucher owed his career to the encouragement and teaching of another sculptor from Nogent, Paul Dubois, twenty years his senior. It was therefore hardly surprising that Boucher, just as

Fig. 1
CH. BOQUET
*Louis-Prosper Claudel
with his children at
Bar-le-Duc: Louise (left),
Paul (on his knees)
and Camille (right),
aged around six*
Photograph, about 1870
Private collection

his Parisian career was beginning, in turn took an interest in the future of the debutant Camille, who was at the very most fifteen years old (fig. 2).[12]

In September 1879, Camille, driven by her all-consuming passion for sculpture, moved with her family from Nogent-sur-Seine to Wassy-sur-Blaise, where her father had just been posted. The Claudels' maid, Eugénie Plé, reminiscing fifty years later, recalls the "imperious Camille dragging her entire entourage over to the Butte du Buisson Rouge to bring back clay for her."[13] And so things continued until, as Paul recalls, "My sister, considering her vocation was to be a great artist . . . succeeded in dragging the whole family to Paris. She wanted to be a sculptress, while I, apparently, was destined to become a writer and my sister a musician . . . To cut a long story short, the family was split in two: my father stayed at Vassy and we moved to Paris, to boulevard Montparnasse."[14] Eugénie Plé's account differs substantially on this point from Paul Claudel's, who described this decision, in his view solely the result of Camille's "terrible will," as a veritable "cataclysm." However, although in 1931 the Claudels' former servant remembered distinctly "Alfred

Boucher advising Camille . . . to go to the capital," it was nevertheless "above all for Monsieur Paul's studies" that Madame Claudel and her three children moved to Paris in spring 1881,[15] while the father stayed on at Wassy to support them. Louis-Prosper, promoted in 1883 to a post in Rambouillet, then in 1887 to Compiègne, where he finished his career in 1893, only saw his family during this period at weekends and on their annual vacation.[16]

THE MOVE TO PARIS

Camille had just turned sixteen when her family moved into 135 bis boulevard Montparnasse. Mathias Morhardt perfectly understood the importance of this event for the young artist: "Paris! A dream at last come true! The freedom to work! The possibility of learning a craft, of working from the model, of posing the model, of being the artist one has to be without having to worry about neighbors peering over the garden wall!"[17] César's famous photograph shows a resplendent Camille who, her brother informs us, "had just arrived in Paris from Wassy-sur-Blaise and was attending lessons at the Atelier Colarossi" (cat. 23 A, p. 18).[18]

The Académie Colarossi was in rue de la Grande-Chaumière on the Left Bank, the part of the city with the highest concentration of artists' studios. Since entry to the École des Beaux-Arts was still barred to women, it was the most judicious of choices for Camille Claudel. As Odile Ayral-Clause points out, "It taught more modeling, it was cheaper, and it gave women the same opportunities as men. Moreover,

Fig. 2
E. CHÉRON
Camille Claudel aged around fifteen
Photograph, about 1879
Private collection

Fig. 2

the school allowed a great deal of scheduling flexibility, thanks to a curriculum that could be as short as a week and as long as ten months."[19] In order to have somewhere to work at will, Camille Claudel requisitioned the maid's room in the apartment in boulevard Montparnasse. The maid, who had followed them "from Villeneuve to Paris via Nogent and Wassy," took umbrage at this and duly left the Claudels' service.[20] The incident spurred Camille to find a proper studio, where she would have space enough to learn her difficult and arduous profession. And so in May 1883, in the catalogue of the Salon of the Société des Artistes Français, where she was exhibiting for the first time, the young sculptress gave her address as 117 rue Notre-Dame-des-Champs (cat. 181). As the Claudel family had moved to number 111 in the same street in the autumn of 1881,[21] one can surmise that Camille moved into her new studio shortly after: it was both close to the apartment where she lived with her family and a street away from the Académie Colarossi.

The archives of this establishment having been destroyed, we do not know how long Camille studied there, the precise nature of the instruction she received or the names of the teachers who taught her.

That Alfred Boucher, "endeavoring to facilitate the hardest of careers for Mlle Camille Claudel," continued to give advice to the young artist after her arrival in Paris is clearly attested by the journalist Paul Leroi in 1886.[22] More problematic, though, is the role played in Camille's artistic education before she met Rodin by the famous sculptor Paul Dubois, to whom, as we have seen, Boucher owed much. Whereas Mathias Morhardt limits Dubois's involvement to a single but nonetheless premonitory visit that Boucher apparently paid him in the company of his young protégée,[23] Paul Leroi maintains that Boucher, having been awarded the Grand Prix du Salon, "had to go to Florence, and asked his teacher, M. Paul Dubois, to continue the advice given to Camille Claudel, which had already produced good results." It was not until "later," according to the L'Art journalist, that "Mlle Claudel became . . . the pupil of M. Auguste Rodin."[24] His version differs from Morhardt's in that the latter maintains Boucher

Cat. 26

personally asked Rodin "to kindly stand in for him"[25] after his departure for Italy in the late summer of 1882.[26] Although it seems unlikely that Dubois, head of the École des Beaux-Arts since 1878, would have had enough time to take a young pupil like Camille Claudel under his wing, his role was nonetheless far greater than the one attributed to him post-Morhardt. This is confirmed by the fact that at the 1883 Salon Camille declared herself to be a "pupil of MM. Rodin, Boucher and P. Dubois."[27] However, after Camille Claudel met Rodin, neither Boucher nor Dubois played the slightest role in the development of her career.[28]

THE OLD WOMAN OR LA VIEILLE HÉLÈNE

What stage in her artistic development had Camille Claudel reached immediately prior to meeting Rodin? Very few works have survived to enlighten us on this. Although, as we have seen, Morhardt was able to examine, albeit in a very bad state, the small *David and Goliath* group Camille Claudel sculpted when she was twelve or thirteen, he nevertheless considers that "the young artist's earliest surviving signed works" date from 1882. He was explicit on this when he compiled what can be considered the

Cat. 15

first catalogue raisonné of Camille Claudel's oeuvre in 1893: "The first work she signed with her name that is still extant is a bust of an *Old Woman*. The patient model was one of Madame Claudel's servants, a woman from Alsace. The work is serious and well thought out. One senses its faithfulness—over-faithfulness perhaps—to the model! Yet there is neither leanness nor dryness. The old woman, with a wrinkled forehead, jutting jaw and prominent cheekbones, is looking straight ahead. Her eyes are gentle and kind. Her whole countenance, moreover, is one of finesse and distinction."[29]

Easily recognizable in this description is the *Vieille Hélène* reproduced in Paul Claudel's 1913 article in *L'Art décoratif* and which he dates precisely to "1882."[30] This first composition is known today by its terracotta version and a Fumière & Cie cast dating from between 1906 and 1926 (cat. 26),[31] both belonging to the Claudel family.

Although the servant who posed for *The Old Woman* does seem to be the "old maid Victoire

Cat. 26
—
CAMILLE CLAUDEL
The Old Woman
1882
Bronze
28 x 18 x 21 cm
Private collection

Cat. 15
—
ALFRED BOUCHER
My Mother
1880
Bronze
55 x 28 x 28 cm
Musée Paul-Dubois –
Alfred-Boucher,
Nogent-sur-Seine

_Fig. 3

Brunet" that Paul Claudel mentions in his *Mémoires improvisés*,[32] which would confirm the bust's similarities with Camille Claudel's 1887 oil portrait *Victoire*,[33] there is still uncertainty as to the origin of the forename "Hélène" Paul Claudel uses when referring to the work. Sculpted when Camille was only seventeen and probably while she was working in the studio in rue Notre-Dame-des-Champs, *The Old Woman* or *La Vieille Hélène* owes much to the advice of Alfred Boucher. The similarities between the Claudel work and Boucher's *My Mother* bust (cat. 15, p. 25), sculpted two years earlier, show this

clearly, although here the teacher shows more restraint than his pupil, imbuing his model with a beautiful dignity somewhat lacking in the Claudels' maid.[34] This notwithstanding, Camille had every reason to be proud of this piece, which she exhibited at the Salon of the Société des Artistes Français in 1885.[35] Nevertheless, although it seems perfectly clear that the choice of model here was above all dictated by practical and economic contingencies, by bringing out all the power and strangeness of the old family servant's features, the young Camille was tackling a theme she would return to throughout her career. For the moment, it is important to establish a connection between this bust and the series of charcoal drawings, in particular the drawing entitled *Woman from Gérardmer (Vosges)* (fig. 3), which the artist executed in a markedly realist vein in 1885 and 1886 (cat. 33, p. 130), several of which were reproduced in *L'Art*.

THE BUST OF "PAUL CLAUDEL AGED THIRTEEN": AN EARLY WORK?

Camille Claudel's *Old Woman* bust is all the more priceless in that it is the only surviving work definitely dating from before she met Rodin.[36] There clearly has to be a complete reexamination of the affirmation by every researcher to have taken an interest in Camille Claudel over the last twenty-five years that the bronze of *Paul Claudel as a Child* in the Musée de Châteauroux dates from 1881 (cat. 30, p. 122). This unique bust, signed by Camille Claudel and neither exhibited, written about nor reproduced before it was donated to the Musée de Châteauroux by Baron

Alphonse de Rothschild in 1903,[37] seems to have been dated to 1881 merely out of a need to see it as a portrayal of Paul Claudel at precisely thirteen years old. Nevertheless, although the model is without a doubt the youngest of the Claudel children, the boy portrayed could hardly be more than eight years old. This is confirmed by a photograph of Paul taken at Nogent-sur-Seine, where the Claudel family lived from 1876 to 1879, in which he could hardly be more than ten (cat. 19, p. 122). Indeed, how could there possibly be only a three-year age difference between the model of this bust and that of *Young Roman*, also known as *My Brother*, portraying Paul Claudel at sixteen (cat. 27, p. 123)? Since it is inconceivable that Camille Claudel could have sculpted a work as accomplished as *Paul Claudel as a Child* when she was barely twelve years old herself, only four years older than her brother, one has to envisage that she may have worked on this sculpture from a photograph later,[38] probably in the mid-1880s while she was modeling the features of her brother aged sixteen, as the stylistic similarities between the two works suggest. On the other hand, it is difficult to imagine Camille hiding an early work as accomplished as this bust from Mathias Morhardt, who would not have failed to praise it. If, "thanks to her incessant activity," the young artist "accomplished much work" before 1882, there was none of it left in her studio when Morhardt frequented it in the 1890s: "The plasters were broken. The sketches have crumbled to dust. The drawings have been burnt."[39]

Having taken an interest in *The Old Woman*, Mathias Morhardt then lingered over a bust of Paul Claudel aged "around thirteen," dating the work to 1883 and describing it as corresponding in every respect to the above-mentioned *Young Roman* portrait of Paul Claudel aged sixteen,[40] a work generally dated to 1884, as indicated by the model himself.[41] This inexplicable error was the source of the misunderstanding regarding the title, and consequently the very date of the bust of *Paul Claudel as a Child*.[42] By postdating the execution of this neo-Florentine-style bust by a few years one can better explain why it "contrasts with the naturalistic vein of, for example, *La Vieille Hélène*," as Bruno Gaudichon revealed.[43] This stylistic gap between what have until now been considered two early works by Camille Claudel was all the more difficult to explain since *La Vieille Hélène*, a work believed to date from a year later than the bust of *Paul Claudel as a Child*, has, again in Bruno Gaudichon's view, just as much "expressive detail and rigorous discipline" as the early *David and Goliath* figure group.[44] One can surmise that this was also true of the "bust of M. Claude père," a work still unlocated which Morhardt mentions along with other works belonging to "this period preceding the moment when the young artist entered Rodin's studio as a pupil."[45]

RODIN IN 1882: ON THE ROAD TO SUCCESS Antoinette Le Normand-Romain

In 1882, Rodin was already forty-one and becoming well known. Although he had shown his marble bust *The Man With the Broken Nose* (fig. 4, p. 30) at the 1875 Salon, it had gone almost unnoticed: he had very purposefully done away with the provocative aspect of the sketchy mask refused by the 1865 Salon for a more conventional image evoking the portraits of ancient philosophers. In 1877, he tried his luck again with a figure[1] he had labored over for almost two years, a study of a male nude in which his aim had simply been, as Bartlett mentions, to make "a study of the nude, a good figure, correct in design, concise in style and firm in modeling."[2] Refusing to employ professional models, from October 1875 he worked with Auguste Neyt, a twenty-two-year-old soldier. He had him try several poses in keeping with his nature until one of them, a pose chosen for its own sake and not as part of a subject, satisfied him completely. The sense that he was on the right track was confirmed to him by a trip to Italy in February-March 1876, during which he discovered Michelangelo, who made a profound impression on him.

The figure (fig. 5, p. 30), shown in Brussels in January 1877, was immediately admired for a "quality as precious as it was rare: vitality."[3] The modeling, enlivened by the play of light produced by the slight swing of the hip and analyzed in depth, muscle by muscle, has all the precision and subtlety of the Renaissance masters. But the statue had neither a title nor any attribute that could identify it. Disconcerted critics could come up with only one explanation, that Rodin had cast from life, an accusation that he took as an insult since it negated his work. At the Paris Salon the following spring, he showed it as *The Age of Bronze,* a title which has the merit of allowing one to guess the new direction his work was taking. If he obstinately rejected all descriptive elements, it was because he was trying to penetrate the inner life of the human being and find a relationship between it and artistic form. He was again accused of casting from life, a terrible blow for him as he had been hoping that the work would be acquired by the fine arts administration, the obligatory departure point for any official career. "How

Cat. 118 B
AUGUSTE RODIN
Saint John the Baptist
1880
Bronze
200 x 55 x 98 cm
Rodin Museum, Philadelphia

29

Fig. 4

Fig. 5

At the age of almost forty he had to go back to work for decorative sculpture contractors such as Legrain, who employed him to produce masks for the 1878 Exposition Universelle, or Cruchet, who so admired his ability that he commissioned him to sculpt a bust of his wife (1879 Salon) (fig. 6). But his morale did not waver and in 1879 he entered two competitions held by the Paris city council. Attracting attention in such competitions and at the Salon, the best place to catch the public eye, was an ideal means for aspiring artists to gain recognition. He therefore submitted his project for a *Monument for the Defense of Paris (The Call to Arms)* for the rond-point de Courbevoie, where the defense of the capital had been organized in 1870. Rodin, who had trained outside official institutions, had a highly personal approach to sculpture guaranteed to disconcert a jury accustomed to traditional criteria. His project was considered too aggressive and was rejected in the first round of judging on November 29, 1879.

Bellona (cat. 117), the bust he submitted in December that year as *The Republic*, suffered the same fate—as did all sixty-three projects submitted. "Ever ready to facilitate his work,"[6] Rose Beuret, with whom Rodin had now lived for almost twenty years and who had borne him a son, Auguste (whom he never recognized), modeled for *The Republic*. However, in the quest for that expressiveness characteristic of Michelangelo and Rude, Rodin gave her the vindictive expression he knew so well. He "did not hide the fact that he had modeled her from life, during the scenes she made."[7] And with the memory

painful it is to see that my figure which can help my belated career as I'm now thirty-six, how painful to see it rejected because of the stain of suspicion," he wrote to the president of the jury of the Salon.[4] And to Rose Beuret, who had stayed on in Brussels, he wrote, "You can see that things are going to be hard as all my money will go into another attempt and let's hope I earn some. The future is looking pretty grim and there is likely to be poverty ahead."[5]

Fig. 4

AUGUSTE RODIN
The Man with the Broken Nose
Marble, 1875
Musée Rodin, Paris

Fig. 5

ANONYMOUS
Plaster model of
The Age of Bronze *in the Dépôt des Marbres, 1880*
Photograph
Musée Rodin, Paris

Fig. 6

Cat. 117

Fig. 6

AUGUSTE RODIN
Madame Cruchet
1879
Terracotta
Musée Rodin, Paris

Cat. 117

AUGUSTE RODIN
Bellona
1879
Plaster
102 x 53 x 43 cm
Musée Rodin, Paris

of his trip to Italy still fresh in his mind, and despite the Phrygian cap being one of the competition's stipulations, he gave her a splendid Renaissance-inspired helmet. The result was a sullen, fierce Republic visibly hostile to any concession, and consequently completely out of step with the desire for peace which the Republicans, then in the majority in Paris, were seeking to manifest.

Yet the bronze mask of *The Man with the Broken Nose* had been accepted for the 1878 Salon despite its fragmented state, and the following year his luck changed at last. In Laoust's studio, Alfred Boucher noticed "a man with a red beard busy preparing large balls of clay . . . then fashioning heads and chubby children's limbs with dizzying speed and sureness." Learning that he was Rodin, "the so-called falsifier" accused of casting from life, he convinced Paul Dubois, Henri Chapu and several others that he was "capable of having executed *The Age of Bronze* without recourse to fraud."[8] A dozen sculptors, all members of the "Néo-Florentin" group, wrote a joint letter to the director of the fine arts administration, Edmond Turquet. The Néo-Florentins, who rejected the idealized modeling of Antiquity, included Paul Dubois, whose *Florentine Singer* (bronze, Musée d'Orsay, Paris) was shown at the 1864 Salon and at the 1867 Exposition Universelle and whom Rodin greatly admired, Henri Chapu, Eugène Delaplanche and Antonin Mercié, whose *David* (bronze, Musée d'Orsay, Paris) and *Gloria Victis* (bronze, Musée du Petit Palais, Paris) were among the most admired works of the 1870s. They endeavored to create the illusion of life using the faithfulness and litheness of bronze. Turquet was won over. On May 2, 1880, he signed an acquisition order for a plaster of *The Age of Bronze* and also commissioned a bronze of the same sculpture (Musée d'Orsay, Paris). The bronze had in fact already been cast and shown at the Salon with the large plaster *Saint John the Baptist* (cat. 118 B, p. 28).

Rodin himself recounted on several occasions how the idea for *Saint John the Baptist* came to him. A peasant from the Abruzzi, Pignatelli, came to his studio one day to propose his services as a model. "Seeing him, I was struck with admiration. The appearance, features and physical strength of this uncouth and hirsute man expressed all the violence but also all the mysticism of his race. I at once thought of a Saint John the Baptist, in other words, of a child of nature, an inspired figure, a believer, a precursor come to proclaim one greater than himself. The peasant undressed and climbed on to the revolving stand as if he had never posed before. He took up his stance, head raised, torso erect, weight on both legs, opened like a compass. The pose was so right, so distinctive and so true that I cried out: 'But it's a man walking!' I at once decided to make what I had seen . . . All I did was copy the model chance had sent me."[9] Photographs of Pignatelli posing (fig. 7) bear witness to Rodin's account and, above all, to his work, which consisted in reinterpreting nature. Rodin deliberately made the figure larger than life, sculpting it directly in its definitive size, reinforcing the expressive power of the modeling by accentuating anatomical character-istics, such as the play of the back muscles, which foreshadows *The Thinker*.

Although it is probable, as Ruth Butler has shown,[10] that "*Saint John . . .* was not a realization of a preconceived idea,"[11] that the subject was indeed inspired by the model himself, it was also, unlike *The Age of Bronze*, one easily understandable by the public at the Salon, where many depictions of the saint had been shown—in 1878, there had been three sculptures depicting the theme. Yet it was received with suspicion and, at the triennial Salon in Paris in 1883, to the indignation of Rodin's admirers, it was relegated to "the obscurest corner of the obscurest row."[12] For some it was "a piece of the first order, one of the most remarkable in contemporary sculpture,"[13] a "marvel of reality, concentrated inti-macy and clear and meaningful execution. The spirit of Gothic man animates this statue."[14] Others were repelled by the realism of a body "as crude as possible in its primitive nudity,"[15] and from which no attribute distracted the eye. Its expressive power does indeed render the gesture sufficient in itself, though, Rodin having done away with the cross he had cursorily indicated in the drawing published in *L'Art* in 1880,[15] and which Gruet in fact cast. As Rodin himself admit-ted in Dujardin-Beaumetz's company, he had wanted to take advantage of a model whom he likened to a "wild beast . . . a wolf" to portray the prophet as a

Fig. 7

fierce, visionary being, closer to Ernest Renan's depiction of him in *La Vie de Jésus* (1863) or Gustave Flaubert's in *Hérodias* (1877) than contemporary pictures or sculptures. But this is also what gives the statue its power, and his fellow sculptor Antoine Bourdelle must have well understood this when, with brilliant intuition, he likened Rodin to Rembrandt:

Fig. 7
ANONYMOUS
Pignatelli posing for
Saint John the Baptist
About 1878
Photograph
École Nationale Supérieure
des Beaux-Arts, Paris

Cat. 124

AUGUSTE RODIN
Albert-Ernest Carrier-Belleuse
1882
Terracotta
48 x 45 x 34 cm
Musée Rodin, Paris

"The mane is all black, the eye in the bony, peasant face is authoritarian, and above all the ensemble conveys the weight of living matter in the fullness of the muscles and heavy frame. Is it a statue or a man, standing, walking before us? . . . One has the impression that the master of Amsterdam, old Rembrandt himself, touched this old Saint John with his glorious brushes, that his magnificent hands molded the whole of this crackpot, fervent statue with its profiles eaten into like one of his large dark etchings."[17]

A bronze of *Saint John the Baptist* (Musée d'Orsay, Paris) was cast after the Salon, and shown the following year with *Adam* (plaster) before its acquisition by the state on July 5, 1881. It was subsequently shown in numerous exhibitions and was the first work by the artist to enter the Musée du Luxembourg, in 1884. The public could no longer consider Rodin an up and coming artist. He had also just been commissioned to sculpt a "decorative door" for the new Musée des Arts Décoratifs to be built in Paris.

Adam was the last of the large figures to be exhibited at the Salon des Artistes Français, where from 1882, Rodin showed mainly busts. In 1882, he exhibited portraits of *Albert-Ernest Carrier-Belleuse* (cat. 124) and *Jean-Paul Laurens* (cat. 125), the first of which embodied the whole of Rodin's early career. Carrier-Belleuse, a sculptor greatly in vogue under the Second Empire, had employed the young Rodin before the 1870 war, and had him come to Brussels in 1871. Now that Rodin had gained in self-assurance and begun to exhibit under his own name—previously Carrier-Belleuse had signed everything he sculpted—relations between the two men suddenly ceased, although less close ties did resume after Rodin's return to Paris in 1877. Rodin certainly learned a great deal from Carrier-Belleuse, particularly in the working of clay, and it was also his former employer who had shown him the example of a sculptor's studio in which many assistants played an important role. The bust, an inspired portrait rendered with elegant freedom, was exhibited at the Salon in terracotta, a medium well suited to an artist who had "something of the fine blood of the eighteenth century, something of Clodion in him."[18] It contrasted sharply with the bust of *Jean-Paul Laurens*, whose bare chest and dry, nervous treatment alluded more to the Florentine Renaissance, and whose material, bronze, further stamped its character on the work. Laurens, a history painter, was an old friend. He had portrayed Rodin as a Merovingian warrior in a fresco depicting the death of Saint Genevieve in the Panthéon, and he asked Rodin to sculpt his bust, which Rodin took great pleasure in doing. The work was acclaimed by the critics, and in particular caught the attention of a journalist belonging to Victor Hugo's entourage, Edmond Bazire. "The sculptor," he wrote, "explains the painter whom nothing can weaken, who deals out brushstrokes like punches. Our thanks to the sculptor."[19] And to help him—at that time Rodin was still in real financial difficulty—Bazire persuaded Victor Hugo to commission a portrait bust,[20] one which would prove to be decisive in Rodin's career since in 1889 it led to his obtaining one of the most prestigious commissions of the period, the *Monument to Victor Hugo* in the Panthéon.

Cat. 125
—
AUGUSTE RODIN
Jean-Paul Laurens
1882
Bronze
58 x 37.1 x 33.1 cm
Musée Rodin, Paris

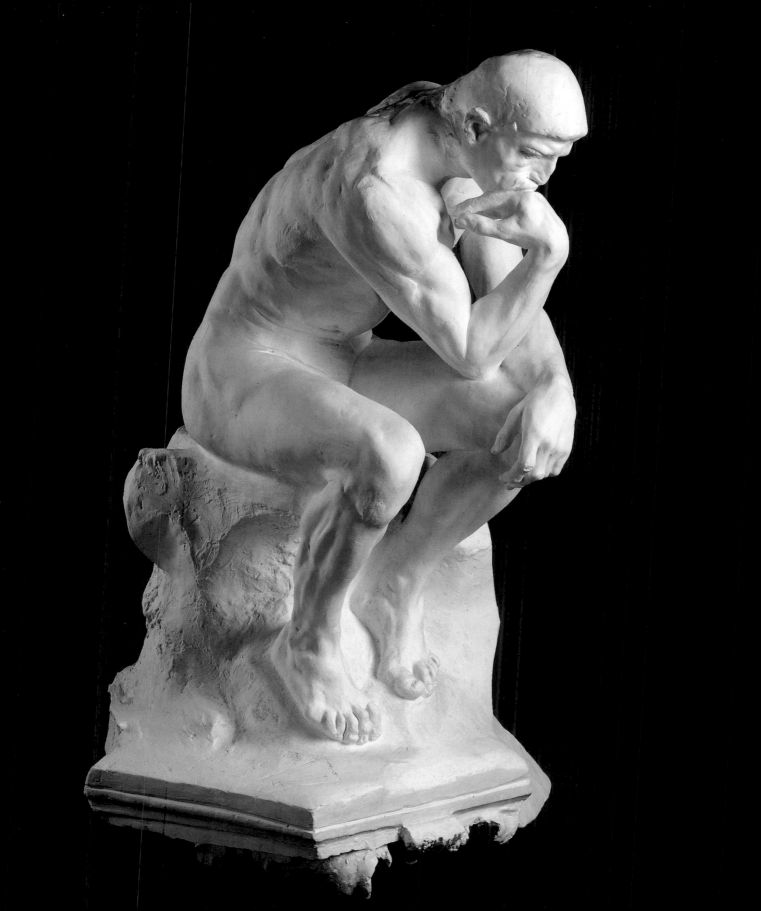

II HAPPY TIMES [1882–1892]

IN RODIN'S STUDIO Antoinette Le Normand-Romain

By order dated August 16, 1880, Rodin was commissioned by the fine arts administration to sculpt a "decorative door" for the future Musée des Arts Décoratifs.[1] It was to be built in Paris on the former site of the Cour des Comptes, destroyed by fire in 1871. The order stipulated that the door had to be "decorated with bas-reliefs inspired by Dante's *Divine Comedy*." For its execution, Rodin was allotted a studio at the Dépôt des Marbres in the rue de l'Université, which from then on became his principal workplace.

He set to work "with a fury," and *The Gates* progressed rapidly, as confirmed by the payment in October of an advance of 2,700 francs, a third of the agreed fee of 8,000 francs. "I have made a lot of drawings and models," he wrote to Turquet, "which I believe I am able to submit to your appreciation and so request that you grant me an advance of a quarter, which would enable me to pay the initial costs of the model's armature."[2] He had first imagined a door divided into panels, like the *Gates of Paradise* door of

the Baptistery in Florence (Lorenzo Ghiberti, 1425–52), but his first model, consisting of ten scenes, five on each side of the central vertical axis, was soon superseded by a second whose overall composition was divided into three areas, the two doors and the tympanum. In the third model (cat. 119, p. 38), in which *The Thinker*, *The Kiss* and *Ugolino* appear for the first time and which undoubtedly dates from very soon afterwards, great strides have been made towards the definitive model which Rodin was hoping to exhibit as early as 1883. A journalist, one of the first to have been allowed in to see what would become *The Gates of Hell*, wrote in April 1882, "Rue de l'Université,

Cat. 120
Auguste Rodin
The Thinker on a
fragment of a capital
About 1880–81
Plaster
87.5 x 59 x 42.6 cm
Musée Rodin, Paris

Cat. 119

in the Dépôt des Marbres de l'État, he worked silently. His studio [is] marked with the letter M—for Master! . . . There is not a hint of luxury. The place is poor, severe, large. No refinements. One could almost be in a monk's cell . . . One is immediately assailed by fantastic visions. What are these veiled shadows looming along the walls? What masterpieces do these damp canvases conceal? And the enormous wooden cabinet rising to the ceiling and which takes up the whole floor, what could that be? 'It's my door,' Rodin replies calmly . . . At the Salon next year everyone will feel small next to this grandiose work."[3]

STUDIOS

We know the first year was largely spent making "dark" drawings inspired by Dante, whom Rodin read again and again. But he undoubtedly resumed modeling in the second half of 1881. As the rest of his career would confirm, drawing was an essential activity for him but bore no immediate relationship to his sculpture. It was directly in clay and from life that he found inspiration for his forms. As he had done for *The Age of Bronze*, he did not work on a preconceived idea but instead sought with his models the poses liable to give the body maximum expressive power. The choice of model was therefore of prime importance. A priceless diary (cat. 179), on the inside front cover of which there are sketches and indications for *The Gates*, gives a record of the presence in his studio between February and early July 1882 of three people. The first two of these were well-known models, Adèle Abbruzzesi and Pignatelli. But we also discover the name of a certain "Camille," a little in February and above all from March to May. "Camille" is increasingly present in the studio: in March, she is marked for the afternoon of the 3rd, 7th, 10th, 11th, 14th, 17th, 18th, 21st,

Cat. 119
AUGUSTE RODIN
The Gates of Hell,
third model
1880
Plaster
111.5 x 75 x 30 cm
Musée Rodin, Paris

Cat. 179
AUGUSTE RODIN
Notebook no. 54
1882
29 x 19.2 cm
Musée Rodin, Paris

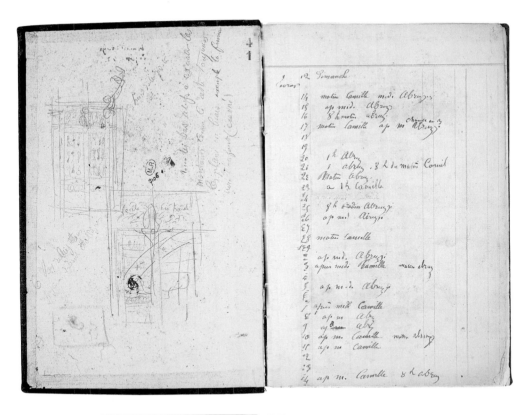

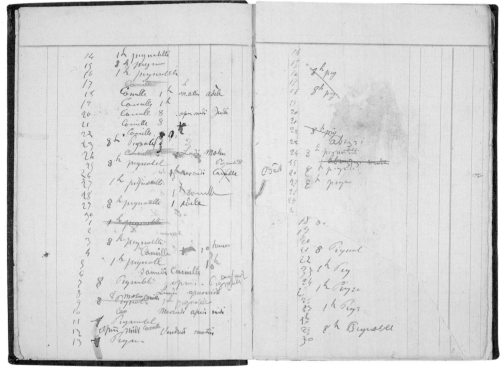

24th and 25th. "Abbruzzezi," "Abruzzi" or "Abruz," who becomes simply "Adèle" from April 18, is there in the afternoon on the 2nd, in the morning on the 3rd, 5th and 8th, in the afternoon on the 9th, and in the morning on the 10th, 14th, 21st, 29th and 30th for eight hours. Pignatelli appears on the 27th and 28th "evening" and for an hour on the 29th. In April, the sessions with Camille are long: eight hours on the 9th and 10th, eight hours again on the 20th and 21st, and ten hours on May 4.

The diary entries pose two questions: is "Camille" the Camille we're interested in, and if so what was she doing in the studio? The answer to the first question seems to be yes, as we know of no other Camille in Rodin's close entourage at that time, and besides Boucher may very possibly have introduced them earlier than is thought. One should not forget that it was he who at the beginning of 1880 had persuaded some twelve other sculptors to rally in defense of *The Age of Bronze* before the undersecretary of state for fine arts. It is harder, though, to reply to the second question. One occasionally reads that Rodin had Camille pose for him, particularly for *The Kiss*. But in February 1882 she had only just turned seventeen, and one can hardly imagine she was then emancipated enough from her very bourgeois milieu to accept to pose in the nude. But there could be another reason for her long hours in the studio and the fact that Rodin refers to her by her first name: the simple fact that he had accepted the young Camille, barely out of adolescence, as a pupil at a time when she had no other place to work.[4] If this was the case, she would have been his only pupil at that time,

which explains why hers is the only name to appear in the diary alongside the models.

Camille's name vanishes from the diary after May 12. Could this mean that she already had the studio at 117 rue Notre-Dame-des-Champs at that date? Alfred Boucher had agreed to supervise her work, but when he was awarded the Prix du Salon in 1881, this enabled him to travel to Italy and he undoubtedly left Paris in the summer of 1882.[5] Rodin stood in for Boucher and, in order to share the expense, Camille was soon joined in his studio by other young women. This is what Léon Lhermitte implied on February 11, 1883, when he thanked Rodin for having taken in one of his protégées, Amélie Casini, "and for the letter in which you were good enough to inform me of the offer by the ladies in your studio to keep a place for her."[6] As Ruth Butler suggests,[7] three of these first "ladies" were undoubtedly Madeleine Jouvray, who signed a letter dated December 29, 1883,[8] Thérèse Caillaux, who exhibited at the 1883 and 1884 Salons as a pupil of Rodin and Boucher, and Sigrid of Forselles, also their pupil, who exhibited a plaster bust of a *Thinker* at the 1884 Salon and gave her address in 1885 as "117 rue Notre-Dame-des-Champs." They were joined in 1884 by two Englishwomen, Amy Singer and Emily Fawcett, and in 1885, according to a letter from Amy Singer to Rodin,[9] by Jessie Lipscomb, who had won several prizes at the Royal College of Art in London and for whom Paris afforded the only opportunity to continue to sculpt.[10] Camille was "naturally, the spirit of the group. She chose the models. She decided on the pose. She dealt out the work. She assigned everyone their place."[11]

Fig. 8

With Rodin, the situation was reversed: it was now he who went to the ladies' studios, where his entourage knew they would find him on certain days. In March 1883, Léon Lhermitte wrote in a note to Rodin, the first document in which Rodin and Camille's names are associated, "My dear Rodin, a thousand pardons for not having been able to come to your studio in rue des Fourneaux yesterday. I had hoped to meet you the next day at your pupils' studio, but as you were told, I arrived shortly after your departure. It was with great pleasure that I saw Mlle Claudel's figure of a man. It reflects greatest credit on your teaching" (cat. 180). This teaching was based on scrupulous attention to nature and recourse to the profiles method he himself practiced: "Model solely by profiles; constantly exaggerate the profiles in a determined and always constant proportion . . . By propagating these principles around him, Rodin shortens a long path for those capable of using them and putting them in the service of beauty."[12]

THE GATES OF HELL AND THE BURGHERS OF CALAIS

The figures destined for *The Gates of Hell* multiplied. As shown in two fascinating photographs showing the clay *Thinker* on a scaffolding in front of the frame of *The Gates* (fig. 8), once modeled, they were tried out in the door spaces, indicated by a wooden frame, then molded and put to one side. "I was only able to see," noted Roger Ballu, inspector of fine arts, on January 23, 1883, "small isolated groups, whose damp drapes were taken off one by one as I looked at them . . . I cannot foresee the effect that compositions all in high relief will have on the massive plane of the large door. To give a fully considered opinion, I would need to see all these groups in place. Albeit, the work of M. Rodin is of the utmost interest. This young sculptor has a truly extraordinary originality and a tormented expressive power."[13] On November 13 he returned to inspect *The Gates* and was again

Fig. 8
VICTOR PANNELIER
The Thinker in front of the
frame of *The Gates of Hell*
About 1882
Photograph
Musée Rodin, Paris

struck by the power of Rodin's work: "The conception of the work will, I believe, be striking. The execution is careful, energetic and strong. M. Rodin's personality, already manifest in his previous works, is asserting itself here and increasing in power . . . When it is finished, parts of this door could appear somewhat bizarre, but they bear witness to the audacity of its author. It will compel recognition as an original creation . . . it will be admired for the deliberate energy of the style which governed its creation. It will genuinely be, in the most powerful sense, a work of art."[14]

As it turned out, *The Gates* were not exhibited in 1883 or even in 1884, but they were cast in plaster for the first time during the second half of 1884 and Rodin felt sufficiently sure of his project to have estimates made for the bronze. Among the privileged few to have seen them were Octave Mirbeau, the first to describe them in the February 18, 1885 issue of

La France, and Jules Dalou, who, on his return from England after the 1879 amnesty, had struck up a close friendship with the sculptor. Rodin exhibited his bust at the 1884 Salon, a bust whose particularly precise and detailed modeling, enhanced here (cat. 127) by the quality of the cast by Pierre Bingen,[15] conveyed the artist's admiration for the bronze foundries of the Italian Renaissance. Soon afterwards, however, relations between the two men deteriorated, Dalou having exhibited a project for a monument to Victor Hugo at the 1886 Salon whose high-relief background appeared to Mirbeau, and no doubt to Rodin, to be a plagiarization of *The Gates*: "This year, M. Dalou has been very influenced by his friend, M. Auguste Rodin, to such an extent that he has used certain movements and motifs belonging absolutely to the great sculptor of the Burghers of Calais and Saint John the Precursor. I understand the vividness of this impression when one has seen *The Gates* of the Palais des Arts Décoratifs. The beauty of this colossal and profoundly original work remains deeply etched in one's mind. But a sculptor should not be dominated by it to the point of reproducing things imagined by someone else."[16] It marked the end of the friendship between the two sculptors.[17]

The casting of *The Gates* was commissioned by an order dated August 20, 1885. However, a new commission[18] had been preoccupying Rodin for some months, to such an extent that he had hardly been able to devote any time to his two English pupils.[19] On several occasions the town of Calais had wanted to pay tribute to the heroism of its burghers, who, in 1347, after a year-long siege, risked their lives to bring the keys to their town to the king of England. None of these projects succeeded until, in 1884, a need was felt to assert the identity of the old town of Calais, which was about to be amalgamated with the neighboring commune of Saint-Pierre and to embark on a renovation program that would entail the demolition of its ramparts. On September 26, 1884, Omer Dewavrin tabled a motion that the city council "erect on a site to be determined later . . . a monument to Eustache de Saint-Pierre and his companions . . . with the aid of a national subscription."[20] A few days later he met Rodin, who set to work without waiting for the commission to be officially confirmed. "He is finding things out; he has borrowed Froissart's *Chronicles* and is reading the chapter on how King Philip of France would not give up the town of Calais, and how King Edward of England took it! . . . Fired by Froissart's complete account, he will now represent not *one* burgher of Calais but all six heroes together; it is impossible to separate them. *Six* for the agreed price."[21] But whereas in November 1884 the first model, which emphasizes the notion of collective sacrifice by presenting the six figures on the same plane, had delighted Dewavrin and clinched the official commission for the monument in January 1885, the one-third life-size model he presented in July got a more reserved reception. "It would injure our Calaisian pride to see the finest hour of our local history represented by the subject that has been submitted to us . . . Nor does the blatant despondency of Eustache de Saint-Pierre and his companions seem to us befitting of a representation of the humblest and most sublime dedication of our fellow citizens . . . We

do not understand why the three principal and most prominent subjects represent an image of pain . . . Monsieur Rodin seems to have overstepped the mark in the desperate pose of the right-hand companion and also in the clothing of the burgher on the left, who, while presenting the keys, cannot hold back his tears."[22] But Rodin took no heed of these criticisms and the modifications he made to his burghers only rendered them even more expressive.

EXHIBITING AND SELLING

Rodin's financial situation was improving. He had begun exploiting the figures of *The Gates* very early

Cat. 123
AUGUSTE RODIN
Ugolino and His Sons
About 1881–82
Bronze
41 x 61.5 x 41 cm
Musée Rodin, Paris

Fig. 9

Fig. 9
CÉSAR
Small Eve, *terracotta,*
in Rodin's studio
About 1882
Photograph
Musée Rodin, Paris

Cat. 128
AUGUSTE RODIN
Eve
Marble, 1888
76.2 x 24.5 x 31.5 cm
The Art Institute of Chicago

Cat. 128

on. Although *The Kiss* and *Ugolino* (cat. 123) were not exhibited until 1887, in Paris, then in Brussels, and *The Thinker* (cat. 120, p. 36), still entitled *The Poet* because clearly a portrayal of Dante, Hugo and Baudelaire,[23] was not shown for the first time until 1888 in Copenhagen, other works such as *Eve*, a scaled-down version (fig. 9) of the life-size figure destined to go with *The Gates* and abandoned, unfinished, in 1881–82, and the *Caryatid* very quickly enjoyed a life of their own. Both were exhibited at the Cercle des Arts Libéraux in Paris in February–March 1883. The marble *Caryatid with a Stone*, now in Boston (cat. 121), is almost certainly the figure which, entitled "Age of Stone" at that exhibition, was renamed "Pain" by Bartlett when he saw it at Bastien-Lepage in late 1887.[24] "Of admirable anatomy, expressing, in a creature crouching beneath some sidereal burden, the profound exhaustion of sadness and hopelessness, such as the illusion of having looked too closely at the mysteries of the stars that crush the reckless,"[25] this marble contrasted interestingly with the *Small Eve*, exhibited in bronze. Very sensual, it enjoyed such success that at least a dozen marbles were made before 1900. In December 1885, Auguste Vacquerie acquired the first, sculpted by Bozzoni, who also carved the *Caryatid*. This purchase by a writer and journalist close to Hugo and the Romantics could not have been better publicity for Rodin, as it was talked about in the press. In *L'Art*, Paul Leroi evoked the "admirable marble" he had seen in Vacquerie's home. When he wrote this, there were already three marbles of the *Small Eve*, and they would soon be joined by many others. In the first,

Cat. 12

PREVIOUS PAGE
Cat. 121

AUGUSTE RODIN
Caryatid with a Stone
Marble, executed
by Bozzoni, 1883
50 x 26.7 x 30.5 cm
Museum of Fine Arts, Boston

Cat. 122

AUGUSTE RODIN
The Crouching Woman
About 1881–82
Plaster
31.9 x 28.7 x 21.1 cm
Musée Rodin, Paris

Cat. 122

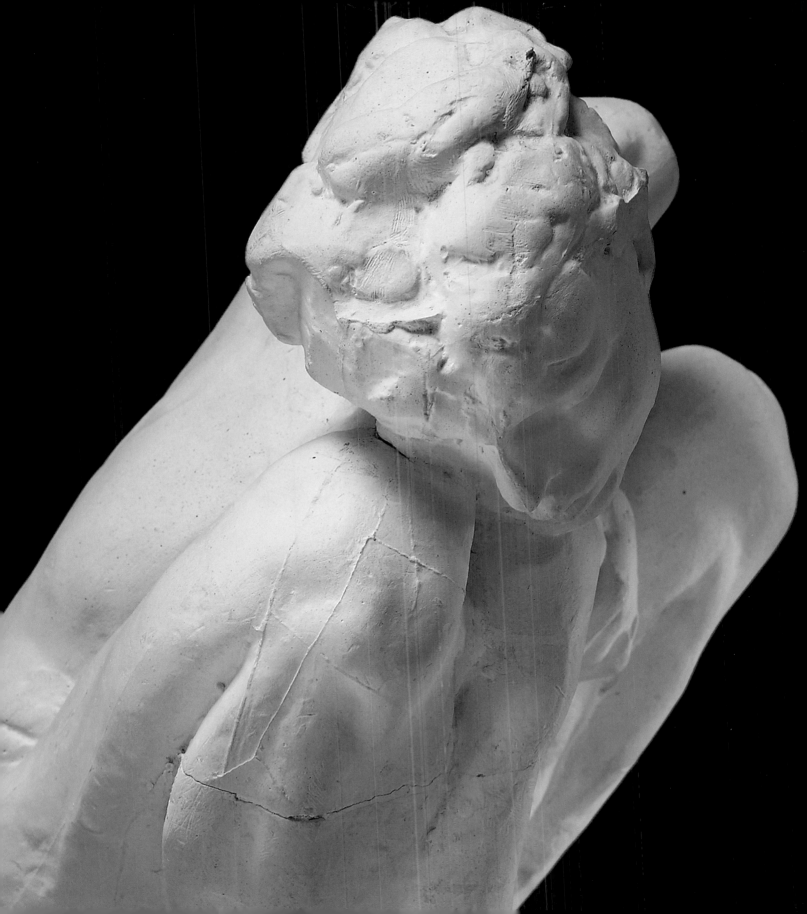

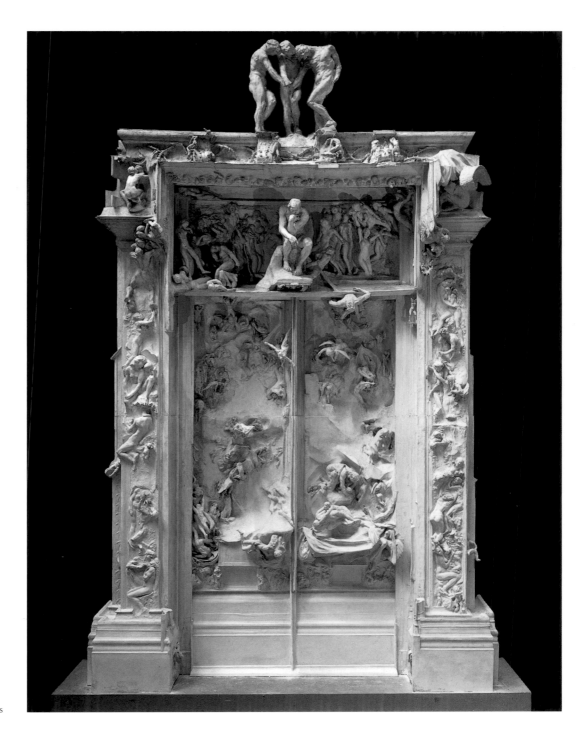

Fig. 10
AUGUSTE RODIN
The Gates of Hell
About 1889–90
Plaster
Musée d'Orsay, Paris

Cat. 146

Vacquerie's, the legs are completely freestanding. The need for reinforcement soon became clear, though: the Chicago *Eve* (cat. 128, p. 44), in gray marble with very prominent veins, undoubtedly the second, delivered to Paul Paulin in late 1887,[25] is supported from behind by a tree trunk. A rock then appeared behind the figure and grew gradually larger in subsequent versions.

Vacquerie's marble *Eve* and the plaster *Caryatid* were exhibited again at the Galerie Georges Petit in June–July 1886, along with "three weary women" (including *The Crouching Woman*, cat. 122, pp. 46–47) and "three studies of human rut" (including *I Am Beautiful*, cat. 141, p. 85). This was the first showing of such a large ensemble of works related to *The Gates of Hell* and made a huge impact on the public, who hardly knew Rodin's work and were unaccustomed to such direct representations. "Eight groups of figures and two busts make up this exhibition, which has upset so many ingrained ideas, highlighted the banality that has become the rule in the annual Salons and revealed a new way of seeing and understanding . . . What is inexpressible in words is the

Cat. 146

AUGUSTE RODIN
Avarice and Lust
About 1887
Plaster
22.5 x 53.5 x 46 cm
Musée Rodin, Paris

Cat. 103

quality of the flesh, the bending of joints, the flexibility of spinal columns, the differences between surfaces, the heaviness of a pelvis, the delicateness of a throat . . . the tension of muscles, the quivering of nerves, the process of breathing . . . And just as Barye has brought to light the moral character of beings through the manifestations of their instincts, Rodin unveils states of mind underlying bodily efforts and the desolation of poses."[27]

Rodin was hoping to exhibit *The Gates* again the following year (1887). But in 1886 he made an important change: *The Kiss* was withdrawn from the left door, because it did not match the tragic atmosphere of the ensemble, and replaced by the *Ugolino* group, formerly on the right, and by the new version of *Paolo and Francesca*, depicted floating in torment as in Dante's text. This new state, known from a series of photographs, the earliest known of *The Gates*, taken by Jessie Lipscomb or her fiancé William Elborne in spring 1887, was quite different from the definitive version (fig. 10, p. 48). The left pilaster appears to be identical to the one we know, but the *Caryatid* has not yet found its place at the top, and on the left door, where the new *Paolo and Francesca* appears beneath *Ugolino*, *The Fortune* is missing, as are *Avarice and Lust* (cat. 146, p. 49) and *Fugit Amor* on the right door. The tympanum has a different rhythm, more vertical for the figures to the left of *The Thinker*, while on his right neither the *Kneeling Fauness* nor the *Torso of Adèle* are yet in place. There are two known sets of these photographs, both including the fine portrait of Rodin, seen in a mirror in front of the plaster of *The Gates*, which are therefore the wrong way round (cat. 103).

At the same time, Rodin was working on *The Burghers of Calais* in his studio at 117 boulevard de Vaugirard. Edmond de Goncourt described its

Cat. 103

WILLIAM ELBORNE
or JESSIE LIPSCOMB
Auguste Rodin at the
Dépôt des Marbres,
in front of The Gates of Hell,
reflected in a mirror
1887
Photograph, albumin print
16.5 x 12 cm
Private collection

Cat. 104

"clay-spattered walls, miserable cast-iron stove, the chill damp emanating from all the huge, wet clay entities shrouded in rags" (cat. 104).[28] The definitive figures (cat. 145, p. 52), quite different from the sketches, were prepared with studies of heads and hands (cat. 138. 139, 143 and 144, p. 53), then, as was customary for Rodin, executed life-size and nude. "I have my nudes, that is, the lower part done, and am getting them right so as not to lose time. You will see that it is what one cannot see, the important part, which is finished," Rodin wrote to Dewavrin on July 14, 1885.[29] The first three burghers, *Eustache de Saint-Pierre*, *Jean d'Aire* and *Pierre de Wissant*, were exhibited in May 1887 at the Galerie Georges Petit and the last cast on December 17, 1888. The group was presented for the first time at the *Claude Monet–A. Rodin* exhibition which opened at the Galerie Georges Petit on June 21, 1889.

This very large exhibition (thirty-six sculptures) marked the climax of the 1880s.[30] It was very important for Rodin because, even though he was sharing

Cat. 104
WILLIAM ELBORNE
Auguste Rodin in his atelier at 117 Boulevard de Vaugirard, in front of a study of Andrieu d'Andres, with Jessie Lipscomb and Camille Claudel
1887
Photograph, albumin print
12 x 16.5 cm
Private collection

Fig. 11

Cat. 145

the bill with Monet, it was his first one-man show. Around the large model of *The Burghers of Calais* (fig. 11), which asserted a new conception of the public monument, no longer narrative but based on the expression of personal feelings, there were several marbles, including the *Danaid* (cat. 154, p. 54 and fig. 12, p. 55) and *Galatea* (cat. 150, pp. 93, 95), bronzes and plasters confirming the direction his work had taken: passionate bodies, hopeless bodies, bodies in motion, bodies imbued with a hitherto unequalled sensuality and expressive power. His sculpture

Fig. 11
AUGUSTE RODIN
The Burghers of Calais
1889
Plaster
Musée Rodin, Paris

Cat. 145
AUGUSTE RODIN
Pierre de Wissant
1887
Bronze
214 x 106 x 118 cm
Musée Rodin, Paris

Cat. 138
AUGUSTE RODIN
Mask Study for
Pierre de Wissant
About 1885–86
Terracotta
27.4 x 20.5 x 11.5 cm
Musée Rodin, Paris

Cat. 139
AUGUSTE RODIN
Study for the Head of
Pierre de Wissant, type C
About 1885–86
Plaster
48 x 28.2 x 28.5 cm
Musée Rodin, Paris

Cat. 138

Cat. 139

Cat. 144

seemed to embody the modern spirit, sweeping away the conventions weighing down artists. It was "a new way of seeing and understanding," Geffroy had emphasized in 1886. But, as Ruth Butler has shown, this exhibition was also in a certain respect a failure. "In 1888, he had made a last desperate effort to complete his *Gates* for the Exposition Universelle . . . Rodin dreamed of receiving official blessing for a major state commission. Instead he found himself sharing space with a painter in a commercial gallery where he had to dicker over percentages."[31] And having believed he could triumphantly hand over a finished work to his client, here he was showing only fragments of it, some of which, *The Thinker* for instance, would become more famous than the work itself. These fragments had nonetheless been conceived as elements of an ensemble—an ensemble never delivered by the artist or even exhibited with all its figures since the only time it was shown, in 1900,

Rodin decided not to include the small groups that gave *The Gates*[32] their full meaning. But the popularity of the figures never waned. In 1900, most of them were shown in the *Rodin* exhibition as independent works, including the only cast of *Awakening*,[33] from the tympanum, now in the Musée Rodin (cat. 130, p. 56). Others had already been purchased. *The Sirens* on the left door, acquired for 6,000 francs by the Montreal collector George Alexander Drummond, had already crossed the Atlantic (cat. 148, p. 57). Two other versions

Cat. 143

Cat. 144
AUGUSTE RODIN
Head of Pierre de Wissant
About 1886–87
Plaster
36 x 24.5 x 27.5 cm
Musée Rodin, Paris

Cat. 143
AUGUSTE RODIN
Left Hand of Pierre de Wissant
About 1886
Terracotta
27 x 18.7 x 13 cm
Musée Rodin, Paris

Cat. 154

Fig. 12

Cat. 154

Auguste Rodin
Danaid
1889
Bronze
35 x 60 x 49 cm
Fondation Pierre Gianadda,
Martigny

Fig. 12

Auguste Rodin
Danaid
Marble, 1889–90
Musée Rodin, Paris

Cat. 130

in marble followed. The work's popularity can be explained by the particularly successful composition of this group of three women, two seen from the front and one from behind, with their intertwined arms forming a garland that seems to emerge from the foam of the wave. This figure group, a magnificent example of symbolism, negating all frontiers between the different forms of artistic expression, was described by Arsène Alexandre in the 1900 catalogue as one of the "most tenderly melodic in Rodin's oeuvre" and compared to the *Rhine Maidens* trio.

COLLABORATIONS

Rodin's intense activity in the 1880s created a need for assistants. During the previous decade he had already used helpers such as Almire Huguet and Léon Fourquet,[34] but his assistants were now more directly involved in the work in progress. Truman Bartlett, who interviewed Rodin at length in November 1887, mentions that he modeled the bodies without bothering about the head, feet and hands, which he left to his assistants.[35] In 1884, Jules Desbois, whom he had known for a long time, joined the studio staff, followed or preceded by Camille. "All those who have frequented the studio in rue de l'Université remember her. Silent and diligent, she remains on her little chair. She hardly listens to the chatting of the idle. Occupied solely by her work, she molds the clay and models the foot or hand of a figure placed in front of her. Sometimes she looks up at a visitor with her large clear eyes whose light is so questioning and . . . so persistent. Then she goes back to her work . . .

Cat. 148

Cat. 130
AUGUSTE RODIN
Awakening
About 1884
Bronze
52.7 x 22.5 x 30.5 cm
Musée Rodin, Paris

Cat. 148
AUGUSTE RODIN
The Sirens
[About 1887]
Marble, executed by
Jean Escoula, 1889–92
44.5 x 45.7 x 27 cm
The Montreal Museum
of Fine Arts

_Cat. 32

_Cat. 31

_Cat. 32

CAMILLE CLAJDEL
Crouching Woman,
without head or arms
Found in 1913
Bronze, about 1913?
35 x 21 x 19 cm
Private collection

_Cat. 31

CAMILLE CLAUDEL
Crouching Woman
About 1885
Patinated plaster
37.8 x 24 x 37.3 cm
Private collection

Fig. 13

Fig. 13
ANTOINE BOURDELLE
Hamlet
About 1891
Bronze
Musée Bourdelle, Paris

Cat. 42
CAMILLE CLAUDEL
Leaning Man
About 1886
Plaster
43.2 x 19 x 28 cm
Private collection

The young artist spreads around Rodin's studio the benefits of her sharp mind, her quick will, her concern for order, her honest and profound sincerity. I said that Mademoiselle Camille Claudel was a pupil of Rodin, but it would be closer to the truth to say that she is becoming his clairvoyant and sagacious colleague. Rodin, who immediately saw the future great artist in her, does not consider her as such. No doubt he imparts as much of his great experience to her as he can. But he also consults her on everything. He discusses every decision with her, and only once they have agreed does he finally make up his mind . . . The happiness of always being understood, of seeing his hopes always surpassed, has

been, he says himself, one of the great joys of his artistic life."[36]

Their respective works of that period are sometimes difficult to tell apart. It is true that Camille worked for Rodin, to what extent it is difficult to determine, but she did not neglect her own work (cat. 55, p. 67), which at the time was strongly influenced by her admiration for her teacher. *The Crouching Woman*, modeled around 1885, could be mistaken for a figure from *The Gates*. This is hardly surprising, as Morhardt notes that it was the first work that Camille sculpted in Rodin's studio,[37] before the bust of her sister Louise. It is presented here both whole (cat. 31, p. 59) and in its fragmentary state (cat. 32, p. 58), the

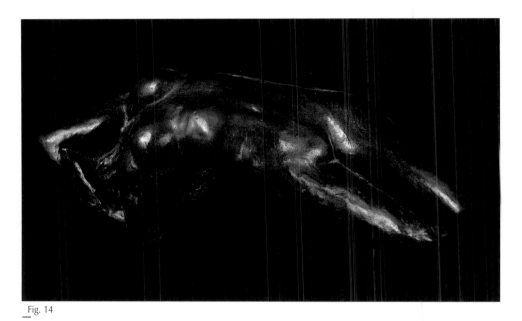

Fig. 14

Fig. 15

figure minus the arms, head and left knee, as reproduced in *L'Art décoratif* in July 1913.[38] The position of the cuts shows that these were not mutilations perpetrated by the artist, but the work of the molder, who had to cut such a complex figure in order to mold it. The limbs were no doubt lost, and when the torso was found in Camille's studio after she was committed in 1913 (by which time public taste had grown accustomed to Rodin's incomplete figures), it was naturally seen as a deliberate choice or the result of a fit of madness rather than the product of chance. But the figure's fragmentary nature emphasizes the modeling of the back. Like that of Rodin's *Crouching Woman* (cat. 122, pp. 46–47), to which Camille's figure is often compared, this is an admirable piece of anatomy. In the *Leaning Man* (cat. 42), there is the same reference to Michelangelo that can be seen in Bourdelle's *Hamlet* (fig. 13). In Camille's work, this is a clear sign of Rodin's influence. *Torso of a Standing Woman* (fig. 15), a twisting torso which Paul Claudel dated to 1888 when he included a reproduction of it in *L'Art. décoratif* in 1913, has the same line curving up the middle of the ribcage emphasizing the spiral composition that can be seen in *Torso of Adèle* (fig. 14). Clearest evidence of the closeness between the two artists can be seen in the comparison of *Head of a Girl with a Chignon* (cat. 43, p. 64) and *The Cry* (cat. 142, pp. 64–65), sculpted by Rodin around 1886: the scale—half life-size—is the same, as is the striated treatment of the hair and the tension pulling the face forward.

Fig. 14
AUGUSTE RODIN
Torso of Adèle
1878?
Bronze
Musée Rodin, Paris

Fig. 15
CAMILLE CLAUDEL
Torso of a Standing Woman
About 1888
Bronze
National Museum of Art,
Bucharest

Cat. 183

As well as the advice they received from Rodin, his pupils and assistants also benefited from the network of collectors and critics he had built up around him. Gustave Geffroy and Octave Mirbeau in 1884, then Maurice Fenaille, whom Rodin met in 1885 through Émile Bastien-Lepage, brother of the painter,[39] and Joanny Peytel, introduced to Rodin in 1888 by Armand Dayot, were members of his close entourage and, when the time came, supported Camille. In the mid-1880s, however, the most important figure was definitely Léon Gauchez, the Belgian art dealer, critic and founder of the review *L'Art*, in which he wrote under the name of Paul Leroi. With Rodin's help, he had gathered around him a group of artists for whom he acted as intermediary for the sale of their works. Gauchez took an interest in Camille and in 1885 bought two bronzes of the bust *Giganti*.[40] These bronzes, like most of those cast in the 1880s, have no foundry mark. They are usually attributed to Gruet, who at that time could not have been Charles-Adolphe Gruet, but they may equally plausibly have been cast by François Rudier or Griffoul et Lorge, since all three foundries worked for Rodin in the 1880s.[41] In 1886, Camille exhibited the bust of her sister Louise and Gauchez bought both the bronze shown at the Salon and the terracotta, with Rodin taking care of the commercial side of the transaction.[42] Gauchez kept the terracotta for himself until 1892, when he donated it to the Musée des Beaux-Arts in Lille (cat. 34, p. 127), and sold the bronze to Baroness Nathaniel de Rothschild, who almost immediately donated it to the Musée Bargoin in Clermont-Ferrand (cat. 35, p. 126). He was also interested in the bust of Paul, and published a drawing of it in *L'Art* in 1887, while the bronze was exhibited at the Salon (cat. 27 and 102, p. 123). He had asked Camille for an accompanying note, but she "got bogged down" in writing it and asked Rodin for help: "Could you correct it for me please and add a nice bit on the movement and quest for trueness to life, etc. . . . I just wasn't able to do it. Send me back the corrected note at the earliest, otherwise you know how M. Gauchez will tell me off again" (cat. 183).

This bronze was cast for Baroness Nathaniel de Rothschild. Née Charlotte de Rothschild, a painter herself and interested in both contemporary artists and the French eighteenth century (two reasons why she liked the bust of *Louise Claudel*), Baroness Nathaniel supported young sculptors to such an extent that, on June 30, 1888, Gauchez suggested to Rodin that they (Claudel, Turcan, Ringel, Escoula, Boucher, Etcheto, Rozet, et al) come together to express "their profoundest thanks and feelings of gratitude for the support and encouragement she has given them and which have enabled several of them to complete their works."[43] Gauchez had also succeeded in interesting the baroness's brother, Alphonse de Rothschild, in his "stable." Owner of the review *L'Art*, elected a member of the Institut de France in

1886, he was the paragon of the art lover and great donor to French museums, and exercised a particular form of patronage which consisted in buying works by young artists and then immediately donating them to public collections. It was to him that Rodin owed his first well-paid commission, in 1885,[44] and Camille in turn greatly benefited from his generosity.[45]

However, the creation of the Société Nationale des Beaux-Arts in 1890 set Gauchez, who supported the Société des Artistes Français, and Rodin at odds. On March 14, 1892, Gauchez sent Rodin back a drawing of *Balzac*, which he had nevertheless asked him for, calling it a "vile smear."[46] After this, correspondence between the two men ceased. The following year Rodin ended his subscription to *L'Art*, which was by this time attacking him violently. In September 1894, Rodin, who was unwell and had retired to the country, complained to Gauchez, "But what consoles me is that you do justice to my pupil, who is a great sculptress because she draws admirably."[47] In his article on the Salon, Gauchez had again mentioned "this brilliant pupil of M. Rodin . . . whilst warning her against her penchant, not for doing pastiches of her teacher, but for drawing attention to herself,"[48] before losing interest in her as he did with all of Rodin's entourage.

Cat. 183
Letter from Camille Claudel to Auguste Rodin
[May–June 1886?]
1 sheet, 17.5 x 11.5 cm
Musée Rodin, Paris

Cat. 43

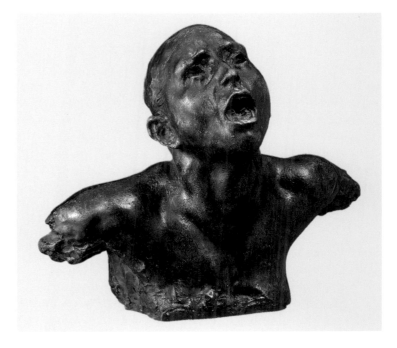

Cat. 14

Cat. 43

CAMILLE CLAUDEL
*Head of a Girl
with a Chignon*
About 1886
Bronze
14.3 x 9.5 x 14.8 cm
Musée Rodin, Paris

Cat. 142

AUGUSTE RODIN
The Cry
About 1886
Bronze
25.2 x 28.7 x 18.9 cm
Musée Rodin, Paris

CLAUDEL OR RODIN? Antoinette Le Normand-Romain

Cat. 147

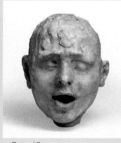

Cat. 44

Cat. 45

Cat. 46

Plasters were exchanged in the studio, and the vagaries of history sometimes deposited works where they do not belong, giving rise to confusion. This is the case with two plasters still in the Claudel family, a small *Head of Saint John the Baptist* which has the same network of seams as the S.679 plaster in the Musée Rodin, from which it differs only in the absence of the neck, and the *Head of Avarice* (cat. 147), close examination of which reveals that it was sawn off a complete version of the figure (which is part of the *Avarice and Lust* group, cat. 146, p. 49). It was therefore not a sculpture by Camille used by Rodin, but a fragment she picked up and later kept with her own works.

Conversely, works by Camille were signed by Rodin, especially when bronzes were cast from plasters at Meudon following Jules Mastbaum's orders for the Rodin Museum in Philadelphia in 1925–26 (cat. 46 and 54). The plasters in Rodin's studio after his death were systematically attributed to him, even though in 1898 Morhardt had noted that "in the very studio of the master her presence was indicated by fragments of great interest."[1] Yet in the cases of the *Slave* and *Laughing Man* heads, there are clays or plasters signed "Camille Claudel" (cat. 44). But she signed the base, which disappeared from the versions in the Musée Rodin (cat. 45). As for *Laughing Man*, the many copies (two terracottas and seventeen plasters) could indicate that this was a work executed in Rodin's

Cat. 147
AUGUSTE RODIN
Head of Avarice
About 1887
Plaster
15 x 10 x 10 cm
Private collection

Cat. 44
CAMILLE CLAUDEL
Head of a Slave
About 1887?
Grey clay (unfired)
22 x 8.5 x 11.5 cm
Private collection

Cat. 45
CAMILLE CLAUDEL
Head of a Slave
About 1887?
Patinated plaster
12.2 x 9.8 x 11.4 cm
Musée Rodin, Paris

Cat. 46
CAMILLE CLAUDEL
Head of a Slave
About 1887?
Bronze
12.7 x 9 x 10.8 cm
Rodin Museum, Philadelphia

Cat. 137

Cat. 53

Cat. 54

Cat. 157

Cat. 55

studio, under his direction as it were, by an assistant who remained anonymous as she was working at the time for him. Comparison of one of the terracottas (cat. 53) with works whose attribution to Rodin has never been questioned, for instance the head studies for *Jean de Fiennes* (cat. 137) or for *Balzac* (cat. 157), approximately the same size, show how similar the two artists' work then was. Working with flattened balls of clay, they both vigorously constructed the face, although

Rodin did so with more freedom than Camille. Rodin modeled almost solely with his fingers, while Camille reworked hers with a tool, particularly a short-toothed spatula, to tamp down the clay. Rodin used the same instrument, especially for the modeling of the small study called *Study C* (1892) for *Balzac*. This is why I suggest dating it to around 1891–92, when Rodin was beginning work on *Balzac*, *Laughing Man* and the small sketch for *Man with Folded Arms* (cat. 55), which until now has

been dated to around 1885. If this sculpture had been one of the works in Rodin's studio instead of belonging to the Claudel family, then it would immediately have been considered a sketch for *Study C*, especially as the small cylindrical onyx base on which it is mounted is similar to the ones Rodin used for his own works or for works in his collection. This is certainly not proof, but it does confirm that one has to pose the question: Claudel or Rodin?

Cat. 137

AUGUSTE RODIN
Sketch for the Head of Jean de Fiennes?
About 1885–86?
Terracotta
15.5 x 12.2 x 12.5 cm
Musée Rodin, Paris

Cat. 53

CAMILLE CLAUDEL
Laughing Man
About 1891–92
Terracotta
20.6 x 9.3 x 11.5 cm
Musée Rodin, Paris

Cat. 54

CAMILLE CLAUDEL
Laughing Man
About 1891–92?
Bronze
12.5 x 9.3 x 11.7 cm
Musée Rodin, Paris

Cat. 157

AUGUSTE RODIN
Sketch for the Head of Balzac
About 1891
Terracotta
23.9 x 9.5 x 14.4 cm
Musée Rodin, Paris

Cat. 55

CAMILLE CLAUDEL
Man with Folded Arms
About 1891–92?
Terracotta
10 x 9.5 x 8 cm
Private collection

Rodin modeled Camille's face for the first time soon after they met. The so-called portrait *with Short Hair* (cat. 126, p. 70) is traditionally dated to 1884, but was doubtless made earlier. If, as Yves Lacasse suggests, César's photograph (cat. 23 A, p. 18) should be dated 1881, the portrait could have been sculpted as early as 1882. Yet it gives us a more familiar image of Camille, close to the photograph by Pannelier showing her in her sculptor's smock with Ghita Theuriet (fig. 16, p. 70) both proudly displaying the tools of their trade. Camille's hairstyle is still almost childlike, the hair hanging down the back with a few loose locks hanging over the forehead, exactly as in Rodin's head.

Rodin did another portrait, most probably a little later, of which the mask (cat. 131) in the photograph of Rodin's studio taken in April 1887 by either Jessie Lipscomb or her fiancé William Elborne (fig. 17, p. 71) is the earliest surviving version. The mask was a mold taken from a clay head modeled extremely spontaneously, with no concern for smoothing the modeling. This is particularly evident around the right eye and on the left side of the nose, where several cursorily squashed balls of clay have been left as they are. The forehead is bare, with the hair flattened back over the top of the head and gathered in two masses at the temples. Perhaps a vestige of a complete head, it in turn gave rise to the *Head Wearing a Bonnet*, which has the same irregularities in the modeling around the eyes and nostrils. But the hairstyle has

been changed, the hair being now completely concealed by a kind of tight-fitting turban. This new head (cat. 132, p. 73) was modeled in clay after an impression of the mask. One notes the difference in treatment between the face, whose very noticeable seam lines are moreover identical to those of the plaster mask, and the hair modeled in the clay itself and then reworked with a tool. There is a narrow crevasse where the two parts join along the cheek. A base rather like a collaret was added, and the head was inclined slightly forward (giving it a slightly thoughtful expression) and mounted on a small round onyx pedestal. There is a plaster made from the mold of this ensemble (fig. 18, p. 72) in the California Palace of the Legion of Honor in San Francisco.[1] Like most of Rodin's works in San Francisco, the plaster was

Cat. 131
AUGUSTE RODIN
Mask of Camille Claudel
About 1884?
Plaster
22.8 x 17 x 16 cm
Musée Rodin, Paris

Cat. 126

Fig. 16

donated by Mrs. Spreckels, whose collection was largely put together by Loïe Fuller. The latter served as Rodin's mediator with America and this is evidently one of the sculptor's works that she liked. On December 16, 1914,[2] Rodin told her that the price of a bronze was 2,500 francs (of which he had already received an advance of 1,000 francs), yet specified

that the pieces "will be delivered progressively as the founder Rudier delivers them to me, the war prevents me from giving dates." In November 1913, Rudier had indeed cast two "heads of a woman with a headband and an onyx base," one of which was exhibited in London in 1914 and was part of Rodin's gift to the English nation (Victoria and Albert Museum, London). At least three casts were made in the ensuing years, the last at the behest of the city of Calais in 1924 (cat. 134, p. 72), most of them mounted on circular onyx pedestals identical in shape to the ones supporting the terracotta and the San Francisco plaster.

The only surviving copy of the first portrait is an early cast that has been identified, without proof, as the "Mademoiselle Claudel, head" included in the

Cat. 126

AUGUSTE RODIN
Camille with Short Hair
1882?
Plaster
27.5 x 21.5 x 21.5 cm
Musée Rodin, Paris

Fig. 16

VICTOR PANNELIER
Camille in a sculptor's smock next to Ghita Theuriet
About 1882?
Photograph
Private collection

Rodin donation in 1916. This cast, whose green undercoat is clearly visible in the declivities, could indeed correspond to the "green bust" in the list of works "to be shown" drawn up by Rodin in July 1910.[3] But the two representatives of the Metropolitan Museum of Art who came to examine them in Meudon showed no interest in them and this portrait, never exhibited, was presumably not intended for public view. The other one, on the other hand, was shown to the public in 1899, since the mask was part of the exhibition in Belgium and the Netherlands, and the following year at the Pavillon de l'Alma (no. 4, *Head of a Woman, Mlle C,*[4] cat. 131, p. 68, and cat. 9 A). During these painful years, in which Camille's face never ceased to haunt him (see "Camille Sublimated," pp. 216–31), Rodin openly paid homage to her: the title, "Mlle C," unambiguously states the identity of the model.

Camille Wearing a Bonnet thus seems to be his official portrayal of the woman he had loved so much. The departure point for *Thought* (cat. 162, p. 224) and *Aurora* (cat. 166, p. 226), it was also reproduced in glass paste by Jean Cros in 1911 (cat. 133, p. 72). Reusing the technique perfected by his father, he made at least two delicately tinted copies[5] in this

Fig. 17

Cat. 9 A

Fig. 17
WILLIAM ELBORNE
or JESSIE LIPSCOMB
Mask of Camille Claudel
with *Avarice and Lust*
in Rodin's studio
1887
Photograph
Private collection

translucent, fragile and precious material, also used for the masks of *Rose Beuret* and *Hanako.*

At any rate, as in César's second photograph (cat. 24, p. 72), the model is gazing unsmilingly straight ahead, eyes wide open, lips tight, with a serious, even impenetrable expression. The impression this firmly structured face gives is already that of a strong yet fragile personality: "A deeply personal nature that attracts by its grace and repels by its savagery."[6] To imagine the attraction she then exercised one has to complement these portraits with Paul Claudel's description of her. "A superb young woman in the triumphant sparkle of her beauty and genius. The superb forehead overhanging magnificent eyes of a blue so rare as to be encountered elsewhere only in novels,[7] the nose which she later loved to think she inherited from the Graces, the wide mouth, even prouder than it is sensual, the powerful mane of hair—that true brown which the English call *auburn* —falling to her waist. An impressive air of courage, frankness, superiority and gaiety. Someone who has received much."[8] His words conjure another Camille, one with whom only benevolent fairies seem to have

Cat. 9 A
ANONYMOUS
The Mask of Camille Claudel
at the Rodin *exhibition,*
Place de l'Alma, 1900
1900
Photograph, aristotype
6 x 4.5 cm
Musée Rodin, Paris

_Fig. 18

_Cat. 134

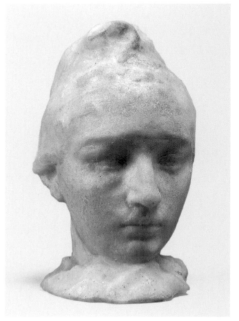

_Cat. 133

_Cat. 24

Fig. 18	Cat. 134	Cat. 133	Cat. 24	Cat. 132
ANONYMOUS	AUGUSTE RODIN	AUGUSTE RODIN and JEAN CROS	CÉSAR	AUGUSTE RODIN
Camille Wearing a Bonnet	*Camille Wearing a Bonnet*	*Camille Wearing a Bonnet*	*Camille Claudel*	*Camille Wearing a Bonnet*
About 1884?	About 1884?	About 1884?	About 1885	About 1884?
Plaster	Bronze	Glass paste, 1911	Photograph, albumin print	Terracotta
Photograph	24.5 x 15 1 x 18.4 cm	24.9 x 14.9 x 17.9 cm	16 x 10.5 cm	25.7 x 15 x 17.7 cm
Musée Rodin, Paris	Musée des Beaux-Arts, Calais	Musée Rodin, Paris	Private collection	Musée Rodin, Paris

_Cat. 132

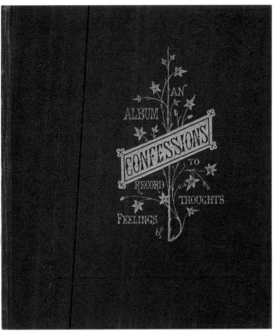

Cat. 191

been concerned, a Camille destined for the most brilliant of futures.

This was undoubtedly how she was seen by her English friends, such as Florence Jeans, whom she met on the Isle of Wight and to whom she wrote regularly from 1886 to 1889 about her work and their friends in common, in particular Jessie Lipscomb, now Mrs. Elborne, whom she had come to detest, and the marriage of her sister. In these letters, she comes across as a young woman like any other, preoccupied with clothes. She sent "Professor Florence," as she called her in memory of the English lessons she had given her, fashion plates and fabric samples of her and her sister's dresses (cat. 192). But this was only a facade and on May 16, 1888, when she was filling in her friend's album of *Confessions: An Album to Record Opinions, Thoughts, Feelings, Ideas, Peculiarities, Impressions, Characteristics of Friends, & c . . .* (cat. 191), she refused to describe

her state of mind—"it is too difficult to tell"—and defines herself as "caprice and inconstancy." In her view, a woman's principal virtue is "to make her husband really angry," and her idea of unhappiness is "to be the mother of many children." She preferred "the color which changes the most and the flower which changes the least," has no qualities—"they are all boring"—and tolerates "all [her] defects but not at all those of others!" True, this was only a game and Camille is being deliberately provocative, yet it is clear that although she has indeed received much, one also senses a fierce independence, a determination to make her mark in a domain in which hitherto virtually only men had succeeded. She showed herself to be, said Morhardt, "extraordinarily strong-willed and tenacious. Perhaps the defining characteristic of her soul is her unwavering determination to affirm, first of all, her aim of becoming a sculptor and, later, to sacrifice anything that might prove a hindrance in the complete and necessary realization of this goal."[9] We know that from birth she had a "slightly lopsided walk" which, according to Robert Godet, the only person to have mentioned this, gave her a "slight limp,"[10] and the will to surmount this handicap had no doubt contributed to forging her character, an untrammeled, dominating character that would bring her nothing but sorrow when she discovered that Rodin was slipping away from her.

As could be expected, she in turn sculpted his portrait, a still young, thin-faced Rodin whose broad forehead and strong nose epitomize the will and power to create. This "patient and thoughtful" work, characterized by its very detailed analysis of his physiognomy, was sculpted in 1888–89 according to Morhardt, abandoned and resumed as Rodin had little time to pose, and fell apart when a mold was made from it.[11] The bust was finished using this mold and the first cast was made by Adolphe Gruet, who invoiced Rodin for the sum of 250 francs on October 8, 1892 (cat. 198). This bronze therefore belonging to Rodin was shown at the Salon of the Société Nationale des Beaux-Arts in 1892. It was engraved by Léveillé (cat. 112) and, considered the official portrait

Cat. 112

Cat. 198

of the artist until 1902, did the rounds of various exhibitions.[12] It later ended up in Rodin's possession, who then parted with it in unknown circumstances, but it seems it could have been the cast Eugène Gruet donated to the Musée Rodin in 1950 (cat. 56, p. 77) since, as far as I know, it is the only one bearing the mark of Adolphe Gruet, who took over from his father, Charles-Acolphe Gruet, as director of the foundry at 195 avenue de Maine in 1890. He made several medium-sized casts for Rodin between 1891 and

Cat. 112

AUGUSTE LÉVEILLÉ
Auguste Rodin,
by Camille Claudel
About 1896
Woodcut
50.5 x 32 cm
Musée Rodin, Paris

Cat. 198

ADOLPHE GRUET
*Invoice made out to
Auguste Rodin for
the casting of his bust
by Camille Claudel*
Dated October 8, 1892
1 sheet, 18.4 x 20.9 cm
Musée Rodin, Paris

1895, then left France for Tunisia. While he was working for Rodin, artists in the latter's entourage naturally made use of his services, Desbois and Camille in particular. Six bronzes cast for Camille bear his mark.[13] Very precise casts, they reproduce all the surface detail. The bust of Rodin therefore bears the cracks, tool marks and seams resulting from its chaotic execution.

In 1892, Edmond Bigand-Kaire, collector, wine grower and sea captain, bought the fine wax-patinated plaster today in Martigues (cat. 57, p. 78). To help the artist, he had offered to acquire the *Old Woman* then on view at the Exposition des Arts Libéraux, even suggesting a "sold" label be put on it: "This will always publicize it."[14] But in her reply, Camille announced that the bust of Rodin had been accepted for the Salon of the Société Nationale des Beaux-Arts, adding, "And I am most pleased about this."[15] Bigand-Kaire, a friend of Rodin, would have no doubt preferred to receive the latter's portrait rather than that of an anonymous old woman, and as a bronze was beyond his means, Camille sold him a plaster, probably for 300 francs,[16] a relatively high amount since she asked the same for the *Mercure de France* bronzes in 1897–98.

Some years later, when Camille was hopelessly embroiled in financial problems, Morhardt succeeded in obtaining an order for fifteen bronzes for the *Mercure de France*, to be cast by François Rudier then finished by her (removal of the seams, engraving of a caduceus and signature). In November 1897, she complained to Rodin about the work this entailed and the little she was making out of it: each bust was sold for 300 francs, of which she received 280, out of which she had to pay the foundry. On the basis of Gruet's fee (250 francs), she was left with only 30 for a week's work. "It takes me a day just to engrave the caduceus," she wrote, "and five to six days to satisfactorily remove the seams" (cat. 215, pp. 206–7). Replying to her on December 2, Rodin recommended abandoning the caducei and the removal of the seams, as "that is not for you to do" (cat. 216, pp. 208–9). At least ten casts were made, however. It was one of the few works Camille managed to sell but, by a kind of twist of fate, at the very time that her relationship with Rodin had definitively ended. "I now have to find a buyer for a bust of Rodin that is very beautiful and of admirable patina," she wrote to Karl Boës, editor of *La Plume* from 1899.[17] Boës acted as middleman or acquired for himself one of the *Mercure de France* casts and exhibited it at the Salon des Cent he organized in the offices of *La Plume* in 1900. In 1903, Loïe Fuller exhibited another in New York,[18] probably the one now in the California Palace of the Legion of Honor in San Francisco and which was included in the museum's

Cat. 56
CAMILLE CLAUDEL
Auguste Rodin
1892
Bronze
40.4 x 24.6 x 28 cm
Musée Rodin, Paris

Cat. 56

_Cat. 57

_Cat. 58

inaugural exhibition in 1924. The cast in the Musée du Petit Palais in Paris (cat. 58) is also definitely one of the François Rudier casts but not reworked, or only minimally. Camille seems to have taken Rodin's advice concerning these casts: the busts with a caduceus beneath the Camille Claudel signature (fig. 21) are rare. In their catalogue raisonné, Anne Rivière, Bruno Gaudichon and Danielle Ghanassia list only two. I myself have examined one—a bronze that has been carefully reworked—and, although there are no traces of the seam, there are deep chisel marks in the beard and hair, as if

Camille had wanted to leave her mark on Rodin's portrait.

Comparison of this bronze (fig. 19) and the one in the Musée Rodin (fig. 20) confirms that the model had been reworked between 1892 and 1897. The modeling of the flesh is smoother and the beard and relief less acute than in the latter. The patina is also different. Gruet was a self-proclaimed specialist in Japanese "patinas," and the cast made in his foundry has a fine patina with green and red reflections that accentuates the modeling and gives it even more depth.

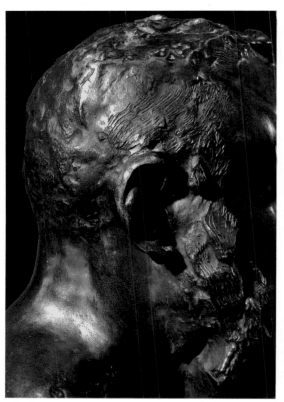

Fig. 19

Fig. 20

Fig. 21

Cat. 57

CAMILLE CLAUDEL
Auguste Rodin
1892
Plaster coated with wax
42 x 26 x 30 cm
Musée Ziem, Martigues

Cat. 58

CAMILLE CLAUDEL
Auguste Rodin
1892
Bronze
40.7 x 25.7 x 28 cm
Musée du Petit Palais, Paris

Fig. 19

CAMILLE CLAUDEL
Auguste Rodin
Bronze, about 1898
Private collection
Detail of the right profile
with incisions made
by the artist

Fig. 20

CAMILLE CLAUDEL
Auguste Rodin
1892
Bronze
Musée Rodin, Paris
Detail of the right profile

Fig. 21

CAMILLE CLAUDEL
Auguste Rodin
Bronze, about 1898
Private collection
Detail of the caduceus

"CAMILLE, MY BELOVED, IN SPITE OF EVERYTHING" Antoinette Le Normand-Romain

Camille must have very quickly aroused intense passion in Rodin. In 1884, at the height of his artistic powers, he expressed his exaltation in *Eternal Spring* (cat. 129, p. 84). This work was exhibited in 1883 at the Galerie Georges Petit simply as "Group, plaster" and was only subsequently given the title *Eternal Spring*, which was inspired by a poem by Victor Hugo.[1] The poem must have echoed the feeling of renewal that Rodin experienced at the beginning of his love for Camille, who, one should remember, was twenty-four years younger than he:

> Let us love one another. Spring is divine
> We feel aroused by the flowers of the ravine,
> By indulgent April, by nests unmorose,
> By the offer of moss and the scent of the rose,
> And by the darkness of the roses in the woods.

Like *The Kiss*, *Eternal Spring* may have originally been destined for *The Gates of Hell* but, if so, was very soon excluded. *The Kiss*, on the other hand, was already in place in the middle of the left door in early 1886 and it was during the ensuing months that Rodin withdrew it. He was going through a difficult period, his relationship with Camille having become almost unbearably tense. By then she had almost certainly been his mistress for some time, but the game she was playing with the totally subjugated Rodin was causing him terrible suffering. The famous letter "to my cruel friend," the first of a series of letters overflowing with

such passion and suffering, could thus have been written in 1886 and, more precisely, early in the year given the allusion to the "Salon," the annual official exhibition that usually opened in early April. In the grip of an all-devouring passion that drove him to the brink of madness, Rodin declares, in a disjointed outflow in which he switches from *tu* to *vous* in the same sentence, that he is ready to give up everything except her. "My poor head is really sick and I can no longer get up in the morning. This evening I wandered [hours] without finding you, our places, how sweet death would be to me and how long my agony is . . . There are moments when frankly I think I will forget you. But in an instant, I feel your terrible power. Take pity, wicked one. I am at the end of my tether. I can no longer go a day without seeing you. Otherwise horrible madness. That's it, I am no longer working, harmful deity, and yet I love you passionately . . . I am already dead and no longer understand the trouble I took over things I am now indifferent to. Let me see

Cat. 156

AUGUSTE RODIN
The Eternal Idol
Before 1891
Bronze
17 x 14 x 7 cm
Musée Rodin, Paris

My cruel friend,

My poor head is really sick and I can no longer get up in the morning. This evening
I wandered (hours) without finding you, our places, how sweet death would be to me and how
long my agony is. Why did you wait so long for me at the studio? What has happened to you?
What pain I had in store for me. I have moments of anemia in which I suffer less, but today,
the implacable pain is still there. Camille, my beloved, in spite of everything, in spite of the
madness that will be your doing if this goes on. Why don't you believe me? I'll give up my Salon,
sculpture; if I could go anywhere, to a country where I would forget, but there isn't one . . .

je ne puis te convaincre et mes raisons
sont impuissantes. ma souffrance
tu n'y crois pas. je pleure et tu
en doute. je ne ris plus depuis longtemps
je ne chante plus tout m'est insipide
et indifférent. je suis déjà mort
et je ne comprends plus le mal
que je me suis donné pour des choses
qui ne sont si indifférentes maintenant
Laisse moi te voir
tous les jours, ce sera une bonne action
et peut être que je m'en trouverai
mieux, car toi seul peut me sauver
par ta générosité.

ne laisse pas prendre à la hideuse
maladie mon intelligence, l'amour
ardent et si pur que j'ai pour toi
aie enfin pitié ma chérie, et toi même un jour
récompensée Rodin

je t'embrasse les mains mon amie,
toi qui me donne des jouissances si élevées
si ardentes, près de toi, mon âme existe
avec force et dans sa fureur d'amour
ton respect et toujours au dessus.
Le respect que j'ai pour ton caractère

pour toi ma Camille et une
cause de cette violente passion.
ne me traite pas impitoyablement
je te demande si peu.
ne me menace pas et laisse moi voir
que ta main si douce marque ta
bonté pour moi. et que quelquefois
je la baise. Adieu mes
transports.

je ne regrette rien. ni le
dénouement qui me paraît funèbre,
ma vie sera tombée dans un
gouffre, mais mon âme a eu
sa floraison tardive hélas. Il
a fallu que je te connaisse. Et
tout a pris une vie inconnue
ma terne existence a flambé
dans un feu de joie! merci car
c'est à toi que je dois
. La part de ciel que
j'ai eu dans ma vie
tes chères mains laisse les sur
ma figure, que ma chair soit
heureuse que mon cœur sente encore
ton divin amour se répandre à
nouveau.
dans quel

Cat. 129

(cat. 141), in which the savage cry of a man abducting an apparently impassive woman expresses all the passion he felt for Camille, who was resisting him. Despite or perhaps because of the promising early career which she largely owed him, Camille felt the need to distance herself from him a little. "With regard to Mlle Claudel, a profound admirer of her master, M. Auguste Rodin, and rightfully so, one can only be reserved about her future prospects," wrote Paul Leroi, alias Léon Gauchez. "M. Rodin is such a powerful personality, his mastery is so superior, that one has to beware of becoming engrossed in an influence so naturally fascinating, in short, the young artist really has to be exclusively Mlle Claudel and not a reflection."[2]

One can imagine that it would have been remarks such as this that prompted Camille to flee to England to stay with Jessie Lipscomb in the spring of 1886. Rodin went to London to spend a few days with her in May–June, but she remained in England all summer, staying later with Amy Singer at Frome in Somerset and then with Emily Fawcett on the Isle of Wight, where she was joined by her brother Paul. The surviving correspondence—some fifteen letters from Rodin to Jessie Lipscomb and two from Camille to Rodin—reveal the two protagonists' states of mind.

you everyday, that would be a good deed and perhaps something better will happen to me, because you alone can save me with your generosity" (cat. 182, pp. 82–83; see the complete translation, pp. 370–71).

THE "CONTRACT"
Although he did not exhibit at the 1886 Salon in June, as mentioned above Rodin showed a number of figures destined for *The Gates of Hell* at the Galerie Georges Petit. One of them was an assemblage, *I Am Beautiful*

Cat. 129
AUGUSTE RODIN
Eternal Spring
About 1884
Bronze
64.5 x 53 x 44.5 cm
Musée Rodin, Paris

Cat. 141
AUGUSTE RODIN
I Am Beautiful
1886
Bronze
69.4 x 36 x 36 cm
Musée Rodin, Paris

Cat. 14

Camille responded to Rodin's anxious passion with a reticence that was a mixture of both fierce independence and, undoubtedly, capriciousness. "I am furious and in despair at not having been to the colonial exhibition at 1:30 on Thursday," he wrote to Jessie shortly after May 30, 1886. ". . . How troublesome and how I fear to displease you, your family and Mademoiselle Camille. I did not expect this unhoped-for chance, and so I cannot benefit from it."[3] And, when Camille was about to return to France: "If it were possible that around the 25th of the month I came to fetch you at Calais, you could see and, before going to Villeneuve, go on a little trip to see towns in France and Belgium. I know all that depends somewhat on your arrangements and on the whim of Mlle Camille . . . My dear artist, you must get me to show you some beautiful towns of northern France, do what you can and, as always, I owe you still more gratitude, yes, do that, and I will be happy" (August 23, 1886).[4]

The "dear stubborn one . . . [whom] we so love, that I really think it is her who directs us all" (cat. 185) maintained her hold over Rodin from a distance. "Dear friend, I am really angry to hear that you are still ill. I am sure that you have again been overeating at your damned dinners, with the damned people I detest, who take your time and health and give you nothing in return. But I will say nothing as I know I am powerless to prevent you from the ill that I see. How do you manage to work on your figure without a model? Tell me, I am very concerned about this. You reproach me for not writing enough to you but you yourself only send me a few banal and indifferent lines which do not amuse me. You can imagine that I am not so happy here. It seems that I am so far from you and that you are such a complete stranger to me! There is always something absent which torments me" (cat. 184).

This letter from Camille, which can be situated at the end of the summer of 1886 as she returned to France in September, and which, despite appearances, is one of the tenderest letters to have survived, raises the question of life modeling sessions. True, she may well have already modeled for Rodin, but no other document confirms this and she does not say enough about the work for which she may have modeled for one to be in any way certain. But it is her jealousy which above all shows through in this letter, a jealousy which, after her return to Paris, would gradually drive her to get Rodin to sign a "contract" whereby he had to place himself at her entire disposition, whereas she granted him only the minimum. Rodin, overjoyed to be with her again, was ready to consent to anything, especially as he must have felt a little guilty: he had not left Rose, who, in his absence, had assumed responsibility for his studio and the work in progress. "How are you, my Darling? I am thinking of you and my mind is at rest my work is in your hands . . . Yours completely your Auguste," he wrote to Rose in late May 1886, despite having left for London in the hope of joining Camille there.[5]

Cat. 184

Letter from Camille Claudel
to Auguste Rodin
[August 1886]
1 sheet, 15.4 x 22 cm
Musée Rodin, Paris

Cher ami,

Je suis bien fâchée
d'apprendre que
vous êtes encore malade,
je suis sûre que vous
avez encore fait des
excès de nourriture
dans vos maudits
dîners, avec le mauvais
monde que je déteste,
qui vous prend votre
temps et votre santé.

et ne vous rend rien.
Mais je ne veux rien dire
car je sais que je suis
impuissante à vous
préserver du mal que
je vois.
Comment faites-vous
pour travailler à la
maquette de votre
figure sans modèle ?
dites-le-moi, j'en suis
très inquiète. Vous
me reprochez de ne
pas vous écrire assez long

mais vous-même,
vous m'envoyez quelques
lignes banales et
indifférentes qui ne
m'amusent pas.
Vous pensez bien que
je ne suis pas très gai
ici ; il me semble que
je suis si loin de vous !
et que vous suis
complètement étrangère.
Il y a toujours quelque
chose d'absent qui
me tourmente.

Je vous raconterai mieux
tout ce que j'ai fait
quand je vous verrai.
Je vais jeudi prochain
chez miss Fawcett, je
vous écrirai le jour
de mon départ d'Angleterre.
D'ici là je vous en prie
travaillez, gardez tout
le plaisir pour moi.
Je vous embrasse
Camille

inv. Ma 108

D'ici au mois de mai je n'aurai aucune femme sans cela les conditions sont rompues.

Si ma commande du Chili s'exécute c'est au Chili que nous irons au lieu de l'Italie

Je ne prendrai aucun des modèles de femme que j'ai connus

Il sera fait une photographie chez Carjat dans le costume que Mlle Camille portait à l'académie toilette de ville et peut être en costume de soirée Mlle Camille restera à Paris jusqu'à mai

Mlle Camille s'engage à me recevoir à son atelier 4 fois par mois jusqu'au mois de mai

Rodin

inv. L.1452

pour l'avenir à partir d'aujourd'hui 12 octobre 1886 je ne tiendrai pour élève que Mlle Camille Claudel et je la protegerai seule par tous les moyens que j'aurai à ma disposition par mes amis qui seront les siens surtout par mes amis influents

je n'accepterai plus d'autres élèves pour qu'il ne se produise pas de hasard de talents rivaux quoique je ne suppose pas que l'on rencontre souvent des artistes aussi naturellement doués

à l'exposition je ferai mon possible pour le placement, les journaux

Je n'irai plus sous aucun prétexte chez Mme ... à qui je n'enseignerai plus la sculpture

Après l'exposition au mois de mai nous partons pour l'Italie et y restons au moins 6 mois commencement d'une liaison indissoluble après laquelle Mlle Camille sera ma femme Je serai bien heureux de pouvoir offrir une figurine en marbre si Mlle Camille le veut bien accepter d'ici 4 mois au plus

inv. L.1452

Cat. 186
Contract between Auguste Rodin and Camille Claudel
Dated October 12, 1886
1 sheet, 18.1 x 22.5 cm
Musée Rodin, Paris

D'ici au mois de mai je n'aurai
aucune femme sans cela les conditions
sont rompues.

Si ma commande du Chili s'exécute
c'est au Chili que nous irons au
lieu de l'Italie

Je ne prendrai aucun des modèles de femme que
j'ai connus

Il sera fait une photographie chez
Carjat dans le costume que Mlle Camille
portait à l'académie toilette de ville
à part être en costume de soirie
Mlle Camille restera à Paris jusqu'à mai

Mlle Camille s'engage à me
recevoir à son atelier 4 fois par
mois jusqu'au mois de mai

Rodin

Cat. 22

Cat. 22
ÉTIENNE CARJAT
Auguste Rodin
About 1886
Photograph, albumin print
16.5 x 10.5 cm
Private collection

Cat. 21
ÉTIENNE CARJAT
Camille Claudel
About 1886
Photograph, albumin print
16.5 x 10.5 cm
Private collection

And so, some weeks after her return in September, Rodin committed himself:

"In future from today October 12, 1886 I will have for my Pupil only Mlle Camille Claudel and will protect her alone by every means at my disposal by my friends who will be hers above all by my influential friends

I will not accept other pupils in order that there should not by chance be rival talents although I do not suppose that one often meets artists as naturally gifted

At the exhibition I will do what I can for sales, the newspapers

I will no longer under any pretext go to see Mme . . . to whom I will no longer teach sculpture

After the exhibition in the month of May we will leave for Italy and stay there for at least six months communally in an indissoluble relationship after which Mlle Camille will become my wife.

I will be very happy to offer a figurine in marble if Mlle Camille cares to accept it within four to five months.

Between now and the month of May I will have no other woman, and if I do, all the conditions are dissolved.

If my commission from Chile is confirmed we will go to Chile instead of Italy

I will take none of the women models I have known

There will be a photograph taken Chez Carjat in the costume Mlle Camille wore to the Academy [when she was dressed] for town, and perhaps one in evening dress

Mlle Camille will stay in Paris until May

Mlle Camille undertakes to receive me in her studio four times a month until the month of May

Rodin" (cat. 186, pp. 88–89; see the complete translation, p. 371).

Cat. 21

Cat. 41

Cat. 150

PREVIOUS PAGES

LEFT

Cat. 41

CAMILLE CLAUDEL
The Young Girl with a Sheaf
1886?
Terracotta
60 x 21 x 21 cm
Musée Rodin, Paris

RIGHT

Cat. 150

AUGUSTE RODIN
Galatea
Marble, before 1889
60.8 x 40.6 x 39.5 cm
Musée Rodin, Paris

Cat. 41

Fig. 22

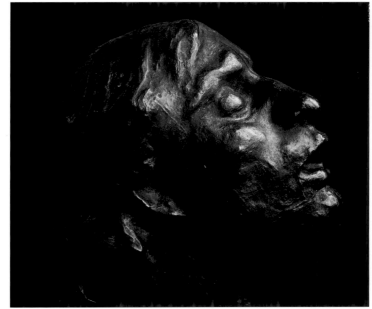

Fig. 23

The contract was adhered to at least at the outset regarding the Carjat photograph of Camille in town clothes and with a matching portrait of Rodin (cat. 21 and 22, pp. 90–91). And perhaps also in the realization of the marble figure that Rodin had promised her. For a long time the connection between Camille's *Young Girl with a Sheaf* (cat. 41, pp. 92, 94 and 95) and Rodin's *Galatea* (cat. 150, pp. 93 and 95) was emphasized and ascribed to their extraordinary communal feeling and inspiration. But could *Galatea* be the figure promised by Rodin? In which case Camille,

subsequently so possessive about her work, would have joyfully accepted that Rodin use one of her pieces as the departure point for one of his works. As for Rodin, what more beautiful homage could he, an already famous artist, pay her than by consenting to do so—even if in the end the marble did not go to Camille but to Eugenia Errazuriz?[6] This Chilean-born collector[7] belonged to the entourage of the Morla-Vicuñas, a couple of diplomats whom Rodin had undoubtedly met in early 1886, when Carlos Morla-Vicuña commissioned the *Monument to General Lynch* in Santiago. The project was never realized, but for a while Rodin thought it would be and therefore hoped to go to Chile. In 1887–88 he was very close to the Morla-Vicuñas.[8] The portrait he sculpted of the ravishing Luisa was so successful at the 1888 Salon that the state wanted to acquire it for the Musée du Luxembourg, to which the young woman consented (marble, Musée d'Orsay, Paris).

Fig. 22

MADELEINE JOUVRAY
Pain
Marble, before 1887
Musée des Beaux-Arts, Lille

Fig. 23

AUGUSTE RODIN
Head in Pain
About 1881–82
Large model, about 1901–2
Bronze
Musée Rodin, Paris

Cat. 50

All of which was bound to make Camille jealous. There are also questions as to the role of Madeleine Jouvray, who has been seen as the "Madame" to whom Rodin promised to no longer teach sculpture. In 1887, Alphonse de Rothschild gave the Musée de Lille a marble sculpted by her, *Pain* (fig. 22), which, although the representation of tears is rather overdone, was clearly influenced by Rodin's *Head in Pain* (fig. 23). But comparisons can also be made with Camille's *The Psalm* (cat. 50). Might Camille have sought to crush her rival by showing that she was capable of better? Her head is admittedly far superior to Jouvray's in the decorative arrangement of the

hood and above all in its expressive intensity. But it also speaks volumes about the tensions reigning in the studio and one can imagine that at a given moment, in a fit of anger or due to lack of money, the two lovers parted with the works which were intended to seal their union. The terracotta, at an

Cat. 50

CAMILLE CLAUDEL
The Psalm
1889
Bronze
47 x 32.5 x 31 cm
Musée Boucher-de-Ferthes
Abbeville

_Fig. 24

_Fig. 25

in September 1889,[11] which enables its identification with the figure of the same name shown at the *Monet-Rodin* exhibition which opened on June 21 that year at the Galerie Georges Petit (no. 16). This marble bears Rodin's very visible signature and has several of his specific characteristics, such as the reference points for its transposition into marble (other French artists effaced them), and an entire part left apparently unfinished. Yet it was indeed finished as far as the artist was concerned, since he had already parted with it: the catalogue of the *Monet-Rodin* exhibition states that it belonged to Madame Errazuriz.

In early April 1887, Jessie Lipscomb also produced a *Mother and Child* group, known only from a photograph, in which the young woman's position is comparable to that of *Young Girl with a Sheaf*.[12] Anne Rivière, Bruno Gaudichon and Danielle Ghanassia

unknown date, became the property of Léon Lhermitte, while, by June 1889, the marble already belonged to Eugenia Errazuriz.

As far as we know, their dates of execution are quite close. The existence of the carefully modeled *Young Girl*, which has vivid accents made with a basting chisel on the face and hair and is signed "Camille Claudel," is attested prior to 1887 by a photograph taken in the studio in rue Notre-Dame-des-Champs, which Camille shared with Jessie Lipscomb[9] (fig. 25). As for *Galatea*, it was reproduced as a work by Rodin in plaster in February 1888,[10] and in marble at the end of an article by Gustave Geffroy published

Fig. 24
AUGUSTE RODIN
Mephistos
About 1880–81
Graphite, pen and
brown ink wash
Musée Rodin, Paris

Fig. 25
WILLIAM ELBORNE
Young Girl with a Sheaf
in the studio in rue
Notre-Dame-des-Champs
April? 1887
Photograph
Private collection

Cat. 41

Cat. 149

Fig. 26

consider that the latter eludes "what one could call the Claudelian vocabulary, particularly the concern with smooth, rounded modeling, absent from the face of this *Young Girl*, whose high cheekbones and pointed chin belong more to Rodin."[13] In fact, it is above all in the woman's Michelangelesque pose and gesture—arm folded against her body and hand on shoulder—that it is similar to Rodin's work: in the gesture of *Young Girl* and *Galatea*, one recognizes the gesture of *David*, *Victory*, *Aurora* and *Night*. Rodin himself had in fact already reused it in a group of works linked to his first studies for *The Gates* in the early 1880s: two drawings (Musée Rodin, D.5609 [fig. 24] and D.5630), the latter annotated "Abruzzesi very beautiful" (the name of the young woman so present in Rodin's studio in the early 1880s), and the

relief at the bottom of the right pilaster of *The Gates of Hell*. Yet the comparison shows that *Young Girl* is more vapid. She is on her own, erect, and has her legs together, whereas in Rodin's couple the young woman is leaning voluptuously backwards, her left leg bent and open (at least in the first drawing, because it later becomes the right leg of the man crouching behind her). Rodin's work is always shot

Cat. 41
—
CAMILLE CLAUDEL
The Young Girl with a Sheaf
1886?
Terracotta
60 x 21 x 21 cm
Musée Rodin, Paris

Cat. 149
—
AUGUSTE RODIN
Galatea,
model for the marble
1887?
Plaster
39.5 x 27.7 x 22.3 cm
Musée Rodin, Paris

Fig. 26
—
AUGUSTE RODIN
Cybele
About 1890?
Plaster
Musée Rodin, Paris

_Cat. 168

Fig. 27
WILLIAM ELBORNE?
Two Children Playing,
terracotta, before 1886,
by Auguste Rodin
Photograph
Private collection

Cat. 168
AUGUSTE RODIN
Brother and Sister
Before 1897
Bronze
38.3 x 18 x 20.5 cm
Musée Rodin, Paris

through with a passion entirely absent from Camille's terracotta. The figure's adventures would continue for some time. It has been customary to compare *Young Girl with a Sheaf* and *Galatea* with a headless female nude, a small model of which (fig. 26, p. 99) was shown for the first time at the *Rodin* exhibition in Brussels and in the Netherlands in 1899, and the following year at the Pavillon d'Alma. But the backward-leaning back shows that it was in fact a reworking of the relief of *The Gates*, as confirmed by the fact that in 1899, this nude was entitled *The Abruzzi*, an obvious reference to Adèle Abbruzesi.[14] Threads are often difficult to spot in Rodin's oeuvre, but once identified they can be seen running from one end of his career to the other: taken from the right pilaster of *The Gates*, the

figure whose head has been removed, perhaps because the artist considered it too anecdotal, was thus a part of his first experimentation with partial forms. It corresponded to the new direction he was exploring so well that he had it enlarged (H. 1.64 m) and he exhibited the second version at the Salon of the Société Nationale des Beaux-Arts in 1905. The first bronze, entitled *Cybèle*, was part of Rodin's donation to the English nation in 1914 and its estimated value (25,000 francs) was the highest of all his bronzes.

When *Galatea* was reproduced in marble it was enlarged by approximately a third. The intermediate stage for this was a plaster (cat. 149, p. 99) in which the young girl is now resting against a kind of rock face, molded at the same time, which means that there must have been a prior state, probably in clay. Indeed, the rock wall seems to have been cut with a wire, as if a space had been prepared for another figure or, on the contrary, a figure had been removed.

But the drawing D.5609 is annotated "Mephistos" and "Do an in-the-round group with crouching figurine." Admittedly, the male figure is placed on the right, not on the left of his companion, but one can nevertheless connect it to the plaster, especially since in the plaster, between the girl's left arm and hip, there appears an element which can be interpreted as a bird's or snake's head, whereas in the marble it becomes merely a bump on the rock. Might Rodin have initially imagined a group of two figures—Leda and the Swan, Acis and Galatea, Pygmalion and Galatea—which in the end he reduced to a single figure because of the size of the block of marble available? He did not completely abandon the idea, however: a child, like several he had modeled in the 1870s and 1880s, joined the young girl, a plaster of which Rodin had kept. Exactly when this happened is unclear since one can only identify the group for certain in an invoice from François Rudier dated May 17, 1897. A dozen casts were made by Rudier and Léon Perzinka before 1900, and almost fifty afterwards, the popularity of *Brother and Sister* (cat. 168) having remained constant, particularly in England. One can understand collectors' enthusiasm for this youthful and charming little juvenile figure group which, it should be emphasized, is probably the only work in which one can see both lovers' hands, and corresponds to an aspect of Rodin's work which, throughout the 1880s, provided an indispensable counterpoint to the tragic universe of *The Gates of Hell*. Another work in this same vein is the group of children which Rodin gave to the Lipscombs[15] (fig. 27).

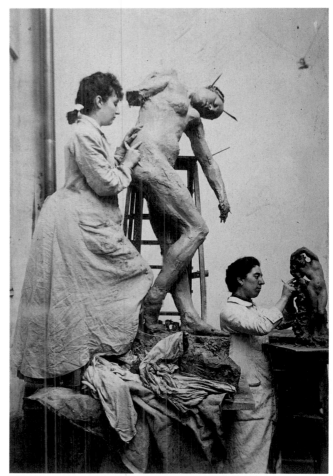

_Cat. 105

SAKUNTALA

Jessie Lipscomb returned to Paris in February 1887, again staying with the Claudels and sharing Camille's studio.[16] Camille soon took umbrage at her presence, however. As early as March 15, Jessie complained to Rodin, "I think I will come and work at yours next Saturday if you do not mind. You know, I would like to say to you frankly, that I came from England specially to have your advice, and you had promised to give this. I am not keen on staying with Mademoiselle

Cat. 105
WILLIAM ELBORNE
Camille Claudel and Jessie Lipscomb in their atelier at 117 rue Notre-Dame-des-Champs
1887
Photograph,
gelatin silver print
15.2 x 9.8 cm
Musée Rodin, Paris

Fig. 28

Claudel if you do not mind, and the discussions you are having with her are none of my business" (cat. 188). In April, with the arrival in Paris of William Elborne, whom she married the following December, things got a bit better: Camille, Rodin and the fiancés went on a day trip to Versailles. "First we visited the palace and gardens then we went on foot through the woods to a very picturesque little village where we had supper at 7 in the evening. From there we returned by starry moonlight, again through the woods, and took the railway two leagues further on. It was great fun, but Will was so tired!"[17] However, by July Camille could no longer stand Jessie and turned her out of her studio. "We have broken off relations forever (at least I hope so) . . . I can't make up my mind whether she is a madwoman or a nasty

Fig. 28

ANONYMOUS
La Folie Payen
1910
Photograph
Musée Rodin, Paris

Cat. 37

CAMILLE CLAUDEL
Study for Sakuntala?
1886?
or
AUGUSTE RODIN
Study for The Kiss?
1880?
Terracotta
11 x 5.2 x 5.1 cm
Musée Rodin, Paris

Cat. 37

Cat. 38

girl devoured by jealousy, but if I allow myself to judge her state of mind from her appearance then I find her as ugly and deformed as can be."[18] Jessie, "excessively ill," left Paris for good and took several months to recover from this crisis.[19]

The year 1887 was also a difficult one for Camille. It was a year of storms and disappointments: the trips to Italy or Chile envisaged in the "contract" never came to be and, as we have seen, *Young Girl with a Sheaf* and *Galatea*, which should have symbolized the couple's union, ended up in other hands. All her energy was now channeled into the realization of the "large group" often mentioned in the letters she regularly wrote to Florence Jeans. *Sakuntala* was inspired by a drama by the Hindu poet Kalidasa. Bewitched by a spell, Dushyanta forgets he has

Cat. 39

Cat. 40

CLAUDEL (Mlle C.). — Çacountala, ou le mariage de l'homme squelette avec la fille de Quasimodo.

Fig. 29

Fig. 29

STOP
"Sakuntala or the marriage of a skeleton man to Quasimodo's daughter", *Salon humoristique illustré* (published by the *Journal amusant*), Paris, 1888

married Sakuntala, who, despairing, flees into the desert, where she gives birth to a son. When her wedding ring is discovered in the stomach of a fish, Dushyanta recovers his memory and relentlessly searches for her until, finally finding her, he kneels at her feet and begs her forgiveness, which she trustingly gives him immediately.

The group is Camille's first truly ambitious work and also one of her largest (H. 1.90 m). She may have begun it before leaving for England,[20] then worked on it in the studio she shared with Jessie Lipscomb (cat. 105, p. 101) and later in the studio at 113 boulevard d'Italie (now boulevard Auguste Blanqui). Her father having granted her an advancement of her inheritance,[21] and thanks also to Rodin, who rented it in his name, in January 1888 she moved into a new studio "on the ground floor at the back of the courtyard, pine floor, roof beams, whitewashed walls, use of the small shed at the foot of the chimney" (cat. 190).

From March 1890, Rodin, to be nearer to her, rented a dilapidated eighteenth-century mansion, the Folie Payen (fig. 28, p. 102), on the other side of the boulevard.[22]

Two studies for *Sakuntala* are still in the artist's family, and there are perhaps two other terracottas in the Musée Rodin. The latter do seem to be both by the same person, but whereas one is close to *Sakuntala*, the other refers directly to *The Kiss*. Until now, they have always been attributed to Rodin[23] since they were in his studio (see "Claudel or Rodin?", pp. 66–67), but one wonders whether they should not be given back to Camille; in which case this one would be part of a figure group close to *The Kiss* (cat. 37, p. 102). The figure that was sitting on the other's knees (therefore presumably the woman) must have later slipped to the ground (cat. 38, p. 102). Despite the former's close relationship with *The Kiss*, these two clays do indeed have similarities, particularly the vertically falling right arm of the seated figure and the color of the clay (underneath, where it was unaltered by any treatment). The seated figure later stood up and took on a distinctly feminine character: standing, leaning forward, bending in an arc to

Cat. 2 B
ANONYMOUS
Sakuntala, *plaster model, by Camille Claudel*
1888
Photograph, albumin print
15.5 x 10.6 cm
Musée Rodin, Paris

Cat. 47
CAMILLE CLAUDEL
Sakuntala
1888
Patinated plaster, broken
190 x 110 x 60 cm
Musée Bertrand, Châteauroux

Cat. 47

press its face to the other's (cat. 39, p. 103), before finding its almost definitive position (cat. 40, p. 103).

Once she had finalized the composition, Camille began the large model. A photograph (cat. 105, p. 101) showing her in front of the clay model of the young woman (for which the difficult Jasmina, whose name crops up several times in correspondence, no doubt posed) can be directly related to a letter to Florence Jeans on November 8, 1886: "My dear Florence, I have been so busy I have not had time to write you a single word. I am now working on my two larger than life-size figures and have two models a day: woman in the morning, man in the evening. You can imagine how tired I am; I regularly work twelve hours a day from 7 o'clock in the morning to 7 o'clock in the evening. Going home I can hardly stand up and I go to bed straightaway" (cat. 187). Despite her capricious models, a mold was made of the group in March 1888[24] and the plaster (cat. 47, pp. 105 and 109; cat. 2 B, p. 104) had some success at the 1888 Salon des Artistes Français, where it received an "honorable mention." In Stop's *Salon humoristique illustré* it was entitled "Sakuntala or the marriage of a skeleton man to Quasimodo's daughter"

Cat. 187

Letter from Camille Claudel to Florence Jeans
Postmarked November 8, 1886
1 sheet, 17.6 x 22 cm
Musée Rodin, Paris

(fig. 29, p. 104), but Paul Leroi reproduced a beautiful drawing[25] by Camille in *L'Art*, rating the work "the most extraordinary at the Salon . . . [this] chastely passionate group by a young woman, Mlle Camille Claudel . . . who, marvelously gifted, has for her art the proudest feeling, which she conveys in a manly way . . . [The] very slight defects are largely compensated for by the most remarkable subtleties of creation, the hand of the young man, for instance, trembling, still hesitating to embrace Sakuntala's body, and the exquisite movement of unconscious abandon of the beloved woman's entire being."[26]

Having put so much of herself into *Sakuntala*, Camille now wanted to sculpt it in marble. Supported by Rodin, she applied to the ministry for a block in October 1889, but as the work was not one of those acquired by the fine arts administration her request was turned down. So she embarked on an entirely different project. Reusing a procedure that Rodin had employed for *The Burghers of Calais*, whereby the same head was used for Jean d'Aire, Jacques de Wissant and Andrieu d'Andres, she made a new work out of a fragment of the plaster, *The Psalm* (cat. 50, p. 97), which Morhardt dates to 1889. Anne Rivière noticed that the face seemed to be the same as *Sakuntala*'s. But, as with Rodin, the different axis of the figure and above all the large hood covering the face have until now prevented one from ascertaining its origin. In *The Psalm*, whose connection to the *Head in Pain* has been discussed above, Camille again appears to be a Rodin disciple, yet, perhaps for the first time, she reveals her genuine originality in the treatment of the hood and the base,

Il me semble que j'ai encore bien des choses à vous dire que j'oublie tout à fait. Je deviens comme Perse

Tout à vous

Camille

11 rue n. d. deschamps

Rappelez moi au souvenir de m. Jeans.

Ma chère Florence

J'ai été tellement occupée que je n'ai pas eu le temps de vous écrire un seul mot. Je travaille maintenant à mes deux grandes figures plus que grandeur nature et j'ai deux modèles par jour: femme le matin et homme le soir. Vous pouvez penser si je suis fatiguée. Je travaille régulièrement 12 heures par jour de 7 heures matin à 9 heures soir, en arrivant il m'est impossible de dormir jamais et je me couche tout de suite. J'ai beaucoup d'ennuis de toutes sortes et je suis très découragée

Je pense souvent au paradis de Shanklin

Je vais envoyer bientôt vos deux dessins, j'attends après celui de m. Jeans qui est à l'Art pour une reproduction.

M. Rodin a trouvé le vôtre très très bien, il est possible que je vous expose à l'Académie l'année prochaine si vous le permettez.

J'ai reçu avant hier seulem. les photographies de Miss Lipscomb, mais

malgré tout ce que j'ai pu dire elle les a collés dans un album et envoyés ainsi. Alors je vous remercie bien pour l'offre que vous m'avez fait de les arranger.

Avez-vous découvert le mystère à la fin?

Vous devriez venir à Paris et hiver, en visite chez-nous ce serait bien amusant.

Je serais si contente.

Miss Florence Jeans
Grantham
Lincolnshire
Angleterre

which transform the face into an autonomous element, now presented as an object in its own right, divorced from the outside world.

The large plaster *Sakuntala* must certainly have gathered dust during its long stay in Camille's studio. And when, via Georges Lenseigne, she donated it to the Musée Bertrand in Châteauroux in 1895, to thank the town for having bought a picture belonging to her, *The Wave* by the American painter Alexander Harrison.[27] she had it patinated by Danielli, who had often worked for Rodin.[28] As soon as the work was installed in the reception hall on the first floor of the museum, it was almost "expelled for immorality."

Geffroy had to come to her defense in *Le Journal* on December 14. "It really is curious to need the help of a man like you," Camille wrote to him, "to defend me for having given a present to the town of Châteauroux: because that is what it was, a simple gift to these gentlemen of Berry. Fortunately, Sakuntala got her revenge by demolishing the staircase of the museum (and also almost crushed the entire commission!). Only one member considered the group less indecent than the others, an abbot, the chaplain of the lycée! While the others buried their head in their hands, he calmly looked at it and explained the legend to them."[29] But the group was ill-fated: after its long purgatory it found its rightful place in a museum —only to be irreparably damaged.[30]

The work, begun in 1886, showed Rodin's influence, which his admirers did not fail to notice. "I read in the papers about the prize the exhibition jury awarded your pupil Camille. My first thought is to ascribe all the merit for this to you and my first sentiment is one of profound gratitude to you," one of them wrote to Rodin.[31] The nudes were indeed modeled with a precision equal to his and while the torso of the young man is reminiscent of certain of Rodin's male torsos, for example *Ugolino*'s children and the *Despairing Adolescent* (fig. 30), the female figure, one knee bent, the other arm hanging vertically, echoes *The Shade* (cat. 140). But the meanderings of inspiration are unpredictable and, just as one can perhaps see reminiscences of *The Psalm* in *Thought* (cat. 162, p. 224), in which Camille's face is emerging from an uncarved block, Rodin also refers to *Sakuntala* in *The Eternal Idol* (cat. 156, p. 80). In both,

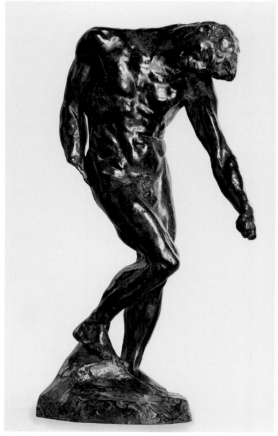

Cat. 140

Cat. 47

a man is kneeling before a woman, but whereas in Camille's sculpture they are united in reciprocal love, in Rodin's the woman is allowing the man to adore her; and the two faces, touching in the first group, are, on the contrary, distant in the second. "Ah, beauty divine, flower that talks, and who loves my darling intelligent flower. My wonderful on two knees in front of your beautiful body I embrace you," Rodin declared to his "cruel friend" (cat. 182, pp. 82–83). Paul Margueritte in turn comments, "She triumphs without pride, a placid but invincible sovereign. And

he, naked, kneeling, humble, weary, in human distress, in passionate fervor, his hands behind his back to clearly show that he is the slave not the master, leans his head against the base of the woman's bosom, against her side, which he kisses like a child adoring a Madonna, like a deeply religious person receiving the host."[32] But the origin of *The Eternal Idol* was two small figures from *The Gates of Hell* which Rodin brought together before February 1891,[33] so, if one situates Camille's pregnancy or one of her pregnancies at that time, could it not be seen

Cat. 47
CAMILLE CLAUDEL
Sakuntala
1888
Patinated plaster, broken
190 x 110 x 60 cm
Musée Bertrand, Châteauroux

Camille who dazzled him when they first met (*Man and his Thoughts*), whom he adored (*The Eternal Idol*), in whom he had believed but who had disappointed him (*Illusion, Sister of Icarus*), and finally with whom he always hoped to be reconciled (*Triumphant Youth*).

THE WALTZ

Camille, now at the height of her powers, was capable of imbuing her works with great emotive power, of reflecting her own feelings "in a passionate embrace with the imagination," to use her brother's beautiful phrase.[35] But she was also intent on asserting herself as an artist and if, because it always took her a long time to finish a work, it so happened that her personal feelings changed, she could not take this into account. And so it turned out that by a cruel twist of fate *The Waltz*, the masterpiece of her early years, whose sensuality expresses the union she thought she could achieve with Rodin, was exhibited after their break-up. This was perhaps why Mirbeau, a close friend of the couple, gave such a pessimistic analysis: "But where are they going? I do not know where they are going, if it is to love, if it is to death, but I do know that from this group there emanates a poignant sadness, so poignant that it can only come from death, or perhaps from a love even sadder than death."[36]

Camille began *The Waltz* just after *Sakuntala*. "I am also working on my Waltzers group which is not yet finished," she wrote to Florence Jeans in February 1889,[37] but its execution was delayed by the intense activity in Rodin's studio. "I am still working a lot at

as a tribute and token of allegiance by Rodin to the woman who was carrying his child?

Some years later, the marble version of the group commissioned by Eugène Carrière[34] was shown at the 1896 Salon along with the marbles *Man and His Thoughts* (fig. 31), *Illusion, Sister of Icarus* and *Triumphant Youth*, in which we can chart the progression of his feelings for Camille: the

_Fig. 31

AUGUSTE RODIN
Man and His Thoughts
Marble, 1896
Berlin, Nationalgalerie

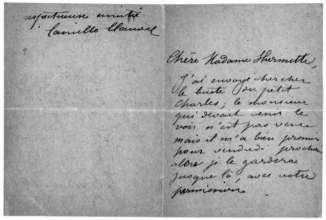

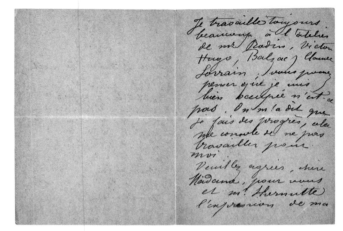

Cat. 194

M. Rodin's studio, Victor Hugo, Balzac, Claude Lorrain," she told Madame Lhermitte, probably around 1891 given the works mentioned. "You can imagine how very busy I am. I have been told I am making progress, which consoles me for not working on my own work" (cat. 194). On February 8, 1892, however, she did make a new request to the ministry for a commission for a marble of "a small, half life-size group entitled *The Waltzers* which several artists and notably Monsieur Rodin think is good."[38] An inspector, Armand Dayot, went to her studio but deemed the work unacceptable as it was. Admittedly, "all the details of this group are of a perfect virtuosity of execution and . . . Rodin himself would not have rendered with more art and conscience the quivering life in the muscles and even the trembling of the skin," but he had two criticisms: the waltzers were heavy and were not turning, which he put down to their nudity. "What is suited to the lightness of the waltz is . . . the rhythmic swirling of the draperies, as though the dancers had wings . . . I therefore thought it right to ask Mlle Claudel to dress her figures." But he reproached her above all for "the violent note of reality exuded [which], despite its incontestable

value, proscribes its placement in a gallery open to the public. The coming together of the sexes is rendered with a startling sensuality of expression which considerably exaggerates the absolute nudity of all the human details" (cat. 195). *The Waltz* is contemporary to the stays at L'Islette and the first, nude version can indeed be seen as a direct reflection of the couple's physical union: "I sleep completely naked to make myself believe you are there but when I wake up it is not the same thing. With love. Camille" (cat. 193, pp. 138–39; see the complete translation, p. 372).

Following the example of Rodin, who always heeded Armand Dayot's observations, Camille complied with his advice. Yet Rodin had intervened on her behalf: "Mlle Claudel requests to do only the nude, in which case let her since it is good and if she does not

Cat. 194
Letter from Camille Claudel to Madame Léon Lhermitte
[1891]
1 sheet, 17 x 25 cm
Private collection

want drapery it is because she would do it badly" (cat. 196). But Camille acquiesced (cat. 199, p. 113), and worked again during the spring of 1892, at L'Islette.[39] When Dayot examined the work again at the very end of 1892 or very early in 1893, he didn't hide his enthusiasm: "No longer do we have two vulgar, heavily coupled nude dancers but a graceful intertwining of forms superbly combining in a harmonious rhythm amidst the twirling encirclement of drapery. Oh, how flimsy the drapery is . . . Mlle Claudel wanted to sacrifice the least nudity possible and she was right. But it was enough to veil certain too visibly realistic details and to indicate at the same time the nature of the subject. The light scarf which clings to the woman's sides, leaving the torso naked, an admirable torso gracefully leaning back as if fleeing a kiss, ends in a sort of shivering train. It is like a torn sheath out of which a winged creature seems to be suddenly emerging! This already so beautiful group, of such striking originality and so powerfully executed, would greatly benefit from being transposed into marble. Mlle Claudel is an artist of very great talent" (cat. 200).

Following this eulogistic report, an order was prepared by the commission . . . but never signed, the director of fine arts, Henry Roujon, having deemed unacceptable[40] that "the couple seems to want to go to bed and finish the dance in lovemaking," as Jules Renard crudely noted in his *Journal* on March 19, 1895. Morhardt was indeed quite alone in seeing "in this idyll a poem persuasive and charming."[41] But even before the opening of the 1893 Salon de la Société Nationale des Beaux-Arts,[42] where it was unanimously acclaimed, the plaster was acquired on

Cat. 199

Armand Dayot's advice by the founder Siot-Decauville, who in August invited Rodin to his shop on boulevard des Italiens to see the bronze cast from this model, characterized by the drapery which comes back over the dancers' heads (cat. 201). "A unique piece, cast with meticulous care by M. Siot-Decauville and coated with a beautiful golden brown patina . . . an original and powerful work [which] avoids the realism of dressed mannequins whilst giving the essential sensation of life and modernism," this bronze (cat. 64) was exhibited at the Salon de la Libre Esthétique in Brussels in 1894, where it was noticed by Emile Verhaeren, who immediately drew a parallel with the "subtle art, both dreamlike and lifelike, of M. Claudel."[43]

Cat. 64

LEFT AND FOLLOWING PAGES
Cat. 64

CAMILLE CLAUDEL
The Waltz, with drapery partially covering the head
1893
Bronze
96 x 87 x 56 cm
Collection Galerie Kaare Berntsen, Oslo

Cat. 199

Letter from Camille Claudel to the director of fine arts
Dated December 21, 1892
1 sheet, 18 x 11.5 cm
Archives Nationales de France, Paris

The Symbolist movement found its perfect expression in this group with such a personal note to it, since one cannot help, like Paul Claudel, identifying his sister with the dancer swept away by her partner "in an exhilarating whirlwind."[44] Although by its very nature a static and mute work, *The Waltz* demonstrates that different domains of perception can mingle to produce, as in Rodin's *Sirens* (cat. 148, p. 57), a vertiginous sensation of music and movement.

The Waltz earned Camille her place among her top-ranking contemporaries. "You know I want to work with modern art. I therefore count on you to help in this," Siot-Decauville declared when he wrote to Rodin on August 11, 1893 to inform him of the completion of the large bronze. Rodin, utterly convinced of Camille's talent, did his best to help, not Siot-Decauville, who had not sold a single copy of the group when he sold his reproduction rights to Eugène Blot,[45] but the artist herself. Camille had produced a small version, which she had cast by a foundry of her choice, and collectors such as Aline Ménard-Dorian and the banker Joanny Peytel, director of the Crédit Algérien, both close friends of Rodin, acquired bronzes (cat. 65, pp. 118–19 and cat. 66). There were also plasters, "all retouched . . . and patinated by Mlle Camille Claudel herself,"[46] more affordable by her entourage (see "Camille Claudel and Claude Debussy: A Friendship," pp. 308–13), in circulation, in which modifications had been made to the first model (removal of the drapery enveloping the dancers' heads; several variations on the dance floor) so that Siot-Decauville, owner of the reproduction rights, could not protest.

_Cat. 64

_Cat. 66

Cat. 66
—
CAMILLE CLAUDEL
The Waltz
[1893]
Reduction with variants, bronze, after 1897
42 x 35 x 22 cm
Private collection

FOLLOWING PAGES
_Cat. 65

CAMILLE CLAUDEL
The Waltz
[1893]
Reduction with variants, bronze, about 1895?
43.2 x 23 x 34.3 cm
Musée Rodin, Paris

CAMILLE CLAUDEL THE PORTRAITIST   Raphaël Masson

In the mid-nineteenth century, a movement advocating greater realism emerged in art. It was a reaction to Romanticism and its visions, which spurned reality for an imaginary, dreamlike conception of the world. As Jacques van Lennep mentions in a brilliant essay,[1] this realist upsurge was slower to influence sculpture than painting. In the sphere of the sculpted portrait, precursors such as Courbet, who modeled several busts, and above all Vincenzo Gemito gradually opened the way for a more flexible and original portraiture. Jean-Baptiste Carpeaux, with his extraordinary virtuosity, took a decisive step. His bust of *Charles Garnier* (bronze, 1869, Musée d'Orsay, Paris), for example, with its stunning treatment of the hair, foreshadows Camille Claudel's *Giganti*. In parallel with these artists, other sculptors such as Carrier-Belleuse developed an approach favoring dazzling, sometimes mannered pictorial effects,[2] which Rodin himself adopted in his early work (fig. 6). In the late 1870s, when Rodin deliberately took the personal path heralded by *The Man with the Broken Nose* (fig. 4), two trends clearly emerged. The first favored realism, a concern for authenticity and likeness; the second centered more on style and effects, pursuing everything that fantasy could suggest, including in the use and treatment of materials. Jean-Léon Gérôme's bust of *Sarah Bernhardt* (1885, Musée d'Orsay, Paris), for example, even uses painted marble to obtain a naturalness verging on Mannerism.

Camille Claudel, in her training, tastes and artistic relations, opted for realism in her portraits, which she skillfully tempered with stylistic references borrowed from the past. This admirable capacity to adapt, visible in her first portraits, is a characteristic that runs right through her oeuvre. One should add that these borrowings were not intended solely to create a simple effect and were not gratuitous. Camille knew, each time she used such borrowings, how to add a personal touch which transcended slavish, empty imitation. I will come back to this.

Camille Claudel's portraits, sculpted over a relatively short period, from around 1880 to 1900, explore a surprising variety of styles, yet all show the same technical mastery. The artist produced some eighty sculptures, more than twenty of which are portraits,[3] executed between 1882 (*The Old Woman*) and 1905 (*Paul Claudel Aged Thirty-Seven*). This

Cat. 19

Cat. 30

relatively limited corpus immediately gives an impression of diversity due to the different styles the artist uses. Yet all the portraits display an obvious technical mastery, verging on virtuosity, and above all a remarkable assimilation of the characteristics of the styles used, no matter how different. Particularly striking are the attention the artist devotes to the drapery that adorns several of these busts (the two portraits of Paul as a boy, those of *Countess Arthur de Maigret* and of her son Christian), and the meticulous care sometimes taken in rendering the hair, the most accomplished examples of this being the various versions of *La Petite Châtelaine* (cat. 72, p. 141, cat. 73, pp. 134, 144–45, and cat. 74, pp. 148–49). The bust of *Countess Arthur de Maigret* (cat. 90, p. 257), shown at the 1897 Salon of the Société Nationale des Beaux-Arts,

perfectly illustrates the heights Camille's dexterity in the carving of marble had reached, especially in the virtuoso rendering of the lace bodice. The critics were quick to spot this. Gustave Geffroy wrote in *La Vie artistique*: "This portrait . . . is a masterpiece of formal amplitude, of inner force, of powerful grace. The beauty of life shines out of the determined forehead, low, square and harmonious like a pediment, the spiritual rose, the forms of the cheeks, the chin, the face

Cat. 19

CAMUS
Paul Claudel
Between 1876 and 1879
Photograph, albumin print
10.5 x 6.5 cm
Private collection

Cat. 30

CAMILLE CLAUDEL
Paul Claudel as a Child
About 1885
Bronze
40 x 36.5 x 22 cm
Musée Bertrand, Châteauroux

_Cat. 27

_Cat. 102

of intelligent beauty in which all is harmony, from the light in the eyes to the shape of the mouth."[4]

Three main influences seem to have inspired the different styles to which Camille Claudel makes explicit reference: the Florentine Renaissance and the style of Donatello; the French seventeenth and eighteenth centuries; and the style of Rodin himself. In the first category, one can place the two portraits of Paul Claudel as a child (cat. 30 and 27) and those of

Ferdinand de Massary (cat. 48, p. 124), Charles Lhermitte (cat. 49 and 3, pp. 120–21), Léon Lhermitte (cat. 78, p. 124) and Count Christian de Maigret in Henry II Costume (cat. 85, p. 257). For the latter, who chose to be portrayed dressed in a costume from the time of Henry II, the artist drew on the Renaissance repertoire for the costume—albeit with a touch of fantasy[5]—but also sought inspiration in the busts of the Grand Siècle by representing her model with a torso and truncated arms. On the other hand, the bust of My Brother is cut off just below the shoulders in the pure Italian Renaissance tradition (cat. 27). The French seventeenth and eighteenth centuries show their influence in the busts of Jessie Lipscomb (fig. 33, p. 132), Louise Claudel (cat. 34 and 35, pp. 126–27), Countess Arthur de Maigret and Countess Christian de Maigret.[6]

Cat. 27

CAMILLE CLAUDEL
My Brother
(Paul Claudel)
1884
Bronze
51 x 44 x 25 cm
Musée Calvet, Avignon

Cat. 102

HENRY DUMONT
Young Roman,
by Camille Claudel,
in LEROI 1887, p. 233
43.2 x 31 cm
Musée Rodin, Paris

Cat. 48

Cat. 78

These busts, all of women, all possess the same cheerful grace and are direct descendants of the female portraits of the eighteenth century, "capturing its frivolous side, as well as its penchant for emotion and the expression of intimate feelings."[7] But this classical inspiration is never slavishly followed and Camille often uses it as a point of departure for an original treatment of the model, notably in the depiction of faces with closed eyes.[8] Rodin's influence can be detected in the busts of *Giganti* (cat. 28), who was Rodin's model (cat. 178), and of *Auguste Rodin* himself (cat. 56, p. 77), which is not surprising, as these works were executed while they were lovers. But also evident is the heritage of precursors such as Jean-Baptiste Carpeaux mentioned above. Only the busts of *La Petite Châtelaine* and *Paul Claudel Aged Thirty-Seven* (cat. 96, p. 291) have a style exempt of any influence from the past, revealing Camille's most personal and freest manner.

Except for the busts of the family of Countess Arthur de Maigret, most of the models Camille chose belonged to her entourage (cat. 107, p. 128): her father,[9] her mother (fig. 68), her brother Paul, her sister Louise, her friend Jessie Lipscomb (cat. 106, p. 129), the old family servant (cat. 26, p. 24), her brother-in-law Ferdinand de Massary, and Back (cat. 5 A, p. 129), the husband of her friend Florence Jeans[10] (cat. 192). They also came from Rodin's entourage, such as Giganti, and the painter Léon Lhermitte, whose success at the 1882 Salon had established him as one of the leading lights of *peinture paysanne*.[11] Lhermitte commissioned from Camille a bust of his son Charles in 1889: "We have just returned from Mlle Claudel's," he wrote to his wife. "If you could only see the little gem of a child it's going to be, she is so pleased with her model, she finds he has such a sculptural head." To the list of models who posed for her, one should add a full-length portrait (fig. 61) which, according to Morhardt, depicted a certain "M.Y.,"[12] as well as the young Marguerite Boyer, the little girl at the Château de l'Islette. near Azay-le-Rideau, who posed for *La Petite Châtelaine*, and of course Rodin, of whom she did a bust but also a portrait in oils.[13] This very short list

Cat. 48

CAMILLE CLAUDEL
Ferdinand de Massary
1888?
Plaster
45 x 30 x 32 cm
Private collection

Cat. 78

CAMILLE CLAUDEL
Léon Lhermitte
1895
Bronze
36 x 25 x 25 cm
Private collection

Cat. 28

CAMILLE CLAUDEL
Giganti
1885
Bronze
30.6 x 30 x 26.5 cm
Musée des Beaux-Arts, Rheims

Cat. 2

Cat. 1

ANONYMOUS
Louise Claudel,
Eyes Closed, *terracotta?,*
by Camille Claudel
About 1886
Photograph, albumin print
9.2 x 5.6 cm
Musée Rodin, Paris

Cat. 35

CAMILLE CLAUDEL
Louise Claudel
1886
Bronze
47 x 18 x 24 cm
Musée d'art Roger-Quilliot,
Clermont-Ferrand

Cat. 34

CAMILLE CLAUDEL
Louise Claudel
1886
Terracotta
49 x 22 x 25 cm
Palais des Beaux-Arts, Lille

_Cat. 34

Cat. 107

WILLIAM ELBORNE
The Claudel family, Jessie Lipscomb, Ferdinand de Massary and his father, on the balcony of their apartment at 31 Boulevard de Port-Royal (at the front: Louise; behind her, Madame Claudel and Camille. Around them, from left to right: Louis-Prosper Claudel, Paul, Monsieur de Massary, Jessie Lipscomb and Ferdinand de Massary)
1887
Photograph, albumin print
16.5 x 12 cm
Private collection

_Cat. 106

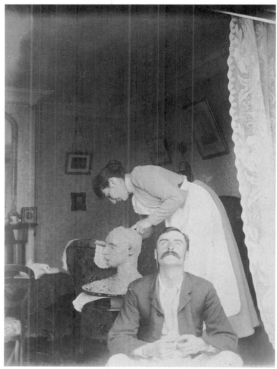

_Cat 5 A

clearly shows that Camille was not really considered a fashionable portraitist—or that she did not have the time to assert herself as one—and that she produced her busts not to order but according to choices dictated by her inspiration or affections or, more prosaically, according to the opportunities that arose. In this domain, Paul Claudel was clearly her favorite family model. She did three busts of him, all remarkable, although in very different styles. These portraits of Paul punctuate her career between the mid-1880s and 1905, and show the profound bond of affection that existed between them.

The same criteria also determined the choices of the models that Camille drew, mostly in charcoal. The Vosgian portraits—such as *Mennie-Jean* (cat. 29, p. 131), *Women from Gérardmer (Vosges)* (fig. 3) and *The Old Lady of the Pont Notre-Dame* (cat. 33, p. 130), a work exhibited here for the first time—were produced during a trip with her uncle Charles Claudel to Docelles in the Vosges in August 1885. The English

portraits—*A Quiet Nap, Fisherwoman* (fig. 32, p. 130), *Old Granny, Doctor Jeans, Florence Jeans* (fig. 35, p. 133) and *Jessie Lipscomb* (cat. 36, p. 132)—were done in 1886, during a stay on the Isle of Wight with her brother and Jessie Lipscomb, at whose home in Peterborough she later stayed (cat. 189). There are also other portraits, all of members of her close entourage, in which she deploys the same gift for capturing the

_Cat. 106

WILLIAM ELBORNE
Jessie Lipscomb, Camille and Louise Claudel in the atelier at 117 Rue Notre-Dame-des-Champs, 1887
Photograph, albumin print
4.5 x 10.5 cm
Private collection

_Cat. 5 A

ANONYMOUS
Camille Claudel modeling the bust of Back
1893
Photograph, aristotype
10.9 x 8.3 cm
Musée Rodin, Paris

Cat. 33

Fig. 32

inner life of her models as she does in her sculptures. Yet, unlike the sculpted portraits, which in turn adopt this or that style, Camille's drawn portraits seem to follow a more regular evolution. The pastel of her sister Louise,[14] done just before her marriage to Ferdinand de Massary in 1888, thus reveals the very strong influence of Manet's style, whereas the last

charcoals reveal a much less naturalistic manner than the portraits of the 1880s, such as *Countess Arthur de Maigret* (cat. 91, p. 256). In all her graphic works, Camille shows her undoubted mastery of the techniques of drawing and painting, even if she has sometimes been criticized, as Morhardt did for *Portrait of Eugénie Plé*,[15] for doing "sculptor's painting, so energetically emphasized are the forms and so solidly established are the planes."[16]

Due to her status as "Rodin's pupil," Camille Claudel was able to exhibit her works fairly early on. Rodin himself endeavored to "push" the young woman and open as many doors as possible for Camille, even if this protection ended up by becoming cumbersome, burdensome even, it systematically placed her in Rodin's shadow. The deterioration of their relationship after their separation and the persecution complex that she gradually developed seem to have had the effect of creating tensions between Camille and the de Maigret family, as she told Lerolle around 1905.[17] Yet this did not prevent Camille from being invited to the Countess of Senlis's home in 1903 and from producing the interesting charcoal portrait of her mentioned above.

Despite her diverse stylistic influences, can one identify a specific Camille Claudel style in her portraits? It can be discerned in the determined carriage of the head, sometimes unexpected, as with the bust of Christian de Maigret, a tendency to give her models a heroic feel at odds with reality, gazes that are extremely studied and sometimes modified —one thinks of the portrait of Louise with closed eyes (cat. 1, p. 126), for instance—and charged with emotion. Most critics agree that Camille's portraits have a special life of their own: "Straightaway the artist notes and makes all these characters clear."[18] Paul Leroi praised she who "instills such character into everything she undertakes."[19] "At last the superb bust, crying out with latent life," Henry de Braisne exclaimed about the portrait of Rodin in the *Revue idéaliste*.[20] Roger Marx praised *La Petite Châtelaine*, in which "the brave artist's constant search for intellectuality again appears in the gesture that implores the *Vanished God*."[21] Maurice Hamel, chronicling the presentation of the work at the Société Nationale

Cat. 29

Cat. 33
CAMILLE CLAUDEL
*The Old Lady of the
Pont Notre-Dame*
About 1885
Charcoal on Cansor paper
mounted on cardboard
60 x 43 cm
Musée Barrois, Bar-le-Duc

Fig. 32
CAMILLE CLAUDEL
Fisherwoman,
charcoal, in *L'Art*,
vol. 42, 1887, p. 149

Cat. 29
CAMILLE CLAUDEL
Mennie-Jean
1885
Charcoal with white chalk
highlights on ocher paper
48 x 37 cm
Musée Eugène-Boudin,
Honfleur

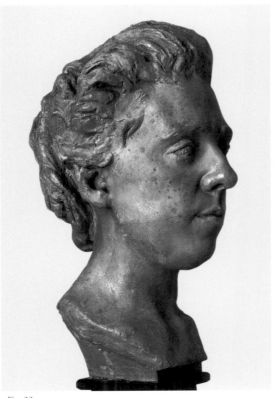

_Fig. 33

_Cat. 36

des Beaux-Arts in 1889, wrote: "A head of a young boy, by Camille Claudel, has the most exquisite delicateness, a charm, a gentleness, a breath of childlike naivety. The truth of nature is taken by surprise, lovingly interpreted."[22] This ability to capture characters, recognized by most critics, is also present in the charcoal and pencil portraits showing us Paul's dreaminess (fig. 34), Countess de Maigret's benevolent geniality and Louis-Prosper Claudel's mischievous kindness (fig. 77). The portrait genre is intrinsically very simple and does not necessarily demand prodigal inspiration. Concentrating on the models she herself chose, not having to confront the throes of ex-nihilo creation, Camille must have practiced it with a serenity and self-confidence that enabled her to exercise her talent completely freely and spontaneously.

The work of Camille Claudel the portraitist, perhaps more than the rest of her oeuvre, is rich in a promise that events unfortunately did not allow to bloom. Blessed by the benevolence of the critics and a genuine gift for bringing her models to life, she lacked the time and the commissions she needed to assert herself as one of the most gifted portraitists of

Fig. 34

Fig. 35

her time. In contrast to the power and realism of Rodin's busts, sometimes stamped with a certain snapshot immobility,[23] Camille Claudel's have a sense of the character and individuality of her models. It is perhaps in this domain that the two artists differed most. Rodin's Camille is an evocation, almost an idealization of the young woman (see "Tête-à-Tête," pp. 68–79), whereas Camille's Rodin goes much further: her rendering *is* Rodin, and allows the grandeur of his genius and the weaknesses of the man himself to show through. Feminine intuition or gift for psychological observation (which

Rodin desperately lacked—as he would often painfully learn), what does it matter? In addition to showing her talent, Camille Claudel, in each of her portraits, demonstrated a capacity to sculpt a soul behind a face.

Fig. 34
CAMILLE CLAUDEL
Paul Claudel Aged Twenty
1888
Colored crayons
Private collection

Fig. 35
CAMILLE CLAUDEL
Florence Jeans
1886
Charcoal
Private collection

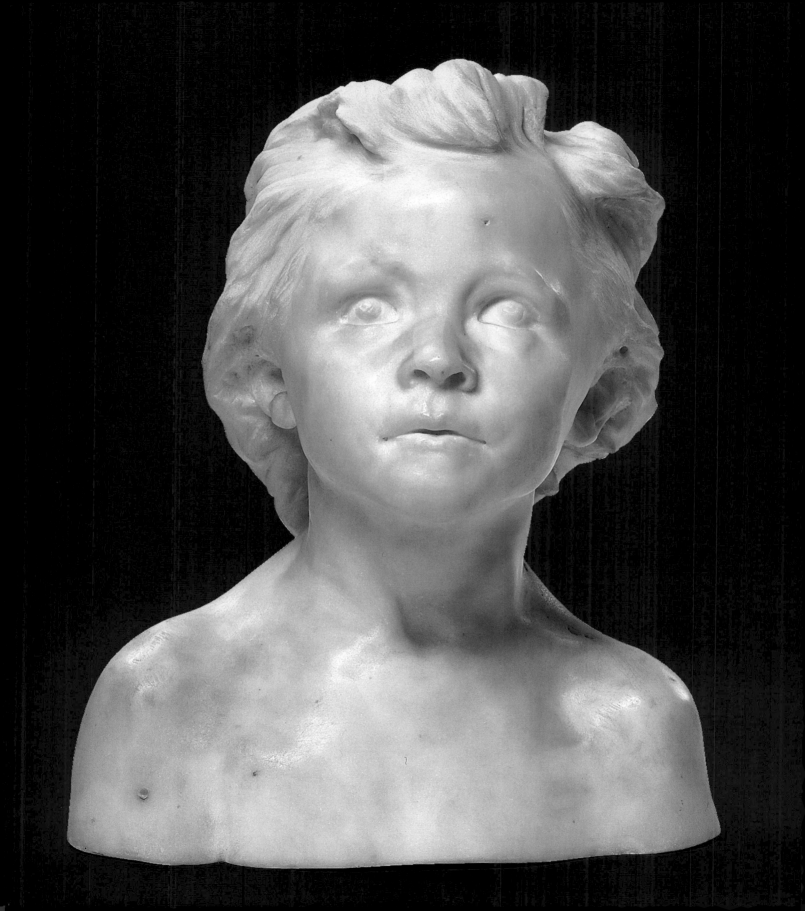

THE STAYS AT L'ISLETTE Bruno Gaudichon

In December 1893, Camille Claudel wrote to her brother to tell him about the new direction her work was taking, and what she felt was the prime advantage of this development: "You see it is no longer Rodin at all" (cat. 202, p. 239). And from then on, for the remaining twenty years of her artistic career, it would be her fierce obsession with independence that would be her driving force. Around 1893, which may therefore have been a turning point in both Camille Claudel's artistic and personal life, one piece stands out, a work begun during her intimacy with Rodin and pursued with her growing need to differentiate herself from him. La Petite Châtelaine was indeed begun in 1892 and still persists in Aurora, the Blot bronze of which was not cast until 1908. But the evolution between the plaster modeled at l'Islette in 1892 and the 1896 marble commissioned by Henri Fontaine reveals the mutation wrought by the inspirational separation—a prelude to the recycling of earlier works that became a hallmark of the artist's work from 1897–98.

In July 1891, the Société des Gens de Lettres, whose president was then Emile Zola, commissioned[1] Rodin to sculpt a monument to Honoré de Balzac to replace the work Henri Chapu left unfinished when he died. Rodin took the project passionately to heart and worked on it over the ensuing seven-year period of his break-up with Camille

Claudel. In July 1891, he replied to A. B. de Farges, "I do not want to start anything before I have as much documentation on Balzac as possible. I am going to go and spend a few days in Balzac's native Tours, and I will do some research in the library there. Meanwhile, I would be glad to receive any information that can be provided on the subject of the life and habits of the great novelist."[2] Rodin had in fact already been to Touraine, with Camille Claudel. In July 1889, they spent time together on the banks of the Loire, a stay that Rodin would use for Les Cathédrales de France.[3] During the summer of 1891, they stayed at l'Islette, a château near Azay-le-Rideau, as the paying guests of Madame Courcelles (cat. 114–115 B and 155, p. 136). The house and its surroundings guaranteed the discretion the couple desired, and Camille Claudel regularly stayed there

135

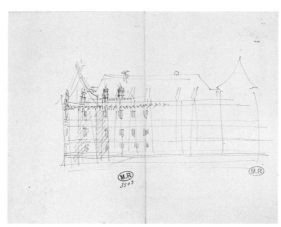

Cat. 155

Cat. 114

Cat. 115 B

AUGUSTE RODIN
Façade of the Château de l'Islette, Cheillé (Indre-et-Loire)
1890 or 1891
Pen and brown ink on watermarked cream paper
18.2 x 23 cm
Musée Rodin, Paris

until at least 1893. Rodin's correspondence confirms his presence at l'Islette in July 1890, and May and August to October 1891, trips which marked an important stage in the development of the *Balzac* project, since they enabled Rodin to find a model who could serve as a living likeness of the writer, several portraits of whom he had procured. He must have been reminded that Balzac's origins were in fact elsewhere, but he insisted on looking for his Balzac double in the Tours region. "Chance sometimes works miracles for the powers of the will: Rodin soon found several individuals resembling Balzac and modeled their masks. He met a young man, a traveling salesman, had him pose and executed a large, very studied bust, then animated his honest, open face with the Rabelaisian joviality and spiritual flame that burned 'in the gold-filled eyes' of the novelist."[4] The Musée Rodin has four photographs of Estager (cat. 4 A), or the "conductor of Tours" as Rodin called him. Rodin sculpted two masks of Balzac (cat. 158, 159) from this model, which served as the departure point for numerous studies that he began at l'Islette.

It seems that the first studies were more concerned with the writer's head than with the monument's overall form; at least this is what a letter from Geffroy suggests: "I do not want to disturb your studies of Tourainians."[5] And Rodin, to accentuate his model's resemblance to his subject, asked Estager to "let his black hair grow into a thick mane."[6] A letter from Camille Claudel to Rodin, who had returned to Paris, leaves a souvenir of the summer of 1891 as an exceptional time for the couple: "Monsieur Rodin as I have got nothing to do I am writing to you again. You cannot

Cat. 114
L. L.
Environs of Azay-le-Rideau. Château de l'Islette
Photomechanical postcard
Undated
9 x 13.8 cm
Musée Rodin, Paris

Cat. 115 B
NEURDEIN FRÈRES
Château de l'Islette (Indre-et-Loire). The Pond
Photomechanical postcard
Undated
9 x 13.8 cm
Musée Rodin, Paris

_Cat. 159

Cat. 4 A

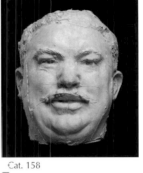

_Cat. 158

imagine how good the weather is at l'Islette. I ate today in the middle room (the one used as a green-house) where one can see the garden on both sides. Madame Courcelles suggested to me (without me saying anything) that if you so wish you can eat there from time to time and even always (I think she really wants to do this) and it's so beautiful there! . . . I went for a walk in the park, everything has been mown, hay, corn, barley, one can go everywhere it's lovely. If you are sweet enough to keep your promise it will be heaven for us. You can have any room you want to work in. The old woman will be on her knees before us, I think. She told me that I [could?] bathe in the river, where her daughter and the maid go bathing without danger. With your permission, I will do so as it's a great pleasure and it will spare me going to the hot baths at Azay. It would be so kind of you to buy me a small bathing costume, dark blue with white trimmings, in two pieces, blouse and trousers (medium size) at the Louvre or au bon marché (in serge) or in Tours! I sleep completely naked to make myself believe you are there but when I wake it is not the same thing. With love Camille Above all do not be unfaithful to me anymore!" (cat. 193, pp. 138–39; see the complete translation, p. 372).

Camille Claudel also spent the summer of 1892 at l'Islette, where Rodin sent her a postal order in early July.[7] In a letter to Edmond Bigand-Kaire, she mentions her forthcoming holiday there: "I am going away to the country for a while, I was going to leave on Tuesday but am now leaving tomorrow due to my molder not having finished. I will not be back until October when I will get to work in earnest and soon, I hope, I will be able to exhibit a few groups that I have not yet dared bring out into the open."[8] It seems that it was during this stay that Camille Claudel used Madame Courcelles's six-year-old granddaughter, Madeleine Boyer, as a model. She posed for sixty-two hours[9] for a first bust or mask, the origin of *La Petite*

_Cat. 159

AUGUSTE RODIN
Balzac, study
for Smiling Mask
1891
Terracotta
28.9 x 15.5 x 14.5 cm
Musée Rodin, Paris

_Cat. 4 A

ANONYMOUS
*Estager, "Conductor
of Tours"*
1891
Photograph,
albumin print
14.4 x 11.2 cm
Musée Rodin, Paris

_Cat. 158

AUGUSTE RODIN
Balzac, mask study
called "The Conductor
of Tours"
1891
Plaster
24 x 21 x 17 cm
Musée Rodin, Paris

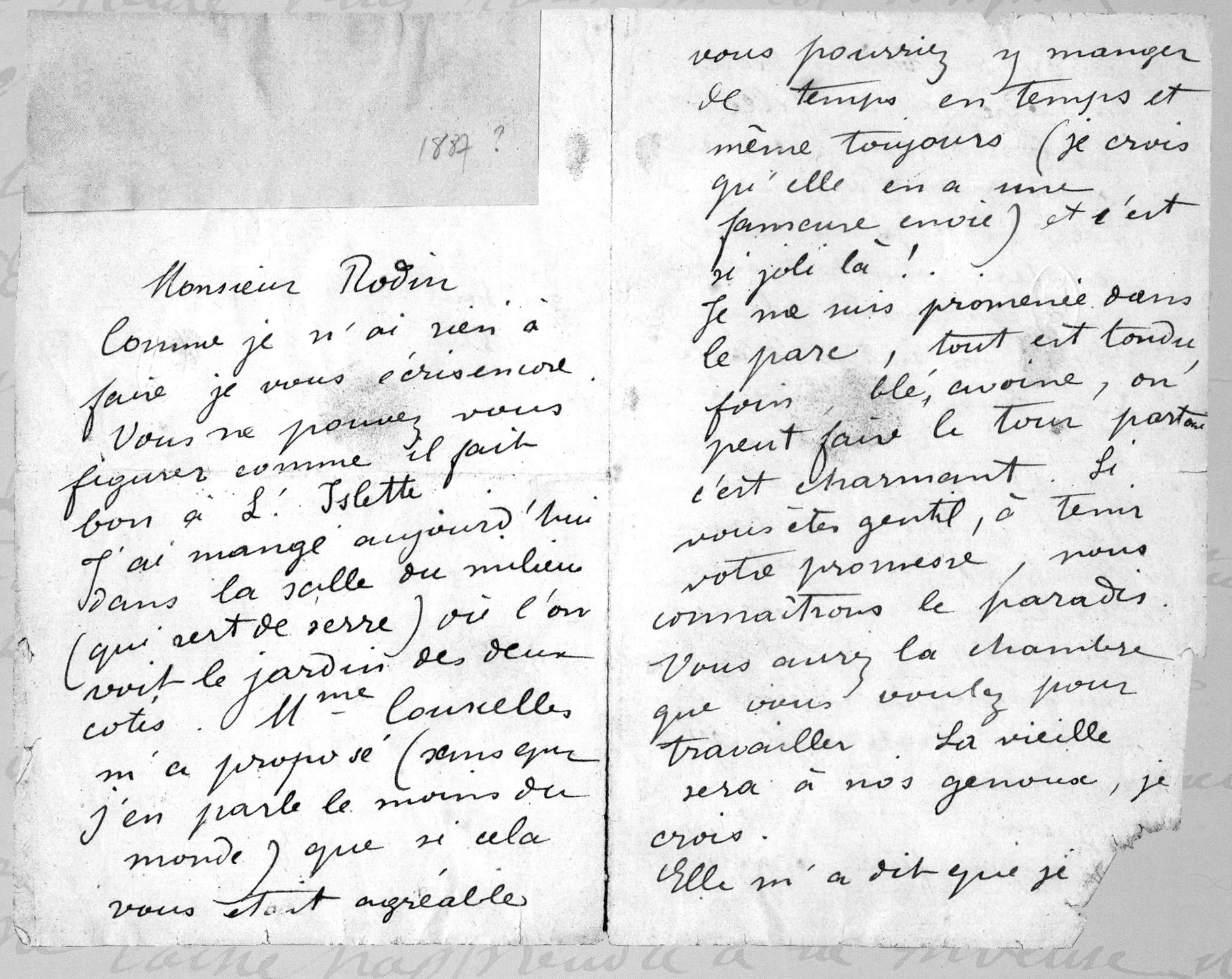

1887 ?

Monsieur Rodin
Comme je n'ai rien à faire je vous écris encore. Vous ne pouvez vous figurer comme il fait bon à L'Islette. J'ai mangé aujourd'hui dans la salle du milieu (qui sert de serre) où l'on voit le jardin des deux cotés. Mme Courcelles m'a proposé (sans que j'en parle le moins du monde) que si cela vous était agréable vous pourriez y manger de temps en temps et même toujours (je crois qu'elle en a une fameuse envie) et c'est si joli là !
Je me suis promenée dans le parc, tout est tondu, foin, blé, avoine, on peut faire le tour partout c'est charmant. Si vous êtes gentil, à tenir votre promesse, nous connaîtrons le paradis. Vous aurez la chambre que vous voulez pour travailler. La vieille sera à nos genoux, je crois.
Elle m'a dit que je

Cat. 193
Letter from Camille Claudel to Auguste Rodin
[July 1891?]
1 sheet, 17.5 x 22 cm
Musée Rodin, Paris

prendre des bains dans
la rivière, où sa fille et
la bonne en prennent,
sans aucun danger.
Avec votre permission,
j'en ferai autant car
c'est un grand plaisir
et cela m'évitera d'aller
aux bains chauds à
Azay. Que vous seriez
gentil de m'acheter un
petit costume de bain,
bleu foncé avec galons
blancs, en deux morceaux
blouse et pantalon (taille
moyenne), au Louvre ou
au bon marché (en serge)
ou à Tours.
Je couche toute nue
pour me faire croire

que vous êtes là mais
quand je me réveille, ce
n'est plus la même chose
Je vous embrasse
Camille.
Surtout ne me trompez
plus.

It would be so kind of you to buy me a small bathing costume, dark blue with
white trimmings, in two pieces, blouse and trousers (medium size) at the Louvre or
au bon marché (in serge) or in Tours! I sleep completely naked to make myself
believe you are there but when I wake it is not the same thing.
With love Camille
Above all do not be unfaithful to me anymore!

Châtelaine. In October, on her return to Paris, she wrote to Rodin, "Monsieur I am back in Paris. I could not bring all my things back from l'Islette as this would have been too expensive. It is agreed that I will go back there next year. I got a little carried away. Merely to Mad. Courcelles I paid 300f and 100f to the molder; 60f journey plus luggage, pieces, etc. I have 20f left and all I brought back was a group and a bust my linen my books my drawings etc. I had lunch with the Vaissiers who were most kind and reassured me."[10]

The stay at l'Islette may possibly have been a period of rest for Camille Claudel, who was recovering from an abortion which, although undated, is attested to by a letter from Paul Claudel to Marie Romain-Rolland: "You should know that a person to whom I am very close has committed the same crime as you and that she has been atoning for it for 26 years in a lunatic asylum. To kill a child, to kill an immortal soul, is horrible, awful."[11] Although there is no certainty that this abortion corresponds to the beginning of work on *La Petite Châtelaine*, the coincidence is striking. In any case, the group and bust in question in the October 1892 letter, and which Camille brought back to Paris from l'Islette, were probably *The Waltz* and the first stage of *La Petite Châtelaine*, on which she was then working.

The long stay at l'Islette in summer 1892 therefore saw the completion of *The Waltz*, begun in 1889, and the beginning of the series of *Petites Châtelaines* that the artist undertook while Rodin was working on his studies for *Balzac*. It is difficult to ascertain what stage the bust that Camille brought back to Paris from l'Islette in October 1892 had reached, but it probably did not differ much from the bronze model which she presented at the 1894 Nationale under the title *La Petite Châtelaine* and which she tried to get the state to purchase: "Monsieur le Ministre, I would like to draw your benevolent attention to a small bust of a child in bronze that I exhibited at the Salon du Champs-de-Mars, where it had the number 36 and to propose its purchase by the state. If I am to believe the encouraging words I have received on the subject of this work I believe I am not being too daring in my solicitation."[12] The artist received a refusal note on July 7. An identical bust was acquired by Baron Alphonse de Rothschild, who in 1896 gave it to the Musée Joseph-Denais at Beaufort-en-Vallée (cat. 72). The work must therefore have matured during the summer of 1893, during another stay at l'Islette, referred to in a letter to Rodin: "I was absent when you came as my father arrived yesterday, I went and had dinner and slept at our apartment. As regards health I am no better since I cannot stay lying down, having to walk around all the time. I expect I shall not leave until around Thursday. Talking of which Mademoiselle Vaissier came to see me and told me all sorts of fables made

Cat. 72

CAMILLE CLAUDEL
La Petite Châtelaine
1894
Bronze
33 x 28 x 22 cm
Musée Joseph-Denais,
Beaufort-en-Vallée

up about me at l'Islette. Apparently I sneak out at night through the window of my tower, hanging from a red umbrella with which I set fire to the forest!!!"[13] Mademoiselle Vaissier is undoubtedly Alix Vaissier, the future owner of the plaster *Implorer* reproduced in Paul Claudel's article in *L'Art décoratif* in 1913.[14] A *Petite Châtelaine* belonged to her sister Marthe, wife of Georges Lenseigne, whom Rodin and Camille Claudel met at l'Islette in 1891—the Vaissier family were from Azay-le-Rideau—and who acted as intermediary, in 1895, with the town of Châteauroux for the purchase of a picture by Harrison which Camille Claudel wanted to sell, and the gift of a large patinated plaster *Sakuntala* for the Musée Bertrand.

The Rothschild bronze version of *La Petite Châtelaine* was finished in late 1893. In December Camille Claudel included it with the works she intended sending to the Libre Esthétique salon in Brussels. She wrote to her brother: "I am taking great pleasure in working. I shall send the small lovers group, the bust with a hood, the bronze Waltz and the little girl from l'Islette to the Brussels Salon"[15] (cat. 202, p. 239). This first version, shown in Brussels as *Contemplation* and as *La Petite Châtelaine* the same year in Paris, is definitely the "petite de l'Islette," that is, the portrait of the little girl who posed for Camille Claudel in late summer 1892 and which she may have updated during her stay in Touraine in 1893. She reused the format of the bust of *Charles Lhermitte* (cat. 49, p. 120) she had shown at the 1889 Salon. Even though the portrait did not attract much attention, it was commented on approvingly by Hamel: "A head of a young boy, by Camille Claudel, has the

Cat. 72

most exquisite delicacy, a gentle charm, a breath of childlike naivety. Nature is caught in its truth, interpreted lovingly";[16] and supported by Leroi: "Mlle Camille Claudel has reproduced, in bronze, the features of M. Charles Lhermitte, son of the painter, adorning the seductiveness of childhood with that touch so personal to the young artist."[17] Alphonse de Rothschild acquired a bronze cast for the Musée de Montauban. This positive collusion was something of a rehearsal for the reception given *La Petite Châtelaine* in 1894: the same perception of an intuitive vision of the world of childhood, the same collector. In this work, Camille Claudel reused the Italianate bust model she had adopted for *My Brother* (cat. 27, p. 123) in 1884 and for *Young Woman With Closed Eyes*, recently acquired by the Musée de Poitiers. After *La Petite Châtelaine*, she returned to this reference

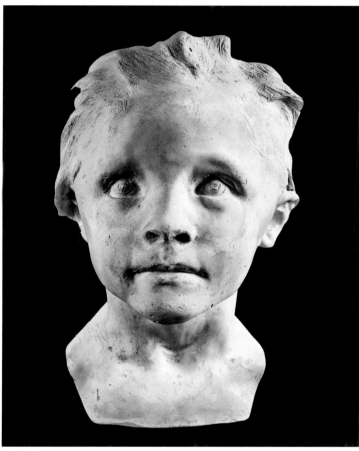

Cat. 71

Insisting like many other critics on the girl's gaze, he covers all the sculpture's states—plaster, bronze, marble—from the first version to the mystical intention of the title she gave the marble in the Peytel Collection, shown at the Nationale in 1895 as *Jeanne as a Child*. "There is . . . in the very disproportion of this already too powerful, already too lifelike head already too open to the eternal mysteries and the delicately infantile bare shoulders, something indefinable that conveys a profound anxiety . . . The bust of Jeanne as a child . . . proves that Mlle Claudel is now a master . . . this model is all her own. It is more lucid and clearer than any signature. It is despotic and passionate . . . It strives above all to translate and evoke the dramatic meaning of forms . . . The young artist . . . has the inestimable privilege of discerning the grandeur, picturesqueness and beauty in even an ordinary passer-by."[19] Camille Claudel's first biographer also dissipates the ambiguity of the title she gave the work in 1895 and which could evoke a "commemoration of Joan of Arc [which] was neither in her mind or her intention and . . . she may have lied to herself and her plan by thinking, in front of the young girl who was posing for her, about the heroine of Orléans. But if she did not think about this, the ardent and resolute eyes of the child, her half-open lips and infantile and powerful forehead necessarily conjure the idea of a miraculous resurrection. And Joan as a child is undoubtedly the best and only authentic portrait of Joan of Arc at Domrémy."[20] This analysis of course begs comparison with Rodin's first studies for *Balzac*, even if the development seems to be the other way round. Rodin certainly sought out a resemblance to

to Alfred Boucher's teaching in *Paul Claudel at Thirty-Seven* (cat. 96, p. 291) in 1905. T. de Wyzewa emphasizes this Florentinism: "Mlle Claudel . . . has given this bust of a young girl something of Mino de Fiesole's ingenious and mischievous gentleness."[18]

In his comprehensive study of Camille Claudel in 1898, Mathias Morhardt discusses *La Petite Châtelaine* at length, rating it as one of her most important works.

lead him to a materialization of his subject and Camille Claudel discovered in her model the essence of an unexpected subject, but one cannot but be struck by the swing from the singular to the universal. Camille Claudel had already historically transposed the bust of her young brother Paul into *Young Achilles* and *Young Roman* (cat. 30 and 27, pp. 122–23), the bust of *Louise Claudel* (cat. 34 and 35, pp. 126–27), "something like one of those delightful prints from the last century"[21] according to Morhardt, and *The Psalm* (cat. 50, p. 97), "loving, human, living, sincere Prayer, simple and true Prayer, like the masters of the sixteenth century showed us."[22] And in 1899 she would again resort to psychological historicization in her model for the bust of *Count Christian de Maigret in Henry II Costume*. But the effect would be quite different.

This vein met with success and Camille Claudel did not hesitate to produce variations on the first version of *La Petite Châtelaine*, notably in the treatment of the plait. She produced a series of patinated plasters as a substitute for the more expensive bronze cast, whose exclusivity she may have granted Baron de Rothschild. The plasters belonging to the painter Fritz Thaulow—which were used for the posthumous edition after 1984—and the Claudel family have now been located. We know nothing of the other plasters in this series known from various sources. There is a plaster mask (cat. 71), probably dating from the same time, formerly belonging to Countess de Maigret, one of Camille Claudel's later patrons (see "A Patron: Countess de Maigret," pp. 250–59).

Three of Rodin's friends ordered marble versions of this first bust. Paul Escudier's, which remained for

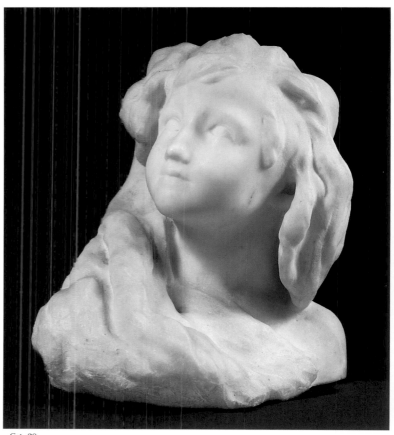

Cat. 89

Cat. 71
CAMILLE CLAUDEL
La Petite Châtelaine, mask
1894
Plaster
28 x 18 x 13 cm
Private collection

Cat. 89
CAMILLE CLAUDEL
Aurora
1900?
Marble
35 x 29 x 30 cm
Private collection

a long time in his family, has a thin curved plait. Joanny Peytel's marble, shown at the 1895 Nationale and acquired by the Musée Rodin in 1968, has a thick curved plait (cat. 73). Fritz Thaulow's has a straight plait. It was exhibited by Blot in 1907, probably after he acquired it at the auction of the Norwegian painter's collection at the Galerie Georges Petit, and is now in a private collection. The rather dry treatment of the marble in the large *Perseus and the Gorgon* (cat. 86, pp. 250 and 252) is very similar to Pompon's. These comparisons and the absence of this version in Morhardt's 1898 article suggest it may have been produced later, between 1898 and 1900. The summary treatment of the hair foreshadows the fluid and vague forms of *Aurora* (cat. 89, p. 143).

Its success is apparent in the accounts of the 1894 and 1895 Salons. For Roger Marx, in 1894, "Mademoiselle Claudel's bust of a chatelaine is endowed with an intense radiance, inspired by young life, and an extraordinarily piercing gaze."[23] The same year Gustave Geffroy paid homage to "this head of a child with wide-open, almost hallucinating eyes, a new expression, expressing the naive, restless, inquisitive."[24] The commentaries, therefore, insisted on a new dimension in the work which, transcending portraiture, becomes a universal expression of the world of childhood, whose anxieties are expressed without distorting the traditional mask of prettiness and false purity. It was this wide-eyed feverishness which struck critics and public alike at the 1894 and 1895 Salons, and which prompted Mathias Morhardt to refer to the plaster he had acquired in March 1895 from the Fonds Puvis de Chavannes as the "little girl."[25]

Cat. 73

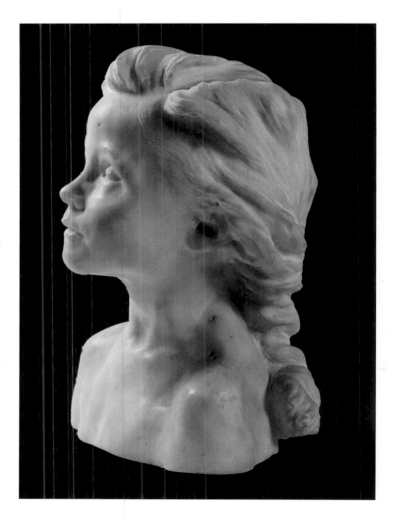

Cat. 73
CAMILLE CLAUDEL.
La Petite Châtelaine
Marble, 1895
34.3 x 28.4 x 22 cm
Musée Rodin, Paris

This bust, even in its first version, is symptomatic of the legions of charming children's busts—portraits, allegories, historical and religious evocations—presented each year at the Salon and intended to appeal to prospective clients for private portraits or publishers of religious or decorative imagery. It is as if the often noted bitterness of the gaze, the assertive pose, the very determined bearing of the tense, tight-lipped face, the discreet disproportion of the skinny, too narrow shoulders and more massive head are an expression of a phenomenon. This assertion of singularity of course poses the question of the abortion, related to the stays at l'Islette and notably to the summer of 1892, the summer of her renouncement of maternity and the birth of *La Petite Châtelaine*, imagined paradoxically both as an improbable child and as the expression of the very essence of childhood.

While Camille Claudel was working on *La Petite Châtelaine*, which she had not yet developed to its full extent, she was also working on two other important pieces. *Clotho* (cat. 63, pp. 152, 154–55) and *The Age of Maturity* (cat. 82, pp. 187–89) also express the pangs of Camille and Rodin's soon to be definitive separation. The plaster model of *Clotho* and the first version of *La Petite Châtelaine*—the threads of old age and a vision of youth—were shown together at the 1893 Salon, and her self-portrait in *The Age of Maturity* group, *The Implorer*, was presented at the 1894 Nationale, in exactly what version is unclear. Its development must surely be linked to l'Islette because Alix Vaissier, whom Camille Claudel had met at Azay-le-Rideau, owned a plaster. The version discovered in Touraine in 1986 has the same Expressionist mane as *Clotho*, which foreshadows the unruly hair of the final version of *La Petite Châtelaine*. It is difficult to date this *Implorer* and therefore to attach it to the stays at l'Islette, but it is interesting that it was for these allegorical portraits that the artist reserved the "exquisitely complicated combinations"[26] that Morhardt discusses apropos of *Clotho*'s skein. At the same time, the hair of *Hamadryad* (fig. 36) and of Thaulow's marble *Les Causeuses* (1896), which we know from the Geneva plaster, are in the same manner and hallmarks of Camille Claudel's style.

At the 1895 Nationale, *La Petite Châtelaine* in the Peytel Collection was noticed by a collector who asked Bourdelle to act as intermediary between himself and Camille Claudel. On May 10, 1895, Camille Claudel replied to the sculptor, whom she had met at Rodin's studio, "Monsieur It would be very possible for me to do another bust in marble like the one I exhibited at the Salon but I would need at least three months and the price would be 1500f. If these terms are acceptable to the collector you have told me about, would you please let me know this as soon as possible. I am very flattered by the admiration you have shown for my works: the approval of an artist such as you is very precious to me."[27] Some time later, Bourdelle having confirmed the commission, she wrote to him, "Monsieur You give me great joy in telling me that you have succeeded in having my small marble bust commissioned and at a higher price than I expected. I shall set to work straightaway and you give me a little of the heart I was beginning to lose. I am very touched, this coming from an artist such as you and spontaneous admiration is a rare and priceless thing. Yours sincerely and gratefully Camille Claudel: P.S Since it is possible I would like a small advance to buy the marble" (cat. 207). Once the commission was underway, she thanked Bourdelle and revealed the identity of the client: "I received today from Mons. Henri Fontaine the sum of a thousand francs as an advance on my small bust which he wants to pay me two thousand five hundred for. I think that is far too much and really this collector's generosity is extraordinary. I undoubtedly owe this to your benevolent protection and allow me to thank you for this again. Your humble Camille Claudel" (cat. 208). Henri Fontaine was an industrialist from the Aisne. He and his brothers Émile and Lucien owned a decorative ironwork and lock factory. The

_Fig. 36

_Fig. 36
_
LÉMERY
Hamadryad, *marble and bronze, by Camille Claudel*
1895–97
Photograph,
in CLAUDEL 1913, p. 39

Fontaine company commissioned Art Nouveau artists such as Alexandre Charpentier and Hector Guimard to create its exclusive designs. Bourdelle had therefore brought Camille Claudel a collector who did not know Rodin but who, via the arts and industry, was instrumental in disseminating Art Nouveau.

The new *Petite Châtelaine* (cat. 74, pp. 148–49) was shown at the 1896 Nationale and, later that year, at the Salon de l'Art Nouveau, at the Galerie Samuel Bing, as "*Bust of a Child*, marble / Belonging to M. Fontaine." Commentators noted the artist's technical virtuosity, Maillard extolling "the admirable head of a child sculpted by Mlle Claudel, in whom a masterly will and absolute conquest of forms are increasingly asserting themselves."[28] And Geffroy

_Cat. 74

unreservedly admires this "portrait of a child of such beautiful vivacity of expression, sculpted with that passionate science peculiar to the artist."[29] Geffroy's commitment to the piece is interesting since it marks a departure from the path he usually appreciated and encouraged in Camille Claudel, her studies from nature (see "The 'Sketches from Nature,'" pp. 236–49). It is a comment all the more remarkable in that it associates the work's aesthetic effect and the sculptor's technical prowess, thereby extolling the independence the artist had gained vis-à-vis Rodin's manner. The virtuosity of the carving here must of course be understood as a mark, a signature, a declaration of independence, in outright opposition to Rodin's manifest preference for modeling. And the stone carving in this version is indeed

extraordinary, associating the striking effect of the hair and the imperceptible hollowing out of the block of marble to render it translucent, to transform matter into light. But Camille's refusal of "Rodinity" is at this point a reply, a vow, one which he does not avoid, if not the quote at least the paternity. There therefore clearly seems to be a very personal intent lying behind the treatment of _Clotho_'s "tout à jour" hair, _The Implorer_ with loose hair, _Hamadryad_ and the Gorgon's snakes (a self-portrait!) in _Perseus_, which took her from 1897 to 1902 to finish. And it was into this self-designating context that she inserted _La Petite Châtelaine_. If this fusion can perhaps be explained by the abortion, or at least if knowledge of this drama puts a very painful reading on the aesthetic effect, it is also interesting to compare this approach to the work of Rodin, who in 1891–92 introduced Estager's mask into a mane to transform the portrait of the "conductor of Tours" into a Balzacian icon.[30] And this reading gives l'Islette a nodal and complex role in the elaboration of the

_Cat. 74

CAMILLE CLAUDEL
La Petite Châtelaine
with hair "tout à jour"
Marble, executed by
Camille Claudel, 1896
44 x 36 x 29 cm
La Piscine – Musée d'Art
et d'Industrie André-Diligent,
Roubaix

_Cat. 74

Fontaine marble and, more broadly, in Camille Claudel's development during this period.

It is therefore interesting to re-situate this version within the overall development of Camille Claudel's work as the final element of a reflection on liberation, that is, that this stage is in equilibrium—or disequilibrium—in the artistic course of an artist who then felt herself at the crossroads of contradictory paths, perhaps even on the threshold of a new life. Stylistically and thematically, *La Petite Châtelaine* is certainly totally different from the studies from nature which the artist had previously undertaken, but at the same time, the sculptor's assertion of her technical prowess is there to be seen, on the same level, in the little girl's hair and the marble-onyx of the Peytel *Causeuses*, which, in 1897, was the final outcome of a project presented to Paul Claudel in 1893. *La Petite Châtelaine* has no obvious connection to *The Age of Maturity* either, yet the Art Nouveau rhythm of the base of the large group shown at the 1899 Salon is disconcertingly similar to the fluid forms of the base from which the bust of the little girl emerges in the Fontaine version, which was shown at the second Salon de l'Art Nouveau at the Galerie Samuel Bing in 1896.[31] Paradoxically, at the same time, no doubt searching for a kind of artistic virginity that would obliterate Rodin's teachings, Camille Claudel was tempted by a more traditional inspiration, not that far removed from the Neo-Florentinism of Alfred Boucher and Paul Debois. And as we have seen above, the Italianate format of *La Petite Châtelaine* is a return to a tradition that the base of the Fontaine version in a sense accentuates by evoking the Renaissance model of the reliquary bust.

The final outcome of the series of *Petites Châtelaines* seems to confirm this development. It is difficult to precisely date *Aurora*, although the smoothness of the marble suggests it was a late version, perhaps around 1900. The model is definitely Marguerite Boyer, though.

Seen in this light, l'Islette seems to lie at the heart of Camille Claudel's entire oeuvre. It is hard to know for sure whether the artist returned to Touraine after the known stay in 1893, but it is certain she remained in contact with Madame Courcelles, the château's owner, if only because of the works she had left there in autumn 1893. This practical detail was the subject of correspondence with Rodin in late 1897: "Morhardt has for a long time appeared to me to be your devoted friend I have neither suspected nor seen any cooling off for you, since without that her husband could not have served you, if only in secret, but this is not the case with Madame Courcelles. There is a solicitor who defends artists, he is one of my friends. If you want to consult him on my behalf here is the address. Auroux 118 Rue de Rivoli 118. As for me it would be difficult for me to demand the dante since in an old letter I told her I would take some of her wine if she gave me back the plaster. I think she is sticking by a former donation. Especially as I must have thanked her for the wine she used to send us without giving her anything in return. I'm not sure about all this. But I gave it to her and cannot ask for it back" (cat. 216, pp. 208–9). In this prosaic conclusion to the studios at l'Islette there was an admission of a new departure, and *La Petite Châtelaine* was, in a way, the story of this transition.

This period of assertion of the new, liberated Camille Claudel that one discovers in the genesis of *La Petite Châtelaine* can also be compared to works with a similar subject by other artists who belonged more or less intimately to Rodin's entourage. Lucien Schnegg, the tutelary figure of what the critics in 1909 entitled "Schnegg's gang," posed at the heart of his artistic reflection the question of the relationship between sculpture and architecture. This exact contemporary of Camille Claudel, before dying very young, developed an oeuvre with great concern for balance, and in obvious reaction to Rodin's art, which had profoundly influenced him. *Pensive* (c.1900, marble, Roubaix / La Piscine, on loan from the Musée d'Orsay), a portrait of the artist's daughter Madeleine, born in 1899, is symptomatic of this ambivalence. The model's anecdotal pose is a far cry from the hieratic pose of *La Petite Châtelaine,* but the overall formats of both busts are not dissimilar in certain respects, even if, in this sense, Schnegg's work is more traditional in spirit. But the hacked-away appearance of the stone block from which the model emerges is a much more modernist reference to Rodin's marbles, far more obvious than the Art Nouveau lines of the base of *La Petite Châtelaine.* Younger, Robert Wérick belonged to the same group who referred to Rodin and whose aim was to recover the rhythms of antique sculpture, particularly archaic Greek statuary. The *Head of a Girl* he showed in 1909, sometimes entitled *Marguerite,* exemplifies this quest for a serene equilibrium. It is above all interesting to compare *La Petite Châtelaine* with his *Petite Landaise* (bronze, Roubaix / La Piscine). Modeled in 1911, it was shown the following year at the Nationale, where it was noticed by Rodin, who said to the sculptor, "It is beautiful like a Donatello, this is the sculpture of the future."[32] The portrait's Italianate bust format and very Gothic elegance most probably explain Rodin's reaction, which is similar to T. de Wyzewa's 1895 commentary on the Peytel marble of *La Petite Châtelaine* and the reference to Mino de Fiesole above. And he praises the freshness and sensitivity of a work conceived with a clear concern for economy and simplicity, for example in the absence of detail of the plait, cut abruptly off above the neck, while Camille Claudel plays with this accessory, even undoing it, theatrically in the Fontaine marble and smoothly in *Aurora,* where it becomes a purely decorative element.

III STORMY TIMES [1892–1899]

OSTEOLOGY OF OLD WOMEN   Antoinette Le Normand-Romain

At the Salon de la Société des Beaux-Arts in 1893, the public discovered an aged, emaciated female nude caught in the strands of her long hair (cat. 63). The hair of this "plaster figurette," as it was described in the catalogue, dense like the roots of a tropical tree, as malevolent as the coils of the snake sent by the gods to suffocate the arrogant Laocoon, transforms it into an octopus or spider. And beneath its thick mantle one does indeed make out two piercing eyes and a mouth contorted into a kind of rictus, a death mask almost, as if the old woman were watching her prey. "Next, the *Fate*, the fearsome *Fate*. Old, emaciated, hideous, her flesh hanging down her in tatters, her withered fallen breasts like dead eyelids, her pitted stomach, her long legs made for terrible never-ending walks, agile, nervous legs whose strides mow down human lives, she laughs behind her death mask. Around her, life, represented by strange banners, by interminable cut selvages and rolls, unfurls, furls."[1] As she had learned from Rodin, Camille pushed realism as far as possible, but far from dwelling on the

sadness and decline that are the lot of advanced age, she transcends this and turns the hideous torso of an old woman (fig. 37, p. 156) into a "Triumph of Old Age," in counterpoint to the penitent Mary Magdalene, one of the most beautiful of which, greatly admired by Rodin and reproduced in *L'Art* in 1911,[2] was Donatello's. "Osteology of an old woman,"[3] "fatal decline of a woman's body,"[4] *Clotho* thus appears to be a vengeance, and all the crueler because Camille is turning what Rodin taught her against him.

LEFT AND
FOLLOWING PAGES
Cat. 63
—
CAMILLE CLAUDEL
Clotho
1893
Plaster
90 x 49.5 x 43.5 cm
Musée Rodin, Paris

153

Fig. 37

Camille Claudel
Torso of Clotho
About 1892?
Plaster
Musée d'Orsay, Paris

Cat. 100

Cat. 100

Jules Desbois
Misery
About 1887–89
Terracotta
37.5 x 24.6 x 17.7 cm
Musée Rodin, Paris

Cat. 153

Auguste Rodin
*She Who Was Once
the Helmet-Maker's
Beautiful Wife*
1889
Bronze
50 x 30 x 26.5 cm
Musée Rod n, Paris

"The only ugliness in art is that which has no character," he would say.[5] Like his predecessors, above all the Greeks, who he believed were rigorously faithful to nature, he was interested in all human bodies and studied them for themselves and not to give morality lessons by showing the ephemeral nature of beauty and youth. Like Delacroix, whose *Massacre at Chios* was violently accused of reveling in the representation of a "gruesome" reality in 1824, he was convinced that the artist can take what is generally considered ugly and "with a magic wand" transform it into beauty. He spoke on the subject at length in his *Discussions* with Paul Gsell: "The fact is that in Art only that which has *character* is beautiful. *Character* is the intense truth of any natural spectacle, beautiful or ugly."[6] He therefore had no qualms about having an elderly woman pose for a nude study, entitled simply *Old Woman* the first time it was shown in public, in Angers in 1889. It was not until two years later, when it was acquired by the state for the Musée du Luxembourg, that it was given its present title (cat. 153), *She Who Was Once the Helmet-Maker's Beautiful Wife*, inspired by François Villon's poem *Ballade de la Belle Heaulmière aux filles de joie. Les regrets de la Belle Heaulmière jà parvenue à vieillesse* (c.1461):

> When I look at myself all naked
> And see myself so very changed
> Poor, dry, thin, meager
> I become almost completely enraged

According to Paul Gsell, it was Desbois who gave Rodin the idea for this figure. "When Rodin saw

Cat. 15

Fig. 38

for Philemon and Baucis. The almost mummified grandmother, who had inspired a masterpiece by Desbois, provided Rodin with an opportunity to create another one: the old *Helmet-Maker's Wife*. One can compare the two artists. Rodin is more abrupt, more haughtily philosophical, more desperate, more distressing, more inexorable . . . Desbois is less immoderate. His *Misery* . . . inspires not horror but pity."[7]

Gsell is, a priori, credible, but he was writing thirty-five years after the event. Can his account, reworked and embellished in 1935,[8] be taken at face value? We know that Desbois's spectacular group *Death and the Woodcutter* (no longer extant), for which he used the old woman for the first time, was not shown until the first Salon of the Société Nationale des Beaux-Arts in 1890, and that a plaster of *Misery* was exhibited in 1894 (fig. 38) and a wood version in 1896. But ten years earlier, Rodin had already incorporated two depictions of old women into *The Gates of Hell*. Octave Mirbeau, the first to describe it in *La France* on February 18, 1885, specifies that on the right-hand jamb, representing limbo, "We see, in a kind of mysterious vapor, tumbling children mingled with horrible figures of old women." The left jamb (cat. 136) is perfectly visible in one of the photographs taken by William Elborne or Jessie

Misery (cat. 100, p. 156) in clay in Desbois's studio, he was dumbstruck, and suddenly had the idea of rivaling his fellow sculptor. He wanted to fashion a sculpture in the same style and asked for the address of this toothless Fate, Caira her name was—almost Chera, the Greek name for 'sister spinsters.' She belonged to an Italian tribe whose every member was a life model, father to son, mother to daughter. The newborn posed for cherubs, the old men and women

Fig. 38
JULES DESBOIS
Misery
1894
Plaster
Musée Jules Desbois,
Parçay-les-Pins

_Cat. 135

_Cat. 136

Cat. 135

AUGUSTE RODIN
Seated Old Woman
About 1884
Terracotta
43.2 x 18.6 x 32.2 cm
Musée Rodin, Paris

Cat. 136

AUGUSTE RODIN
*Left Jamb, bottom section,
of* The Gates of Hell
About 1884–85
Patinated plaster
188.5 x 47 x 30 cm
Musée Rodin, Paris

Lipscomb in 1887,[9] which shows it already in its present-day state with, in the lower part, an old woman seated in profile. In fact, it is merely half an old woman since it is a bas-relief: the clay study was cut in half, one half being used for *The Gates*, while the other is still in the storerooms of the Musée Rodin (cat. 135, p. 159). This study, and also undoubtedly a clay sketch of a torso (fig. 39) with withered breasts falling "like dead eyelids," to use Mirbeau's phrase, and a wrinkled and swollen stomach, can be dated to

_Fig. 39

AUGUSTE RODIN
Torso of an Old Woman
About 1884?
Terracotta
Musée Rodin, Paris

1884 and no later, given the date of Mirbeau's article on *The Gates*, and hardly earlier, since it was when Mirbeau first met Rodin. But Mirbeau himself told Edmond de Goncourt that he "found Rodin modeling an admirable thing from a ninety-two-year-old woman . . . and that, a few days later, when he asked him how the clay was going, the sculptor said to him that he had broken it up . . . He subsequently regretted the destruction of the work praised by Mirbeau and has produced the two old women on exhibit"[10]—that is, an assemblage of two identical copies of *She Who Was Once the Helmet-Maker's Beautiful Wife*, exhibited in 1889 at the Galerie Georges Petit in Paris under the title *Dried-Up Springs* (fig. 40). It was also certainly in 1884 that Desbois joined Rodin's studio, but six years would pass before he exhibited a work in which he used an old woman as model. Recounting his relentless labor in 1911, Gustave Coquiot describes him shut up in his studio, where he worked "ceaselessly, with a thoughtful, tenacious conscientiousness, even copying for *three years* the fantastic model he had found for the figure of Death (*Death and the Woodcutter*) and which he later retained for the statue of *Misery*."[11] In Coquiot's view, these three years were a considerable length of time: three years but not six.

This article has enabled the dating of the first studies for *Misery*[12] to c.1887–88, which has led some authors to date *She Who Was Once the Helmet-Maker's Beautiful Wife* to 1888.[13] Perhaps then, Rodin, spurred on by Desbois's work, may have completed it by giving it its autonomy. But since his work dated back to 1884–85, it must surely have been he who had been the first to discover the beauty of an old woman's body and the first to immerse himself, as Anne Pingeot puts it, "in the voluptuousness of the devastating realism which fascinates the sculptors of troubled times."[14] However, to put the date forward (or rather, return to the date indicated by Grappe in his catalogue of the Musée Rodin[15]) poses the question of the model herself, generally identified as Marie Caira. On the back of a letter sent by Léon Lhermitte on December 5, 1888, asking him for addresses of models and in particular "an old, <u>thin</u> and <u>tall</u> woman (for my own pupils)," Rodin noted down: "Caira (the old woman) / 67 years / 7 rue du (Congo?)."[16] For all that, one cannot conclude that he used her. In 1888, Desbois was thus working on both *Death and the Woodcutter* and *Misery*, with an elderly female model, perhaps indeed Marie Caira, despite her having left no trace, whereas several other models of that name in Paris at that time did,[17] and it is very possible that it was he who gave Rodin the information requested by Lhermitte.

"The story of the 92-year-old model is rather curious," continues Goncourt, who had been told it by Mirbeau. "She was the mother of an Italian model, who came on foot from Italy to see him before she died, and the son said to her, 'Mother, I'll throw you out if you don't pose.' And he suggested her to Rodin, without telling him she was his mother." Mirbeau wrote a story about it, *L'Octogénaire*, published in *L'Écho de Paris* on January 11, 1889:[18] "When I entered the studio, an old woman, completely naked, was sitting on the model's table, posing." Frederick Lawton, who did Rodin's secretarial work from March

Fig. 40

to May 1905, confirmed this anecdote.[19] Goncourt, Mirbeau and Lawton all describe a woman over ninety years old, which seems to correspond better to the presumed age of *She Who Was Once the Helmet-Maker's Beautiful Wife* than the sixty-seven years of the woman whose address Rodin gave to Lhermitte. But fourteen months later, on February 22, 1890, Rodin announced to Victor Peter, charged with transposing the figure into marble (fig. 44, p. 163), that "the old woman [was going] to come to Paris in the next

Fig. 40
Auguste Rodin
The Dried-Up Springs
1889
Plaster
Musée Rodin, Paris

few days I have had her return from Italy you will therefore have as much nature as you want to continue my work."[20] But could a woman over ninety years old have possibly gone back to Italy, then returned?

Could there have been two old women? What little information we have seems to refute this. Comparison of *She Who Was Once the Helmet-Maker's Beautiful Wife* and the study for *Misery*, exhibited side by side in the Musée Rodin, could indeed lead one to believe so: the bone structure of the former's back is more prominent; the pelvis of the latter seems wider and her limbs are longer and

thinner; the face of *Misery* is more triangular, with a more pointed and more prominent chin. In Rodin's sculpture, the face is unquestionably a portrait, prepared by a tiny, nut-sized study, whose structure—including a hollow at the left temple, the features and hairstyle—is indicated strikingly precisely with a few spatula marks (cat. 152 and fig. 41). But the face remains the same, from the relief of *The Gates of Hell* (for which one can nonetheless envisage that it may have been modified after 1884–85, since the clay *Old Woman* has a different head) to *Winter*, and it is still recognizably the same in a later group of sculptures, which means that the model lived until at least around 1900 and therefore makes it more probable that she was sixty-seven in 1888 rather than eighty in 1885. One of Rodin's pupils, Anna Golubkina, during her second stay in Paris in 1897, exhibited a huddled figure entitled *Old Age*[21] at the 1899 Salon. Her face, like the *Bust of an Old Woman* executed in Paris in 1900–1 by the Portuguese sculptor Antonio Fernandes

Cat. 116
FRANÇOIS POMPON
A Good Old Woman
1883
Terracotta
24.5 x 10.2 x 16.5 cm
Musée des Beaux-Arts, Dijon

Cat. 152
AUGUSTE RODIN
Sketch for the Head of She Who Was Once the Helmet-Maker's Beautiful Wife
Before 1889
Terracotta
3.3 x 2.7 x 3.4 cm
Musée Rodin, Paris

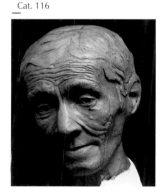

Cat. 116

Cat. 152

Fig. 41

Fig. 42

Fig. 43

Fig. 44

de Sá (fig. 42),[22] and that of a seated naked old woman modeled no doubt about the same time by Henri de Bideran, an amateur sculptor and pupil of Bourdelle, and a head of an *Old Woman Singing* by Bourdelle himself (terracotta, Musée Bourdelle, Paris), definitely seems to have been sculpted from the same model as *She Who Was Once the Helmet-Maker's Beautiful Wife*. Henri de Bideran's figure is, incidentally, so close to the latter that one wonders whether he might not have reinterpreted it without recourse to a model.

The general public were put off by the almost excessive realism of this "cry of humanity"[23] echoing Bonnat's *Job*, which had triumphed at the 1880 Salon, but the figure fascinated artists, critics and art historians such as Desbois, Claudel, Geffroy and Kenneth Clark, who considered it one of the "unforgettable nudes of pity" created in the late nineteenth century,

and also Henry Moore, who, at the beginning of his career, did "a figure of an old man standing because [he had] been very impressed by the figure of an old woman [by Rodin]."[24] Even though one can cite a great many portraits of old men and women, such as Pompon's bust of *A Good Old Woman* (cat. 116), part of the renewal in realism in the last quarter of the nineteenth century, Rodin appears as the immediate heir of Pigalle (*Voltaire*, 1776, marble, Musée du

Fig. 41
AUGUSTE RODIN
She Who Was Once the Helmet-Maker's Beautiful Wife
1889
Patinated plaster
Musée Rodin, Paris

Fig. 42
ANTONIO FERNANDES DE SÁ
Bust of an Old Woman
Marble, 1901
Museu Nacional de Soares dos Reis, Oporto

Fig. 43
RENÉ DE SAINT-MARCEAUX
Winter
Marble, 1902
Musée des Beaux-Arts. Reims

Fig. 44
AUGUSTE RODIN
Winter
Marble, 1890
Musée d'Orsay, Paris

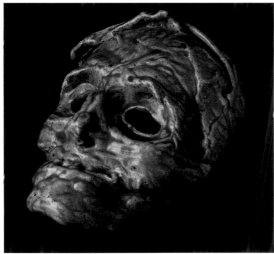

Louvre, Paris) and, in turn, drew a great many artists into his wake, including those hostile to him such as René de Saint-Marceaux: "René has done two bas-reliefs—One, *Winter*, with an old Italian woman [fig. 43, p. 163], the other, *Autumn*, delightful in feel-ing," his wife noted in her *Journal* on October 15, 1897.[25] But it was obviously those closest to Rodin who were the most influenced by him, especially Desbois and Camille Claudel, who were at his side during the first studies of old women. Indeed, the connection between the three figures is a perfect demonstration of the studio phenomenon, a veritable

artistic greenhouse in which new ideas germinate like seeds and develop more or less quickly and in differ-ent directions depending on each person's personality. It is worth noting, incidentally, that *Clotho* is exactly contemporary with *Misery* and that her grimacing face is not unrelated to hers. Desbois, however, would go further by bestowing an autonomous existence on the mask derived from this face, *Death*, of which he had Jeanneney execute stoneware copies (cat. 101). These are later than 1900,[26] like the stoneware heads of Balzac produced by the same ceramicist,[27] and again one wonders whether it was Rodin or Desbois who had the idea of transposing his works into a material so attractive in the range of refined tints it afforded.

Meanwhile, at the banquet given in Puvis de Chavannes's honor on January 16, 1895, Morhardt had launched a subscription to aid Camille by commis-sioning a marble version of *Clotho* for the Musée du Luxembourg. Rodin, worried about her, gave 1,000 francs, almost doubling the sum collected, which mainly consisted of the balance of the Puvis de Chavannes committee. The marble, slightly smaller than the plaster,[28] "a gem . . . clear, rich, as brilliant as a fine Alsatian ivory,"[29] was exhibited at the Salon of the Sociéte Nationale des Beaux-Arts in 1899. It then remained in Camille's possession and she tried to sell it (even though it belonged to the Puvis de Chavannes committee),[30] and was subsequently kept by Morhardt until 1905, when it was handed over to Rodin. Rodin, whom Camille accused of having "stolen" it from her, had it delivered, as agreed, to the Musée du Luxembourg, where it was "naturally" refused by the museums council. There is no trace of it from then on,[31] and we know it solely from the reproductions included by Paul Claudel in his 1913 article (fig. 45 and 46). The disappearance of this figure, whose quality of execution must have been comparable to that of *Vertumnus and Pomona*, is particularly regrettable in an oeuvre comprising so few pieces.

"Irrespective of the technical merit of a sculptor in approaching such a subject," Louis de Fourcaud complained in front of *Clotho* in 1899, "he is depriving himself of the purest expressive resources of his art. By overindulging in *intellectualism*, he ceases to be intelligible in form: he abandons himself to curiosity instead of serving the popular ideal, in the noble, antique sense of the word."[32] He was thus echoing the analysis of *She Who Was Once the Helmet-Maker's Beautiful Wife* published in *L'Artiste* ten years earlier: "Whether one approves of or condemns the choice of subject, it is impossible not to see a great artist behind this small bronze, one who knows how to mold with her thumb and conjure out of clay, what? Life, the essential element of art; life, in a both general and individual form."[33] For Rodin, all that mattered was attentive observation of nature, whereas *Clotho* and *Misery*, more dramatic, evoke Gothic sculpture and its *memento mori*. Desbois and Camille Claudel both felt the need to resort to allegory, an allegory which, at least for the latter, cannot be properly understood without being considered in its historical context. In a young woman, the locks of hair covering the face were considered a symbol of femininity and eroticism: here, the Fate *Clotho* spins both the threads of life, which her sister Atropos will cut, and the threads of the liaison that united Camille and Rodin.

Fig. 45   Fig. 46

In 1892. Camille moved into 11 avenue de La Bourdonnais but kept her studio in boulevard d'Italie. She had not completely broken off relations with her parents, yet they now no longer wanted to see Rodin whereas before they had received him willingly. She therefore took care to warn him of their visits: "Do not come here as here is the letter I have received," she wrote to him on the back of a note from her mother fixing a rendezvous for the next day. "We must avoid trouble. Other than that, I am feeling better" (cat. 197, p. 166). Rodin remained close, but their ties loosened, of her volition, and without this preventing her from finishing *The Waltz* (cat. 64, p. 112) for the 1893 Salon. As in 1886, when she went to England, it is probable that certain critics weighed heavily in this evolution: "Nothing is worth originality, Mademoiselle," Paul Leroi reproached her in 1892, "and when one has it—such is

Fig. 45 and 46
LÉMERY
Clotho, *marble, front and back, by Camille Claudel*
1899
Photographs,
in CLAUDEL 1913,
pp. 22, 23

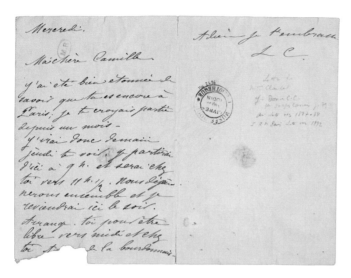

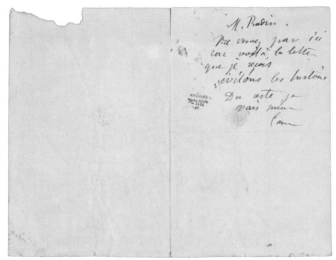

Cat. 197

*Letter from Louise Claudel to
her daughter Camille Claudel*
(recto)
*Letter from Camille Claudel
to Auguste Rodin* (verso)
[May–June 1892?]
1 sheet, 17.6 x 22.6 cm
Musée Rodin, Paris

your good fortune—it is a gross fault to put oneself in
the tow of anyone at all. Content yourself, therefore,
with being yourself."[34] The following year, she was
accused of having pasticched *She Who Was Once the
Helmet-Maker's Beautiful Wife*: "I would have you
note," she wrote to Maurice Guillemot, who had a
special interest in the affair because Rodin had given
him a drawing of his figure,[35] "that I owe my works
only to myself, since I have too many rather than not
enough ideas."[36] In January 1893, Armand Dayot had
noted that "her personality is highly apparent and
[that] she will manifest herself daily with more freedom in the isolation which she now lives with her art"
(cat. 200). The break had therefore taken place.
Camille had tried to get "Rodin to repudiate his poor
old Rose, who had stood by him through hard times
and shared his long years of misery. [But] he [had not
been able] to reconcile himself to this even though he
loved her passionately, both as an artist and as a
man."[37] Frightened by her violent character, Rodin in
turn decided to flee and moved in with Rose, who
represented comfort for him, at Bellevue in April
1893, then at Meudon at the end of the year.

Yet he missed Camille and made this known to
her, as she did, through the language of allegory.
The point of departure for one of the marbles he
exhibited at the 1896 Salon, *Triumphant Youth* or
Fate and the Convalescent (cat. 164 and fig. 47) was
*She Who Was Once the Helmet-Maker's Beautiful
Wife*, in which Fate, having thrown her scissors
behind her, is protecting a young girl sitting on her
lap. But Camille would have none of this and set out
her version of events in *The Age of Maturity*.

Fig. 47

Cat. 164

Fig. 47

AUGUSTE RODIN
Triumphant Youth
Marble, 1896
MAK, Vienna

Cat. 164

AUGUSTE RODIN
Triumphant Youth or *Fate
and the Convalescent*
About 1895
Plaster
50.5 x 46.7 x 33 cm
Musée Rodin, Paris

THE AGE OF MATURITY OR FATE   John R. Porter

The future is what lies beyond the outstretched hand.[1]

—Louis Aragon

It is impossible to overemphasize the importance of *The Age of Maturity*, the summit of Camille Claudel's art and supreme illustration of her genius. It is a work into which she put everything, and which sums up her life, both in its narration and treatment. Although it marked a turning point, expressed a hope and aspiration, this terribly premonitory work would lead to the ruin that the artist herself feared. *The Age of Maturity*'s evolution, narrative content and critical fortune are also inseparable from the figure of Rodin. Yet it is a powerful work whose universal significance transcends the subjacent dynamics of the various ties binding Camille and Rodin. In this context, it is hardly surprising that the work has been abundantly discussed since it was first exhibited in 1899.

The Age of Maturity is the encounter of two destinies or, more exactly, the separation of two destinies, the rift between two artists, one at the height of his powers, the other still striving to emerge. *The Age of Maturity* is the impossible conjugation of two singulars, the final outcome of their conflict, of two paths that met but had to part. Two trajectories, two ages, two sexes, two temperaments opposed but drawn to one another, whose break-up or scission would be triggered by a third player, Time, aided by their

twenty-four-year difference in age. *The Age of Maturity* is the ages of life, of life that passes and that, one day, confronts us with the unanswerable.

A PROTRACTED BREAK-UP

The process of Camille Claudel and Rodin's break-up, which coincided with the creation and first showing of *The Age of Maturity*, lasted from 1892 to 1899. In this sense, *The Age of Maturity* is the subject, illustration and staging of episodes Camille lived through.[2] If this process dragged on for so long, it was because the bonds between the two protagonists were manifold and complex, and reached beyond their original amorous and artistic complicity. From 1892, Camille manifested a fierce desire for independence, giving free rein to her unbridled and difficult temperament,

Cat. 68
CAMILLE CLAUDEL
The Age of Maturity,
first version
About 1893
Plaster
87 x 103.5 x 52.5 cm
Musée Rodin, Paris

169

Cat. 205

while more than ever Rodin wanted to concentrate on his art, refusing to jeopardize his material security and the comfort of ingrained habits. And so their cohabitation came to an end. Although Camille kept the studio at 113 boulevard d'Italie[3] (now boulevard Blanqui), in 1892 she decided to move to 11 avenue de la Bourdonnais, near the Eiffel Tower. And Rodin took advantage of this opportunity to distance himself from her, moving out of the old house in rue des Grands-Augustins and out of Paris, to Bellevue, in April 1893 and then to Meudon before the end of the year.

Cat. 205

Letter from Auguste Rodin
to Octave Mirbeau
[May 1895?]
1 sheet, 8.4 x 12.6 cm
Musée Rodin, Paris

The purchase of the Villa des Brillants in 1895 definitively closed the door on any amorous rapprochement.

Rodin's refusal to repudiate his long-term companion Rose Beuret, as Camille had demanded, undoubtedly exacerbated her rancor. Despite her fading beauty, the possessive, simple-hearted Rose had one steadfast quality: fidelity, humble fidelity. She had always been Rodin's efficient servant, faithfully obeying his every command and respecting his routines. However, as a working woman who had received very little education, she was incapable of providing anything like the companionship that nourished Rodin and Camille's relationship during its happy years. In this context, and given her fiery temperament, one can easily understand how humiliated Camille must have felt by Rodin's choice and her intense jealousy and hatred for poor Rose. Having felt rejected, she opted for solitude and withdrew into herself. The critic Henry de Braisne stressed how hard it was to win Camille Claudel's confidence, describing her as a "very inward" artist "with great reserve for those unwelcome."[4] Rodin himself confirmed Camille's silent withdrawal in the rather "discouraged" letter he wrote to the novelist and pamphleteer Octave Mirbeau in 1895, in which there is question of a project that would enable the "misunderstood artist" to finally obtain the success she deserved: "I do not know whether Mademoiselle Claudel will agree to come and see you and me on the same day. We have not seen or written to each other for two years. So I am not in a position to tell her anything. All that is up to you. Mademoiselle Claudel will decide whether I should be there or not" (cat. 205).

Although Rodin continued to act as Camille's protector, he manifested a certain apprehension as to her reactions. Edmond de Goncourt wrote in his *Journal* on May 10, 1894: "[The critic Roger] Marx told me this morning about the sculptress Claudel, about her closeness to Rodin for a time, during which he saw them working together amorously, just as Prudhon and Mlle Mayer must have done. Then, one day, who knows why, she escaped from this relationship for a while, resumed it again, then completely broke it off. And when this happened Rodin came to see Marx in a terrible state and, weeping, told him that he no longer had any authority over her."[5]

But Rodin evidently remained in love with his old flame. In 1895, their paths crossed by chance at an exhibition opening, and the letter that the "contented and happy" sculptor then wrote to his "sovereign" and "divine friend" speaks volumes: "I am still sick and yet if am to heal, I will, because the opening at which I saw you was for me the beginning of a consolation that will restore me to health! My very dear friend how kind you were how your intelligence pleases me . . . nor copy in your soul, which I feel is so beautiful; with what pain I am stricken, and how great my fault has been; but I feel that in seeing you there was a destiny I could not flee" (cat. 206, pp. 172–73; see the complete translation, pp. 372–73).

From then on Rodin would increasingly come to Camille's aid, orchestrating interventions by one and all[6] in favor of she who, he wrote, "has the gift of reigning over everyone."[7] Yet relations between the two protagonists remained occasional and were not matched with reciprocal visits to their studios. More often than not, they kept in contact via intermediaries, with the Swiss journalist and poet Morhardt playing a prime role in this. Morhardt, touched by Camille's fate, often invited her to dinner and, with his wife's help, took care of her, securing commissions, generally promoting her work and finding sculptors to produce marbles of her sculptures.[7] Rodin, for his part, did as much, exploiting the influence of his network of friends, journalists and politicians. In May 1895 he wrote to the journalist Gabriel Mourey, banking on the interest he had already shown in Camille Claudel: "Do something

1893?

inv. L1454

ma souveraine amie

Je suis toujours malade et cependant si je dois guérir, je guérirai, car le vernissage où je vous ai vu est pour moi le commencement d'une consolation qui me rendra à la santé! ma bien chère amie Que vous avez été bonne et que votre intelligence me plait, tous est quelque chose de nouveau n'est insignifiant, pas de ...

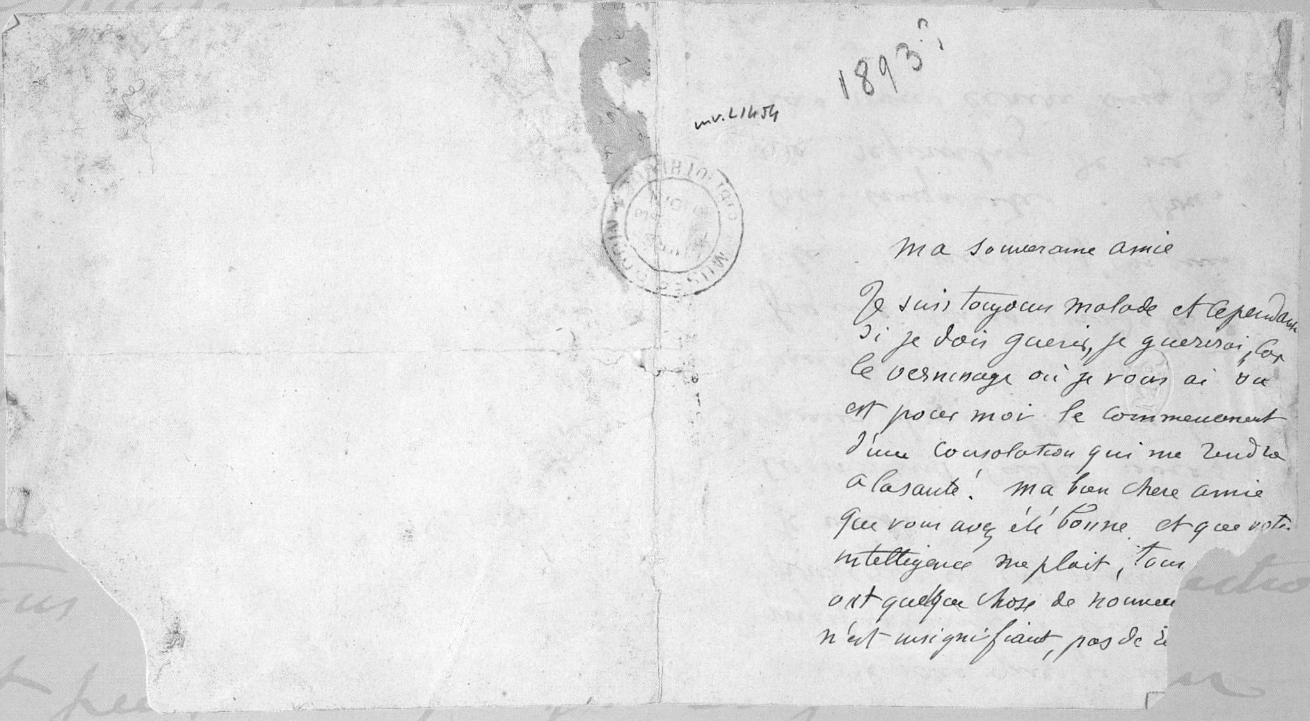

Cat. 206

Letter from Auguste Rodin to Camille Claudel
[May 1895?]
1 sheet, 13.5 x 24.9 cm
Musée Rodin, Paris

My sovereign friend
I am still sick and yet if am to heal, I will, because the opening at which I saw you was for me
the beginning of a consolation that will restore me to health! My very dear friend how kind you were
how your intelligence pleases me, all . . . have got something new . . . nor copy in your soul, which
I feel is so beautiful; with what pain I am stricken, and how great my fault has been; but I feel that
in seeing you there was a destiny I could not flee. Ah my divine friend. You will be happy be patient,
one has to pay for everything in this world. I was paid for my work. I'm paying for my faults and
my continuing pain is a striking example of justice . . .

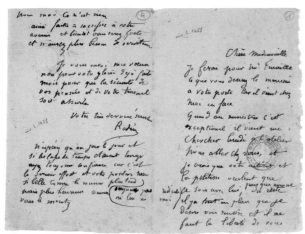
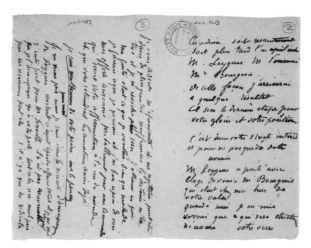

Cat. 209

for this woman of genius (this is no exaggeration) whom I love so much. for her art. and for whom you have been so vigorously benevolent" (cat. 204).

The following month, he wrote another of his clumsy letters to Camille, in which mention is made of the many approaches to the authorities he was orchestrating in the hope that these would be "crowned probably by a commission which will be your affirmation in the eyes of the world." To this end he literally begs Camille to agree to see him when the minister of public instruction and the fine arts,

Georges Leygues, visited her studio: "As for me I will see you only when strictly necessary the sight of you terrifies me and would perhaps pitch me into the greatest of suffering . . . So make this sacrifice for your future and soon you will be strong and will no longer need a servant" (cat. 209; see the complete translation, pp. 373–74).

Whatever the exact consequences of Rodin's specific approaches, his efforts did bear fruit because the following month Camille finally obtained her first state commission, which would lead to the creation of *The Age of Maturity*.[8] And once the commission had been obtained, Camille asserted her independence more than ever and made a point of distancing herself markedly from her illustrious protector. Rodin, though, manifested a certain relief in a letter to Hélène Wahl dated February 5, 1896: "I hope to be out of my troubles as I am working and sleeping, I feel that I am happy, or am going to be. I can feel

Cat. 209

*Letter from Auguste Rodin
to Camille Claudel*
[June 1895?]
1 sheet, 18 x 23 cm
Musée Rodin, Paris

youth coming back my head is full of enthusiasm. And the tyrannical passions seem well and truly over I love women just as much but in another way."[9]

Despite these remarks, he continued to aid Camille in every way he could, sometimes overstepping the mark. After he had informed her that he wanted to introduce her to the president of the Republic, Camille politely rejected the idea under the pretext that she did not have a suitable outfit for such an occasion (cat. 212).[10] A few months later, in September that year, Camille expressly asked Morhardt to ensure that Rodin kept his distance. In the context of *The Age of Maturity*, then in progress, it is important to understand the various motives underpinning Camille's behavior: "Would you kindly do everything in your power to ensure that M. Rodin does not come to see me on Tuesday. I do not like showing unfinished things and studies in progress; they can be viewed at leisure when they are completely finished and why should one make all one's ideas known before they are fully formed? If you could at the same time gently and subtly inculcate in M. Rodin the idea of not coming to see me anymore, you would be giving me the greatest pleasure I have ever felt. M. Rodin is well aware that many spiteful

Cat. 212

Cat. 212

Telegram from Camille Claudel to Auguste Rodin
Postmarked April 25, 1896
1 sheet, 13.1 x 11 cm
Musée Rodin, Paris

people have imagined that he did my sculpture: why then do all one can to give credence to these lies. If M. Rodin really does wish me well it would be possible for him to do so without on the other hand leading people to believe that it is to his advice and inspiration that I owe the success of the works on which I am aboring so hard" (cat. 213, p. 176).

For years Camille's talents had flourished in Rodin's shadow, had benefited from the great sculptor's advice. Again in 1892, she did not hesitate to take advantage "of M. Rodin" and his reputation when needed. Clearly, this situation had been beneficial for a time, but had had the perverse effect of rendering her name inseparable from Rodin's and hindering her pursuit of her own career. She therefore sought to come out from Rodin's shadow,

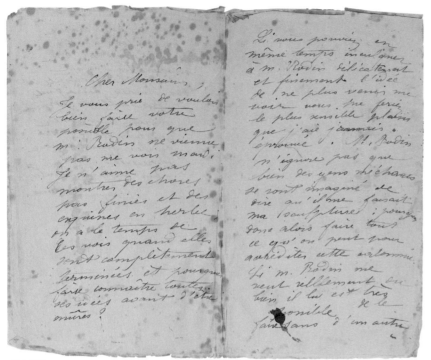
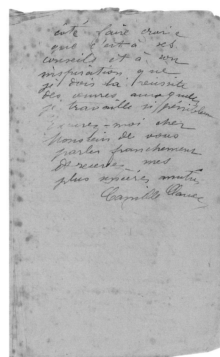

thereby responding to the injunction of Paul Leroi, alias Léon Gauchez, who in 1892 beseeched her to at last be herself rather than the reflection of another.[11] One consequently better understands the distance she sought to maintain between Rodin and herself, both in the literal and figurative sense, and that she did all she could to prevent him from visiting her studio.

The Age of Maturity's critical fortune from 1899 to 1908 would substantiate Camille Claudel's concerns. In the shorter term, it is entirely understandable that she should have insisted on being allowed to develop The Age of Maturity in complete secrecy, far from Rodin's eyes, since its very subject was guaranteed to annoy the great man,[12] who persisted in wanting to protect and help her. Camille's aim in The Age of Maturity was therefore twofold: on the one hand to realize her most ambitious work as a way of asserting her own genius loud and clear, a genius distinct from

Cat. 213
Letter from Camille Claudel to Mathias Morhardt
[September 1896?]
1 sheet, 21.5 x 50 cm
Société des Manuscrits des Assureurs Français, Paris

Rodin's; and on the other to publicly unveil her former relationship with Rodin and denounce the fact that he had in the end preferred his old mistress, Rose.

THE GENESIS OF THE WORK

The genesis of *The Age of Maturity* lies in a letter Camille wrote to her brother in December 1893, the month of her twenty-ninth birthday, in which she was eager to tell the diplomat Paul Claudel, then in New York, about her various projects in progress. She mentioned *The Age of Maturity*, which, incidentally, did not yet have a name: "I am still working on my group of three, I am going to add a leaning tree to express fate; I have a lot of new ideas which you would like a lot, you would be absolutely enthusiastic." Further on, she tells him she wants to show her group of three at the next Salon if she has finished it, adding: "Here's how it will be [annotated drawing] very wide," concluding with a phrase which speaks volumes: "You see, it is no longer Rodin at all and it is dressed." It should be said that Camille was already showing signs of paranoia, as this order to her brother attests: "I am confiding these finds to you only, do not show them" (cat. 202, p. 239).

Contrary to what Camille hoped, her three-figure group would not be ready for the 1894 Salon. But she did show a sculpture entitled *The Vanished God*, probably a reference to Rodin, who had left her a year before. In the July 15, 1894 issue of the *Magasin littéraire*, Henry Bordeaux described it as follows: "From Mlle Claudel, a kneeling woman, her face pleading, her arms outstretched toward her vanished hopes, a work of great rigor, à la Rodin." The piece was bound to please the latter, who did not fail to suggest one of his journalist friends mention it in an article.[13] Conversely, Camille was probably annoyed by the brevity of Bordeaux's commentary, especially as Paul Leroi's was somewhat along the same lines. Regretting that the brass wire hair spoilt Camille Claudel's sculpture, Paul Leroi warned her yet again about "her penchant, not of doing pastiches of her master, but of calling attention to herself, instead of contenting herself with producing works bearing the unmistakable stamp of an elevated personality."[14] Morhardt was more positive and enthusiastic about Camille's plaster in his major article published in 1898, making express mention of a "young woman kneeling, her left hand raised to breast height, [who] is reaching with her right hand above her head in a movement of marvelous eloquence."[15] And it is his description of *The Vanished God* that enables us to link the imploring female figure to the first version of *The Age of Maturity*, then in progress.[16]

The plaster of the first version of *The Age of Maturity*, in the Musée Rodin since 1952, differs by its overtly narrative nature (cat. 68, p. 168). Although the male figure is beardless, his profile, with its highly

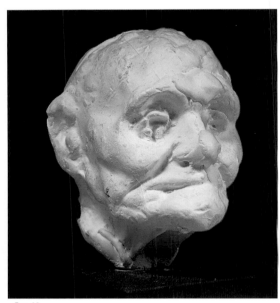

Cat. 69

of four caricatures Camille drew in 1892 (cat. 59 to 62, pp. 198–201) and which she sent to Rodin in a spiteful gesture channeling all her frustration and jealousy. These caricatures are in a certain sense the trivial and terrible pendant to *The Age of Maturity*, a work in which Camille succeeded in sublimating her innermost feelings. In them, Rose plays the role of a horrible shrew armed with a broom holding the man prisoner and preventing him from acting.[17]

And what should one make of the old woman's balding head. which corresponds to a small study that has fortunately survived (cat. 69). Camille kept this emaciated and wrinkled head for a long time. It still belongs to her family and was exhibited for the first time at the retrospective at the Musée Rodin in 1951. According to her brother Paul, Camille, who always loved skulls, powerfully demonstrates her talent as a sculptress here by transcending the initial repulsiveness of the subject. There is not the slightest refinement, only the emergence of an idea and the urgency of capturing its expression with keenly applied pellets of clay. This is a sculptural idea in its primal state that has lost none of its original intensity.

characteristic forehead and nose, is clearly comparable to Rodin's. As for the figure of the old woman, she has the sniggering face of *Clotho*-Rose, while the figure of Camille is associated with the figure of the young woman kneeling.

One is of course initially struck by the strangeness of this group of three nudes, with the off-balanced man with his huge feet and hands as the central figure. What a contrast also between the young woman's full forms and the old woman's sagging breasts and emaciated thighs. And if she has not yet grabbed hold of the man, she is readying herself to do so as she gives the implorer a defiant look, shaking her right fist menacingly. The figure of Rose being closely associated with that of the old woman, it is hardly surprising that she was the object of cruel mockery in the series

Cat. 68

Cat. 68
CAMILLE CLAUDEL
The Age of Maturity.
first version
About 1893
Plaster
87 x 103.5 x 52.5 cm
Musée Rodin, Paris

Cat. 69
CAMILLE CLAUDEL
*Head of the Old Woman from
The Age of Maturity group*
About 1893
Plaster
11 x 7.5 x 10 cm
Private collection

In 1895, the attempts made to secure a state commission for Camille Claudel bore fruit, and the critic and arts inspector Armand Silvestre was appointed by the director of fine arts to commission her a bronze or marble bust. When he visited the studio in boulevard d'Italie, Camille took this opportunity to interest him in her three-figure group, already in an advanced state. Silvestre referred to it in the report he wrote for the undersecretary of state on July 3: "Mlle Claudel showed the model for a group of really interesting composition and for which the studies are already very advanced. It represents the Age of Maturity, portrayed by a man whom Old Age is luring and whom Youth is greeting with a [illegible word]. Its movement is truly lyrical and the preoccupation with Rodin manifest. The artist would have preferred that the state commission this work, a marble of which she claims she can make for 5,000 francs. Without raising her hopes at all on this matter, I promised to submit her wish to you. It really is a very noble and very advanced work for a woman."[18]

How should one interpret the reference to Rodin? Does Silvestre's comment imply a link with the work's subject or its treatment? Symptomatically, an official letter was prepared to notify Rodin of the inspector's favorable appraisal of Camille Claudel's work, but it was decided not to send it.[19] It was rather as if Camille had now escaped Rodin's system of protection. At any rate, on July 27, 1895, Camille Claudel officially informed the ministry of fine arts that she gladly accepted its commission of a plaster of her group "The Age of Maturity" for the fee of 2,500 francs.[20]

In February 1896, Silvestre wrote in his second report on The Age of Maturity: "The group's figures are anatomically finished, and there remains only the modification of the parts to be clothed with drapery. One can therefore consider the work at least two thirds executed. Mlle Claudel, who has already spent considerable time on it and has had to pay models, requests that an advance of 1,000 francs be granted her. I believe her request should be given consideration" (cat. 210).

Two and a half years later, on October 14, Camille Claudel was at last able to inform the fine arts administration that her group was finished.[21] In his third and final report dated November 1, 1898, Silvestre sheds light on the considerable evolution Camille Claudel's composition had undergone since his visit in February 1896: "In a previous report, I described this composition comprising three figures and representing man at the end of his maturity, vertiginously drawn away by age while he reaches needlessly toward youth, who would like to follow him in vain. The artist has made only a few modifications to her model. Mlle Claudel has separated the hand of her principal figure from that of the figure of Youth to better express his being taken away. She has also enveloped the figure of Age in billowing drapery to emphasize the speed of her step. These three figures are well studied from nature and comprise fine pieces of anatomy. As it is, the group is interesting and very modern in treatment. It deserves the bronze cast which the artist requests and I can but give my favorable opinion on this wish. The impression of Rodin is blatant in this work but, since it is treated infinitely consciously one can say that it is by his qualities of invention and movement that she proceeds, only with the master's treatment and not his deliberate negligence" (cat. 217). As in his 1896 report, Silvestre evokes the figure of Rodin in ambiguous terms—"the impression of Rodin"—open to diverse interpretations.

After five years of effort, Camille Claudel was now at last nearing her goal. Despite all the obstacles, she had succeeding in seeing her great project through. *The Age of Maturity* was indeed an act of artistic self-assertion on Camille's part, but this was done at the price of emotional overload. On a human level, Camille was more fragile than ever. Her paranoia had intensified during the years she worked on

her figure group. In her staging of old age and death battling with youth and love, she was expressing her acrimony toward her former protector, who had distanced himself and abandoned her.

In November 1897, in a letter to Rodin, she attacks Morhardt, her most unconditional defender, trying to discredit him by throwing his fidelity and goodwill into question. Even though Morhardt and his wife selflessly took care of her every time she was ill, she attacks their "clan," recalling in passing their foreign origins and the fact that they are Protestants [22] Rodin was appalled by his protégée's words and tried after a fashion to get her to see reason in the letter he wrote to her on December 2 that year: "One has to remain faithful to friends. We have friends in life; if you distrust them you have no more support." He advises her to take a soft approach, to be patient, emphasizing her genius and his admiration for her. Aware of Camille's growing instability, he attempts to convince her of the need for the major article just written by Morhardt to be published, even though Camille had questioned its relevance.[23] The first biography of her, and a glowing plea in her defense in which Morhardt insists on the powerful assertion of the artist's personality, it was published in the *Mercure de France* in 1898.

On another note, it is necessary to return to a highly significant aspect of the disturbing letter which Camille wrote to Rodin in November 1897. In passing she fiercely attacks women in general, and in doing so sheds light on *The Age of Maturity*: "Besides, you know well the utter hatred all these women show me as soon as I appear, until I return to my shell they use any weapon they can, and further-more, as soon as a generous man tries to help me out of difficulty, there is his wife holding his arm to prevent him." This expression of an acute persecution complex immediately brings to mind the enraged fist and "utter hatred" of the old woman in the first version of *The Age of Maturity*, as well as the figure who in the second version is holding the man by both arms to prevent him from acting freely.

Camille's fragile mental state manifested itself again before the end of the year over a mere technicality concerning the final payment for the plaster of *The Age of Maturity*. Despite having been asked to await the availability of new funds in 1899,[24] she believed herself to be the victim of intrigues and wrote an acrimonious complaint to Henry Roujon, director of fine arts, denouncing in passing the presumed interventions of Rodin and Morhardt to block the payment owed her (cat. 218).

In 1898, Camille definitively broke all ties with Rodin by moving (apartment and studio) to 63 rue de Turenne. By the end of that year, however, she was already envisaging moving again. In January, she had to move to 19 quai de Bourbon, into a seventeenth-century mansion that had been divided up to be let. She lived and worked there, on the ground floor in the courtyard, from 1899 to 1913, and was living there when the plaster of *The Age of Maturity* was finally shown.

THE AGE OF MATURITY ON DISPLAY

Camille, who had been allowed by the fine arts administration to keep the plaster of the *The Age of Maturity* "with a view to [its] definitive execution," took advantage of this to show the work at the Salon of the Société Nationale des Beaux-Arts in 1899. The catalogue lists it as "The Age of Maturity (fantastic group), plaster (property of the state)." The work did not go unnoticed. Ivanhoë Rambosson thought it a "stormy masterpiece," describing as it follows: "Youth, portrayed kneeling is desperately reaching out to the man leaving her and whom Old Age, toward whom he is falling, is regretfully already drawing away and guiding. Nothing could be more dramatic or more alive in the fantastic so expressive is the movement of the walking man and the two women."[25] Gustave Geffroy appreciated "the power and nervous life of the overall movement."[26] Gabriel Mourey, commenting on both *The Age of Maturity* and the marble *Clotho*, also shown at the Salon, saw the fruits of the artist's "ardent imagination."[27] And André Fontainas, while wondering about the "powerful and tender" work, mentions that it "reveals the rare qualities of plastic realization, in a beautiful overall form both firm yet floating, flowing drapery, the expressive coloring of the plaster obtained by various thicknesses of patina, the harmonious sureness in every part of this perfect ensemble. It is a beautiful thing, truly moving and captivating."[28]

The reviews were also enlightening in their emphasis or absence of emphasis of the filiation of Camille's oeuvre with that of her protector. Roger Marx, although he recalls that Camille is a former pupil of Rodin, insists that she has a "gift for composition and also a tragic, fantastic imagination which fills one with enthusiasm in an age in which the mind so rarely animates matter."[29] Maurice Hamel shows interest in Camille while reflecting more broadly on "the definitive place that Rodin will have in the evolution of French art,"[30] and Charles Saunier affirms more categorically that "Mlle Camille Claudel is very influenced by Rodin,"[31] and Félicien Fagus notes that the artist "has managed to draw inspiration from the poignant grandeur of the master" while "keeping her own sensibility."[32]

But it was undoubtedly Jean Bernard who best summed up the critics' views in words that the artist, who wanted more than ever to remain distant from Rodin, must have appreciated: "Mlle Camille Claudel. Yes, a woman. And why not? Few men have the power, personal touch and nervous poetry that make Mlle Claudel one of the great contemporary sculptors. It is said that Mlle Claudel is a pupil of Rodin. That may well be. In which case one has to congratulate both the master and the disciple; but what is certain is that Mlle Claudel has succeeded in carving out her own personality and one can only see the lessons of the studio in a concern for modernity happily satisfied."[33]

Although some critics wondered about the meaning and significance of the allegory Camille Claudel had depicted, no one linked it explicitly to the master and pupil's past affair. But Rodin could hardly have failed to grasp the public declaration that Camille was making him, especially as she had made sure that there could be no ambiguity about this seven years earlier when she sent him four drawings expressing her bitterness (see "Camille Claudel: Vitriolic Caricatures," pp. 198–201). For Rodin, the exhibition of *The Age of Maturity* was a new declaration of their break-up, one that this time displayed his private life in public. From now on he could no longer "keep apart" the woman and the artist.[34] Nor could he have been fooled by the silence the art world had kept on this and this is why he from then on went about safeguarding his reputation at the very time when his career was reaching its apogee.

Following on from Anne Pingeot's 1982 hypothesis,[35] everything indicates that Rodin intervened to prevent a bronze or marble version of the plaster from being made. In early June 1899, five months after the payment of the remainder of Camille's fee for the plaster of *The Age of Maturity*, an order form for its casting in bronze was made out. But on June 24, having decided to postpone the commission until the

Fig. 48

following year, the director of fine arts, Henry Roujon, with no apparent motive, ordered its cancellation. In this respect, it is imperative to take into account the report Dujardin-Beaumetz wrote in 1907, which alludes to the probable motive for Roujon's cancellation order, referring to "reasons not mentioned in the dossier and which must have to do with the work's very nature."[36]

One should note in passing the irony of the game of hide-and-seek that Camille and Rodin had been playing from *The Age of Maturity*'s inception to its public exhibition. Rodin had done all he could to get Camille an important state commission, but from 1895 to 1899 was unaware that this commission was for *The Age of Maturity*. In parallel, Camille, in the utmost secrecy, had created a masterpiece meant to undermine the master and assert her own talent. And then, when it was finished, Rodin went about denying its permanence!

For Camille, instead of the expected triumph, *The Age of Maturity* marked the beginning of a long and impossible struggle with the state[37] and a descent into hell that would only increase her fragility and

exacerbate her mental condition. In May 1899, her instability was manifest. She unreasonably changed her mind more than once and missed her meetings with the nevertheless conciliatory and admiring Ottilie McLaren, a Scottish student she was intended to teach.[38] In the end it was Rodin himself who accepted to take over from Camille as teacher of Ottilie and one of her friends, and did his best to find excuses for her:[39] "[Rodin] says he thinks poor Miss Claudel has overworked and that she is really ill. That this mania against seeing anyone is really an illness."[40]

But "Rodin and his gang" were already being demonized by Camille, who would blame them for all her difficulties and disappointments even if, in reality, her former teacher continued to help her in various ways behind the scenes, notably by paying for the execution of certain works by the woman he continued to admire.[41]

Over the ensuing difficult years, Camille could always count on the staunch support and friendship of the "generous" men who defended *The Age of Maturity* and saved such an important and fragile work from oblivion.[42] Others before me have highlighted the remarkable roles played by Georges Lenseigne, Louis Tissier, Eugène Blot and Philippe

Fig. 48
CAMILLE CLAUDEL
The Age of Maturity
1899
Bronze
Musée d'Orsay, Paris

Berthelot. After Lenseigne's two vain attempts in 1900 and 1901 to persuade the director of fine arts to commission a bronze of *The Age of Maturity*, it was finally a soldier, Captain Louis Tissier, who succeeded in "saving the work from destruction by having it cast," despite his modest means. Camille, an acknowledged anti-Dreyfusard,[43] would clearly not have been indifferent to the admiration "of an officer who . . . always frankly speaks his mind."[44] Tissier, a friend of the painter Léon Lhermitte, was fascinated by *The Age of Maturity*, particularly by the figure of the *Woman on Her Knees* or *Imploration*.[45] The friendship he developed with Camille prompted him to have *The Implorer* cast by Adolphe Gruet, entrusting his father with the work because he had to set sail for China with the French expeditionary force. When he returned to Paris two years later, in late 1901, he was keener than ever to own a complete bronze of *The Age of Maturity*. Various steps led to a cast being undertaken by Thiébaut Frères, Fumière et Gavignot, under the supervision of the artist, who personally made the necessary cuts in the plaster to facilitate the transport Tissier's career moving from garrison to garrison entailed.[46] Camille and Tissier were completely satisfied with the sand cast and Tissier paid in

nine installments between February 28, 1902 and February 2, 1903. The work remained in the Tissier family until its acquisition by the Musée d'Orsay in 1982 (Fig. 48).

Shortly before the Thiébaut foundry began casting, Tissier commissioned a small bronze head of the group's male figure. The work was carried out before the end of January 1902 by François Rudier (cat. 70, p. 186), whom Tissier had initially hoped would undertake the casting of the entire group.[47] The head is striking in many ways. The old man's withered and inscrutable face expresses renouncement, withdrawal and failure, while his strikingly big ears do not heed the cries of the imploring woman.

Camille was clearly only too glad for Tissier to buy some of her works. In a letter she wrote to him on March 16, 1902, she made this friendly but caustic suggestion: "Make sure you shake up the people of independent means among your acquaintances! . . . even though this may be hard! . . . don't be too cross with me."[48] Earlier in this letter she refers to the bronze of the kneeling woman Tissier had bought some time before, saying she could not part with it for less than 400 francs, even wondering whether "people in the provinces" [would like] "this figure." There is therefore every reason to believe that having initially refused Tissier's offer to give her *Implorer* back for nothing,[49] Camille finally accepted her patron's offer due to her dire need of money for the completion of her large marble of *Perseus and the Gorgon* (cat. 36, pp. 250 and 252).

As the Société Nationale des Beaux-Arts refused to exhibit the plaster of *The Age of Maturity* at the

Cat. 70

toward him. He no longer sees her, or rather he has turned his tear-veiled gaze away from her, and his arm is reaching back to her in a gesture of regret and definitive adieu . . . as he follows the other woman, like a prisoner under sentence of death following the hangman. Ah! How difficult it is to get old. I have not had the honor of meeting Mlle Claudel; I believe that she is, and I hope that she is, still very young; but her *Age of Maturity* resembles a work by a recalcitrant and revolted eighty-year-old Romantic. And to better express this revulsion and this drama, she has accentuated the veins, tendons and muscles and protuberances, suddenly piercing the skin with deep cavities; she has modeled the painful and decrepit bodies with a somewhat messy vehemence—this is a sculpture of feeling, similar to M. Bourdelle's *Beethoven.*"[51]

Other critiques, in the *Gazette des Beaux-Arts*, *La Petite Gironde* and *La Revue de Paris*, closely associated Camille Claudel's work with Rodin's. Romain Rolland even declared *The Age of Maturity* to be "something of a caricature of Rodin's genius."[52]

Exposition Universelle of 1900, Camille Claudel decided to resign from the association, exhibiting there for the last time in 1902. The bronze of *The Age of Maturity* belonging to Captain Tissier was therefore exhibited at the Salon des Artistes Français in 1903.[50] Of all the descriptions of *The Age of Maturity* by critics, André Michel's is the most noteworthy in several respects: "The Age of Maturity is a small bronze group—or rather three bronze statuettes placed single file but linked by their action. A man in his forties showing all the signs of somber hopelessness is following an emaciated ghost, an old woman leading him away, while behind him, a younger woman, kneeling, imploring him in vain, has her arms outstretched

Cat. 70

CAMILLE CLAUDEL
Head of the Old Man from
The Age of Maturity group
About 1893
Bronze
18 x 9 x 9 cm
Private collection

Cat. 82

CAMILLE CLAUDEL
The Age of Maturity
1899
Bronze
121 x 181.2 x 73 cm
Musée Rodin, Paris

Cat. 82

Cat. 82

Fortunately for Camille, Charles Maurice's judgment was more nuanced: "Among the sculptural works, it is Mlle Camille Claudel who is the most worthy of attention. Her group in bronze, *The Age of Maturity*, quivering with bitterness, is worthy of the fine name this courageous woman has made for herself. She is reproached for resembling Rodin. How admirable they

Cat. 82

CAMILLE CLAUDEL
The Age of Maturity
1899
Bronze
121 x 181.2 x 73 cm
Musée Rodin, Paris

are these people who want everyone to owe nothing to anyone. How more rightly I would condemn artists insensitive to the greatest statuary of this century!"[53]

Camille Claudel would soon find another champion in the person of Eugène Blot, foundry owner, publisher, art dealer and treasurer of the Société des Amis du Musée du Luxembourg. He was introduced to her by the critic Gustave Geffroy, an avowed admirer of her. In 1905 he in turn would in vain approach the fine arts administration concerning *The Age of Maturity* and its sculptress, an "unfortunate woman whose great talent many envy but whom nobody looks after."[54]

Blot decided in 1903 or 1904 to acquire the reproduction rights of the kneeling figure of *The Age of Maturity* (see "Take this Helping Hand I Am Holding Out to You," pp. 260–73). In 1907, he bought the rights for the complete group of three figures, to be reduced in size by a third for a limited edition of six casts to be exhibited in his gallery at 11 rue Richepanse from October 24 to November 10 that year as "Youth and the Age of Maturity."[55] In the exhibition catalogue, the critic Louis Vauxcelles brought out the genius of a full-fledged sculptress who, until then, had never given up rivaling her male competitors: "Contemplate at length this group in which science is the ally of emotion, and whose casting and patina do great honor to its caster. The man whom youth is imploring and would like to hold back with her muscular arms has half turned away from her, but the decrepit emaciated woman is irresistibly drawing him away to his death. I do not know what one should admire most in this artist more virile than many of her male colleagues, the fullness of her volumes, her lines, her lyrical boldness of mind, or the impeccable faithfulness of her execution. Berthe Morisot was the only female painter of the century. Camille Claudel is incontestably the unique sculptress on whose forehead shines the sign of genius."[56]

On July 25, 1907, Camille took, as it were, a last stand concerning *The Age of Maturity* when she wrote to the ministry for the last time "to obtain the conclusion of an affair that has dragged on in the fine arts administration for years."[57] She confusingly leads the ministry to believe that she is yet again reopening the old file that Lenseigne and Blot had already grappled with. In fact, Camille's request concerns an entirely different commission, the *Wounded Niobid* (cat. 234).

Until the time she was committed to an asylum in 1913, Camille continued to worry about her plaster's future. In a letter to her brother Paul around 1909, she writes: "I tremble over the fate of The Age of Maturity, about what will happen to it, I can't believe it!"[58] But even though the state had bought the plaster of *The Age of Maturity*, she would never part with it, disobeying the repeated orders to this effect from the ministry of fine arts, who wanted the work to be stored not at the artist's studio but at the Dépôt des Marbres.[59] She supervised the work's casting in September 1902 to ensure that the original work was damaged as little as possible. What mattered for her "was to obtain a good result while sparing the plaster group."[60] Around 1909, just as in 1893 when the idea for the "group of three" had come to her, Camille was

Cat. 82

still afraid her ideas would be stolen and that pastiches of her work would appear.[61]

Following Camille's committal to an asylum in April 1913, a board of guardians was formed and Paul, then posted to Germany, asked his close friend, the diplomat Philippe Berthelot,[62] to be a part of it. It was Berthelot who took care of Camille's belongings in her apartment on quai de Bourbon, notably her remaining works, which he stored at his home.

Cat. 84 A

belonged, which he was then showing as *Youth and the Age of Maturity*. In 1905, Blot exhibited a large and small version of *The Implorer*. Five large versions (cat. 83) and fifty-nine small versions (cat. 261) were sold, the second largest sale of a work by Camille. One of these casts, formerly in Joanny Peytel's collection, was acquired by the Musée Rodin in 1968 (cat. 84 A).

The casts of *The Implorer* put on the market by Blot clearly aroused the interest of the critics. Although in their commentaries they often referred to Rodin, they almost systematically insisted on the specific qualities of Camille's art. For Émile Dacier, "The poignant *Imploration* is certainly by someone."[64] For François Monod, Camille Claudel "has put a nuance of her own in her *Implorer*."[65] In Vauxcelles's view, "The lessons which she received from Rodin at the outset certainly taught her the grammar even the syntax of statuary, but she is as profoundly herself as Rodin is."[66] For the critic of the review *Psyché*, Camille has "perhaps a mystical manner that Rodin, more down to earth, lacks."[67] And Gustave Kahn considered that Camille Claudel had "found her own style after her apprenticeship with Rodin."[68]

Undoubtedly aware of the necessity of ensuring the survival of the second version of *The Age of Maturity* in his care, he deemed it his responsibility to have a cast-iron cast made (cat. 82). The circumstances under which this was carried out remain obscure and we do not even know whether Paul Claudel had anything to do with his friend's decision. The cast bears the inscription "Cire perdue Carvillani" (lost wax Carvillani) and it was most probably because of the use of the lost-wax casting process that the plaster disappeared. In addition, the quality of the half-size bronze which Paul Claudel gave to the Musée Rodin in 1952 is nowhere near that of the Musée d'Orsay version as there are numerous drill holes.

Due to Eugène Blot, the figure of the kneeling woman, sometimes called *Imploration*,[63] sometimes *The Implorer*, became more widely known than the whole group. He acquired the reproduction rights in 1903 or 1904 and showed it in his gallery in boulevard de la Madeleine in December 1905 and then in his new showroom in rue Richepanse in December 1908, where it was entitled *Youth*, no doubt to reestablish the link with the group to which *The Implorer*

Cat. 84 A

Camille Claudel
The Implorer
1899
Bronze
28.4 x 30.3 x 16.5 cm
Musée Rodin, Paris

Cat. 83

Camille Claudel
The Implorer
1899
Bronze
66.5 x 74.5 x 32.5 cm
Private collection

Cat. 83

In the letter Eugène Blot wrote to Camille on September 3, 1932, and which the authorities of the Montdevergues psychiatric hospital at Montfavet never passed on to her, he takes us right to the heart of the drama of *The Age of Maturity*. The memory he recalls is as poignant as the heart-rending *Implorer* figure associated with Camille Claudel. It is crucial testimony concerning the subject here since it emphasizes Rodin's passionate love for Camille, even a long time after their break-up Regarding *The Implorer*, Blot writes: "I cannot look at her without feeling an indescribable emotion. I seem to be seeing you again. The half-open lips, the flared nostrils, that light in the eyes, all that proclaims everything that is the most mysterious in life. With you, we were going to leave the world of false appearances for that of thought. What genius! The word is not too strong. How could you have deprived us of such beauty? One day when Rodin paid me a visit I saw him suddenly stand stock-still in front of this portrait, contemplate it, gently caress the metal and weep. Yes, weep. Like a child. It is now fifteen years since he died. The truth is he never loved anyone but you, Camille, I can say this now. Everything else, his pitiful affairs, the moving in society circles—he who, deep down, remained a man of the people—were the writ of execution of an excessive nature. Oh, I well know, Camille, that he abandoned you, I am not trying to justify this. He caused you too much suffering. I mean every word I have just written. Time will put everything back in place."[69]

INTERPRETATIONS OF *THE AGE OF MATURITY*

Given that *The Age of Maturity*, including the separate casts of *The Implorer*, occupied such a central place in Camille Claudel's personal and professional development, it is hardly surprising that the work has given rise to a great many enlightening and contrasting commentaries. The work's various titles immediately give a measure of its diverse interpretations. In 1893, Camille associated the "group of three" with the expression of "destiny." Having probably been enlightened by Camille, Armand Silvestre spoke as early as 1895 of "The Age of Maturity, represented by a man whom old age is drawing away and whom youth is holding back." In 1898, just over a year before the work was shown for the first time, Matthias Morhardt entitled it "The Path of Life." In 1905, in a letter to the inspector

of fine arts, Henry Havard, Camille used a new title, indicative of her state of mind, *Fatality*.[70] Three years later, Blot adopted the title *Youth and the Age of Maturity* to emphasize the singular nature of the figure of the young implorer.

All things considered, the critics of the time were unanimous in their definitions of *The Age of Maturity*'s protagonists. The old woman was associated with old age, death, aging and "cruel destiny," while the implorer evoked youth, the joys of life, desire, beauty and "sweet destiny." The mature man "in his forties" or "at the end of his maturity" appears torn between his destinies, though.[71] Certain critics of course wondered what the true subject of the sculpture was, Louis de Fourcaud accusing the work of an "intellectualism" that hampered its appreciation: "Mlle Claudel, pupil of M. Rodin, has conformed to Romantic theories. On a fragment of terrain that looks like it has been made out of pieces of curved coachwork, she shows us a stooping old man walking along with a heavy step and pestered by Death. Behind him, on her knees, a naked young woman is reaching out to him with imploring arms. The title of the work is The Age of Maturity. There is of course no lack of talent, but I still feel this is a sculpture imagined as an illustration of a ballad."[72]

In 1951, Paul Claudel in a certain sense withdrew the veil of mystery shrouding the work by insisting on its autobiographically allegorical nature: "But no, this naked young woman is my sister! My sister Camille, imploring, humiliated, on her knees, superb, proud, that was how she portrayed herself. Imploring, humiliated, on her knees and naked! It's all over! This is what she left us to look at forever. And do you know what is being torn from her in that very moment, before your eyes? Her soul. Her soul, genius, sanity, beauty, life, all at the same time."[73]

Paul Claudel's interpretation from then on is final: "My sister's oeuvre, what gives it its unique interest, is that it is completely the Story of her life."[74] Earlier, on October 19, 1943, he noted in his *Journal*: "My sister! What a tragic existence! At thirty, when she realized that Rodin would never marry her, everything fell to pieces around her and she lost her reason. This is the drama of *The Age of Maturity*." Clearly, then, for him the male figure was Rodin and old age was his long-time mistress Rose Beuret, alias "convenience," and of course the imploring figure was Camille. Everything indicates that this interpretation was for a long time prevalent in the Claudel family, who cast Rodin, the abuser and abandoner of Camille, in the role of the villain. It is also sympto-matic that, despite Morhardt's and Berthelot's approaches,[75] Paul for a long time blocked the project of a permanent tribute to his sister Camille within a museum devoted to the works of the despised Rodin. Besides, after her death, Camille could obviously no longer compromise her brother's career. And now that his own genius had been consecrated by numer-ous honors, he could at last concern himself with the all too rare traces of his sister's genius, notably the two versions of *The Age of Maturity*.

It was Paul Claudel's largely justified interpretation of *The Age of Maturity* that to a great extent colored the rediscovery of Camille and her work in the early 1980s. While some insisted on the work's universal significance, transcending the events of the artist's life, others saw it as a self-portrait twinned with a kind of *Ecce Homo* showing Rodin as she saw him.[76]

Given the narrative nature of the tragedy of *The Age of Maturity*, associated with a gesture of breaking-off by the person who had staged it, sculpted it and cast herself in the lead role,[77] it seems appropriate or at least enlightening to interpret the two versions of *The Age of Maturity* as two episodes of the same drama and to do this irrespective of the two works' very different status. Silvestre had seen this evolu-tion from the outset, when he visited Camille's studio in February 1896 and November 1898. Some fifty years later, Paul Claudel in turn summed up the play's two acts: first the man is hesitating, then he has chosen; the vengeful old woman defiantly shakes her fist before triumphing, while the young woman, having entertained vain illusions, is losing the fight of her life. And this was how the tragic rondo of the plaster of the "group of three" would end, in a sad waltz for two echoing the abandonment of the imploring young woman. In this sense, Paul Claudel was right to speak of "two chapters of the same drama."

Danielle Arnoux, having aptly described the complexity of the bonds between the two protagonists, enables a fuller understanding of the reasons for their "break-up . . . which dragged on and on."[78] That said, both in the plaster first version and the bronze second version, the artist opted for an appropriate distance, avoiding the banal realist details[79] of everyday life and sublimating her preoccupations in an allegory charged with emotion. At least this was how most contemporary critics interpreted it.

However one interprets it, *The Age of Maturity* stands out on account of its formal qualities, which make it one of the masterpieces of French sculpture. It is clearly a mature work, the work of a mature person in its self-assertion and treatment. Camille was striving for an autonomous career distinct from Rodin's. She was striving for maturity, for the artistic age of maturity whose corollaries are public recognition, honors and prestigious commissions. She wanted to be considered a sculptress in her own right and to at last be able to reply to Paul Leroi's hurtful accusations. This was why she was so secretive about her ideas, notably about the composition and execution of the "group of three" that she first sketched in 1893. This was why she put so many hopes into *The Age of Maturity*, a powerful work evoking the past but looking to the future.

A HIGHLY STRUCTURED WORK

Irrespective of its interpretations, the bronze version of *The Age of Maturity*, with its strong diagonal and horizontal changes in level reinforcing the work's dynamism and the singularity of its components, immediately appears to be a very structured work. The configuration of the base, extremely evocative in itself, immediately situates the action on a seashore. A wave is clearly indicated on the left, an Art Nouveau-inspired naturalistic motif that Camille had used in 1897, influenced by the famous print by Hokusai. The interplay of the terrain's natural changes in level, like a rocky staircase, has the effect of heightening the composition's instability. This is the staircase of the ages of life that mark our changes, separations and abandonments. The man has just ascended a level, reached a new stage, is about to escape the encroaching water, while old age is already high and dry, controlling the game from a higher outcrop while the beautiful young woman has been abandoned several levels lower. The man is making off, drawn on by old age, leaving the contorted implorer stranded where she is. Although the young woman's arm follows the axis of the old couple's progress, her legs do not, creating an effect of torsion accentuating the separation. They are standing and in motion, she is on her knees and can only fall.

Whereas the old woman has the evening breeze with her and is gripping the man tightly, youth is reaching out in the vain hope of touching him in both the physical and figurative sense. The whole of the sculpture's tension is concentrated in the space separating the hands of the man and the imploring young woman, on the verge of toppling over. The message is clear: without Rodin's support, Camille can only fall. The only thing still evoking the bond between Rodin and Camille is the man's left hand, which, obeying a strange robotic impulse, is pointing toward the young woman but has already inexorably let go of her. Rodin's wide open hand and Camille's reaching fingertips will never touch again. The crucial moment of contact, as though between two sleepwalkers, has gone. During the first years of their relationship, Rodin "created" Camille and supported her as her talent began to bloom, rather like Michelangelo's God giving life to Adam. But the opposite is happening here: life is withdrawing, the god has vanished, a page is being turned, eyes are parting, contact is being broken off.

The striking solitude and the expressions of each figure confirm the breaking-off effect. The distraught young woman is not even looking at the hand abandoning her; the inscrutable mature man is gazing blankly ahead with an expression of renouncement, toward the ground not toward the horizon; the sinister old woman is looking back, contemplating her obedient prey, who is not even looking at her.

On a textural level, one should emphasize the treatment of the faces, feet and hands of the two protagonists on the left. Despite the power which the man's muscular anatomy exudes, the signs of age are clearly there on his extremities. The critic Charles Morice was struck by what he considered an "excessive physical disgrace," noting that "the knotted, sick fingers and toes and tanned, wilting flesh add nothing to the somber effect of dramatic sadness which the gestures are enough to suggest."[80] Evidently, Camille, who for a long time modeled the hands and feet of Rodin's sculptures, had lost none of her talent in this domain. To heighten the effect of parting, she also played on the textural contrasts between the group of two and the person being abandoned. The former are textured, while the latter is smooth. The same goes for the hair: the young woman's, worn up in a chignon, is controlled and soothing.[81] Conversely, the hair of *Clotho-Rose* resembles a pair of downward pointing horns and emphasizes her sneering witchlike demeanor.

Camille succeeded in integrating these contrasts into a coherent whole by using the beautiful diagonal discussed above. The diagonal is enhanced by the artifice of the large veil which, while adding powerful movement to the ensemble, has the effect of softening the staircase effect. As Paul Claudel rightly emphasized, "The drapery . . . has much the same role as the Wagnerian melopoeia which, repeating, enveloping and developing the theme, gives it unity in its total brilliance."[82] The strategy the artist adopts here calls to mind that of the amorous couple of *The Waltz* of 1893, only here the man is about to dance his last dance with old age not youth. The large veil billowing in the wind in the rear part of the sculpture is rather like a cape which, out of a kind of flower or corolla, forms two waves or twirls on either side of the old woman's body. This treatment is absolutely typical of Art Nouveau, the segmented motif of the wide-brimmed hat recalling the characteristic movements of the American dancer Loïe Fuller, whom Parisians first saw at the Folies-Bergères in 1892.[83] It is therefore incontestably in its drawing, treatment, wave movement, drapery and effects of imbalance that *The Age of Maturity* clearly manifests its modernity.

Even though Camille Claudel clearly asserted her own style during the work's genesis, she did not entirely free herself of Rodin and his influence, despite having declared this ambition to her brother Paul in 1893 when she first had the idea for the group. It may therefore be symptomatic that she again used allegory to convey her personal feelings,

an option far less modern in subject, treatment and scale than that of the *Causeuses* group. Just as Rodin had done earlier, for *The Age of Maturity* she also opted for the half life-size scale. In short, one cannot help associating her figure of the man gravely walking toward his destiny after a difficult choice with one of *The Burghers of Calais*. Like *Eustache de Saint-Pierre*, Camille's man is not looking back. He has renounced life and is now alone with his destiny.

THE AGE OF MATURITY AND CAMILLE'S DESTINY

The Age of Maturity will remain forever inseparable from Camille's destiny. It is also important, in summing up, to reflect on the symbolic significance of her masterpiece as expressed in her brother Paul's favored interpretation. In doing so, one is struck more than ever by the biographical message conveyed by the ensemble, above all when one relates it to certain high points in Camille's life, both before and after the years of the group's development.

In Rodin's famous letter to his "cruel friend" in 1886, he begged for her pity, declaring that only her generosity "could save him," ward off the "hideous and slow illness" and prevent him from dying. "On his knees" and begging, he wrote: "Do not threaten me and let yourself see that your so very gentle hand marks your bounty for me and sometimes leave it there so that I can kiss it in my transports." He adds further on: "Your hand Camille, not the one which is withdrawn, no happiness in touching it if it is not proof of a little of your tenderness" (cat. 182, pp. 82–83; see the complete translation, pp. 370–71). Five years later, in a letter Camille wrote Rodin from the Château de L'Islette, near Azay-le-Rideau, she mentions the figure of the owner, Madame Courcelles,[84] making clear that the hostess of their idylls would do everything to be pleasant to them, using this jealous phrase: "The old woman will be on her knees before us, I think."[85] She adds that she could "bathe in the river, where her daughter and the maid go bathing without danger," ending by telling him that she "sleeps completely naked to make [herself] believe [he is] there" (cat. 193, pp. 138–39; see the complete translation, p. 372).

But in *The Age of Maturity* the tables had now been turned. "The old woman" is no longer kneeling but standing triumphantly, even dominating the man who has reached maturity. And the young woman who once reigned over the man's soul is still naked but kneeling, abandoned, vainly imploring the man who once begged her. Camille is no longer bathing safely in the river near the Château de L'Islette waiting for Rodin, but about to fall, to drown in a tragic scene of ruin. "She had placed all her hopes in Rodin, and lost everything with him. The beautiful vessel, tossed around for a while on bitter waves, went down without a trace."[86]

In the end one has to accept that *The Age of Maturity* conveys a powerful premonitory feeling echoing Camille's avowed fears both for her oeuvre and her own fate. Like it or not, *The Age of Maturity* heralds the last pages of Camille's destiny. From her confinement in 1913 to her death thirty years later, she was the living personification of her implorer, turning in vain to "her dear mother" and toward [her] "petit Paul" to

get them to put an end to her incarceration and enable her to return to Villeneuve, to the countryside of her childhood. In a certain sense, her intransigent mother took over from the old woman in *The Age of Maturity*, while Paul, above all preoccupied by his reputation, success, diplomatic career and the apotheosis of his literary genius, took on the role of the mature man. Ironically, the imploring woman in the Montdevergues psychiatric hospital at Montfavet ended up resembling the figure of Old Age in *The Age of Maturity*, becoming, in Paul Claudel's words "old, old, old" and "ruined," "pitiful, with her mouth dotted with a few horrible tooth stumps."[87]

Light years away from this terrible, sinister vision of Camille, the beautiful figure of *The Implorer* has remained forever frozen, petrified in the moving beauty of her youth. Kept isolated from her friends of yesteryear, Camille never received the moving letter that her faithful admirer Eugène Blot wrote her on September 3, 1932, in which he concludes by these heart-rending words that still ring in our ears: "What can I do for you now, dear Camille Claudel? Write to me, take this helping hand I am holding out to you. I have never ceased to be your friend." A message in a bottle that never reached Camille's desert island.

CAMILLE CLAUDEL: VITRIOLIC CARICATURES   Jacques Vilain

These four drawings (cat. 59 to 62), two of which were drawn on halves of the same sheet (D.7631, cat. 60, and D.7632, cat. 61), were very probably by the same person. They first appeared in 1982, when they were published by Anne Delbée, who, with her inimitable exaggeration, wrote, "I saw the drawings. Riddled with jealousy, howling out their despair."[1] They were included in the Musée Rodin's inventory of drawings in late 1983 and were finally shown for the first time in 1984, first in Paris, then in Poitiers.[2]

The circular "Musée Rodin / Bibliothèque / Livres d'Auguste Rodin" stamps prove that they came from the collection of Camille's letters and manuscripts in the museum archives, all of which bear the same stamp. Nevertheless, it is surprising they were not included in the first retrospective, organized by Cécile Goldschneider and Paul Claudel in 1951. They were probably found between 1952 and 1982, filed in the archives and later, definitively, in the department of drawings.

As early as the 1983 inventory, they were described as attributable to Camille or Auguste Beuret, the son Rodin never officially recognized. Nonetheless, they were still part of Rodin's 1916 donation —the artist habitually kept and accumulated everything, even documents which, a priori, would not show him in a flattering light. The hypothesis that they could be by Auguste Beuret, recently advanced within the Musée Rodin, although at first seemingly attractive has been ruled out, the caption "Le Réveil. / Douce remontrance par Beuret" (cat. 60) being an inscription, not a signature. Previous exhibition catalogues and catalogues raisonnés have been inclined to copy each other on the subject of these drawings, so in an attempt to unravel this tangle, a series of psychiatric and graphological investigations of the document (the latter conducted by Rosine Lapresle-Tavera), together with purely historical analyses, have been undertaken. Two psychiatrists examined the four sheets (drawings and inscriptions), knowing in advance neither the name Camille nor Auguste Beuret. Their diagnoses both point to Camille. One notes:

—That the drawings reveal a complicated mind as opposed to a frustrated character.

—That in the pose of Rodin enchained, described as Christly, like Christ with his hands bound, there is unde- niable tenderness for the man.

—That these are drawings by a woman: the negation of Rose's body, without buttocks and with sagging breasts, could not have been the work of her son,

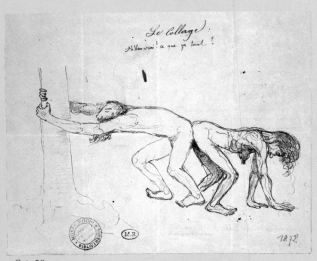

Cat. 59

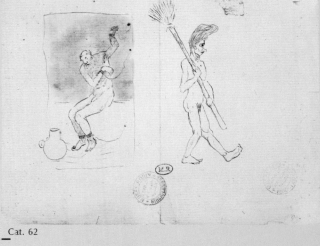

Cat. 62

Cat. 59

CAMILLE CLAUDEL
The Collage
1892
Pen and black ink on verso
of circular letterhead of the
Palais du Champ-de-Mars,
Secrétariat, Société Nationale
des Beaux-Arts, 189[2],
signed by secretary general
Hippolyte Durand-Tahier
21 x 26.2 cm
Annotated in pen and
black ink upper center:
*Le Collage/Ah! ben vrai!
ce que ça tient?*
Annotated lower right: *1892?*
Musée Rodin, Paris

FOLLOWING PAGES
Cat. 60

CAMILLE CLAUDEL
Le Réveil
Rodin and Rose embracing
1892?
Pen and black ink on
cream paper with notched
upper and left edge
17.8 x 26.7 cm
Annotated in pen
and black ink, lower right:
*Le Réveil/Douce
remontrance/par* BEURET
Annotated lower right: *1892*
Musée Rodin, Paris

FOLLOWING PAGES
Cat. 61

CAMILLE CLAUDEL
The Cellular System
Rodin in Chains and
Rose with a Broom
1892?
Pen and black ink wash on
cream paper with notched
upper and left edge
18.3 x 27.2 cm
Annotated in pen
and brown ink lower left:
Le système cellulaire
Musée Rodin, Paris

Cat. 62

CAMILLE CLAUDEL
*Rodin in Chains and Rose
with a Broom*
1892?
Pen and brown ink wash
on cream laid paper
21 x 26.8 cm
Musée Rodin, Paris

Cat. 60 (recto)　　　　　　　　　　　Cat. 60 (verso)

especially one who bore the name of his mother, who is described as a sad shrew, even—as the broom attests—a witch.

The behavioral study also prefigures a dual and very complex personality capable on the one hand of tenderness and sensitivity, and on the other of extreme brutality and vulgarity—traditionally male attributes. It is also worth noting that maternal sensitivity is exaggeratedly mimed. This is the psychological profile of someone who does not get on with their mother yet refuses to part from her. Analyses of the handwriting on the four sheets with the drawings hidden, and of Camille's and Auguste Beuret's handwriting in their letters, also immediately singled out Camille, and reveal a number of character traits discussed elsewhere in this catalogue. The various authors quoted above have all dated these drawings to between 1892 and 1894, the pencil inscription "1892?" on *The Collage* and on *Le Réveil* being thought to have been added at a later date.

No attention was ever paid to the verso of *The Collage* (cat. 59), which is a circular letter from the secretariat of the Palais du Champ-de-Mars, "Société Nationale des Beaux-Arts, . . . 189[?]". The letter, signed by the general secretary, H. Durand-Tahier, invites exhibiting artists to check and retouch their works on exhibit on Sunday, May 1, 189[?]. It so happens that in the 1890s, May 1 falls only twice on a Sunday: in 1892 and 1898. Hippolyte Durand-Tahier became secretary of the Société Nationale des Beaux-Arts in 1890 and remained so until his death in 1899. One cannot therefore draw any conclusion by favoring 1892 rather than 1898, or vice versa. The text of the circular letter does however merit being included

_Cat. 61 (recto)

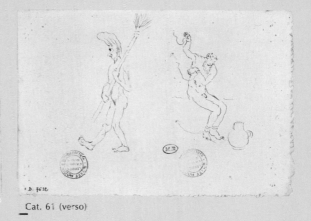

_Cat. 61 (verso)

in its entirety: "Palais du Champ-de-Mars / Secretariat / Société Nationale des Beaux-Arts, Paris, . . ., 189… / Dear Sir, You are invited to come and check or retouch your works exhibited on Sunday, May 1 from midday to 6 in the evening. On presentation of your exhibitor's card in the secretary's office you will be given the number of invitations to the opening that you have been allocated / for the delegation / the Secretary General / H. Durand-Tahier." The 1898 Salon in fact opened on Saturday, April 30, as the press attests. This date must therefore be excluded, unlike 1892, which confirms the annotation mentioned above. The chronology can thus be reconstituted, from Sunday, May 1, when exhibitors came to "check or retouch" their works, to Saturday, May 7, the date of the Salon's official opening. Camille exhibited the bronze _Auguste Rodin_ (no. 1482), which soon became the sculptor's official portrait and which he loved to show at his many exhibitions in France and abroad until 1902. A veritable homage by Camille to her teacher, the bust is an allegory of the famous sculptor's physical power and energy. Like all exhibitors, Camille received the circular letter from Durand-Tahier. In 1892 the two lovers were drifting apart, although they had not yet definitively separated, but Camille, by drawing on the circular letter, is reminding him that she too exhibited at the Salon. But there are two messages here: the official one shown to the public on the Champs-de-Mars, and the more intimate one, in which she tells Rodin in a caustic way exactly what she thinks of him. The duality of Camille's character is expressing itself to the full.

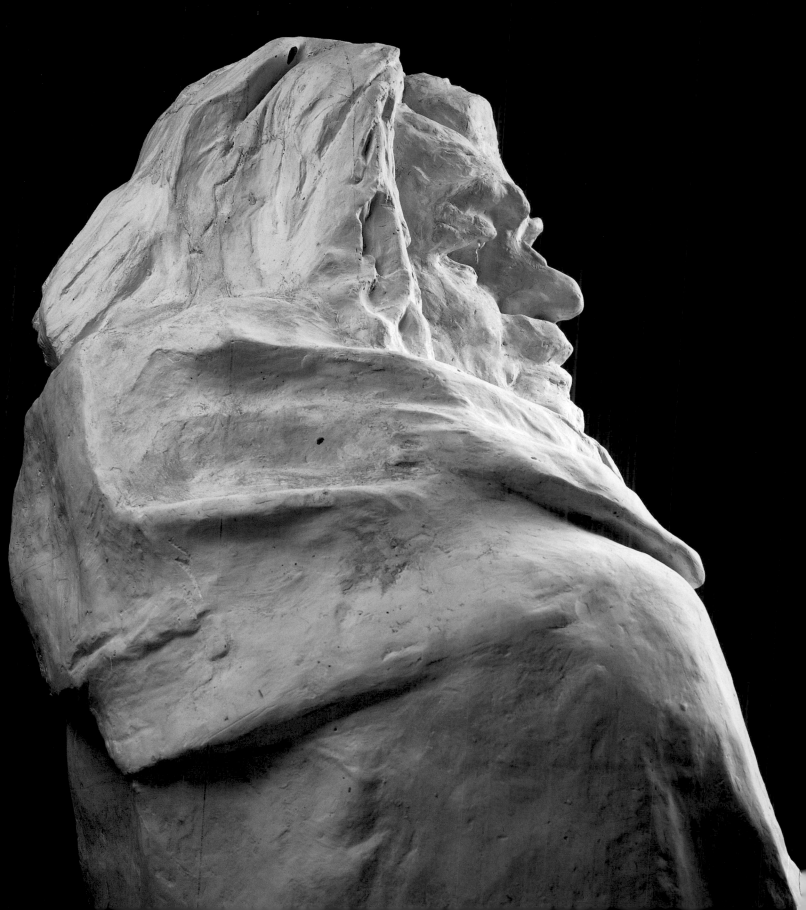

BALZAC   Antoinette Le Normand-Romain

In July 1891, after a long prehistory and the failure of the initial Chapu commission, the Société des Gens de Lettres, whose president was then Émile Zola, entrusted Rodin with the realization of a monument to one of its first presidents, the man of letters and novelist of genius Honoré de Balzac. A man of passion to the point of excess, he was the author of *The Human Comedy*, the series of novels including *Old Goriot*, *The Lily of the Valley* and *A Harlot High and Low*, which describe a society driven by violent passions and dominated by the thirst for wealth. Rodin promptly and eagerly started work on the project, but the creation of the figure would take seven years,[1] with the difficulties he encountered along the way exacerbated by the crisis of his break-up with Camille. "A more intimate and more agonizing cause compounded his torment. No one was aware of it and it was not until long afterward that he spoke to me about it," Judith Cladel wrote.[2]

In January 1892, he submitted three projects to the Société des Gens de Lettres, who chose a standing Balzac dressed in the monk's habit he habitually wore when working. Rodin had amassed a considerable amount of research material, but was also intent on finding a model who resembled the novelist, and he found him at Azay-le-Rideau in the person of Estager, the famous "Conductor of Tours." In 1892, he sculpted a series of figures from him known as the *C Studies* (fig. 49, p. 205), showing Balzac nude (Rodin always made nude studies of his figures before dressing them) with legs wide apart and arms crossed over a prominent stomach. The project greatly displeased his clients, who found it "shocking, deformed." "The advocates of verisimilitude were indignant . . . about its excessive resemblance. . . . Balzac, in short, was a kind of real-life monster. It was the duty of a sculptor aware of his glorifying mission to tidy him up for public view,"[3] and so it was suggested that Rodin should depict him "at a less potbellied age, when fat had not yet eliminated his neck."[4] Rodin acquiesced and produced a new, completely different model. The face was still based on the known portraits of Balzac, the canvas by Louis Boulanger (1837) and Bisson's daguerreotype (1842), rather than the bust by David d'Angers (1844), which he found "solemn and rather cold,"[5] but the novelist looked younger, had his head tilted back in a more imposing

Cat. 169
———
AUGUSTE RODIN
Balzac
1898
Patinated plaster
277.5 x 116.2 x 125.5 cm
Musée Rodin, Paris

But the Société des Gens de Lettres was growing impatient. Rodin had undertaken to deliver the model within eighteen months—in February 1893. But on July 3, 1893, he could merely promise to "show his work nearing definitive completion toward the month of October,"[6] and when Zola visited his studio at the end of the year, we learn that he was hoping to finish the model during the winter. In 1894, however, the monument hardly progressed at all. Rodin was going through a difficult time. There was the break-up with Camille Claudel and he was overwhelmed with work. The mayor of Calais was pressing him to cast and install *The Burghers of Calais* and he had to see through his two projects for the *Monument to Victor Hugo*. Following the controversy which wracked the Société des Gens de Lettres during the autumn of 1894 and which led to the resignation of its president, Jean Picard, and several members, Rodin had to return the 10,000 francs advance he had received to retain his freedom of action.

But "Rodin now has his *Balzac*," said an article in *Le Soleil* on January 28, 1896. "He has it well in mind. He has been setting him up since the month of September, and one can see him in his studio,

pose with his left arm tucked behind his back, and was holding a manuscript in his right hand. This was the so-called *Balzac in Monk's Habit* (cat. 160) whose torso Rodin liked particularly. Yet he remained attached to the previous project, although certainly aware the figure was in no way suited for a public monument. He therefore returned to the *C Study*, accentuating its characteristics instead of effacing them, and draping it. The resulting *Nude With a Fat Stomach and Open Robe*, no doubt executed in 1894, is thus the most extreme point of this first phase of work.

Cat. 160
—
Auguste Rodin
Balzac in Monk's Habit
About 1893
Bronze
108 x 50 x 37 cm
Fondation Pierre Gianadda,
Martigny

Fig. 49

Fig. 50

standing, solidly portrayed, with his solid muscles and powerful head . . . Before long the model will be definitively finished. The artist is still working on the expression of the face: he has to capture the physiognomy of the great observer, of he who foresaw the whole modern world, creating models which have had too many Impersonators." The year 1895 had indeed seen the inauguration of the *Monument to the Burghers of Calais* and it was one of the nude studies for it that put Rodin on the track of the definitive *Balzac*. Its departure point, the *Nude Study of Balzac*

as an Athlete (fig 50), was produced by grafting the torso of *Jean d'Aire* onto the legs of *Balzac*.

It was not until summer 1897, however, that Rodin arrived at the definitive model. In April, at last satisfied with the nude, he had, it seems, begun work on the drapery, which he finalized during the spring and summer. Four clothed models have survived. Although the first already has no belt, the robe still has a hood like that of a religious habit and regular, vertical folds down the back. The garment is open at the front, revealing a half-undone shirt with a ruffle,

Fig. 49
AUGUSTE RODIN
Balzac, C Study
1892
Plaster
Musée Rodin, Paris

Fig. 50
AUGUSTE RODIN
Nude Study of Balzac as an Athlete
1896
Plaster
Musée Rodin, Paris

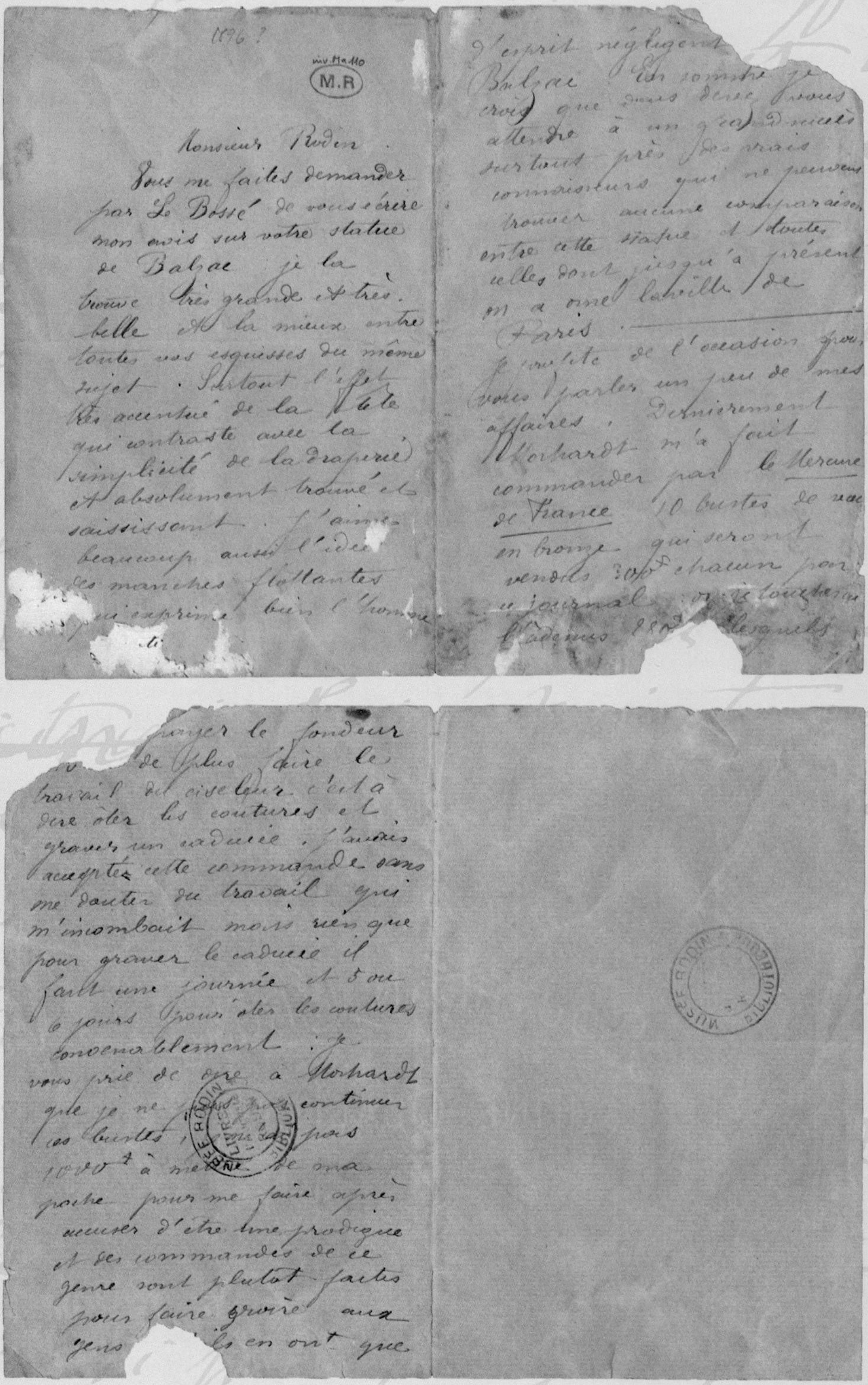

Monsieur Rodin.
You have had Le Bossé ask me
my opinion on your statue of Balzac:
I find it very great and very beautiful
and the best of all your studies of
the same subject. Especially the very
accentuated effect of the head, which
contrasts with the simplicity of the
drapery and is so well-found and
striking. I also love the idea of
the billowing sleeves, which well
convey Balzac's negligent nature.
In short, I think you should expect
great success with it, above all with
true connoisseurs, who could find
no comparison between this statue
and all those which have until
now decorated the city of Paris. . .

Cat. 216

Letter from Auguste Rodin to Camille Claudel
Dated December 2, 1897
Manuscript copy by Rodin's secretary, René Chéruy
2 sheets, 17.7 x 22.1 cm
Musée Rodin, Paris

The benevolence with which
you have judged my balzac
reassures me somewhat as I could
have done with your advice in
the black abandon in which I was
left for dead, I think. I would like
you to one day come and see my
Balzac of which I had a very light
cast made and which I sometimes
put out in the courtyard to see
the effect in the open air. There
you could judge it with me.

_Fig. 51

the left hand is visible, and the head is turned to the left. But at this stage Rodin felt the need for an even more precise study and procured himself a woollen dressing gown, which he rigidified and made a mold of to obtain an extraordinary wearerless garment (fig. 51). He made at least three subsequent models, each increasingly simplified. By now the head had changed direction and was tilted back to better reveal the lower face, and the hands were hidden beneath the robe. The robe, revealing the neck but concealing the

_Fig 51
AUGUSTE RODIN
*Balzac, Study for
the Dressing Gown*
1897
Plaster
Musée Rodin, Paris

shirt, was gradually stripped of superfluous detail to lead the eye toward the most important thing, the face.

The enlargement, carried out by Henri Lebossé, was begun during the summer for completion in late October 1897. It was delivered to Rodin on October 25, but Camille had seen it before then and expressed her admiration to him. "I would like," Lebossé asked Rodin on December 17, "to obtain in writing the warm appreciations she expressed in my studio in front of my employees when examining your enlarged statue of Balzac." Rodin passed on the request and Camille obliged him: "You have had Le Bossé ask me my opinion on your statue of Balzac: I find it very great and very beautiful and the best of all your studies of the same subject. Especially the very accentuated effect of the head, which contrasts with the simplicity of the drapery and is so well found and striking. I also love the idea of the billowing sleeves, which well convey Balzac's negligent nature. In short, I think you should expect great success with it, above all with true connoisseurs, who could find no comparison between this statue and all those which have until now decorated the city of Paris" (cat. 215, pp. 206–7; see the complete translation, pp. 374–75).

Rodin was deeply moved by this letter. "The benevolence with which you have judged my balzac reassures me somewhat as I could have done with your advice in the black abandon in which I was left for dead, I think. I would like you to one day come and see my Balzac of which I had a very light cast made and which I sometimes put out in the courtyard to see the effect in the open air. There you could judge it with me" (cat. 216, pp. 208–9).

The various processes of retouching and casting took several more months. On March 15 the next year, Henry Houssaye, president of the Société des Gens de Lettres, asked Rodin what had become of the statue: "Is the plaster finished? Do you intend to exhibit it this year? Or are you already working on the bronze? I absolutely need this information to reply to the questions I am bound to be asked during the next general meeting."[7] And one can well imagine the immense satisfaction Rodin had in replying: "The Balzac is finished and I have to send it for casting. If you and the Committee should wish to see it at the exhibition it would have to be the plaster. Which would delay things a little."[8] On March 31, 1898, Houssaye therefore announced that the statue was finished. Rodin would have liked to have kept "for months longer, well out of view, the statue to which I have however given the final finishing touches . . . as one can only judge well with a certain distance, when the fever of conception no longer envelops one's work."[9] But he had offered to exhibit it and he could no longer go back on this.

The Salon of the Société Nationale des Beaux-Arts was inaugurated on April 30, 1898, and the keenly awaited Balzac (cat. 169, pp. 202, 212–13) instantly became its main attraction, but the impression it made on the Société des Gens de Lettres, the press and the general public could hardly have been worse. On May 9 the Société therefore made it known to the artist that it could not accept a work in which "it did not recognize" Balzac. "What does 'not recognize' mean?" Rodin retorted. "For me, modern sculpture cannot be photography. The artist must work not only with his hands but with his brain as well."[10] He was thus calling into question the nature of the public monument, whose guiding principle throughout the nineteenth century had been a didactic preoccupation with easy identification of the model through gesture and dress, with the additional use of allegorical figures and anecdotal bas-reliefs to specify and develop its meaning. But as his research had continued, he had distanced himself from existing portraits of Balzac, which, incidentally, neither clothing nor pose helped identify. He who now knew Balzac's physical details better than anyone gradually discarded them, keeping only the essential elements, which he pushed almost to exaggeration to express the novelist's creative power: the bull's neck, the lion's mane, the large, ironic, sensual mouth and above all the fiery eyes that had so struck Balzac's contemporaries. This process can be seen as the logical outcome of his artistic development: the Rodin of the 1890s was the Rodin who, having devoted himself to the study of movement as the means of expressing emotions, was now turning to a sparer sculpture, reduced to the absolute essential. While he accorded fragmentary figures such as *Iris*, *The Earth* and *The Inner Voice (Meditation)* the status

Cat. 169
AUGUSTE RODIN
Balzac
1898
Patinated plaster
277.5 x 116.2 x 125.5 cm
Musée Rodin, Paris

Devant la statue

Les efforts d'intellectualité.

_Cat. 20

of finished works, he purified *Balzac* of everything not indispensable. "This *Balzac* has no legs, arms, neck, nothing; nothing but two eyebrows, two holes, two eyes, and then a lip. In favor of the eyes and the lip, Rodin perhaps deserves to be forgiven for the missing arms and everything else which is not there. I can picture Rodin making his *Balzac* as complete and finished and marvelously executed as the hero of his *Kiss*, and then erasing everything, spending months taking away muscles, arms, legs, everything that has no use and does not express solely what this man saw with his eyes and felt with that lip."[11]

Although in *The Age of Maturity* (cat. 82, pp. 187–89), then nearing completion, Camille had taken the exact opposite position, she immediately understood that Rodin's *Balzac* had turned over a new leaf in the history of sculpture, which, now liberated from the obligation to describe, could merely suggest. In her footsteps, those who advocated or represented modernity in art were overtly enthusiastic, whether critics or artists such as Monet ("Let it be proclaimed from the rooftops, never have you gone so far; it is absolutely beautiful and great, it is superb and I cannot stop thinking about it"),[12] Cézanne, Gauguin, for whom Rodin was "if not the greatest sculptor, at least one of the rare great sculptors of our time,"[13] and the young sculptors, "the Charpentiers, Desbois, Besnards, Bourdelles, Baffiers and Carrières who haughtily declare themselves disciples of the master [and] bravely face up to detractors."[14]

But Rodin's experiments were incomprehensible both for the general public and the press, who had a tremendous time lampooning and caricaturing *Balzac* (cat. 20). The figure was described as a seal, a block of salt left out in a shower, a toppling dolmen, a snowman in a straitjacket. Even a sculptor like the American Augustus Saint-Gaudens declared that he

_Cat. 20
Caran d'Ache
(Emmanuel Poiré)
"Before the Statue.
Intellectual Effort,"
Psst...!, no. 17, May 28, 1898
40.3 x 28 cm
Alain Beausire collection,
Paris

was "stunned by Balzac's habit, [which gave him] the impression of a dripping candle."[15]

The scandal spurred the "true connoisseurs" into action. Rodin received two offers of purchase, from the Belgian writer and politician Edmond Picard, who was planning Rodin's first one-man exhibition in Brussels the following year, and the industrialist and art collector Auguste Pellerin, who already owned a copy of *Eve* and was aware that here was an opportunity "to procure a masterpiece [he could] never have expected."[16]

Meanwhile, however, the idea of a collective protest had taken shape. Mathias Morhardt took the lead and with a number of Rodin's friends wrote a circular letter clearly establishing that the rejection from the Gens de Lettres was a blow struck at creation. Signatures came flooding in, especially those of prominent Dreyfusards, even though Zola himself abstained, and Rodin took fright at the association that could be made between the two "affairs": "Do you want me to further add to my difficulties? The struggle for sculpture takes all my time and energy. And I am not even managing to triumph."[17] Despite the subscription having been a financial success, he therefore announced on June 4 that he would not pursue the matter further, nor Pellerin's proposal to acquire it, which nevertheless tempted him. Aided by Morhardt and Carrière, he wrote individual letters of thanks to all the subscribers: "I would like to resume, in the silence of the studio, my work which this quarrel has threatened to momentarily interrupt. Permit me therefore to decline the generous proposition you have made me. The statue of Balzac is the logical development of my life as an artist. I take complete responsibility for it. And it is my desire to remain its sole owner."[18]

The plaster was only exhibited once in his lifetime, in 1900, at the Pavillon de l'Alma, where it was placed in the central entry aisle, as though waiting for and scoffing at the public. Several years later, Rodin was deeply moved when he saw the famous photographs Edward Steichen had taken at night: "It is Christ walking in the desert," he said, before continuing after a long silence, his arms round Steichen's shoulders. "Your photographs will make my *Balzac* understandable to everyone."[19] Despite the incomprehension he had encountered, he was still convinced he was right and reaffirmed this in *Le Matin* on July 13, 1908: ". no longer fight for my sculpture. For a long time it has known how to defend itself . . . My life is a long path of study . . . If truth must die, then my Balzac will be broken up by generations to come. If truth is imperishable, I predict my statue will make its way in the world . . . This work that has been laughed at, that people took great care in scorning because they could not destroy it, is the result of my whole life, the very linchpin of my aesthetic."

CAMILLE SUBLIMATED   Antoinette Le Normand-Romain

As soon as Rodin chose Rose by moving to Bellevue in April 1893, Camille closed the door to him. Nevertheless, despite or perhaps because of his remoteness from her, her face continued to haunt him and he embarked on an admirable series of allegorical portraits in which he expressed his utter confusion. All stemmed from one or the other of the masks made at the beginning of their affair: "Many times he interpreted her purebred French features in images that have the tender fullness of certain figures at Chartres. His poet's imagination turned her into *Thought, France, The Young Warrior*, and the lovely face of *Aurora*."[1] Around the same time, the beautiful classical face of Mrs. Russell became *Minerva*, of which Rodin produced a number of variations, even placing a small model of a Greek temple on her head (fig. 52, p. 218). But with Camille he took this essentially rather simple game of correspondences much further. The emotional complexity that these portraits embody instills them with a deeply moving dimension. In *Thought, The Farewell* and the vision of menacing madness produced by *Assemblage of the Mask of Camille Claudel and Left Hand of Pierre de Wissant*, Rodin allows us a glimpse of how he lived these years. "Despite the congenital egotism of the superior man, he never got over this sorrow. Heartbroken by their break-up, his courage for a long time faltering, he continued to draw inspiration from the clear and harmonious features he had repro-

duced so many times."[2] Rodin himself noted nostalgically in a notebook much later, but before 1913, "I remember the glory we had together . . . Your courage. CCC. I consider you a divine woman. Would you like it better if I was incapable of rendering your extraordinary side, your gentleness. You are at my side, do you hear me! Divine character you exalted me to your level."[3]

These rarely shown portraits are difficult to date. One can, however, identify two groups, those derived from the head *with short hair* (cat. 126, p. 70) and those from the head *with bonnet* (cat. 132, p. 73). The former are more dramatic and all allude to Camille's increasing isolation; in the latter she becomes a kind of tutelary figure, a distant muse.

Spread over the ten years which elapsed between the break-up and Camille's committal to an asylum, the three works made from *Camille with Short Hair*, the first portrait he did of Camille, tell us that Rodin

Cat. 165
AUGUSTE RODIN
Assemblage: Mask of Camille Claudel and Left Hand of Pierre de Wissant
About 1895?
Plaster
32.1 x 26.5 x 27.7 cm
Musée Rodin, Paris

217

Fig. 52

Fig. 53

never gave up hope. *Assemblage of the Mask of Camille and Left Hand of Pierre de Wissant* (cat. 165), no doubt the earliest, is the most poignant and even premonitory. "A burning, steel-gloved giant's hand is pressing down on my head, and my ideas, frightened off by this menacing hand, are bashing against the walls of my skull like birds in an aviary," Alfred de Musset complained on the verge of a fit of cerebral fever.[4] The assemblage, all the more powerful because it is uncluttered, was never shown, but since a copy of the mask was exhibited on its own at the *Rodin* retrospective at the Pavillon d'Alma in 1900[5] (cat. 131 and 9 A, pp. 68 and 71), it is generally dated after 1900—that is to say, during the years in which Camille, believing herself threatened by imaginary enemies, shut herself up in her studio. Yet I believe the work can be dated to around 1895, when Rodin was preparing the casting of *The Burghers of Calais*, whose large nudes, it should be remembered, were executed in 1886–87, in Camille's presence and certainly with her help. Nothing here is innocent: might this menacing left hand (cat. 143, p. 53), enormous compared to the young woman's face, be a malevolent pendant to *The Hand of God* (fig. 53), which was derived from *Pierre de Wissant*'s right hand and can be exactly dated to 1895?

The departure point for both *Convalescence* and *The Farewell* was an assemblage of the same mask and, this time, two hands joining in front of a mouth, the ensemble linked by drapery and placed on a large rectangular base whose upper part was originally a wooden plank with carefully softened edges, faithfully reproduced by the mold. There were two successive states of this plaster: the original assemblage, comprising fabric elements, is only known by the photograph (maybe by Bulloz) reproduced in Judith Cladel's book in 1908 (cat. 7, p. 221), while the other reached us in the form of two casts, one presented here (cat. 170, pp. 220–21), the other used for the execution of the marble.[6] Both these casts were made from a *moule à pièces*, itself made from the second state of the original assemblage, and

Fig. 52
Auguste Rodin
Minerva at the Parthenon
Marble and plaster,
about 1910?
Musée Rodin, Paris

Fig. 53
Auguste Rodin
The Hand of God
1895
Plaster
Musée Rodin, Paris

Cat. 165
Auguste Rodin
*Assemblage: Mask of
Camille Claudel and Left
Hand of Pierre de Wissant*
About 1895?
Plaster
32.1 x 26.5 x 27.7 cm
Musée Rodin, Paris

Cat. 16

Cat. 7

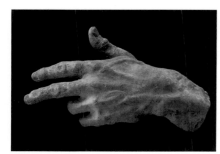

Fig. 54

Cat. 170

Cat. 7

ANONYMOUS
The Farewell,
plaster model, first state,
by Auguste Rodin
About 1898?
In CLADEL 1908
36.5 x 28 cm
Private collection

Fig. 54

AUGUSTE RODIN
Left Hand
Before 1898
Terracotta
Musée Rodin, Paris

Cat. 170

AUGUSTE RODIN
The Farewell, second state
About 1898?
Plaster
38.8 x 45.2 x 30 6 cm
Musée Rodin, Paris

Cat. 17

Cat. 175

most probably destroyed during the molding process. The plaster had been modified from one state to the next: the left hand, with bent fingers, was replaced by a different hand with straight index and middle fingers and the thumb bent to one side (fig. 54, p. 221), the same hand that had also been used in one of the studies for the bust of *Madame Fenaille*.[7] This hand was placed obliquely whereas its predecessor was horizontal, and the drapery was simplified: the drapery falling onto the base at the front disappeared. One of the plasters, probably the second, was described by Rilke in 1907: "And here is another thing: a silent face, with this suffering hand, and the plaster has that transparent whiteness it only has when fashioned by Rodin. On the plinth, I read this word, already crossed out: *Convalescente*."[8] The connection with the bust of *Madame Fenaille* prompts one to date the second plaster to around the same time, that is, around 1898, and one could see the inscription Rilke described as confirmation of this: in 1897 Camille had accepted to rekindle relations with

Cat. 176

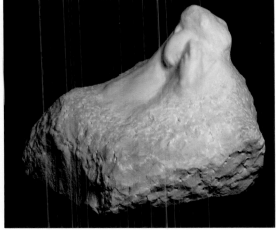

Fig. 55

Rodin, who may thus have thought that things could go even further.

Marble copies were made of both versions and are today entitled *The Convalescent* (cat. 176) and *The Farewell* (cat. 175). The former is traditionally dated to 1892, which is impossible given the work's style. In his 1916 inventory of the Donation Rodin, Bénédite states that the marble was the work of Matruchot, adding that "Rodin worked a great deal on this figure himself, at Mengue's studio, particularly the hands, whose very particular trembling of the flesh is his; he worked from nature, slowly, close up because of his short-sightedness, but with great art." Yet Rodin did not use Matruchot until 1908–9 onwards. Jean-Marie Mengue, on the other hand, received payments in 1906 for a bust entitled *The Farewell*, which he delivered on August 1, 1907. At around the same time, he did the marble version of *Young Girl Telling Her First Secret to Isis* (Zurich, private collection), whose treatment, particularly the sinuous folds of the drapery, is reminiscent of the

marble today in Norfolk. This marble was photographed by Bulloz (cat. 171, therefore after 1903–4, in a very advanced state but not quite finished, as indicated by the pencil marks in the hair. It was reproduced in 1910 in *Die Kunst für Alle*,[9] and acquired in 1913 by Max Sulzberger, who obtained an explicative note from Rodin: "Document, for Monsieur Sulberger. This sculpture, the <u>Convalescent</u>, is a bust of a young girl in a chaise longue or bed. She says little but thanks those who have come to see her, she sends kisses. White marble, resembling Greek marble a little. This sculpture may, should the opportunity arise, be made in marble once more and twice in bronze. This is the first time, left my studio

Cat. 176

AUGUSTE RODIN
The Convalescent
Marble, begun by Jean-Marie Mengue, 1906–7?; completed by Émile Matruchot, about 1914
48.5 x 71 x 56 cm
Musée Rodin, Paris

Fig. 55

AUGUSTE RODIN
Madame Fenaille with Hand
Marble, 1912–13
Musée Rodin, Paris

Cat. 162
—
AUGUSTE RODIN
Thought
1895
Marble, executed
by Victor Peter
74.2 x 43.5 x 46.1 cm
Musée Rodin, Paris

_Cat. 163

_Cat. 109

_Cat. 6

undoubtedly hoping she would get better. The convalescent says little, but sends kisses. However, no matter what the work's relationship to his innermost feelings, the dynamics of the studio went on relentlessly and the first marble having been sold, Rodin hastened to order another from Matruchot, who had just completed a second version of the bust of *Madame Fenaille with Hand*, in which there is the same softening of the face by a kind of *sfumato* effect (fig. 55, p. 223). This new portrait of Camille, in which she seems to be gradually sinking into an uncarved block suggesting nothingness, definitely belongs in the last years of Rodin's career. But how

in August 1913."[10] A record confirms this: "The <u>Convalescent</u>, sold in marble to Mme Shutzberger 1500 and authorizing rep. of 1 marble and 4 bronzes Sept 15, 1913."[11] A cast was made of the marble[12] and the following year Matruchot worked on a bust of a "young convalescent," later called "bust of a young girl," for which he received 1,300 francs.

It therefore seems likely that the bust produced by Mengue in 1906–7 corresponds to the one still called *The Farewell*, and if the title of the second copy changed to *The Convalescent* this is perhaps explainable by the date—August 1913, five months after Camille was committed—when Rodin was

Cat. 163

AUGUSTE RODIN
Thought
Marble, executed
by Raynaud et Durand,
1900–1
76.2 x 43.4 x 46.1 cm
Philadelphia Museum of Art,
Philadelphia

Cat. 109

D. FREULER
*Thought covered in a veil,
plaster, by Auguste Rodin*
1895?
Photograph, salted
paper print
24.2 x 17.6 cm
Musée Rodin, Paris

Cat. 6

ANONYMOUS
*Auguste Rodin in front
of his atelier at the Dépôt
des Marbres, with* Thought
in the background
About 1895
Photograph, albumin print
9.7 x 7.4 cm
Musée Rodin, Paris

can this be reconciled with the sequence of plasters? It corresponds to the first of the two models. Given the complete absence of information on this, one can simply imagine that the two marbles were begun almost simultaneously, around 1905–6. One was momentarily put to one side and resumed again later by Matruchot, while the other was completed in 1907 but remained in the studio until 1913.

The second group has its roots in two works that can be quite precisely dated: *Thought* (1895) and the *Apollo* of the *Monument to Sarmiento* (1898). Exhibited in 1895, *Thought* (cat. 162 and 163, pp. 224–25) is one of the masterpieces of the 1890s, both in its execution and the perfect appropriateness of form to subject, even if this is by chance. And it is perhaps this which explains its originality, Rodin having in this work completely renewed a hackneyed theme: the intensity of the face alone, which, leaning slightly forward, seems concentrated on itself, evokes the power of the mind and its capacity to direct the world. Victor Peter, entrusted with the marble version of the portrait *with a bonnet*, "told how the idea came to the master to leave the block unfinished beneath the head. Assuming, because of the bonnet, that Rodin might want to complete the costume with a collar, Peter had left the stone intact from the bottom of the face down. But when Rodin saw the effect this produced, he said to him, 'Don't touch it, leave it as it is!' A friend exclaimed rather amusedly that it was thought emerging from matter, and this was how the subject got its name."[13] Even though the anecdote was altered by Léonce Bénédite when he told it much later, it is still highly indicative of the way Rodin

Fig. 56

Fig. 57

worked, of his receptiveness to exterior circumstances, a receptiveness, it should be emphasized, that had been aided in this instance by *The Psalm* (cat. 50, p. 97), executed shortly before by Camille and whose features can be found in *Thought*. In both cases, the base transforms the head from portrait into allegory. It was the first time but not the last that Rodin would sublimate Camille's face like this.

Already in progress in 1893,[14] the marble beside which Rodin seems to have liked to have himself

Cat. 166
AUGUSTE RODIN
Aurora
About 1895–97
Marble
56 × 58 × 50 cm
Musée Rodin, Paris

Fig. 56
AUGUSTE RODIN
Rose Beuret
About 1898
Marble
Musée Rodin, Paris

Fig. 57
MEDARDO ROSSO
*Boulevard Impression:
Lady with a Veil*
1892–93
Wax on plaster
Musée des Beaux-Arts, Lyon

Fig. 58

photographed (cat. 6, p. 225) was exhibited at the Salon of the Société Nationale des Beaux-Arts in 1895 and acquired the following year for 7,000 francs by the Durands, who agreed to its being shown at the Pavillon d'Alma in 1900,[15] then donated it to the Musée du Luxembourg in 1902. Rodin promised not to make a copy, but this did not deter him from accepting to make a second marble for the Memorial Hall in Philadelphia in 1900. The order was cancelled, as that institution's rules forbade the purchase of sculptures,[16] but as work on the marble had already begun, Alexander Harrison, who had acted as intermediary between the two parties, offered the work to John G. Johnson. On March 8, 1901, Harrison informed Rodin that Johnson was "eager to buy it for his collection which is very famous and this will be a better place for your work than the other."[17] Johnson confirmed his interest on April 8, 1901, and on July 20 informed Rodin of the marble's arrival. "Your

lovely marble has at last arrived and fascinates me with its entrapped charm and with all it suggests. You have made that coldest of all things—marble—warm with life. I can recall nothing happier in conception, or more mastery in creation. It is in all ways worthy of your genius."[18] The marble was executed by Durand and Raynaud in 1900–1 from a cast of the upper half made from the first marble, a mold which was used again after Rodin's death when Jules Mastbaum wanted to obtain a bronze for his Rodin Museum in Philadelphia.[19] The two marbles are very similar, although the contrast between the finished face and the roughly hewn surface of the block is more marked than in the Musée d'Orsay version, in which only the base's top side has been cut away with a small pointed chisel. The Philadelphia version has this chisel effect over the whole block, which very faithfully retains the form and volume of the original block, to the extent that the difference between the top surface and the large flat vertical areas remains perceptible despite the more uniform treatment. Although still having the "charm" that Johnson had appreciated, the work has lost some of its spontaneity.

Was it in order to emphasize her mysterious side or simply to embark on a new experiment that Rodin next put a veil over the head of *Thought* (cat. 109, p. 225)? This experiment can be compared to the *Veiled Torso of the Age of Bronze* (plaster, Musée Rodin, S.3179), which, however, was molded, meaning that Rodin wanted to keep it. Neither work is dated, yet D. Freuler worked for Rodin from 1893 to 1897, which enables the dating of the photograph of *Thought* to the time of the execution of the marble.

Fig. 58
AUGUSTE RODIN
Apollo Slaying Python
Marble, 1899
*Monument to President
Sarmiento*, Buenos Aires

One can imagine that it was the success of *Thought* which prompted him to try again with *Aurora* (cat. 166, p. 226), the second metamorphosis of the same mask (cat. 131, p. 68). Also very carefully executed but vertical, whereas *Thought* is leaning slightly forward, the face evokes the appearance of the sun in the early morning mists by the contrast between its very smooth, almost polished appearance, giving the impression of radiating light, and the uncarved block from which it is emerging. Never, to my knowledge, exhibited or reproduced in Rodin's lifetime, *Aurora* is traditionally dated to c.1898 due to its similarity to the portrait of *Rose Beuret*, whose conception is similar (fig. 56, p. 227). But it should perhaps be dated to a little earlier, around 1895, immediately after *Thought*, since the treatment of the marble is more reminiscent of the works of the beginning of the decade than its end. As in *The Gates of Hell*, much earlier of course, Rodin truly succeeded

in suggesting a space that continues well beyond the work's material limits. Can one see a point in common with the experiments of Medardo Rosso? In 1893, at La Bodinière, Rosso exhibited four "impressions," including *Lady with a Veil*, "female physiognomy seen in the fleeting space of a fraction of a second, but caught exactly as I saw her"[20] (fig. 57, p. 227), *Child at the Breast* and *Jewish Child*. Rodin went to the exhibition and an exchange of works—Rosso's *Laughing Woman* and Rodin's *Torso Study for Walking Man*—sealed the two men's reciprocal admiration. Yet in Rosso's work, the face seems to

_Cat. 173
AUGUSTE RODIN
Study for France
About 1902–3
Bronze
49.8 x 46.3 x 36.5 cm
Musée Rodin, Paris

_Cat. 172
AUGUSTE RODIN
Minerva in a Helmet
About 1902–3?
Plaster
49.8 x 50.1 x 36 cm
Musée Rodin, Paris

Cat. 18
—

flee and dissolve into the ambient atmosphere, while in Rodin's it constitutes a dense form solidly occupying space. The triangular-shaped block is exploited in highly unconventional fashion, since one of the points is directed at the viewer. Perfectly frontal, impenetrable, the face, a "powdered face animated only by the eyes and mouth," as Jules Renard described it in his *Journal* on March 19, 1895, appears more like a figurehead in a space whose emphasized depth creates a distance between it and the viewer.

The same face, a face of maturity, heavier than the first portrait and this time with abundant hair evoking the "powerful tuft of brown hair" described by Paul Claudel, is again recognizable in the high-relief decorating the plinth of the *Monument to Sarmiento* in Buenos Aires (1900). The contract was signed in November 1895 and the model of the relief enlarged in 1898 before being transposed into marble in 1899. *Apollo Slaying Python* (fig. 58, p. 228), Apollo defeating the ignorance against which Sarmiento had struggled, or the truth (of Rodin's feelings) imposing itself on Camille? Could it have been then that, full of

hope, he wrote "convalescente" on the assemblage today known as *The Farewell*?

Rodin used the face for the last time around 1902–3, giving it a kind of helmet to obtain the work initially known as *Byzantine Princess* or *Late Roman Empress*, then *Saint George* in 1904 and finally *France* in 1912. Apart from a magnificent variation, with a more clearly represented breastplate and a winged helmet (cat. 172, p. 229), we know of two other states, a bust thought to be the study (cat. 173, p. 229) and the definitive version, in high-relief, in which the face is turned to the right and therefore with only the left profile visible, the Musée Rodin version facing in the opposite direction being a unique case (cat. 174). An intermediate state, which disappeared a long time ago, can be reconstituted by a photograph of the high-relief by Bulloz (cat. 18), which shows how the work arose from a sculpture of the young woman, undoubtedly in clay. A demarcation line is clearly visible at the base of the neck and in the middle of the forehead, and the modeling of the bust and hair, only summarily indicated with broad knife strokes, contrasts strikingly with that of

_Cat. 18

JACQUES-ERNEST BULLOZ
France *during execution, plaster, by Auguste Rodin*
After 1903–4
Photograph, gelatin
silver print
35.5 x 26.5 cm
Musée Rodin, Paris

_Cat. 174
—
AUGUSTE RODIN
France Turned Leftwards
About 1904
Bronze
57 x 43 x 29 cm
Musée Rodin, Paris

the face, which is carefully finished. As Chéruy noted, the ensemble was then placed against a plaster panel in the middle of which there had been cut an arched opening, the background being filled in with clay, identifiable by its darker color.[21]

On April 3, 1904, Guillaume Mallet, who had initially intended to acquire a large model of *The Benedictions*, asked the price of the bust "that Monsieur Rodin calls St Georges or Courage."[22] It was destined for the library of his property, Bois des Moutiers, at Varengeville, where it was to be installed next to a tapestry by Burne-Jones, *The Adoration of the Magi*.[23] The bronze was finished in June and delivered in October. "I have observed," Rodin wrote to Mallet, "what a happy choice you have made as I had never seen this work in bronze."[24] It was therefore the first bronze cast of the high-relief, the first of the bust being, if one is to believe Rodin, the one acquired by Mrs. Simpson in 1906 (Washington, National Gallery of Art).[25]

Unlike the previous works, *France* became known to the public very early on. It was exhibited in 1904 and numerous bronzes were cast. In 1906, Rodin gave a cast of the high-relief to Glasgow University to express his gratitude for the honorary doctorate they had conferred on him. But the apotheosis came in 1912 with the project for the *Monument to Samuel de Champlain* on the banks of the lake named after him in the United States.[26] "What can, what should France do?" Gabriel Hanotaux, president of the Comité France-Amérique, asked himself. "What stone worthy of the monument could she contribute? There is only one solution, that

Cat. 174

this stone should be *precious* . . . We went to Rodin's studio. We know how popular he is in America. . . . We went through the rooms of the Hôtel Biron . . . and there among so many masterpieces that the imagination exhausts itself, we discovered—this is the *mot juste* because the proud modesty of the master hardly pointed it out to us—a bronze bust: *France*. Imagine our emotion at this encounter. We were looking for an image, a symbol, I would even dare to say a signature of our country to send over there, and we found France herself, a lovely France full of grace, vivacity and courage . . . her hair like a helmet, protected by her finery as though by a breastplate. We were looking for a French thought and we found the very image of France."[27]

POETIC VARIATIONS ON *AURORA*   Véronique Gautherin

Antoine Bourdelle, who joined Rodin's studio as an assistant in the early 1890s (the first written traces of their collaboration date from September 1893, but it probably began earlier), knew Camille. Although not close— in her letters she addresses him as "Monsieur"—he was in regular contact with her at least until 1898. A recently discovered letter from Camille reveals that he sent her an invitation to visit the exhibition of his work at the Galerie Georges Petit that year.[1] Throughout these years, during which Camille was gradually sinking into isolation, Bourdelle constantly expressed his admiration for her and attempted to help her as best he could. It was thanks to him that the collector Henri Fontaine commissioned the so-called *with hair "tout à jour"* version of the bust of *La Petite Châtelaine* executed in 1896 and today conserved in the Musée d'Art et d'Industrie, Roubaix (cat. 74, pp. 148–49). In a letter, probably written in 1895–96, she wrote, "You would cause me great joy by telling me that you have managed to have my small bust commissioned at a higher price than I thought. I shall set to work straightaway and you have given me back some of the courage that I was beginning to lack. I am very touched by this, from an artist such as you. Spontaneous admiration is a rare and precious thing" (cat. 207).[2] In a second letter, in which she informs him that she has just received a 1,000-francs advance and that Fontaine was intending to give her 2,500 francs, she adds, "I find this far too much and really the generosity of this art lover is extraordinary. I undoubtedly owe this to your kindly protection and allow me to thank you yet again" (cat. 208). At the studio in rue de l'Université, Bourdelle witnessed the genesis of the sublimated faces of Camille Claudel. Alluding to her then intimacy with the older Rodin, who at that time fascinated him, he one day admitted to Camille that

he envied seeing "the grand silent spectacle that unfolds when this man is alone, far from the others who are only a third his brothers, and when, in his thoughts, as though in an immense world of snow, one by one or in droves, his immortal offspring take shape."[3] He was a witness to their creation—a troubled witness, as he reveals in a draft for a sonnet entitled Aurora, inspired by one of these portraits, which are like odes to an absent woman, at the time of its creation around 1898.[4] Thirty years later, immersed in nostalgic contemplation one day in February 1926, he suddenly felt compelled to rewrite this sonnet twelve times.

The poem evokes Camille's "burning, pale, shapely and supple" face, like a "reflection of the night in which the sun trembles," a "face of wilting gold pierced with shadows, like a cold sky moving and coming alive at dawn." The allusions in the introductory lines of what was probably the first draft invite one de facto to see it as a transcription of the marble composition that was never exhibited or reproduced during Rodin's lifetime and that appears for the first time in a photograph taken by Harlingue after 1905 in the Pavillon de l'Alma, which had been re-erected at Meudon (fig. 59). Its present-day title,

Aurora, appears only in the notes written by Léonce Bénédite when she made her donation to the state in 1916. Nevertheless, the allusions Bourdelle makes to the theme it depicts suggest that Rodin himself had given it this title very early on, as a deliberate reference to the character of his young lover. The memory of this person he considered divine was still painfully alive in the 1910s, as some of his notes and Bourdelle's poem demonstrate. "You have a fire that I have not and which has made you a poet," Rodin wrote with a hint of envy to his assistant while they were working together.[5] The way Bourcelle uses language to convey the richness and complexity of the feelings aroused in him by the contemplation of the idealized face of Camille is touching. Fixed in her block of marble, she had been transformed by her lover into an eternal symbol of the inspiration of beginnings and of the woman eternally in love. And, according to the legend, this was in fact the fate—weighing on her like a curse and somewhat reminiscent of Camille's destiny— of Aurora "with rose-colored fingers," whom Aphrodite punished for having slept with Ares. In a draft of the poem contemporary with the first draft, Bourdelle describes (accompanied by the note "to be completed") the face as "a woman's face in which her alert senses put golden flames on the forehead . . . a face like a beautiful freshwater lake whose waves, undulating in the hollow that pushes her, make the mirror tremble in wide rings of pure gold" (cat. 219. 3). He was alluding to the passionately amorous state in which he had known her when she joined Rodin's studio. Her face was lit up with large clear eyes whose

light was so questioning and persistent. Evoking the "tragic attraction"[6] of this "head of eternity,"[7] "built out of hope and sparse shadow,"[8] Bourdelle talks in isolated snatches of verse of the "flight of love,"[9] dwelling on the "burning forehead"[10] that Paul Claudel described as "superb, overhanging magnificent eyes of that dark blue encountered elsewhere only in novels."[11] Bourdelle describes her now-marble gaze as "filled with lukewarm gold,"[12] playing on the allusion to the golden yellow color that the French adjective *aurore* then designated, at one point "opal,"[13] the next "full of metamorphoses."[14] But Bourdelle seems to have had difficulty in precisely defining the impressions that came to him in his meditation on this "head snatched from the gods,"[15] "unshading herself in the last fires of the sun,"[16] attempting between the lines to combine the evocation of the face of the woman who had been its venerated model and whose powerful charm,

a blend of gentleness and sensual pride, he still vividly remembered. The twelve abundantly altered drafts he wrote of his poem in February 1926 bear witness to this inability. The comparison in the seventh version of Camille's face with that most quintessentially enigmatic creature, the sphinx, is an admission of this. How can one express the mystery of this singular being—"flower of the summits"[17] that has become "flesh of crystal, still damp with life"[18]—when the mystery, by its very essence, remains resistant to all description? To attempt to do so could only consist in plumbing its depths. Nothing more, nothing less.

III

Fev 1926

Le visage de Camille Claudel.

~~Chair pure de cristal pas entièrement éclose encore~~

faite d'espoirs, de désirs et reflets de soleil

structure d'ombre d'aube et de matin pareil

au glaçon qui se prend au glacier de l'aurore.

Tête d'Éternité, que du sang humain, dore

Chef d'immortalité Souffle de neige tiède, fait austère et vermeil

~~Ovale~~ épure des candeurs des lune en éveil

Trait chef d'immortelle fleur que le fastif adore.

Tragique ~~attrait~~. ~~[illegible]~~ vestige enflammé de l'eau douce

dont le front transpercé de source, qui le possède

[illegible] épuisé le sourire est [illegible], [illegible] d'or pur.

marbre apaisé du beau ouvert sur les paupières closes:

Et ~~cette~~ l'agonie de l'aube en son éclair obscur

Dans le regard, expire d'or tiède à reflets roses.

Ant

nouvelle copie

Février

19.26

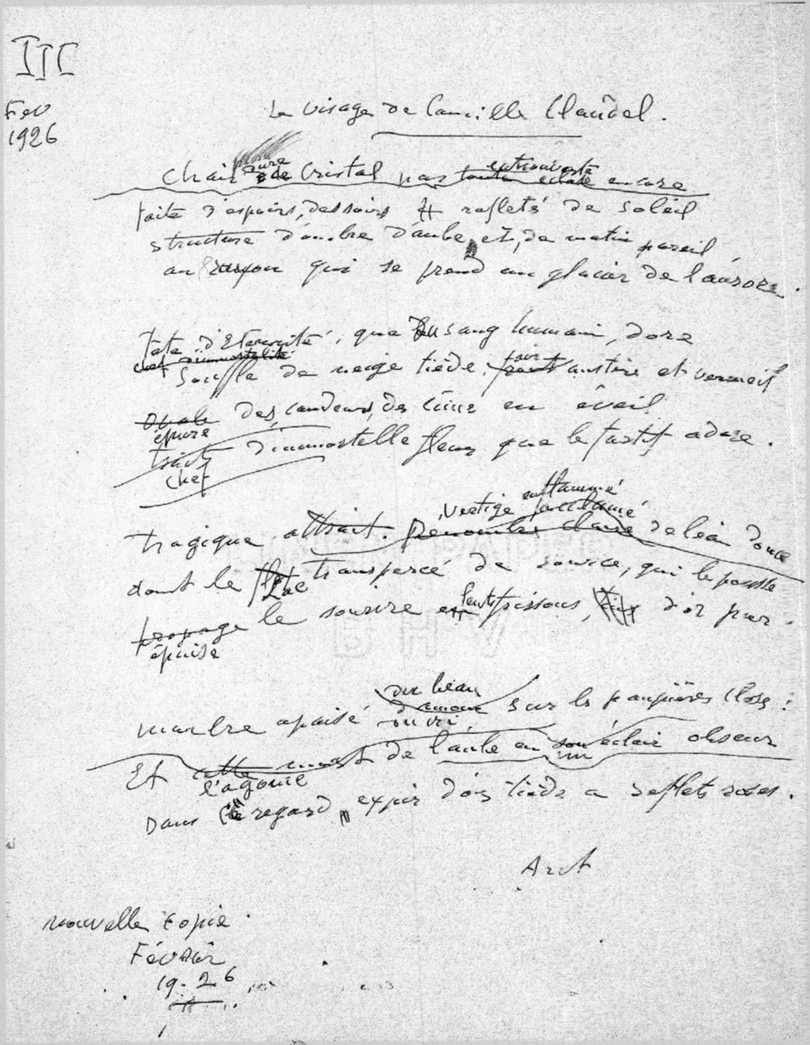

Cat. 219. 3

Antoine Bourdelle

The Face of Camille Claudel, III

February 1926

1 sheet, 21.1 x 27.1 cm

Musée Bourdelle, Paris

IV

THE FREEING OF CAMILLE CLAUDEL [1895–1905]

THE "SKETCHES FROM NATURE" Laure de Margerie

WHICH NATURE?

Camille used the phrase "sketch from nature" three times to describe her works at exhibitions, even entitling them as such. In the catalogue of the 1895 Salon of the Nationale des Beaux Arts, work no. 23, the plaster of *Les Causeuses* (cat. 76, p. 238), is listed as "Sketch from nature, group." In 1897, no. 24 is listed as "The Wave, sketch from nature (group plaster)" and in 1898, no. 36 is listed as "*Deep Thought*—sketch from nature, statuette bronze, belonging to M. P." Camille used this appellation again in a letter to Gustave Geffroy, probably written in April 1895: "Dear Sir, Your note encourages me to pursue a path I am at present only groping along (that of the sketches from nature) and which excites me enormously. I have others in the same genre, come and see them when you wish, but on Sunday afternoons I am always there. Your devoted Camille Claudel" (cat. 203).

It has since been customary to group in this category an ensemble of sculpted works of similar inspiration (everyday life), size (their "miniaturization") and

material, or more precisely, the combination of materials used in the definitive works (bronze and stone or bronze and marble onyx). They are *Les Causeuses* (cat. 77), *The Wave* (cat. 79, p. 242) and two fireside compositions, *Deep Thought* (cat. 80, p. 240) and *Fireside Dream* (cat. 88, p. 240). Also included are *The Painter* or *Sketch by an Amateur* (fig. 61, p. 241). *Head of an Old Blind Man Singing*, of which only a study for the head has survived (cat. 75, p. 241), *Dog Gnawing a Bone* (fig. 60, p. 240) and works which have disappeared such as *Two Street Urchins* and *Study of a Japanese Man*.

A priceless letter from Camille to Paul Claudel written in late 1893 reveals that she was planning

Cat. 77
—
CAMILLE CLAUDEL
Les Causeuses
Marble onyx and
bronze, 1897
44.9 x 42.2 x 39 cm
Musée Rodin, Paris

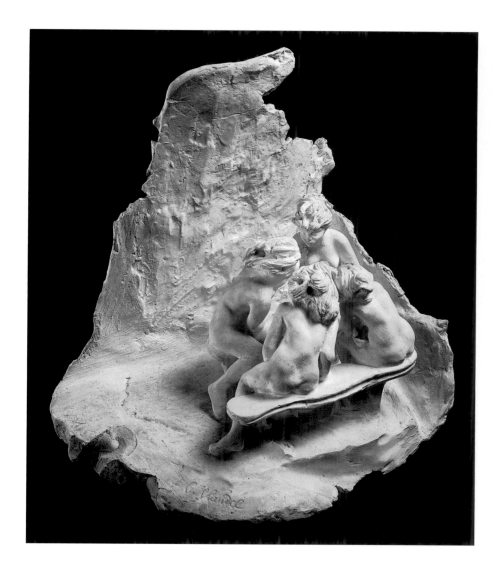

Cat. 76

CAMILLE CLAUDEL
Les Causeuses
1895
Plaster
40 x 40 x 40 cm
Musée Rodin, Paris

other pieces in the same vein. As well as *Confidence* (*Les Causeuses*), she describes, with the aid of quick ink drawings, *Grace* ("tiny figures around a large table listening to grace before a meal"), *Sunday* ("three men in the same new blouses perched on top of a cart on their way to mass") and *Fault* ("a young girl crouching on a bench crying, her parents looking at her surprised") (cat. 202). She may perhaps have already made sketches or models of them and they might therefore have been among the works she invited Geffroy to come and see. They might also have been the works that struck Mathias Morhardt in the studio on boulevard d'Italie: "These tiny incidents of life . . . have inspired the young artist to produce groups of inconceivable beauty. The cupboards in her studio are peopled with figurines that are the abundant

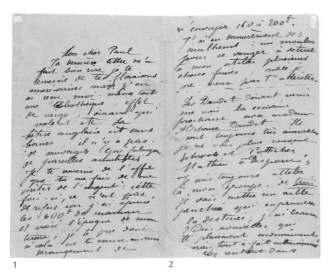

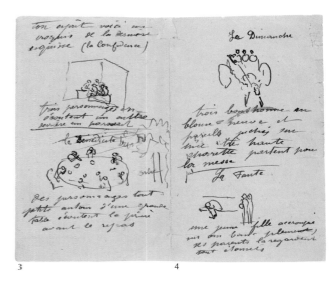

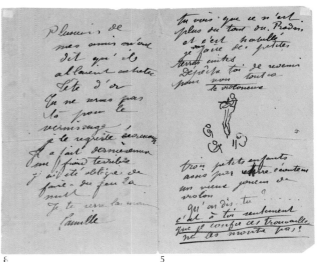

Cat. 202

*Letter from Camille Claudel
to Paul Claudel*
[Late 1893 or early 1894]
2 sheets, 17.5 x 22 cm
Société des Manuscrits des
Assureurs Français, Paris

Cat. 80

Cat. 88

Fig. 60

harvest of her long retreat."[1] They may have fallen victim to the fits of destruction Camille often had from 1906. Or they may only ever have been mere sketches on paper.

Critics were quick to note Camille's declaration of intent. all the more willingly because she herself had invited them to do so. This was the case with Geffroy, who emphasized: "Mademoiselle Camille Claudel, who will soon realize her own personal art of direct observation, if I am to believe the precious indication of this 'Sketch from nature.'"[2] But he was not the only one, because in 1895 Octave Mirbeau filled his imaginary visitor to the Salon, Kariste, with an "enthusiastic joy before an admirable group, of such absolute beauty that nothing purer or more powerful could have been found at Pompeii and Tanagra, when divine artists were full of amazement at nature and the worship of life."[3]

This reference to the art of Pompeii and Tanagra, also made by other commentators,[4] poses the question of the sculptor's sources of inspiration. Until

then, apart from *The Old Woman* (cat. 26, p. 24), she had produced few naturalistic works. This was less true of her drawings. The charcoals she produced in 1885 during a stay with her uncle at Gérardmer in the Vosges (cat. 33, p. 130 and fig. 3) and in 1886 on the Isle of Wight with her friend Jessie Lipscomb (fig. 32) show the etched features of old peasant women and fisherwomen. Before the series of "sketches from nature," her naturalism seems therefore to have been focused on representing the reality of old age.

Were these new subjects really sketched from scenes which Camille had witnessed? Only Morhardt mentions that "four women sitting opposite one

Cat. 75

Fig 61

another in a narrow railway compartment and who seem to be sharing who knows what precious secret must have suggested this masterpiece: *Les Causeuses*."[5] However, Camille's *Causeuses* are naked, as are her bathers. Yet Camille, in the above-mentioned letter to Paul, declared: "You see it is no longer Rodin at all, and it is dressed."

Even if the idea for the subject may have come from observation of reality, Camille strips her figures bare and divests them of any subjective connotation, thus assimilating them to the previously identified themes such as, in the case of *Les Causeuses*, the *sacra conversazione* between saints and martyrs, the nine Muses or witches' Sabbaths. The very bench on which the gossipers are sitting is devoid of style, the wall against which they are gathered is unidentifiable (the vague undulations in the marble onyx version could, if one wished, evoke Louis XV-style wood paneling) and even the women's features are timeless. Some saw their faces as prehistoric (William Sarment: "these little prehistoric women"[6]), others as simian (Alain-Fournier in his correspondence with Jacques Rivière: "The Conversation. Primitiveness. Bodies listening, confiding in one another, bodies on

the lookout: three naked women seated—like three apes"[7]). Only their Helleu-style chignons put them in fin-de-siècle Paris.

The other works in the series in no way conceal the fact that they are inspired by everyday modern life. The clothes of the woman by the fireplace and those of the painter are completely ordinary. The few accounts of Camille's daily environment during those

Cat 75
CAMILLE CLAUDEL
Head of an Old Blind Man Singing
About 1894?
Plaster
21 x 10 x 11.5 cm
Private collection

Fig. 61
CAMILLE CLAUDEL
Sketch by an Amateur
About 1894
Patinated plaster
National Museum of Art, Bucharest

_ Fig. 62

years insist on her isolation in her new studio in boulevard d'Italie, where she moved in 1888, and on the very working-class nature of the Glacière quarter. Once more, it is Morhardt's article which provides the information:

> Alone in this deserted quarter, in her studio at the back of the huge courtyard—the *Cour des Miracles* as it is called on boulevard d'Italie— she spends the hours she is not working watching passersby. This is no prison, of course, she can come and go as she pleases. She often goes to the Musée du Louvre or the Musée Guimet for long periods of study. She often goes out walking, wherever she pleases, watching with all the power of her wide-open eyes the incomparable spectacle of the streets. It is the streets and her walks which above all inspire her. A passerby here, a group of people glimpsed there or a swarm of workers busy working suggest a thousand other works to her. As soon as she gets home she starts immediately, with an enthusiasm untrammeled by material difficulties or that heavy and persistent solitude from which she suffers in her deserted studio, noting down the perceived impression, the poses of the groups she has encountered, the gestures of passersby, the movements of workers. For hours, she feverishly searches to recapture, to reconstruct the life which, in ever different, always striking and dramatic forms, reveals itself to her.[8]

But what remains of this popular proximity? Where are the swarms of workers going about their work, where are the workers whose movements she sketched? In the gallery of her bronze founder and dealer, Eugène Blot, Camille's sculptures were shown alongside miners, boat haulers, sowers and ragmen by the German Bernard Hoeger, the fisherwomen of the Swedish sculptor Ruth Millès and the workers of Jean-François Raffaëlli. But social study does not seem to have been Camille's preoccupation. Not at all interested in politics or in any way politically committed, Camille was most probably entirely absorbed in her individual struggle as a woman and female artist. When she did her "sketches from nature," what mattered to her was to escape for a while from the constraints of the life model, the

_ Cat. 79

CAMILLE CLAUDEL
The Wave
Marble onyx and bronze,
executed by Camille Claudel
and François Pompon,
1898–1903
62 x 55 x 50 cm
Musée Rodin, Paris

_ Fig. 62

CAMILLE CLAUDEL
The Wave, *plaster*,
in SILVESTRE 1897

_ Cat. 79

portrait, and the historical, allegorical, mythological and autobiographical repertoire, even if the latter dimension is never completely absent from some of her works. Real life, real people's emotions, this was the new universe she sought to capture. It mattered little in the end whether she had witnessed the scenes she described or not, whether her sketches were from life or memory. "The artist who looks at life and wants to faithfully capture it has to have a supreme independence of spirit to seek and invent the means the most capable of achieving his idea . . . It is because she knew she was capable of reconstructing the essential form of the movement that she was recalling that she realized this project."[9] During these years of separation from Rodin, she needed first of all to find her roots in real life again in order to reconstruct herself.

LIFE, ABOVE ALL

Many critics remarked on the formidable energy which *Les Causeuses* and *The Wave* exuded: "a gentle intensity of life,"[10] "the feeling of life,"[11] "proof that art has a power, capable of creating ensembles,"[12] "this group so intense,"[13] "It is alive, constantly alive."[14] They also praised the "apparition of an intimate truth"[15] and the expression exuded by the figures' poses.

The raw power of the sea unleashing itself on land, the wave, contributes to this expression of energy. In the same way, the diagonal composition of *The Wave*, which was accentuated between the plaster, whose marine wall was almost vertical, like a multiheaded Cerberus looming over the three women

(fig. 62, p. 243), and the marble onyx version, in which there is confrontation (cat. 79, p. 242), suggests, as in many other sculptures by Camille, a movement caught in its instantaneity, in its happening. Paul Claudel wrote: "Always the suspended gesture."[16] The disequilibrium thus introduced is dynamic, there is nothing frozen about it.

The Wave's Japanese inspiration has been emphasized many times. We know that Camille took Claude Debussy with her to the 1889 Exposition Universelle, where they admired *Great Wave off Kanagawa*, a print by Hokusai dating from the early 1830s. Jean-Michel Nectoux mentions in the same catalogue how the composer reused the motif for the score of *La Mer*. And in a text written in 1925 during his second stay in Japan, Paul Claudel also uses the image of the print: "I compare French poetry to Hokusai's famous wave which, after immense and powerful undulations, finally breaks over the shore in a plume of spray and small birds. Those marvelous birds are the phrases of Maurice, Guérin and Arthur Rimbaud."[17] At the Exposition Universelle and at the gallery of the great dealer of Japanese art in France, Siegfried Bing, who bought two of her sculptures and exhibited one of her busts, Camille also discovered kimonos and curios with no practical use that depicted miniature genre scenes. Their production, essentially for the western market, developed from 1887 onwards within the Tokyo School of Art.

The Wave's very material brings to mind Oriental sculptures. When *Les Causeuses* in onyx was shown at the Salon of the Société Nationale des Beaux-Arts in 1897, it was listed as being in jade, a frequently used material for Chinese and Japanese objects. Whether it was a deliberate mistake on Camille's part or an error in the catalogue, it at least shows that the Orient was present in people's minds. Armand Silvestre made no mistake when he published *Sculpture in the 1897 Salons*, a poem dedicated to "Mlle Claudel—The Wave" and decorated with a Japanese-style border.[18]

Thanks to the gemologist Martine Droit,[19] who analyzed the stone of *The Wave* with the scanning electron microscope at Nantes University, we know that it is marble onyx or calcareous onyx, generally called onyx because of its resemblance to real onyx. In fact there is nothing Japanese about this stone at all. In a letter to Morhardt written while she was working on *Les Causeuses*, Camille says she went "to the onyx merchant (Bastille)."[20] It may have been H. Journet et Cie, Société des Marbres-Onyx de l'Algérie, who had premises at 29 rue Popincourt and 24 boulevard des Italiens. Journet was listed in the 1880 *Bottin du commerce*[21] as the successor to Eugène Cornu, himself successor to G. Viot and Alphonse Pallu, founders of the Compagnie des Marbres-Onyx de l'Algérie in 1858. Journet owned the quarry at Aïn Tekbalet in Algeria and was the main supplier of marble onyx at that time. *Les Causeuses* was therefore probably carved out of a block of Algerian marble onyx, a material which rapidly became very fashionable in the 1860s due to the World's Fairs in Paris, London and Vienna and to its use in sculpture, principally by Charles Cordier, and in architecture by Charles Garnier, for example. We know from a letter written by the founder Eugène

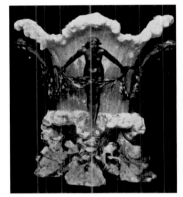 

_Fig. 63   _Fig. 64

Blot[22] that the marble onyx used for *The Wave* came from Mexico. Camille again used this material for the fireplace of certain copies of *Deep Thought* and in 1905 she proposed that Eugène Blot produce a *Siren* on a green onyx rock,[23] but this was never made. Camille carved her stone works (marble or marble onyx) herself. She participated more than most of her contemporaries in the execution of her works, as this extract from a letter to Mathias Morhardt, probably written in March 1896, shows: "You asked me whether I will be showing much at the Salon this year. Alas, you and M. Rodin know how long and difficult marble is and how much delay I have had due to my workers. I am doing everything I can to finish my little *Causeuses* in marble, which are coming along fine, I think, but I need someone intelligent

Fig. 63
HENRI VIAN
Wave, crystal vase, marble and gilt bronze, in CHAMPIER 1902, p. 164

Fig. 64
CHARLES RAPHAËL PEYRE
Lame, edition by Eugène Blot, in THOMAS 1901, p. 183

Fig. 65

right now to help me to add the <u>corner</u> while I polish the small women. If you or M. Rodin could send me someone you would be doing me a great service" (cat. 211). Her brother notes: "My sister claimed to have discovered the polishing technique in use in Bernini's time: using a sheepskin."[24] But she also employed marble carvers ("my workers," as she called them when she frequently complained about them). François Pompon's ledger[25] shows that in 1900 Camille employed him to finish the carving of *The Wave*, which he did not complete until 1902.

The marble onyx and bronze version was contemporaneous with works more decorative in inspiration, such as the vase exhibited by Henri Vian at the 1900 Exposition Universelle, decorated with a nude woman in gilt bronze on a background of crystal spray (fig. 63, p. 245).[26] A work very close in iconography to *The Wave* but rendered different by the change in scale of the aquatic element was *Lame*

Fig. 65
FÉLIX VALLOTON
Interior with Red Chair and Figures
1899
Gouache on card
Kunsthaus, Zürich

(fig. 64, p. 245) by the sculptor Charles Raphaël Peyre produced around 1901 in bronze and possibly marble onyx by Eugène Blot.[27]

ENCROACHING SHADOWS

The two compositions showing a woman alone by a fireplace, produced only a few years later, have often been described as anecdotal, and even as examples of bad taste. A letter from Blot to his successor Leblanc-Barbedienne accredits this opinion: "As [*Fireside Dream*] sold well and the great artist was always short of money, she did me another figure in front of a fireplace called *The Yule Log* [*Deep Thought*]" (cat. 249 and 88, p. 240). And Camille even suggested producing a third fireplace piece, *La Frileuse*, adding, "it will be the most beautiful for a night light."[28] *Deep Thought* was cast by Blot and transformed into a night light by adding a lamp at the back of the hearth. The founder had acquired the reproduction rights for the group, which he sold as *Intimacy*. Its conversion into a utility object is surprising and disconcerting. Paul Claudel disapproved: "Later, she sold the woman kneeling in front of a fireplace to the dealer Blot. One has to earn a living! A red lamp in the fireplace and the woman becomes a silhouette. The effect is amusing."[29]

But beyond their anecdotal dimension, these works are laden with meaning. From life, we are passing to a half-death, to a place of melancholy. Whereas in *Les Causeuses* the spoken word is the principal subject—even if, as Bouté pointed out, it is "the first work to attempt to do exactly what is impossible for a sculptor, to sculpt words, <u>to give words to</u>

Cat. 51

Fig. 66

form"[30]—in the *Fireside* series it is silence that reigns. Gone the babble of *Les Causeuses* and the crash of *The Wave*. We are in the realm of intimacy, which her brother Paul described so well: "From then on proscribed from public places and the open air, sculpture, like other arts, retired to the solitary room where the poet harbors his forbidden dreams. Camille Claudel is the foremost craftswoman of this interior sculpture."[31] In October 1940, he devoted a text to "Sitting and looking into the fire": "She is happily sitting alone, there is no one but her, everyone is dead or as much . . . Of course this is not hopelessness, but it is a sweet feeling to be rid of hope, to have retreated into oneself, to commune with the present with one's entire being."[32] By "ridding oneself of hope," one abolishes the future. All that remains is the present and the past which cannot be effaced. The central element of these compositions is of course the fire itself. Due to its hypnotic power, its contemplation leads to a semi-dreamlike state in which the mind leaves the body to roam in an elsewhere that is almost the beyond.

In these compositions, Camille Claudel transcends the state of introspective solitude described by the Danish painter Hammershoï. She joins Valloton, who in his works (fig. 65) so powerfully evokes the atmosphere of latent drama sometimes hanging over bourgeois drawing rooms.

"IT IS NO LONGER RODIN AT ALL"

Was Camille warding off ill fortune or was she trying to persuade herself that she was now free when she wrote to her brother in December 1893?: "You see it is no longer Rodin at all"? She had distanced herself from the sculptor, but had not yet reached the stage where she would communicate with him via other people. They still saw each other occasionally, as demonstrated by the two etchings *Rodin Working* (cat. 51 and 52.2) and *Rodin Looking at the Subject*

Cat. 51

CAMILLE CLAUDEL
Rodin Working
About 1890–92
Drypoint, about 1896
19.9 x 25.7 cm
Musée Rodin, Paris

Fig. 66

AUGUSTE RODIN
Despair
About 1890–93
Bronze
Musée Rodin, Paris

(cat. 52.1, p. 248), probably commissioned in 1896 by Léon Maillard for his book *Auguste Rodin Statuaire*, and the telegram Camille sent to Rodin on March 30, 1896: "Tomorrow you will probably be paid a visit by Léon Maillard who has had me do two engravings of you (price agreed 200). As he is being difficult about paying me, I told him you do not want the sketches published (do not contradict me on this)."[33]

Camille probably did the engravings from earlier drawings. Morhardt confirms this when he writes about "a series of drawings she did either at home or in the studio in rue de l'Université" while she was working in Rodin's studio, specifying that "Mlle Camille Claudel has produced engravings of four of

these drawings for a book (not yet published) by Léon Maillard entitled *Auguste Rodin*." His description of one of them very clearly suggests the silhouette and pose Camille gave her teacher in her etchings: "It is Rodin himself, at work, in the midst of his figure groups and statues: it is Rodin leaning, diving, straightening, holding a ball of clay at the end of his straight arm, or almost falling over backwards to better judge a lofty outline."[34] One should also point out the very great similarity between Rodin's features in the etching *Rodin Looking at the Subject* and in the famous drawing *The Collage* (cat. 59, p. 199): same straight forehead, same nose prolonging the line of the forehead, same rectilinear eyebrow, same slit eye.

But what is the "piece" that Rodin is leaning over? The rounded outline of the crouching body, as though inside an egg, the left hand reaching forward, the head down between the knees and the large block serving as a base are enough for us to recognize the figure Rodin entitled *Despair*. The work, of which there exists a plaster, a bronze (fig. 66, p. 247), a bronze assemblage on stone in the Musée Rodin and other casts in public collections, was photographed by Eugène Druet in Rodin's studio.[35] Dating from between 1890 and 1893, it corroborates, together with *The Collage*, drawn in 1892, the dating of the drawings that Camille used for her engravings in around the early 1890s.

When the book was finally published by Floury in 1899, a year after Morhardt's article, it was the first monograph on the sculptor ever published. Léon Maillard had previously written several books on illustrators and engravers (Henri Boutet, André

Des Gachons) and the painter Auguste Boulard. He had also published the short-lived illustrated weekly newspaper *Le Parisien de Paris* (1897–98) and articles and critiques, including one on the 1897 Salon in which he discusses Camille Claudel. He was certainly a collector of engravings. His book on Rodin was his last.

The second etching, *Rodin Looking at the Subject* (cat. 52.1), known from Maillard's book, leads us to the statuette *The Painter* or *Sketch by an Amateur*. Maillard, when he discusses the bronze shown at the Salon of the Société Nationale des Beaux-Arts, suggests that it shows "Rodin painting."[36] Admittedly, his garment, the prominent beard and backward-leaning pose are close to the etching *Rodin Looking at the Subject*. According to Morhardt,[37] its origin dates back to sketches of a painter, "M. Y.," done on Guernsey in the summer of 1894, during a stay there with Madame Ménard-Dorian. The model could have been Georges Hugo. Other names have been suggested for the figure: the painter and friend Léon Lhermitte[38] and, more recently, Camille's first teacher, the sculptor and painter Alfred Boucher.[39] We will never know. It is clear, however, that this is a statuette in whose conception the study of nature played a definite role, as in the series of "sketches from nature" we are concerned with here.

Camille was intent on distancing herself from Rodin and critics remarked on this with some satisfaction. "No, Mlle Claudel really has her tone, her style, her signature . . . she will always know how to find an original subject which she will render originally and like a profound poet,"[40] Henry de Braisne noted. When she placed her *Causeuses* in the hollow of *The Wave*, she was succumbing to what Bruno Gaudichon called the "Rodinian habit"[41] of using her own creations as a repertoire of forms. While she was working in Rodin's studio, Camille would certainly have seen the storeroom full of the sculptor's "limbs." Mixing materials was also something that Rodin often did: his sawn-off plaster bodies emerging from antique cups are giant steps toward the destruction of form and a disgust with the likeness, alongside which Camille's compositions seem quite tame.

And yet the modernism of *Les Causeuses* and *The Wave* is undeniable. Camille was using a new language, just as her brother Paul was using a new kind of metrics in his poetry. Morhardt emphasized Camille Claudel's new contribution to the history of modern sculpture: "I think I am right in saying that hardly any modern work has the scope of *Les Causeuses* . . . It bears no precise similarity with anything known. It has the providential clarity of creations which do not proceed from known creation, which do not confirm an already established habit, whose mysterious filiation cannot be explained, and yet which suddenly, according to the inexplicable and unforeseeable will of genius, *are*."[42]

Camille said the same thing in different words: "I will have you note that I owe my works only to myself, since I have too many rather than not enough ideas."[43]

A PATRON: COUNTESS DE MAIGRET   Anne Rivière

In the spring of 1905, when Camille Claudel wrote to Gustave Geffroy, "I envy those who at the beginning of their lives find a benevolent protector instead of a sly and relentless enemy: it simplifies everything, the way is all paved,"[1] she was conveniently forgetting that she had found this "protector" in Auguste Rodin before she was twenty. She is glossing over the fact that throughout her artistic career, Rodin was very present and attentive, both on a professional level and regarding her material well-being. She was showing her ingratitude even though Rodin sent collectors to her, got articles written about her and granted her a monthly allowance, continuing to do so for a long time after their separation.

At the turn of the century, Camille Claudel met Countess Arthur de Maigret. Madame de Maigret, née Marie Chandon de Briailles, was then the widow of Count Arthur de Maigret, whom she had married in 1875. She owned a mansion at 22 rue de Téhéran and a house at Senlis, where she frequently stayed. Her son Christian divided his time between Paris and the château in Burgundy he had inherited from his father.

It seems possible that a distant cousin of her mother, Henriette de Vertus, introduced Camille Claudel to Countess de Maigret. In the autumn of 1913, from the nursing home at Ville-Évrard, she wrote a letter to "Mademoiselle de Vertus / 22 rue de Téhéran / Paris," with the instruction "Please forward."[2] The address is that of Madame de Maigret's home, which was sold by her heirs in 1913. The "Please forward" suggests that Camille Claudel was not sure whether her cousin was still living there but that if she had moved then it would have been recently, the consequence perhaps of the mansion having been sold. Mademoiselle de Vertus may have had a role in the de Maigret household or been in the countess's employment and thus acted as intermediary between the artist and her patron. It is extremely improbable that it was purely by chance that Mademoiselle de Vertus should have gone to live, after 1910 (the year Countess de Maigret died), at 22 rue de Téhéran, a mansion that contained works by her cousin Camille Claudel.

One can trace relations between the artist and Countess de Maigret back to 1897. They are attested by the mention Mathias Morhardt, Camille Claudel's first biographer, makes of them in his article "Mlle Camille Claudel," a key text even today. This article

was almost finished in autumn 1897 since, on October 5, Morhardt wrote to Rodin, "would you mind coming up to avenue Rapp[3] for a moment as I would like to read you the article on Mademoiselle Claudel,[4] and on page 754 of his article Morhardt writes, "We will see, in forthcoming exhibitions . . . the *Perseus and the Gorgon* group in marble and bronze that she is executing for the mansion of Madame the Marquess of Maigret."

If Morhardt refers to a "group in marble and bronze," this is because the project for the mansion in rue de Téhéran was already in an advanced state of completion in spring 1898. The "life-size" plaster was exhibited at the Salon du Champ-de-Mars in 1899, but the marble, smaller than the plaster, was not shown until 1902 (cat. 86). At that time, the artist had left the studio in boulevard d'Italie, first for rue de Turenne in 1898, then for her last address, 19 quai de Bourbon, in late January 1899. Although only thirty, she was "tired to the point of hopelessness,"[5] and it was Pompon and his assistants who undertook the preparation and carving of the marble of *Perseus*, the *Fireside Dream* statuette in pink marble, also destined for Countess de Maigret[6] (1899), and the white marble version for Baron de Rothschild. They also completed *The Wave* in 1900 (cat. 79, p. 242).

According to Pompon's ledger (cat. 221), the plaster model (2.46 x 1.32 x 1.10 m) was reduced by a quarter for the marble and paid in several installments as work progressed. These advances were paid via several intermediaries, including Peytel (probably on Rodin's behalf) and Rodin himself, who continued to help Camille at least until 1906.

Camille Claudel supervised every stage of work on the marble in Pompon's studio at 3 rue Campagne-Première. In July 1901, she wrote to Geffroy, "In the afternoon I sometimes go to work on the large statue of Perseus which is going to cause me such suffering and tears and which is in a studio near boulevard Montparnasse" (cat. 220). On December 13 that year Maurice Pottecher wrote to Geffroy, "I saw Mlle Claudel yesterday. She begged me to come and see a marble group she is working on, Perseus, slaying the Gorgon, a powerful and noble work, and one of the most important she has done . . . If you would like me to accompany you to Mlle C's, at 3 rue Campagne-Première, I am at your disposal."[7]

When the work was shown at the Salon of the Société Nationale des Beaux-Arts in 1902, the artist complained to Peytel, hoping that he could get Rodin to intervene, that her "poor statue," exhibited outside, "is constantly in the rain, hail, frost, wind, etc." and that "in this bad weather nobody sees it as they stay inside" (cat. 223). She even threatened to write to Rodin himself and to withdraw the marble from the Salon. The group received varied critical receptions and although her unconditional admirers compared the work to those of ancient Greece,

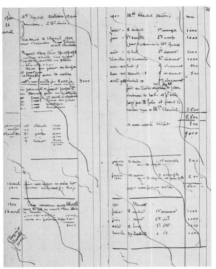

_Cat. 221

Benvenuto Cellini and Giambologna,[8] Henry Marcel, for example, thought that the "hero has very rickety legs" and that "the horror of the haggard mask bristling with snakes is diminished by all the vulgarity of a kind of shrew."[9] Gustave Babin's judgment, however, is fairly typical of most reviews of the figure group: "Rather gangling in arrangement but original in conception . . . And if this is undoubtedly not a complete work in every respect, it is at least something before which one can only feel a mixture of sympathy and admiration."[10] It was in poetical terms, however, that Paul Claudel analyzed his sister's last work. "This sinister figure in which loomed the conclusion of a painful career before the definitive darkness beckoned," seeing "this head with bloody hair," as an image of madness and remorse.[11]

Although one can imagine that the artist, seemingly lacking in inspiration since 1898–99, remembered an early work, David and Goliath, still in the studio in rue de Turenne in 1897–98 (see "Camille Claudel: the Early

Cat. 221
François Pompon
Ledger
Vol. 1 (July 1884–
August 2, 1908)
Fol. 75 verso, April 14,
1901–April 11, 1902
32 x 13.8 cm
Musée d'Orsay, Paris

_Cat. 87

_Cat. 8

Cat. 87

CAMILLE CLAUDEL
Perseus and the Gorgon
About 1899
Bronze
51 x 30 x 25 cm
Private collection

Cat. 8

ANONYMOUS
*Camille Claudel in
her atelier at 19 Quai de
Bourbon, with the plaster
of* Perseus and the Gorgon
About 1899
Photograph, gelatin
silver print?
Approximately 17 x 12 cm
Bibliothèque Marguerite-
Durand, Paris

Works," pp. 18–27), one should also hypothesize that she reused *Crouching Woman* (cat. 31, p. 59), sculpted some fifteen years earlier, for Medusa's body. The composition is nonetheless the culmination of specific, cultivated and mature reflection. On the same almost horizontal plane cutting across the vertical of the body of Perseus dominating the monster, the severed head of the Gorgon (which can be seen as a self-portrait[12]) stands out. It is brandished at the end of the left arm, behind the left shoulder, the hero's head and the shield/mirror held by the outstretched right arm. The artist is showing both the moment of victory and how this victory came about—by means of the mirror—but also the fact that, since Medusa's head retained its petrifying powers despite its decapitation, Perseus,

"he who kills without looking,"[13] can only behold the proof of his victory in the mirror before, as the myth goes, concealing it in a bag.

When this statue, forgotten at the foot of the staircase of Countess de Maigret's mansion for decades, was finally located, the shield was missing. Given Morhardt's description of "the group in marble and bronze," but also the photograph of the artist with the life-sized plaster (cat. 8), in which the shield is missing but not its strap, it was agreed that it was the shield that was bronze, and perhaps even polished like the shield in the myth. The combination of two materials as different as marble or onyx and bronze was very much in the artist's manner during those years. Her inspiration was running dry and her quest

Fig. 67

Fig. 68

for buyers prompted her to produce more decorative works, such as *The Wave* or the so-called *Fireside* series (*Deep Thought* and *Fireside Dream*), versions of which were produced in marble and bronze, in marble onyx or entirely in marble.[14]

However, a recently discovered photograph of the group exhibited at the 1902 Salon (fig. 67) illustrates the text of the critic Maurice Hamel: "Mademoiselle Claudel has kept her perceptive and strong personality. Her *Perseus and the Gorgon* group is a nervous, elegant and tormented work which renews an old subject with a novel note."[15] The work was not completely finished since there is still a marble support linking the hero's right arm and thigh. And, surprisingly, the shield is also marble. The artist may have

envisaged the use of marble and bronze but, since she had entrusted the carving of the marble to Pompon, it was he who chose marble, or else it could have been the client who preferred marble to bronze.

The white marble reduction of *Perseus* (H. 52. 3 cm, fig. 68) now in the Musée Rodin, Paris, belonged to Joanny Peytel and was acquired from his heirs in December 1963. None of the correspondence between the artist and Peytel mentions a purchase by

Fig. 67
CAMILLE CLAUDEL
Perseus and the Gorgon
Marble, 1902
In HAMEL 1902, p. 174

Fig. 68
CAMILLE CLAUDEL
Perseus and the Gorgon
Marble, about 1902
Musée Rodin, Paris

the latter between 1898 and 1902. Reine-Marie Paris and Arnaud de la Chapelle's hypothesis is that, having shared in the financing of the marble executed in Pompon's studio, Peytel obtained a reduction of *Perseus* from the latter.[16] In which case, it would be possible to attribute the softer treatment and a certain prettiness in the features of Perseus and even Medea to Pompon's manner. But perhaps this reduction of *Perseus* should be seen instead in the context of the artist's production at that time. *Deep Thought,* in white marble, which also belonged to Peytel and is now in the Musée de Poitiers (cat. 80, p. 240), and *Aurora* (cat. 89, p. 143), which is a very dull version of *La Petite Châtelaine,* have the same opaque and "soapy" treatment of surface and none of the translucent polish of *La Petite Châtelaine* in Roubaix (cat. 74,

pp. 148–49). Similarly, earlier works such as *The Waltz* (cat. 64, pp. 112, 114–16) and the variant of the female figure in *The Fortune* (cat. 92 A, p. 260), *Abandon* (cat. 94 A, p. 267) and *The Implorer* (cat. 84 A, p. 190), once they had been retouched and reduced for Eugène Blot, forfeited a little of their power for that elegant and decorative prettiness that would appeal to the maximum number of clients.

Around 1904, Camille Claudel asked Blot to intervene to get the state to commission "a large statue of Perseus in bronze."[17] Eugène Blot produced a three-quarter-size version of *Perseus* from a plaster that seems extremely close to Joanny Peytel's marble reduction. When Blot sold the reproduction rights to Leblanc-Barbedienne, it was stipulated that only six copies were to be made (cat. 254, p. 267), whereas in the catalogue of the exhibition of Camille Claudel's works at Blot's gallery in 1905, thirty were envisaged. There is nothing to indicate that the version presented here (cat. 87, p. 254) belongs to this edition, for it bears no stamp and the dimensions are different.

During the four years it took to finalize and execute *Perseus and the Gorgon,* Countess de Maigret commissioned and acquired several works. As well as the pink marble version of *Fireside Dream* mentioned above, which also seems to have been ordered the same year, in 1899, she commissioned a marble bust of her son Christian de Maigret and in 1900 her own bust and that of her daughter-in-law Marie d'Anterroches.[18] In 1905, Countess de Maigret acquired a major work, the marble version of *Sakuntala* entitled *Vertumnus and Pomona* (cat. 93, pp. 274 and 277). She also owned a mask of *La Petite*

CAMILLE CLAUDEL
Countess Arthur de Maigret,
née Marie Chandon
de Briailles
1903

Charcoal with chalk and pastel
highlights on cream paper
66 x 53 cm
Musée du Pays de
Château-Gontier

Cat. 85

Cat. 90

Châtelaine (cat. 71, p. 142) and a charcoal drawing of Countess de Maigret executed at Senlis in 1903 (cat. 91), both of which were probably gifts of the artist.

In *Dix ans d'art français*, the naturalist writer Paul Adam devotes a eulogistic passage to the bust of Christian de Maigret (cat. 85) that deserves to be quoted in its entirety: "In sculpting the *Portrait of M. le Comte de M . . .*, Mlle Camille Claudel has produced a masterpiece. An audacious, virile youth. The powerful, vulgar nose defies space. An adolescent moustache adorns his sensual lips. Everything is of such superb arrogance, from the severe forehead mirroring the light to the sharply delineated flesh of the devouring mouth.

A lust for life asserts itself in his resolute allure, which is heightened by the collar and bouffants of the Henry II costume. Aware of his young vigor, the male is presenting himself to the world, which he is going to tame and which he almost affably scorns, so easy it seems to defeat. The mastery in art that one expected from Camille Claudel has been completely attained. Few museum pieces, even in the Louvre, communicate both such a mental and living impression."[19]

Yvanhoë Rambosson was one of the rare critics to have noticed the bust at the 1899 Salon, eclipsed as it was by the plaster of *Perseus* and by the interest shown in *The Age of Maturity*, also exhibited at the

Cat. 85

CAMILLE CLAUDEL
Count Christian de Maigret Dressed as Henry II
Marble, 1899
66 x 65 x 43 cm
Private collection

Cat. 90

CAMILLE CLAUDEL
Countess Arthur de Maigret, née Marie Chandon de Briailles
Marble, 1902
78 x 48 x 47 cm
Private collection

Fig. 69

Fig. 70

same Salon. He noted that "the *Portrait of M. le comte de M* evokes the fine things, both mannered and proud, of the Renaissance."[20] The choice of dress, the inscription of the family motto—*Pro Christo et contra inimicos ejus*—on the plinth and the heavy necklace emphasize the young man's roots in History. Yet the artist, perhaps playfully, breaks the portrait's historicism and turns Christian de Maigret into a contemporary figure by including, on the medallion hanging on the chain, the figure of *Perseus*, then still unfinished.

The bust of *Countess Arthur de Maigret* was shown at the 1902 Salon (cat. 90, p. 257) with the large *Perseus*, after its rejection by the 1900 Exposition Universelle had led to the artist's resignation from the Société Nationale des Beaux-Arts. In a letter to Gustave Geffroy, Maurice Pottecher wrote:

"You know that at the Exposition her bust was rejected—the one that the model, a Countess de Maigret, had commissioned from her in the hope that it would be exhibited. This rejection is inexplicable since even if the bust had possessed even less merit (and it did have merit—I saw it), given the position which its author has won for herself, she deserved better treatment."[21]

For some authors, in addition to the marble bust and the charcoal drawing, there exists another portrait of Countess de Maigret by Camille Claudel.[22] They identify Madame de Maigret in a plaster bust of a woman owned by the artist's family (fig. 70), a work shown for the first time in Paris and Poitiers in 1984. Displayed unrestored under the title *Bust of a Woman*, the sculpture at the time presented traces of patina and a small piece of plaster at the tip of the nose.[23] The nose has since been restored and the descendants of Madame de Maigret are said to have "recognized" their ancestor.[24]

Yet when I first saw this work, I saw a strong resemblance between this bust and the known photographs of Madame Claudel as an old woman, but with no written sources or mention of a *Bust of Madame Claudel* being exhibited, I have preferred to keep a more evasive title for this bust.[2] The hair parted in the middle and drawn into a chignon on the top of the head is indeed similar to the way Madame Claudel wore her hair, whereas the bust, the charcoal portrait and a photograph of Madame de Maigret show her hair falling in curls over the forehead. Certain anatomical features—the position of the eyes, the shape of the ears, the corners of the lips joining the shadow cast by the cheekbone, and the sagging oval shape of the face and double chin—seem to me to match the artist's mother's facial structure (fig. 69). The head, furthermore, is set slightly forward on the bust and turned slightly to the left—many photographs show that Madame Claudel spontaneously bent her neck forward and to the left. Perhaps, at around fifty, she may have had cervical arthritis, which would have prevented her from maintaining a straight posture. The famous photograph taken on the balcony of the apartment in boulevard du Port-Royal, at Louise's engagement party in 1886, shows her already like this (cat. 107, p. 128).

The portrait, certainly not flattering, is difficult to date. In the 1886 photograph Madame Claudel looks much older than forty-six, but she seems not to have changed much over the following years. In 1888, Camille Claudel left home for 113 boulevard d'Italie and, in 1893, after Monsieur Claudel's retirement, her parents moved to Villeneuve for good. The ensuing chronology is known and from then on the artist had only distant and tense relations with her mother. I therefore think that this work should be dated to before 1890, along with the series of portraits of family and friends sculpted in the 1880s.

Camille Claudel's relations with Countess de Maigret seem to have ceased after June 1905, when the Vertumnus and Pomona group was shown at the Salon. The artist, in a letter to Henry Lerolle, alludes to a quarrel while she was finishing the group: "I would like to have taken you to Countess de Maigret's as promised but since I am no longer in her good books, my dear mother who dreamed only of installing my sister in my

place in this house and Lhermitte, whom I hindered from getting his foot in the door completely, have been so busy scheming they have deprived me of the affection of this woman, my only buyer."[26] And indeed, after 1905, Countess de Maigret seems to have neither commissioned nor purchased any more sculptures by her.

Although the busts executed for Countess de Maigret between 1897 and 1900 have lost something of the "Rodinity" of her early works, this is not because Camille Claudel wanted to efface her debt to her teacher, but rather because she was catering to what her client expected of a society portrait. Yet despite this she asserts her vigorous savoir-faire and concern for expressive detail. These portraits are also extremely interesting in that they are among Camille Claudel's few original works after 1898. As we have seen, Perseus is probably a reworking of a very early work. David and Goliath (1876), Fortune reuses the dancer of The Waltz (1889–93), Aurora is a variation of La Petite Châtelaine (1892–96), Niobid is derived from Sakuntala (1886–88), not to mention Vertumnus and Pomona, and perhaps even The Siren should be compared to Young Woman with a Sheaf (1887). By enabling the artist to prove her talent once more when her inspiration was running out, Madame de Maigret, although not the sculptress's "only buyer," was certainly one of her most important mainstays during the last years of her artistic life.

"TAKE THIS HELPING HAND I AM HOLDING OUT TO YOU"
EUGÈNE BLOT, FROM BRONZE FOUNDER
TO ART DEALER   Catherine Chevillot

Eugène Blot occupied a unique place in Camille Claudel's oeuvre since he was the only person to have sought to produce editions of her work.[1] He served as her dealer during her second creative period and remained on very friendly terms with her. He was not at all a typical bronze founder. The milieu of traditional bronze founding had developed considerably between the 1840s and 1880s, with the growing division of labor and the quasi-industrial production of multiples.[2] It had been in this milieu that Eugène's father, François-Louis Blot, established himself in 1854, at the age of twenty-six,[3] at the heart of the bronze makers' district, at 8 rue des Enfants-Rouges.[4] Like Barbedienne, Thiébaut and Siot-Decauville, the Blots followed the art scene closely to secure contracts for new works: "At the Salon des Artistes Français, the only one then existing, in the old Palais de l'Industrie, today demolished, my father and I went to look above all at the sculpture, to buy works to make editions of in our bronze foundry in the Marais quarter."[5]

Having probably started from practically nothing, but at a favorable time, Blot *père* bought a modest two-room apartment "for use as a workshop" in 1854, and the following year the building at the back of the courtyard, where he installed workshops and storerooms. Over the years, he extended the premises, renting more and more space until, in 1875, he became the owner of the three buildings at 84 rue des Archives.[6] The business therefore seems to have prospered considerably, which perhaps explains the family's apparent affluence during Eugène's youth.

On tax inspectors' forms filled out in 1862, Blot is declared as a "wholesale bronze dealer, gilding and silvering on metal." It is highly probable that, like Thiébaut, he began by contracting for art dealers then, as success came, began buying models and selling multiples of them himself. His advertisements later state "Workshop for various artistic bronzes and cast irons. Pewters, works for the Salons, *objets d'art* and furnishings and lighting." He produced editions of works by artists known for having specialized in "industrial art" and who sold their models to other manufacturers (Carrier-Belleuse, Moreau, Salmson), and editions of works by second- and even third-rate sculptors, known for their Salon works (Hébert, Leroux, Dumaige, Poitevin).

Cat. 92 A

CAMILLE CLAUDEL
Fortune
Before 1904
Bronze, edition by
Eugène Blot
Early 1905
48 x 35 x 17.5 cm
Musée Sainte-Croix, Poitiers

His son, Eugène Blot (fig. 71),[7] moved in cultivated and progressive bourgeois circles. His friends
included Gustave Geffroy, Arsène Alexandre and
Théodore Duret, and he first traveled to England
when he was seventeen, then to Belgium and
Germany. Eugène Spuller, Gambetta's advisor, was
a friend of the family. Édouard Delpeuch, Spuller's
nephew and later a secretary of state, became a
friend of Eugène. Very early on, the latter frequented
the first collectors (Camondo, Personnaz, Have-
meyer) and dealers (Portier *père*, Martin *père*,
Vollard, Bernheim) in Impressionist painting, and
himself started to collect. The photographer Dachery,
who worked for his father and took the pictures of the
company's pieces, also collected Impressionist painting and introduced him to new dealers.

Increasingly keen to give up mass production,
Eugène began thinking about rendering the most
recent trends accessible to the general public and
was one of the first to offer limited editions. "Around
1899," he wrote, "I thought about leaving the rue
des Archives and aiming my commercial editions for
export at the art lovers' and collectors' market by
showing works directly in a gallery on the boulevard. I tried to get a few Rodins, I had acquired the
right to produce editions of two pieces,[8] then some
Constantin Meuniers and, guided by Gustave
Geffroy, whom I met because of our mutual admiration for Cézanne, I went to see the great sculptress
Camille Claudel, who for a long time worked for
Rodin, executing his finest marbles for him."[9]

The emergence of dealer-founders such as Blot
was characteristic of the change in fashion and taste

_Fig. 71

that took place around 1900. "A happy movement in
art has banished dull bronzes from modern interiors.
The gradual clearing of the Salons of all this tasteless
insipidity was a good deed done by decorative art
and the Japanese influence . . . The most noteworthy
of the dealers vigorously striving to accredit and
further new artists, and thereby accomplish the most
useful and interesting of tasks, is Eugène Blot."[10]

Blot, a founder and treasurer of the Société des
Amis du Musée du Luxembourg in 1895, president
of the Salon d'Automne in 1903, a great collector of
Impressionist painting and later, of works by Cézanne,
Gauguin, Bonnard, Vuillard, Matisse, Marquet and

Jean Puy, was clearly more fascinated by painting than sculpture, but collected it nevertheless (four Carriès were sold at the Blot auction in 1906).[11] Pursuing the new goal he had set himself, he produced editions of works by Rodin, Claudel, Hoetger, Meunier, Carabin and Maillol. The choice of artists corresponded perfectly to the tastes he discusses in his memoirs, both in painting and sculpture. In the Impressionists he liked "the impulsive joy, the sudden emotion, the lyricism encapsulated . . . the emotive, heartfelt, radiant definitive impression of their blond and pink spring morning light," and appreciated their "study-like," even "sketchy" aspect because it had more life than works produced with too much professionalism. In his view, "Camille Claudel was to Rodin what Berthe Morisot was to Manet: the same great art of life, less powerful because less brutal, more feminine and gentler, but surprisingly curious, original, spiritual and alive."[12]

"Too Soon, Always Too Soon!"

He left us many accounts of his failure at selling bronzes: "So I set up shop at no. 5 boulevard de la Madeleine in a large premises where I tried—in vain—to sell my bronzes by Claudel, Rodin,

Constantin Meunier, Carabin and Maillol. Alas! The public showed little interest—except for a few rare connoisseurs . . . It was too soon, always too soon!"[13] In 1899, he auctioned 240 of his pictures,[14] and had to do the same again in 1906 after moving to rue Richepanse to concentrate on picture dealing: "Having had to get started, buy a commercial lease and move in—the boulevard and the bronzes cost me dearly—I thought about a second auction."[15] He often returns to this experience, which clearly upset his finances for a time: "Sorting through my papers last month," he wrote to Camille in 1932, "I came across letters from you. I reread them. They were all written in 1905, the year I organized the exhibition for you in my gallery which the critics loved but, alas, had nobody reaching for their wallets."[16]

Yet one can imagine that, from the moment that Blot decided to produce editions of her works, given his knowledge of his trade and milieu, and assuming he contracted out the founding as is thought, he would have managed to ensure if not low prices then at least attractive and stable ones. Yet, by his own account, the business ran at a loss: "I have never been able to recover even half of my outlay . . . yet . . . how low I set prices for her! Her 'Imploration' at 160 Frs (before raising it) and her 'Firesides' at 225 Frs."[17] It is interesting to compare his sale prices with those of other founders at the time. His prices seem quite reasonable compared to those listed in the catalogues of Barbedienne, Susse, Siot and Thiébaut. Even taking into account that the 160 francs for *The Implorer* is commensurate with its small size (29 cm), it still seems low compared to the price of Fix-Masseau's *Secret* (Siot-Decauville, 28 cm,

Fig. 71
Anonymous
Eugène Blot
Photograph
Private collection

Cat. 67

Cat. 257

Cat. 250

275 francs), Aubé's *Dante* (Thiébaut, 22 cm, 225 francs) and Chapu's *Joan of Arc* (Barbedienne, 23 cm, 180 francs, 30 cm, 250 francs). Rodin's *Triumphant Youth*, cast by Thiébaut, although only 52 cm high, was sold for 1,325 francs.

The lovers, defenders and buyers of his bronzes, cited by Blot himself, were prominent personalities: Armand Dayot acquired *The Waltz* from Siot, and Henri Marcel, director of the Musées Nationaux, organized the exhibition of Camille Claudel bronzes from the Blot Collection in Rome in 1912. Among his buyers were the sculptors Hoetger and Bartholomé (*Abandon*; cat. 249), and above all Doctor Viau (a group of *The Age of Maturity*), Vollard (*Fortune*, bust of *Auguste Rodin*), Louis-Bernard Goudchaux[18] and Albert Pra.[19] But they tended to be collectors of painting with an occasional interest in sculpture rather than out-and-out sculpture collectors.

THE CHRONOLOGY OF THE EDITIONS

The question of the date when Blot began buying works by Camille Claudel can be resolved unequivocally. A rather over-literal interpretation of Blot's memoirs, written in 1934, for a long time had us believe that the visit he paid to Camille's studio with Geffroy took place in 1900. Bruno Gaudichon and Anne Rivière have already questioned this, notably in their meticulous exegesis of the sculptor's letters. Numerous clues lead one to fix the date of the beginning of the Blot editions as 1905, or at the earliest 1904.

Cat. 67

CAMILLE CLAUDEL
The Waltz
Reduction with variants,
bronze, edition by
Eugène Blot
Early 1905
47 x 34 x 22 cm
Musée Sainte-Croix,
Poitiers

Cat. 257

GALERIE EUG. BLOT
Group The Waltz by
C. Claudel, *edition record
(no. 1860) illustrated with
a photograph by Larger*
Undated
28 x 18.7 cm
Archives Nationales
de France, Paris

Cat. 250

GALERIE EUG. BLOT
The Implorer by C. Claudel,
*edition record (no. 1465)
illustrated with a photograph
by Larger*
Undated
28 x 18.7 cm
Archives Nationales
de France, Paris

_Cat. 251

_Cat. 258

_Cat. 97

Although Blot is evasive as to the precise date when he met Camille ("around 1900"), in three different accounts he never budges on the fact that he initially bought, in quick succession, a group of two sculptures, *Imploration* and *Fortune* (or *Fortune* and *Imploration*, depending on the account), and then, some time later, the others at different times. One finds this order in his memoirs (1934),[20] in the letter to Mathias Morhardt (1935),[21] and in his long letter to Gustave Leblanc-Barbedienne in 1936 (cat. 249), in which he explains the circumstances of the purchase and casting of the different pieces: "When I was taken by my friend

G. Geffroy to see the great artist Camille Claudel . . . I first bought from her the figure *Imploration* in its original size (roughly half life-size) . . . The second piece (which G. Geffroy so liked) was *Fortune*." One should note that these two works are at the top of the list of pieces by Camille Claudel in Blot's commercial catalogue (*The Implorer*, no. 1465; *Fortune*, no. 1752; cat. 250–58[22]), but it has been shown that in certain cases the order of the numbers given to the illustrations or plates in a publisher's collection can be significant pointers as to the order in which the collection was acquired.[23] *Fortune* (cat. 251 and 92 A, p. 260) was not finished until 1904 (Salon d'Automne, no. 1730). One can therefore presume that Blot bought *The Implorer* (cat. 250 and 84 A, p. 190) a little earlier,[24] but not much. As Bruno Gaudichon and Anne Rivière have pointed out, in 1902 Camille had sold another cast directly to Captain Tissier, for

Cat. 252

Cat. 253

Cat. 81

a friend of his.[25] The first trace of business relations between the sculptor and Blot dates from 1902[26] and the first letters exchanged between Camille and her dealer and founder seem to date from 1904. It is in the letter written in autumn 1904 that the artist first mentions a reduction made by Blot: "Do not forget that I am swooning waiting for the arrival of my reduction."[27] This may well be the beginning of the production of *The Implorer*, since the purchase of *Fortune* is first attested to in the letter written in March–April 1905, in which Camille herself, having thanked Geffroy for having brought Blot to her studio, wrote, "I have just seen Blot, we have agreed on terms . . . He has bought *Fortune* and *Thought*."[28] The purchase of *Fortune*, at any rate, constitutes a fixed point around which one can attempt to situate the other transactions.

The next to appear in correspondence[29] are: *The Siren* (cat. 258 and 97, p. 265) in April 1905 ("The siren is ready, you can send someone for it"[30]); a "small kneeling figure" in autumn 1905, which may possibly have been *Deep Thought* (cat. 253 and 81) rather than *The Implorer*;[31] and *Abandon* (cat. 256, 94 A; cat. 95, p. 279) and *Les Causeuses* in autumn 1905 ("I have an admirable montage of Les Causeuses 1st style which are not in circulation (300 f. 4 figures)"[32]); and lastly a "small head" "that I am giving to you for all the trouble you are taking."[33] *The Waltz* (cat. 257 and 67, p. 264), still with Siot-Decauville in March–April 1905,[34] is listed in the 1905 exhibition as being produced by Blot.[35]

One should bear in mind that Blot could buy isolated works in addition to producing editions. This is perhaps the meaning of the letter from Camille on March 16, 1902 advising Captain Tissier to go to

Cat. 252

GALERIE EUG. BLOT
Fireside Group by
C. Claudel, *edition record (no. 1778) illustrated with a photograph by Larger*
Undated
28 x 18.7 cm
Archives Nationales
de France, Paris

Cat. 253

GALERIE EUG. BLOT
Intimacy by Camille
Claudel, *edition record (no. 1788) illustrated with a photograph by Larger*
Undated
28 x 18.7 cm
Archives Nationales
de France, Paris

Cat. 81

CAMILLE CLAUDEL
Deep Thought
[1898]
Master model, bronze,
for the edition by Eugène
Blot, about 1905?
23.5 x 21 x 27.5 cm
Musée Sainte-Croix, Poitiers

Cat. 254

Cat. 255

Cat. 256

Cat. 94 A

Blot's to see a "Head of a Brigand" (*Giganti*?), which he is showing "with orders to let it go for 600 F."[36] This would explain why this work is mentioned in Blot's account to Barbedienne (if indeed it was the *Neapolitan Bust*[37]) but never appears in the list of editions. After 1905, Blot continued to exhibit in his gallery in rue de Richepanse works by Camille that he had not cast (the "onyx and bronze" version of *The Wave* in the 1905 exhibition,[38] and the original marble of *La Petite Châtelaine* in 1907[39]).

Reconstructed in this context, the unfolding of events is logical. Blot opened a gallery at 5 boulevard de la Madeleine in 1900 to sell works in a different way from his industrial production in the rue des Archives (fig. 72, p. 268). However, he ran into financial difficulties that obliged him to auction part of his collection of paintings and very probably reconsider his expenditures. He certainly did not simultaneously sign contracts with all the artists he mentions. It is also logical that, having undertaken to buy the Claudel works, he would have organized an exhibition of her work as soon as possible (1905)

(cat. 225, p. 269) to commercially "launch" his editions. His acquisitions of models for editions were very probably spread over a very short period: of the fourteen works we are certain he actually produced editions of, only four were missing from the 1905 exhibition. In addition to the two *Busts of women*, there was above all *The Age of Maturity* (in the 1907 exhibition[40]) (fig. 48) and *Aurora* (included in the

Cat. 94 A

Camille Claudel
Abandon
1905
Reduction of the marble, bronze, edition by Eugène Blot
Early 1905
43 x 36 x 19 cm
Musée Sainte-Croix, Poitiers

Cat. 254

Galerie Eug. Blot
Perseus by Camille Claudel, *edition record illustrated with a photograph by Larger*
Undated
15.9 x 10.2 cm
Archives Nationales de France, Paris

Cat. 255

Galerie Eug. Blot
Bust Aurora by C. Claudel, *edition record (no. 1864) illustrated with a photograph by Larger?*
Undated
28 x 18.7 cm
Archives Nationales de France, Paris

Cat. 256

Galerie Eug. Blot
Group Abandon by C. Claudel, *edition record (no. 1784) illustrated with a photograph by Larger*
Undated
28 x 18.7 cm
Archives Nationales de France, Paris

_Fig. 72

1908 exhibition[41]) (cat. 255, p. 267). Until 1907 Blot and Camille were still hoping the state would commission a bronze of *The Age of Maturity*, and he was unable to acquire the plaster of *Aurora*, which belonged to Thaulow, until the Thaulow auction on May 1 and 6, 1907.[42]

In all, the number of Camille's works produced by Blot, which are precisely documented by the archives of their sale to Barbedienne or indicated in old sources, comes to a total of fourteen (see the table, p. 273). Even if he had had more success, Blot could hardly have done more. The acquisition of pieces stopped in 1907, and in the six ensuing years before Camille was committed to an asylum, she produced nothing more. As regards earlier works,

there are good reasons why Blot did not handle them. It was clearly not his policy to deal with portraits, due no doubt to the circumstantial nature of this type of work. As for the others, *Giganti*, *The Psalm* and *La Petite Châtelaine* had been ordered in bronze by Baron Alphonse de Rothschild.[43] *Wounded Niobid* was a state commission, so the rights were not acquirable. *The Wave* and the rights to it had been bought by Henri Fontaine and Blot only exhibited the "onyx and bronze" copy financed by Fenaille. Every time there was the slightest doubt as to the ownership of rights due to the circumstances of the sale (and as to the ownership of the plaster model), Blot abstained, preferring to concentrate on works for which he was sure he had free rein. The few exceptions to this are *The Implorer* (Gruet cast 1899), *The Waltz*, bought for an edition by Siot-Deauville, the *Head of the Old Man* from *The Age of Maturity* group (cast by François Rudier; cat. 70, p. 186) and *The Age of Maturity* (cast by Thiébaut, 1902). Again these exceptions are easily explained. For the bronzes prior to *The Implorer* and *The Age of Maturity*, Tissier, who commissioned them, had dealt directly with Camille and she had kept the model. For *The Waltz*, Blot duly acquired the rights, probably in late 1905.[44]

OWNERSHIP OF THE MODEL, OWNERSHIP OF THE RIGHTS[45]

We will probably never know the precise terms of Blot's agreement with the artist in 1905. Indeed, to the historian's despair, Blot wrote in 1937, at the

_Fig. 72

Eugène Blot Galerie,
in VAUXCELLES
Bibliothèque Marguerite-
Durand, Paris

time he was selling his editions to Barbedienne: "In all the time I have been a producer of editions of sculpture, that is, for nigh on sixty years . . . I have habitually, like most of my colleagues, destroyed many contracts after ten years. We never had to show them and I will have you note that the auctioneers (it was almost always M. Lecoq) auctioned our models without having us produce the slightest contract. The very fact that we were producing editions was the best proof that we had the right . . . I understand your scruples and will not insist if you are so determined. I will only regret this for the magnificent work of Camille Claudel, which to my mind it was interesting to continue to produce . . . It is known that I have remained the sole owner of almost all her works . . . I cannot even remember, since it is over twenty years ago that Claudel was locked up in Avignon, if we entered into proper contracts."[46]

When he discusses *The Age of Maturity* in his memoirs, Blot specifically states that he bought it outright.[47] Barbedienne, for his part, writes, "I have decided to accept your kind offer that I reproduce certain works that you have acquired outright and of which you possess the bronze models."[48] Barbedienne is of course above all trying to establish in writing that he will have no royalties to pay, and explicitly stipulates, "You are the owner not only of the models in bronze but also of the reproduction rights and . . . I am exempt of any royalties to the artists in paying you the bonus stipulated in the contract for each piece sold."[49] The contract drawn up between the two in 1937 (cat. 259, 260 and 261) clearly shows that there were no royalties to be paid

Cat. 225

Cat. 260

to either Camille or her family. There is no trace of payment of royalties, by either Barbedienne or Blot, in any archive document concerning Camille directly or indirectly.

The question as to whether Blot may have been a founder as well as a dealer has never been fully elucidated. It is possible that the first Blot company may have comprised a foundry: a vague mention in the *Calepin des propriétés bâties* does indeed seem to indicate, at 28 rue des Archives, in a pencil correction concerning the premises bought by Blot, a "foundry" opposite the description of one of the workshops in use.[50] However, one cannot assume from this tenuous

Cat. 225
—
*Exposition d'œuvres
de Camille Claudel
et Bernard Hoetger,
du 4 au 16 décembre 1905*
Catalogue
21.2 x 15 cm
Bibliothèque Nationale
de France, Paris

Cat. 260
—
*List of models turned
over by Eugène Blot to
maison Barbedienne
in 1937 and 1938*
1937–38
1 sheet, 27 x 20.8 cm
Archives Nationales
de France, Paris

evidence that Eugène Blot cast his "artists'" bronzes himself. Of course, the state commission for *Wounded Niobid* in 1907, the execution of which Camille entrusted to Blot and which bears the inscription "Eugène Blot Paris," would tend to support this interpretation. But the archives of the sale of rights to Barbedienne seem to indicate the contrary. They mention Rudier[51] as subcontractor. When Barbedienne points out that the second size of *The Implorer* is missing from the models delivered, Blot explains that it "was I remember at the Rudier company, who cast several for me, when I had them transported to you; the same goes for the no. 2 *Beethoven*, which was at Rudier with my bust of *Wagner*."[52] He adds, concerning *The Age of Maturity*, "Having immediately sold 4 casts I have neither the photograph nor the exact dimensions, which are those of the model cast by Rudier and which is around 1 m 20 cm long."[53]

THE "ABANDONMENT" OF THE BRONZES

Blot's move to rue Richepanse in 1906 after the relative failure of his limited edition bronzes and his subsequent concentration on picture dealing does not, however, imply that he gave up these editions. His new gallery had two windows on the street in which he could "put his limited edition collectors' bronzes on show"[54] next to his canvases. To publicize his new gallery, he organized a Daumier exhibition.

It seems that he never entirely stopped producing bronzes, an industry which, during economic hard times, he had subsisted on by producing lamp accessories.[55] Blot seems to have kept the workshop on rue des Archives until he died and, in his gallery on boulevard de la Madeleine, one could also see lamps and chandeliers by Blanchot and by Follot, and by "ring boxes, dishes, electric lamps, small clocks, vases, inkwells, statuettes, animals, groups and busts and artistic curios of all kinds in bronze, pewter and silver, all interesting, ingenious and charming and original in style."[56] Blot explains to Barbedienne that for "Cinderella—woman sitting by a fireplace" and "the yule log," "I sold a great many, above all of the former, by placing a red light bulb behind the logs in these fireplaces to turn them into night lamps" (cat. 249, 252, 253, 80 and 88, pp. 266 and 240). In his memoirs he talks about exchanges with other picture dealers, from whom he received pictures in return for electrical objects.[57] Félicien Champsaur gave him three Forain drawings for an electric lamp. Rosenberg *père* exchanged a Hoetger for a Bonnard.[58] In 1932, he spoke to Camille about the bronze *The Implorer*, which was still his gallery's "center-piece." The letterhead he used in 1936 for his correspondence with Barbedienne still gives his address as rue Richepanse and "workshop 84 rue des Archives." Blot, who wrote to Barbedienne, "In all the time I have been a producer of editions of sculpture, for almost sixty years now," must therefore still have considered himself one. One can thus assume that the phrase "when I stopped doing bronzes"[59] means rather that he had stopped buying models but was continuing to sell casts. Why deprive himself of this continuing source of income? Even after he had sold the rights to Barbedienne, Blot was still entertaining the idea of continuing to sell them because he asked his colleague, "There is still a question on which I would like to be informed, at what price would you deliver to me the work which I frequently sell, the Claudels, the *Beethoven* and *Wagner* bust [by Jouant], for instance, and above all the medium size *Imploration* No. 1b."[60]

EUGÈNE BLOT AND CAMILLE CLAUDEL

"You have done," Camille wrote to Gustave Geffroy, "everything you could for me, particularly by sending me M. Blot, who has been of great help to me,"[61] and she continued to hold him in high esteem as she did no other. The tone of her letters to him is unique. Never does she use the reproachful or accusing tone she did with so many others. Even when she is asking for money, her words are full of familiarity and humor, even if this humor is, as always with her, very sardonic "Try to bring me a client, I am in great need of money to pay my October rent, if not I shall be woken one of these mornings by the amiable Adonis Pruneaux, my usual bailiff, who will come and seize my possessions with his usual delicacy. Of course, he will only be able to seize the artist herself, an operation which, for me, would have nothing attractive about it."[62] She describes herself as "his devoted supplier of sculpture";[63] readily beseeches him: "Unfortunate dealer of objets d'art, tremble at the sight of this ill-fated writing that brings back so many terrible memories to you . . . the sight of the Siren on view in your gallery whets her ferocious appetite";[64] or feigns outrage: "Monsieur and venerated patron . . . You asked me the different dates of the works you listed. What horror! Do you want to know my age!"[65] But only feigns it. She thought of Blot as a kind of protective, benevolent, affect onate genius

Camille, who fell out with one of her most steadfast supporters, Mathias Morhardt, because he was a Dreyfusard, never did so with Blot. Yet, as Gustave Kahn recalls, "It was he who at the height of the Dreyfus Affair commissioned the good sculptor Jouant to make a bust of Zola and thus played his part in propaganda."[66] And, in return, Blot considered himself her friend: "I have followed her as dealer and friend since the day, around 1900, my excellent friend Gustave Geffroy took me to her studio on quai Bourbon . . . I was proud to produce her work and happy to be of service to her, as she sold very little, and such superb works so cheaply . . . but I could count on friendship, and Geffroy knew this, he who had sent me to her to get her to accept his kind offers, such as the Blanqui monument."[67]

In his last letter to Camille, dated September 3, 1932, which Camille never received, the publisher casts a melancholic eye back over the years they worked together, and is manifestly as fond of Camille as ever: "It should never be forgotten that into the scheming world of sculpture, Rodin, you and perhaps three or four others introduced authenticity . . . The copy of the first cast [of *The Implorer*], enriched with your signature, is one of the centerpieces of my gallery. It fills me with inexpressible emotion every time I look at it. It is as if I were seeing you again. The half-open lips, the trembling nostrils, the light in the eyes, all that cries out everything that is most mysterious in life. With you, one was going to forsake the world of false appearances for that of thought. What genius! The word is not strong enough. How could you have deprived us of such beauty . . . Write to me, take this helping hand I am holding out to you. I have never ceased to be your friend."[68]

Appendix: Editions Produced by Blot

The chart opposite is divided into two parts. The first is an analytical synthesis of the information in the archive documents concerning Blot's sale of works to Barbedienne (1937–38, ANF), cross-referenced with the information in the catalogues raisonnés and the catalogues of Blot's exhibitions in 1905, 1907 and 1908. It should be emphasized, however, that the indications given in these three catalogues concerning the number of casts is totally unreliable and therefore cannot be used as a scientific basis. The second part lists the works which Blot is thought to have produced editions of, although there are no reliable documents to confirm this.

In compiling this chart I have also used the information collected by Florence Rionnet for the latest version of the RIVIÈRE / GAUDICHON / GHANASSIA catalogue raisonné, and which could be seen as its first draft. It is also the result of a detailed discussion with Antoinette Le Normand-Romain.

Concerning the identification of works with ambiguous titles, I have for a long time thought that the work entitled "Bust of Old Woman" was *La Vieille Hélène*. I finally chose the title *Head of an Old Woman* from *The Age of Maturity* group, since no "Blot" cast of *La Vieille Hélène* has ever been identified and there exists a post-1905 cast bearing the inscription "FUMIÈRE ET CIE SUCRS / THIEBAUT FRES / PARIS." It is therefore highly unlikely that Blot decided to cast it at the same time. On the other hand, the heads from *The Age of Maturity* group bearing the Blot stamp are documented, and it seems that one cannot rule them out from the confusion between *Head of an Old Woman* and *Head of an Old Man*, when they are cast separately: I therefore suggest that in the case of *Old Woman* and *Old Man* Blot is in fact referring to the same head taken from *The Age of Maturity*.

The bronze of the *Wounded Niobid* does not appear in this table, even though it bears Blot's stamp, because it was a one-off and not an edition.

Title	Blot Exhibitions	Blot No.	Number of Casts (sold / total)	Delivery to Barbedienne	Archive sources	Rivière Gaudichon Catalogue	Catalogue R.-M. Paris
1 Abandon (Sakuntala, Vertumnus and Pomona) large format small format	1905, no. 9 1908, no. 3	1784	13 / 25 14 / 25	1937 1938	Letter from Blot to Barbedienne, December 17, 1936; catalogue annotated by Blot; letter from Jacques Blot to Barbedienne, February 2, 1937, transported to rue de Lancry (ANF)	23	62
2 The Age of Maturity	1907, no. 1 1908, no. 1	no	4 / 3	1938	Letter from Blot to Barbedienne, December 17, 1936 (ANF)	45	42
3 Les Bavardes or Les Causeuses	1905, no. 11	no	6 or 10	no	Blot auction, Hôtel Drouot, June 2, 1933, no. 111, edition of six; letter from Blot to Morhardt, September 21, 1935, edition of ten sold out (AMR)	41	43
4 The Yule Log (Deep Thought, Intimacy)	1905, no. 6	1788	10 / 25	?	Letter from Blot to Barbedienne, December 17, 1936 catalogue annotated by Blot (ANF)	57	53
5 Bust of Aurora	1908, no. 5	1864	6 / 25	1938	Letter from Blot to Barbedienne, December 17, 1936, card annotated by Blot (ANF)	63	34
6 Cinderella (Fireside Dream)	1905, no. 4	1778	65 / unlimited	?	Letter from Blot to Barbedienne, December 17, 1936; card annotated by Blot (ANF)	61	55
7 Fortune	1905, no. 5 1908, no. 10	1752	15 + 1 / 50	1938	Letter from Blot to Barbedienne, December 17, 1936 (ANF); card annotated by Blot; Rivière/Gaudichon/ Ghanassia 2001 (plus one belonging to Blot)	58	56
8 Imploration (Youth, The Implorer) large format medium format small format	1905, nos. 1–2 1908, no. 2	1465	5 / 10 5 / 20 59 / 100	1937 1938	Letter from Blot to Barbedienne, December 17, 1936 (ANF); card annotated by Blot; letter from Jacques Blot to Barbedienne, February 2, 1937, transported to rue de Lancry (ANF)	44	41
9 Perseus[69]	1905, no. 3 1908, no. 9	no	6 / 25	1938	Letter from Blot to Barbedienne, December 17, 1936; erroneously entitled Thought in the lists typewritten by Barbedienne; card annotated by Blot (ANF)	54	57
10 Siren (Flute Player)	1905, no. 8	1792	6 / 25	1938	Letter from Blot to Barbedienne, December 17, 1936; card annotated by Blot (ANF)	64	60
11 The Waltz large format small format	1905, no. 10 1908, no. 4	1860	24 / 50 4 / 25	1938 (both)	Letter from Blot to Barbedienne, December 17, 1936; card annotated by Blot (ANF)	33	28
12 Bust of Old Woman (study for The Age of Maturity) = Bust of Old Man?	1905, no. 7 1908, no. 6?	no	? / 50 (1905 exhib.)	no	Letter from Blot to Barbedienne, December 17, 1936 (ANF). The title Old Woman, taken from The Age of Maturity, appears only in the 1905 catalogue, while in the 1908 catalogue the only head cast from The Age of Maturity is Old Man. I believe them to be the same work. A cast-iron copy by Blot no. 1 cited in Paris 2000, no. 40	45	40
13 Bust Woman = Young Girl with a Chignon? (Head of a Negress)	1908, no. 7	no	? / 25?	no	Not in the list Blot gave to Barbedienne. Identified here with Young Girl with a Chignon, including one bronze bearing the inscription Eug. Blot, no. 1 in the Musée Rodin	70	24
14 Bust Woman = Study for Hamadryad, or Head of a Child?	1908, no. 8	no	? / 25?	no	Not in the list Blot gave to Barbedienne. It could be Study for Hamadryad of which a Blot no. 2 cast appeared in 1979 at a sale at the Hôtel Drouot on February 28	50	46
15 Neapolitan Bust (Giganti?)	no	no	Not cast?	no	Letter from Blot to Barbedienne, December 17, 1936 (ANF)	19	16

Casts figuring neither in the archives of the transfer to Barbedienne nor in the 1905, 1907 and 1908 exhibition catalogues

1 Study for the Burghers of Calais	no	no	?	no	Not in the list Blot gave to Barbedienne. A bronze bearing the inscription "E. Blot no. 1" is identified as being in a private collection in both catalogues raisonnés	17	12
2 Study for a Hand	no	no	?	no	Not in the list Blot gave to Barbedienne. A bronze bearing inscription "E. Blot" (but apparently without a number), former Louise Vetch Collection	34	15
3 Clotho	no	no	?	no	Not in the list Blot gave to Barbedienne. Totally hypothetical edition based on an allusion in Blot's letter to Morhardt (September 21, 1935), Rivière/Gaudichon/Ghanassia 2001. It may in fact have been the head of Old Woman (see above)	37	31

"HE NEVER LOVED ANYONE BUT YOU"

A *NIOBID* WOUNDED BY AN ARROW   Antoinette Le Normand-Romain

"Quai de Béthune, in this picturesque and stately area of old Paris, against the peaceful backdrop of the Seine, which drags with it the smell of the apples filling the boats, Mlle Claudel is working on her piece for the Salon.

When I enter the ground-floor room which an artist's caprice has turned into a studio, I at first make out only a vague form bent over a marble and chestnut hair tied with a cherry ribbon.

'You've caught me at work; excuse the dust on my blouse, but I sculpt my marbles myself. I could not bear to hand my work over to the "zeal" of a marble carver,' the young artist says as she puts down her file.

'It's hard work! Modeling clay is tiring enough for a woman, so I can imagine what working marble is like. You must be the only woman, Mademoiselle, to dare sculpt marble?'

'What else can I do? It's a matter of conscience: I will only deliver a work I'm completely satisfied with.'

'This is your piece for the Salon?'

'Yes,' the artist replies, turning the turntable a little. *Vertumnus and Pomona*."[1]

Gabriel Reval's text, with a photograph of Camille at work—complete with ribbon in her hair (fig. 73, p. 276)—is the only document that gives an idea of the time it took to produce the marble: at least two years, as the picture was published on May 1, 1903 and the marble was finished just in time for the 1905 Salon des Artistes Français, which opened on May 1. "I am still coughing and sneezing as I angrily polish the group that has destroyed my tranquility," Camille wrote to Geffroy in early April. "It is with teary eyes and convulsive coughing that I am finishing the hair of Vertumnus and Pomona. Let's hope that despite the various accidents they will be finished in a logical manner and as befitting perfect lovers, God willing. I am fed up with blowing on the sculpture while waiting

Cat. 93
CAMILLE CLAUDEL
Vertumnus and Pomona
Marble, carved by
Camille Claudel, 1905
92 x 80 x 42.5 cm
Musée Rodin, Paris

enough. A few weeks later she had to sell a painting that Henry Lerolle had given her: "I know you will forgive me, you who know the panic of artists at bay."[4]

The struggle with hard substances such as marble and onyx, her favorite materials for a few years, was undoubtedly a means of exorcising her inner demons. Encouraged by the success of *Perseus* and the understanding she received from the Countess de Maigret (see "A Patron: Countess de Maigret," pp. 250–59), but perhaps also because she already no longer felt capable of creating a completely new work, she decided to realize an old dream: the transposition of *Sakuntala* (cat. 47, p. 105), a commission which she had so hoped to obtain in 1888. Following *The Wave* (cat. 79, p. 242) and *Les Causeuses* (cat. 77, p. 236), and like *Clotho* (fig. 45), this marble illustrates Camille's very particular interest in the medium. Whereas Rodin and other sculptors influenced by him played on the material's raw aspect, Camille gave it a highly finished appearance and, by polishing it "for a long time and carefully,"[5] obtained a golden patina similar to Renaissance marbles. The "lamento d'amour" group,[6] a "work of the highest order in which feminine weakness huddles up in the moved tenderness of man,"[7] had some success in 1905, above all because

for 1,000-francs notes."[2] Madame de Maigret acquired the marble (cat. 93), but it must certainly have been a costly undertaking for Camille. The previous autumn, she had repeatedly written to Blot asking for money and, although Rodin paid her 200 francs a month in 1905 and 1906,[3] as he had done in 1902 (cat. 222), in March 1905 "she was having great difficulty paying the rent, the bailiffs had taken her furniture, etc." Convinced he was doing what Rodin wished, Joanny Peytel advanced her the 326 francs 95 centimes she owed her landlord, to "avert her imminent misfortune" (cat. 224). But this was not

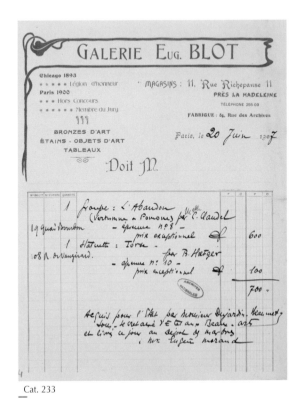

_Cat. 233

of its lyricism. Maurice Hamel, for instance, enthusiastically praised this "pure masterpiece" in which one feels "not the chisel of the sculptor's assistant but the hand of the artist."[8] And Paul Claudel was one of the few to draw attention to the quality of its execution: ". . . the marble of the 1905 Salon, so silky, just like skin, that it gladdens the hands with the eye."[9]

The new version of the group, differing from the 1888 plaster in the drapery passing through the legs of the male figure and in the young woman's braided hair, was also transposed into bronze by Eugène Blot, who had acquired the reproduction rights (two sizes: H. 63 and 42 cm). This was a third model, a third smaller than the marble, undoubtedly made from the plaster that had served as model for the latter and that was itself a half-size reduction of the 1888 model. A copy 63 cm tall was exhibited at the Salon d'Automne in 1905, then by Blot in the *Claudel-Hoetger* exhibition in his gallery on boulevard de la Madeleine, where the bronze had almost more success than the marble: out of the twenty-five that were planned, eighteen casts of the large model were made. The eighth was acquired by the fine arts administration (cat. 95 and 223). The title of the Blot bronze was *Abandon*, a simpler title than the previous one, more easily understandable by the public and corresponding more closely to the reality of Camille's life.

When it was transposed into marble, *Sakuntala* had been rebaptized *Vertumnus and Pomona*, after the heroes of one of Ovid's *Metamorphoses*. Rodin had on several occasions, and even during the time he and Camille were close, sought titles for his own works in Ovid's text. Camille delved into it in turn and chose the end of the fable, when Vertumnus, renouncing the guise of an old man that he had taken to approach Pomona without frightening her, appears to her "as brilliant as the god of the sun when he triumphs over the clouds" and conquers the nymph.

_Cat. 233
GALERIE EUG. BLOT
*Invoice for the purchase
by the state of Abandon
(bronze) by Camille Claudel*
Dated June 20, 1907
1 sheet, 27.5 x 21.4 cm
Archives Nationales
de France, Paris

_Cat. 95
CAMILLE CLAUDEL
Abandon
1905
Reduction of the marble,
bronze
63 x 67 x 24 cm
Musée des Beaux-Arts,
Cambrai

Should one see a fit of pride in this representation of a united and confident couple harking back to Rodin and the 1880s? Or was this, as the gratuitous loops and curlicues of certain capitals in the letter she wrote to Florence Jeans on November 8, 1886 (cat. 187, p. 107)[10] seem to suggest, her illness inexorably enclosing her in a circle whose beginning and end join? Convinced she was the victim of organized persecution, she increased her tirades against "old Rodin who, as usual, is trying to keep me away from Paris for the opening . . . The Old Weasel always making sure I don't have any money,"[11] and her figure group's exhibition at the Salon seems to have triggered a genuine persecution mania that she expresses openly in her correspondence: "M. Rodin (whom you know) has amused himself this year by cutting off my livelihood everywhere, having forced me to leave the Salon de la Nationale due to the horrible things he did to me."[12] Or again: "I know the malevolent hand working behind the scenes to divest me of all my friendships, all the goodwill, so that I'm forced to beg him for aid and again make him look like a benefactor. The means he employs are so well spun, so invisible, so indirect that it is impossible to prove anything at all."[13]

At the same time, another artist who had been part of Rodin's close entourage some ten years earlier, Medardo Rosso, was also accusing him of the basest villainy: "There are two categories of madmen. Those one locks away . . . and those with whom one has to deal on a daily basis. Clairvoyant rogues, well knowing the impact of their deeds. Committing crime after crime, legally. [There follows a list of the things he

_Cat. 35

reproaches him for.] I foresaw his fraud. Tell me who you frequent and I will tell you who you are. That has always been seen to be true. I always resented his idiocy, the indecency of his never even replying to my note. At the Salon, when he came toward me, offering me his hand, greeting me, I turned my back on him."[14] Like Camille, but with one notable exception, *Ecce Puer*, Rosso was by now almost incapable of creating. The pieces he exhibited at the 1904 Salon d'Automne (where he refused to shake hands with Rodin), in Vienna in 1905 and in London in 1906 were old works, complemented in Paris by the *Torso* which Rodin had given him and photographs of works by Rodin, including *Balzac*. In 1904, there was also an important series of Rodin exhibitions in Germany (Düsseldorf, Dresden, Weimar, Leipzig), while the large *Thinker* was shown in London, then at the Salon de la Nationale in Paris. The two major fragmentary figures, *Ariadne* and *Cybele*, which Rodin exhibited the following year, again at the Nationale, are among the works that opened the way for twentieth-century sculpture. They foreshadow the *Walking Man* (1907) which, finally liberated from any concerns linked to subject matter, can be considered the manifesto of a profound renewal. Rodin was indeed one of those artists whose late works give meaning to their entire lifetime. At the same time, with Maillol's *Mediterranean* a return to Classicism was evident at the 1905 Salon d'Automne in the use of simpler forms and a rejection of violent feeling, rather than in references to mythology. For an artist whose energy was beginning to wane, the comparison was harsh indeed.

Although slightly younger than Maillol, Camille remained faithful to the passionate symbolism of the closing years of the nineteenth century, giving her last testament to it in *Wounded Niobid*. In April 1905, she had turned down the commission for the *Monument to Blanqui* that Mirbeau and Geffroy had obtained for her (and that was then given to Maillol, who produced *Action Enchained*). "First, I am too tired and life-size statues wear me out; second, it [the statue] is not paid enough given my way of working, which always costs me a lot of money."[15] *Vertumnus and Pomona* had been the last effort of a great artist.

Her chronic lack of money, despite help from her parents and Rodin, and her poor health now prevented her from seeing an entirely new work through to completion. She also tried yet again to obtain a commission for *The Age of Maturity* from the fine arts administration.[16] On March 8, 1906, Eugène Blot intervened on her behalf: it would be "one of the finest clauses [of your testament as minister]—artistically speaking—and one of the most <u>necessary</u>, I can assure you, and you would be once more doing a fine and good deed" (cat. 226). An order for the commission of a "statuette in plaster," for a fee of 1,500 francs, followed on April 26 (cat. 227). Camille was informed on April 30, Eugène Blot on May 9. Camille delayed replying, as she was "sick from the consequences of the bad treatment I have endured and from lack of the care my health necessitates." She proposed 500 francs more, for an "original sketch in clay" that had cost her dearly because, she said, she used "a French model of rare beauty who made me pay a lot."[17] Her request was refused, and on May 30 she accepted the 1,500 francs and demanded an advance (cat. 228). As was customary, an inspector of fine arts was sent to report on her progress. On June 30, Armand Dayot, who had taken an interest in her since *The Waltz*, declared that he had seen "the almost finished model" of a *Wounded Niobid*, "full of remarkable qualities. I consider," he continues, "that it should be accepted urgently and that the artist, who is in the direst need, should be granted an advance of 800 francs."[18] The sum was authorized on July 9 (cat. 229). On October 6, Camille notified Dujardin-Beaumetz that "on M. Armand Dayot's choice [she had] executed a Niobid mortally wounded by an arrow" (cat. 230). She delivered it to the Dépôt des Marbres on October 16,[19] and was paid the remainder of her fee two days later.

A bronze was commissioned by ministerial order the following year, on February 15, 1907, for the sum of 3,000 francs (cat. 231). Having said that she hoped to deliver the figure in mid-March, she declared that the commissioning letter had been stolen "by people used to crafty tactics and fraud" and that she had not been able to retrieve the plaster she needed to cast the bronze. She openly accused Rodin of all these obstacles, which no doubt existed only in her imagination: "It apparently depends on him. What's more, he bragged several times about having the state under his thumb and being more powerful than a minister. And so I have not the slightest chance of succeeding in my procedures as I refused outright to see him knowing full well what is going on and the reasons why this gentleman wants to see me. Having tried by every possible means to get his hands on my ideas, on different sketches he took a liking to and having encountered fierce resistance from me, he

Cat. 231

Cat. 238

wants to forcibly, by the misery with which he knows how to overwhelm me, reduce me to delivering what he wants, this is his usual means. This is the infamous exploitation to which this great genius has to resort to conquer ideas he lacks" (cat. 232). The undersecretary of state, Dujardin-Beaumetz, did everything he could to reassure her. She was able to withdraw the plaster from the Dépôt des Marbres in September, and announced that the bronze, by Blot, had been finished "for a long time" (cat. 235). Eugène Morand was then

Cat. 231

MINISTÈRE DE L'INSTRUCTION
PUBLIQUE, DES BEAUX-ARTS
ET DES CULTES
*Purchase order for the
Wounded Niobid (bronze)
by Camille Claudel*
Dated February 15, 1907
1 sheet, 31 × 21 cm
Archives Nationales
de France, Paris

Cat. 238

ARMAND DAYOT
*Report to the Ministre
de l'Instruction publique,
des Beaux-Arts et des Cultes
on the* Wounded Niobid
(bronze) by Camille Claudel
Dated December 15, 1907
1 sheet, 31 × 21 cm
Archives Nationales
de France, Paris

charged with inspecting it but, on October 15, he refused to do so as he had received "postcards of such coarseness and envelopes containing such malodorous rubbish that I wish to have nothing to do with Mlle Claudel, who has conducted herself in the same way and at the same time with M. Rodin. Although these vile acts were of course anonymous, the similarity of the writing and the coincidence of their posting following my letters clearly point to Mlle Claudel" (cat. 236). Armand Dayot returned to Camille's studio and on December 15 wrote his report to the director of fine arts. "The work is beautiful and, looking at it, I could only rejoice in having found it ready-made in the artist's studio and in not having ordered a new sculpture which, at present, would be impossible for her to execute," he admitted (cat. 238, p. 281). The bronze was registered at the Dépôt des Marbres on December 20, 1907 (cat. 98, p. 282, and cat. 239 and 240).

Just as *Perseus* (cat. 86, pp. 250–52) had been an adaptation of the male figure of *The Waltz* (cat. 64, pp. 112, 114–16), and *Fortune* (cat. 92 A, p. 260) a reworking of the female figure of the same group, the *Niobid* is quite simply *Sakuntala* or *Pomona* detached from her male partner. Her isolation brings out Rodin's influence, and if Camille was accusing him of having stolen his idea, was this not precisely because the figure clearly showed her debt to him? The position of the legs, the forward-hanging arms and the head leaning to one side so that the other shoulder is higher situate the figure midway between *The Shade* (cat. 140, p. 109) and *Meditation*.

Meditation, modeled around 1881–82,[20] appears in the tympanum of *The Gates of Hell* as the small

Damned on the far right hiding her face with her bent arm and with her weight all on one leg to keep her balance. At that time she had neither feet nor a left arm, but a few years later Rodin finished her by making some modifications (cat. 151, p. 283). He did two variations, differing particularly in the treatment of the head and the presence of a tear under the left breast in the second, and used the figure for his pen drawing illustrating the poem "Beauty" in Paul Gallimard's copy of Baudelaire's *Les Fleurs du mal* (fig. 74), whose first lines are inscribed on the base of *I Am Beautiful* (cat. 141, p. 85). Camille witnessed the first phase of the figure's existence but it was the complete *Meditation* she remembered, as did for that matter Joseph Bernard in *Harmony* (1908–10) and Desbois in the allegory of *Painting* of the *Monument to Puvis de Chavannes* (1924), which he had just completed (Rodin had been awarded the commission but never finished it).

But *Meditation* continued to evolve. Around 1894, Rodin used it in several compositions (*Christ and Mary Magdalen, Constellation*), and above all in *Monument to Victor Hugo*, in which it first represented the Muse in Hugo's *Les Orientales*. In order to integrate it, he had to remove the outer side of the left leg, the left knee and the arms from a complete version of the figure (cat. 161 and fig. 75, p. 286). Hesitating over the position of the arms, he decided to enlarge it and exhibit it as it was in 1897 with the whole of the monument, but also on its own in Dresden and Stockholm: "The study of nature is complete, and I have put my every effort into rendering art as whole as possible. I consider this plaster one of my most finished, most probing works," he declared to Prince Eugene of Sweden on January 2, 1897.[21]

With this admittedly partial but in his view totally accomplished figure, Rodin was taking an entirely innovative direction, that of sculpture reduced to the essential by the removal of all redundant details. "Rodin's armless statues," Rilke wrote, "lack nothing necessary. One is before them as though before a whole, a finished whole that will tolerate no complement."[22] Morhardt understood this before Rilke and—how ironic!—did not hesitate to write in 1898 in his article on Camille Claudel that *Meditation*, *The Tragic Muse*, *Earth* and *Iris* "will mark a culminating point in the history of modern sculpture. They indeed prove that Rodin, who has always striven for a better and more complete realization of life, has at last received due reward for this patient quest. His eyes are now wide open"[23] (cat. 167, p. 287).

For Camille in 1907, on the other hand, recourse to an attribute, in this case an arrow in the right breast, remained indispensable to give her work meaning. After *Vertumnus and Pomona*, the *Niobid* with closed eyes, destabilized by the absence of man and infinitely moving in half life-size, is a way of admitting her inability to renew herself. It is a statement of defeat. Her career was over; never again would she who had received so much be capable of creating.

Fig. 74

AUGUSTE RODIN
Beauty
Pen and brown ink on a
copy of the first edition of
Baudelaire's *Fleurs du mal*,
formerly belonging to
Paul Gallimard, 1887–88
Musée Rodin, Paris

Fig. 75

Cat. 161

Fig. 75

AUGUSTE RODIN
Third model for the
Monument to Victor Hugo
1895
Plaster
Musée Rodin, Paris

Cat. 161

AUGUSTE RODIN
The Inner Voice
or *Meditation*
About 1894
Plaster
54 x 18 x 16 cm
Musée Rodin, Paris

Cat. 171

AUGUSTE RODIN
Meditation with Arms
After 1900
Bronze
158 x 78 x 66 cm
Fondation Pierre
Gianadda, Martigny

Cat. 167

AUGUSTE RODIN
The Inner Voice or
Meditation, large model
1896
Bronze
146 x 75.5 x 55 cm
Musée Rodin, Paris

Cat. 171

Cat. 167

CAMILLE'S EXILE, RODIN'S GLORY   Line Ouellet

CAMILLE AND PAUL

The last truly original piece that Camille produced and that has survived is a bust of her brother Paul, then just thirty-seven years old (cat. 96, p. 291). The time is September 1905 and Camille, now forty, had just returned from a trip to the Pyrenees with her brother. Paul, home on leave from his post as French vice-consul at Fuzhu in China, was getting over a terrible disappointment in love. Earlier that year, in April, Camille had exhibited *Vertumnus and Pomona* (cat. 93, pp. 274 and 277) at the Salon des Champs-Élysées, and Paul had just published his eulogistic article "Camille Claudel, Statuary" in *L'Occident*. The piece, an invaluable source of information on the artist, was reprinted in *L'Art décoratif* (cat. 244, p. 290) with forty-seven illustrations of Camille's works.

Camille had already produced three portraits of her brother before 1905: two busts, *Paul Claudel as a Child*, most probably executed from a photograph (cat. 30 and 19, p. 122) and *My Brother* (cat. 27, p. 123), and a drawing, *Paul Claudel Aged Twenty* (fig. 34). Apart from her sister Louise, whose bust she sculpted between 1886 and 1887, before her affair with Rodin became known, distancing her from her family until the couple's break-up, Paul was the only one she portrayed from childhood to maturity, a fact indicative of the importance of their relationship for Camille. The sober, classical treatment of *Paul Claudel Aged Thirty-Seven* (cat. 96, p. 291) fully brings out the personality of her younger brother, now a famous, respected author and a very determined, self-confident man. Camille has given Paul a slenderer neck than in real life, hence his rather haughty bearing. His features are both purified and emphasized, with a central axis running from the furrow between the eyebrows down the bridge of the nose and ending on the jutting chin, giving the model an almost stubborn air. An edition of six bronzes was cast, including the one in this exhibition.[1] This cast, acquired by the Musée Rodin in 1982, formerly belonged to the painter Maurice Denis. The surviving plaster (fig. 76, p. 291) is slightly different from the above mentioned bronzes, however. The shoulders have been removed here to show the bottom of the neck, and the hair is thicker on the left side of the head.

Cat. 108

WILLIAM ELBORNE
Camille Claudel at the Montdevergues public asylum at Montfavet
1929
Photograph, gelatin silver print
8 x 5.5 cm
Private collection

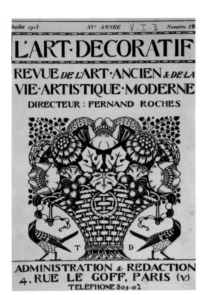

Paul and Camille's relationship was fundamental and had a decisive influence on their respective lives. With time a role reversal came about. Camille, four years older, had dragged him to Paris with her and had been the first to set out on the path of creation. After countless struggles, however, she gradually become the one in need, the one who waited, while her deep attachment to her brother never wavered in the slightest. Paul, on the other hand, would become increasingly famous both as a playwright and as a diplomat and in doing so gradually amassed the fortune that enabled him to buy the vast Château de Brangues in Isère in 1927. Camille had been confined inside the Montdevergues asylum near Avignon since 1914. The bust of *Paul Claudel Aged Thirty-Seven*, sculpted in 1905, in some respects closes the period during which brother and sister admired one another—or at least admired their respective works.

FROM ISOLATION TO EXILE

Camille's father, Louis-Prosper, was clearly concerned as early as 1904: "It appears we will be going to Gérardmer next month, invited by Marie, who has rented a chalet there for us to join her. Which is all very well but it will break my heart to leave Camille to her isolation. What a tragedy all these discussions and family discord is and a cause of immense sorrow for me. If you could help me restore harmony what a great service you would be doing me!"[2]

Louis-Prosper, whose pencil portrait (fig. 77) Camille drew in 1905, had always been her most faithful ally. He was most probably the one most affected by her gradual impoverishment and the deterioration of her mental health. Camille had shut herself off from the world. Her distrust of others had constantly increased, developing into a full-blown paranoia which eventually prevented her from leaving the studio on the quai de Bourbon on the Île de la Cité that she had been renting since 1899. In a letter to Paul written around 1909, she maintains she is being copied by other artists: "After the *Small Fireplace*, that year everywhere in Paris all one saw was fireplaces with a seated or reclining women, etc. The same goes for *The Age of Maturity*, they will all do it one after the other. Every time I put a piece into circulation millions

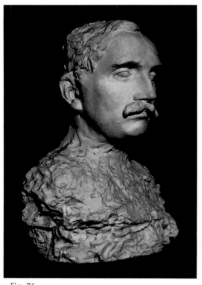

Fig. 76

Cat 96

Fig. 77

are made by foundries, molders, artists and dealers, and what do I get . . . 0 + 0 = 0" (cat. 242).

In 1909, Louis-Prosper, ever faithful to Camille, wrote to his son Paul, then back in Paris: "Until now nobody has wanted to take care of her. For ages now, I have been hoping your mother would go and see her and see to her linen and furniture—because I have never been able to get Camille to listen to me without bringing on sickening scenes . . . I would like Camille to come and see us from time to time. Your mother will not hear of it, but I wonder whether this might be a way of calming, even healing that enraged madwoman."[3]

At that time Camille was financially dependant on her family and friends. She had not exhibited at the Salon since 1905 and her last commission, *Wounded Niobid* (cat. 98, p. 282), was cast in bronze in September 1907. On September 5, 1909, Paul

wrote in his *Journal*: "In Paris Camille mad. Wallpaper ripped off in long strips, one broken, torn armchair, horrible filth. She enormous and dirty-faced, incessantly talking in a monotonous, metallic voice" (cat. 241). In a letter she wrote to her cousin Henriette Thierry after the death of her cousin Henri Thierry in December 1912, we realize the terrible fate that awaited Camille's works during the last years in the studio on the quai de Bourbon: "This death affected me greatly, I cannot get over it. When I received your death notice, I was so angry I took all my sketches in

Fig. 76
CAMILLE CLAUDEL
Paul Claudel Aged Thirty-Seven
1905
Plaster
Private collection

Cat 96
CAMILLE CLAUDEL
Paul Claudel Aged Thirty-Seven
1905
Bronze
43.2 x 52.5 x 31.5 cm
Musée Rodin, Paris

Fig. 77
CAMILLE CLAUDEL
Louis-Prosper Claudel
1905
Charcoal
Private collection

wax and I threw them in the fire, which made a big blaze and I warmed my feet in the glow of the fire; that's what I do when something unpleasant happens to me, I take my hammer and I smash a figure."[4]

Louis-Prosper Claudel's death on March 2, 1913, which was kept from Camille, brought things suddenly to a head. Paul, in Paris, procured a medical certificate confirming that Camille—then forty-eight years old—was mad and Madame Claudel signed the authorization for her to be committed. On March 10, 1913, Camille was taken to the asylum at Ville-Evrard, from where, in 1914, because of the war, she was transferred to the Montdevergues asylum. She remained there for the next thirty years until her death on October 19, 1943 at the age of seventy-eight.

Throughout those long years of confinement, Camille constantly wrote to her family, her only link with the outside world, but also to people who could help her. Many of these letters were lost, but those that have survived show how Camille's intellectual coherence, despite her persistent paranoia concerning "Rodin and his gang," remained surprisingly intact and that she could maintain warm and attentive relations with her mother, Paul and others. Yet it had been they who had not only requested her committal—probably inevitable given the state of abandon and mental distress she was in—but also demanded that any visit or letter by or from someone not a member of her immediate family be forbidden. This extreme decision was probably motivated by fear of scandal. But scandal broke out nevertheless when Camille's cousin Charles Thierry alerted the regional paper, *L'Avenir de l'Aisne*, in September 1913, six

Cat. 14

Cat. 110

Cat. 111

months after attempting but failing to see Camille. *L'Avenir de l'Aisne* and a Parisian paper, *Le Grand National*, stirred up a controversy that lasted from September to December 1913 and in a certain sense put the Claudel family on trial. The family did not comment on the matter and the storm passed without Camille ever knowing about it.[5]

Camille lived in almost total isolation. Neither her mother nor her sister ever visited her. Paul saw Camille less than ten times over this long period. His daughter Marie occasionally visited her aunt in the 1930s. In August 1943, Marie's mother-in-law, Nelly Méquillet, spent a week at Camille's bedside when she was in an extremely weak state due to malnutrition. The only photographic records we have of Camille at Montdevergues were taken by her old friend Jessie Lipscomb, who, after obtaining Paul's authorization, visited her in 1929 with her husband, William Elborne, who took the two photographs in question. In one of them, Camille, alone, looking old and drawn, almost sixty-five, her head slightly tilted, is looking at the camera. Her gaze, although not lifeless, is devoid of hope but her thin, tightly closed lips show she has not lost the determination, the will to survive (cat. 108, p. 288).

RODIN AND CAMILLE

In 1914, Rodin, through his friend the art critic Mathias Morhardt, tried to come to Camille's aid when he heard that she had been committed (cat. 245). Now seventy-four, Rodin had escaped from the clutches of the Duchess of Choiseul after a seven-year affair which, despite the happiness it gave him, distanced him from his most faithful friends. He did several portraits of this woman who insinuated herself into his life with an authority he had never previously tolerated. A 1911 marble (cat. 177) shows Choiseul smiling and evokes the gay atmosphere she managed to create around the aging Rodin.[6] Since the exhibition at the Pavillon de l'Alma in 1900—the pavilion was reerected in the garden of his house at Meudon (cat. 14)—Rodin "was clearly seen as the most famous artist in the world."[7] On April 21, 1906, a large version of *The Thinker* donated to the state by public subscription was unveiled in front of the Panthéon (cat. 111) and major collections of his works were being amassed in Europe and America. In 1911, Paul Gsell published his discussions with the artist (cat. 243), which were translated into English in 1912 and German in 1913. Rodin, concerned about posterity, wanted to make the Hôtel Biron (cat. 110, p. 193),

Cat. 111
MARCEL HUTIN
*Inauguration in
The Thinker in front
of the Panthéon,
April 21, 1906*
1906
Photograph, albumin
print
11.7 x 16.6 cm
Musée Rodin, Paris

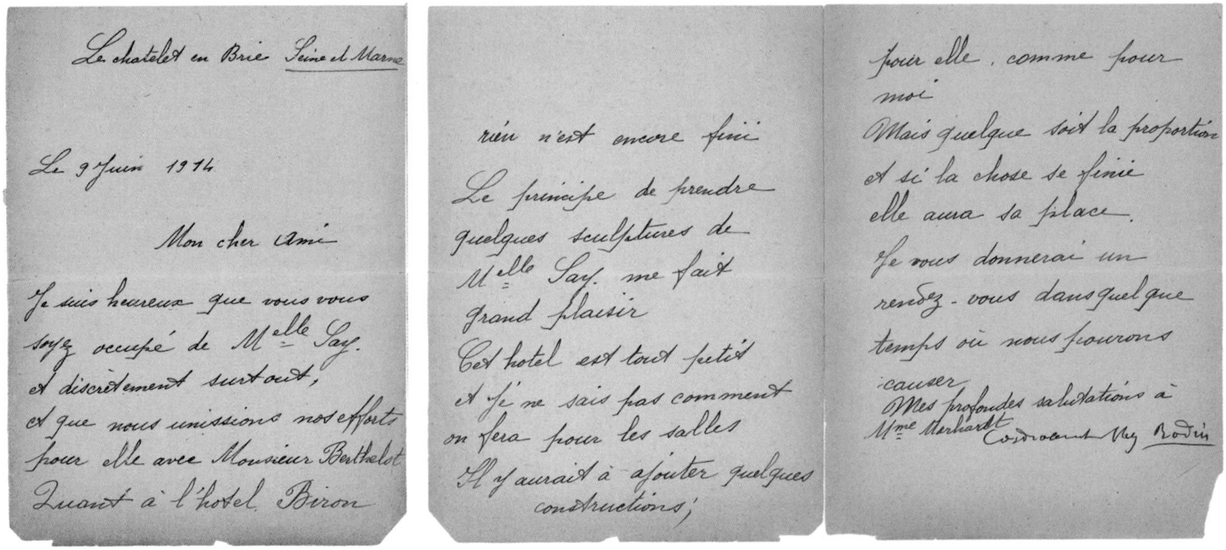

Cat. 247

Cat. 247
Letter from Auguste Rodin to Mathias Morhardt
Dated June 9, 1914
1 sheet
Société des Manuscrits des Assureurs Français, Paris

which he had discovered thanks to Rilke in 1908, into a Rodin museum. It was in this context that Morhardt suggested to him: "I would like you to consent to reserving a room in the Hôtel Biron for the work of Camille Claudel" (cat. 246). To which Rodin replied on June 9, 1914: "The principle of taking several sculptures by Mlle Say [the codename Rodin used for Camille] pleases me greatly" (cat. 247). However, the Claudel room would not become a reality until 1952, shortly after the first *Camille Claudel* retrospective, with Paul Claudel donating the plaster of *Clotho*, two versions of *The Age of Maturity* and *Vertumnus and Pomona*. Since then, the Musée Rodin's excellent Claudel collection has constantly grown and today comprises some twenty sculptures, several works on paper and an important collection of archive material concerning the artist.

Camille's medical file proves without a shadow of a doubt that she was a victim of her paranoia concerning Rodin's role in her being committed to an insane asylum. Not only did he play no part in this decision—as we have seen above, it was Louise Claudel, her mother, and her brother Paul who made this decision—but he helped Camille financially several times after their separation, particularly from January 1902 to December 1906 (see "A *Niobid* Wounded by an Arrow," pp. 274–87).

This aspect of Camille and Rodin's relationship is now clearer, thanks to the exhaustive research by, among others, Odile Ayral-Clause,[8] who devoted seven of the twenty-three chapters of her biography of Camille Claudel to her thirty-year confinement and her posterity. As Antoinette Le Normand-Romain so aptly emphasizes when she quotes the bronze

Fig. 78

Cat. 113 A

(*Giganti* and *The Old Woman*), when she was twenty-one, and finished *The Age of Maturity* at thirty-four. But Camille's meteoric career was to be short-lived: it came to an end in 1907 after *Wounded Niobid*, when she was forty-five. Rodin was already forty-two when he met her, they worked together on his masterpieces, *The Gates of Hell* and *The Burghers of Calais*, and he carried on producing well into his old age.

While Camille withdrew into isolation from 1904 onwards, Rodin had a full social life, as shown by the photograph of the sculptor with the friends who gave a party in his honor at Vélizy on June 30, 1903 to celebrate his Legion of Honor (cat. 113 A). His celebrity made him the center of a veritable court of men of letters, artists, politicians and women constantly trying to attract his attention. And of course there were the many models who posed for him at the Hôtel Biron: "In this monastic retreat, he likes to shut himself away with the nudity of beautiful young women and record in innumerable pencil sketches the fluid poses they do for him"[10] (fig. 78). Jacques Vilain rightly emphasizes that "Rodin was always a man of two women (the one and the other, the other not always being the same), and that was the primary

founder Eugène Blot: "Time will put everything back in place."[9] I shall simply emphasize here the extent to which the artists' careers followed opposing courses. Rodin's began laboriously after he failed the entry exam to the École des Beaux-Arts three years running, in 1857, 1858 and 1859, and did not succeed in exhibiting at the Salon until 1875 (*The Man with the Broken Nose*), at the age of thirty-four. Camille, on the other hand, exhibited for the first time at the Salon des Artistes Français in 1885

Fig. 78
AUGUSTE RODIN
Female Couple
Graphite and watercolor,
assemblage of paper cut-outs
Musée Rodin, Paris

Cat. 113 A
JEAN-FRANÇOIS LIMET
*Reception in honor
of the presentation
of the insignia of
Commander of the
Legion of Honor to
Auguste Rodin, at
Vélizy, June 30, 1903*
1903
Photograph, aristotype
17.4 x 23.5 cm
Musée Rodin, Paris

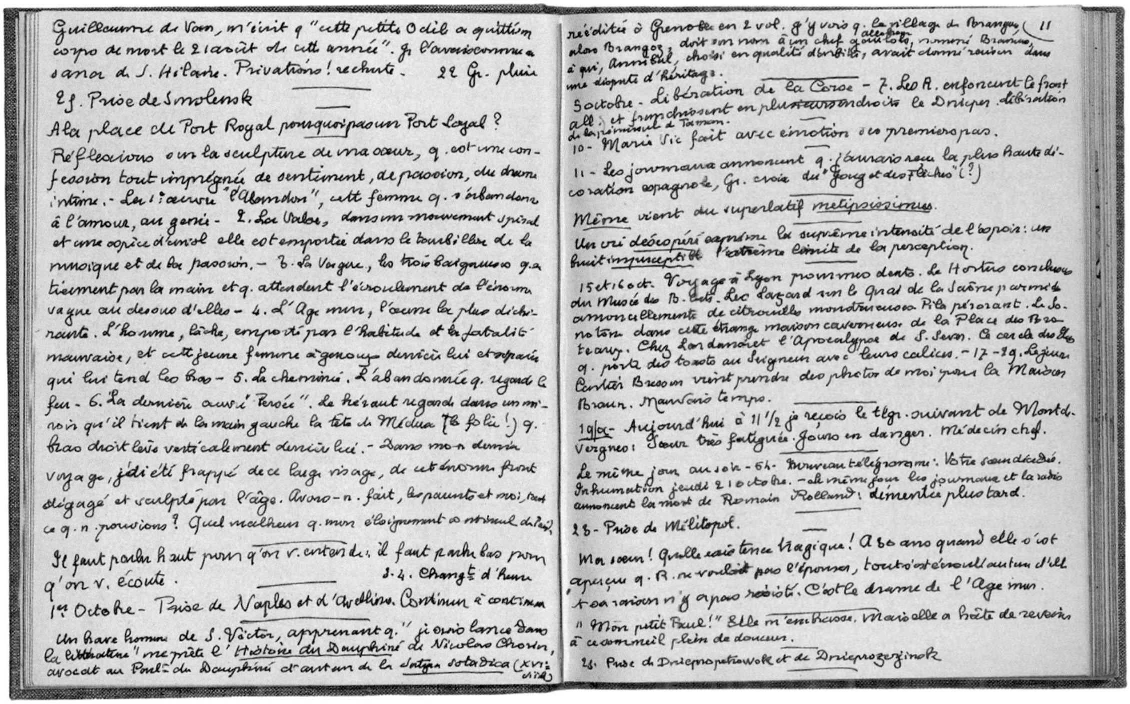

Cat. 262

Cat. 262

PAUL CLAUDEL
Journal
Vol. 9 (1943–49)
Fol. 110 verso
and 111 recto,
September–October 1943
43 x 26.5 cm
Société des Manuscrits des
Assureurs Français, Paris

reason for his rupture with Camille."[11] He finally married his most faithful companion Rose Beuret (cat. 13) a few weeks before she died on February 16, 1917.

The deaths of Rodin and Camille Claudel occurred at an interval of twenty-six years. He died just before his seventy-eighth birthday, during the First World War, on November 17, 1917 in his cold villa at Meudon. Camille died on October 19, 1943, a victim of the terrible food shortage at the Montdevergues asylum during the Second World War. After so many years of isolation, she gradually grew weaker and, in 1942, Paul was twice alerted by the asylum's doctor. He visited her for the last time in September 1943, and talks about this in his *Journal* where, following this visit, he reflects on the close relationship between his sister's life and work: "Reflection on my sister's sculpture, which is a confession completely impregnated with feeling, passion and inner drama. The 1st work, *Abandon*, this woman who abandoned herself to love, to genius. 2 *The Waltz*, in a spiral movement and a kind of taking flight she is swept away by the whirlwind of music and passion. 3 *The Wave*, the three bathers holding hands and waiting for the enormous wave looming over them to break. 4 *The Age of*

Cat. 13

Cat. 25 A

Maturity, the most heart-rending work of all. The weak man, led away by habit and bad fate, the young woman on her knees behind him and separated reaching out to him. 5 *The Fireside*, the abandoned woman gazing into the fire. 6 The last work *Perseus*. The herald looks in the mirror he is holding in his left hand, the head of Medusa (madness!) held up vertically behind him with his right hand. During my last visit I was struck by her broad face, the enormous forehead laid bare and sculpted by age. Did we, our parents and I, do everything we could? What a misfortune my continual absence from Paris" (cat. 262).

The day after Camille died, Paul wrote in his *Journal*: "October 19, 1943 Today at 11 A.M. received the following telegram from Montdevergues: Sister very tired. Fears for her life. Head doctor. The same day in the evening—5 P.M.—another telegram: Your sister has died. Burial Thursday October 21 . . . My sister! What a tragic life! When she was thirty, when she realized Rodin did not want to marry her, everything

collapsed around her and she lost her reason. This is the drama of *The Age of Maturity*; 'Mon petit Paul' She hugs me. But she is in a hurry to return to that sleep full of gentleness" (cat. 262).

Only a few nuns attended the artist's funeral in the cemetery at Montdevergues on October 21. Ten years later, her remains were transferred to a communal grave. What a contrast between her funeral and Rodin's at Meudon (cat. 25 A), with its succession of orators. Clemenceau devoted the entire front page of his newspaper, *L'Homme libre* to it. Rodin was buried at Meudon, alongside Rose, and *The Thinker* keeps watch over their tomb. The Musée Rodin was created during Rodin's lifetime, at the

Cat. 13

Anonymous
Auguste Rodin and Rose Beuret in the garden of the Villa des Brillants at Meudon, March 25, 1916
1916
Photograph, gelatin silver print
21.1 x 16.3 cm
Musée Rodin, Paris

Cat. 25 A

Pierre Choumoff
The funeral of Auguste Rodin at Meudon, November 24, 1917
1917
Photograph, gelatin silver print
17.2 x 22.4 cm
Musée Rodin, Paris

Hôtel Biron in Paris (opened to the public in August 1919) and at Villa des Brillants at Meudon. It comprises the sculptor's entire production and collection and has promoted the dissemination and defense of his work worldwide.

ARTISTS ABOVE ALL

Throughout her exile, Camille never stopped thinking of herself as an artist. Two pathetic letters, sent on March 3, the day she considered to be the date of her "abduction" (even though her confinement proper did not begin until March 10, 1913, the third being the day after her father's death) and which she seems to have had the habit of commemorating by writing a letter to Paul, attest to this. On March 3, 1927, she wrote, "It is 14 years ago today that I had the unpleasant surprise of seeing two henchmen enter my studio armed to the teeth, helmeted, in boots, menacing in every way. A sad surprise for an artist: instead of a reward, this was what happened to me!"[12] And on March 3, 1930: "Today, March 3, is the anniversary of my abduction to Ville-Evrard:

Cat. 248

*Letter from Camille Claudel
to Paul Claudel*
Dated March 3, 1930
2 sheets, 17.5 x 22.5 cm
Société des Manuscrits des
Assureurs Français, Paris

it has been 17 years since Rodin and his dealers in objets d'art sent me to serve my penitence in lunatic asylums. Having divested me of the work of a lifetime . . . Because I have to stay at their discretion! This exploitation of woman, the crushing of the artist they wanted to see sweat blood . . . I am so sick of this slavery. I would so like to be in my own home and close the door tight shut. I don't know whether I will be able to realize this dream, of being in my own home" (cat. 248). The many tearstains still visible on this document express, if need there were, Camille's utter dismay and her slim, increasingly unrealistic hopes of ever seeing her confinement come to an end.

Of all the roles she might have continued to play—pupil, model, lover, mother, artist—Camille chose only one: artist. Rodin would have said, "When women have bronze, marble and the creativeness of clay as rivals, they have a very poor lover in the sculptor."[13] In the "Testament" the sculptor left us at the end of his famous discussions with Paul Gsell, several pieces of advice are noteworthy: "Nature should be your only goddess. . . Work relentlessly. . . Exercise your art ceaselessly. You have to inure yourself to your trade. . . Patience!. . . Be profoundly, fiercely truthful. . . Love your mission passionately." And when he confides, "The great thing is to be moved, to love, to hope, to tremble, to live. Be a man before an artist!"[14] one is tempted to think that for Rodin life and art were one and the same thing. For both artists, creation was the sole thread running through their lives: for Camille, it led to exile, for Rodin, to glory.

Montdevergues 3 Mars 1930

Cher Paul,

Aujourd'hui 3 Mars, c'est l'anniversaire de mon enlèvement à Ville-Evrard : cela fait 17 ans que Rodin et les marchands d'objets d'art m'ont envoyé faire pénitence dans les asiles d'aliénés. Après s'être emparés de l'œuvre de toute ma vie en se servant de B. pour exécuter leur sinistre projet ils me font faire les années de prison qu'ils auraient si bien mérités eux-mêmes. B. n'était qu'un agent dont on se servait pour te tenir en respect et t'employer à exécuter ce coup d'audace qui a réussi à leur gré grâce à ta crédulité et à celle de maman et de Louise. N'oublie pas

que la femme de B. est un ancien modèle de Rodin : tu vois maintenant la combinaison dont j'étais l'objet !... C'est beau ! Tous ces millionnaires qui se jettent sur une artiste sans défense ! car les messieurs qui ont collaboré à cette belle action sont tous plus de 40 fois millionnaires. Il paraît que mon pauvre atelier, quelques pauvres meubles, quelques outils forgés par moi-même, mon pauvre petit ménage excitant encore leur convoitise ! — S'imaginer le sentiment, le nouveau, l'imprévu qui sort d'un esprit développé étant chose fermée pour eux, têtes bouchées, cerveaux obtus, éternellement fermés à la lumière, il leur faut quelqu'un pour les leur fournir. Ils le disaient : « nous nous servons d'une hallucinée pour trouver nos sujets »

Il y en a au moins qui auraient la reconnaissance du ventre et qui aur aient donné quelques compensations à la pauvre femme qu'ils ont dépouillée de son génie : non ! une maison d'aliénés ! pas même le droit d'avoir un chez moi !...... Parce qu'il faut que je reste à leur discrétion ! c'est l'exploitation de la femme, l'écrasement de l'artiste à qui l'on veut faire suer jusqu'au sang. Il paraît que le principal bénéficiaire de mon atelier est le sieur Hébrard, éditeur d'art, rue Royale. C'est là que sont engouffrés toutes mes esquisses (plus de 300)

que je sois malheureuse lui mort comme vivant. Il a réussi en tous points pour pour être malheureuse, je le suis ! Cela ne peut pas te déranger beaucoup mais je le suis ! On fait semblant de temps en temps d'adoucir mon sort, mais cela ne dure pas c'est de la frime ! Dernièrement on a construit une grande cuisine, au loin à plus d'1 km du pensionnat : on m'a donné la permission d'aller chercher la nourriture avec les hommes et les femmes de peine ; cela me faisait une sortie et une promenade. Cela n'a pas duré... j'ai reçu l'ordre de ne plus y aller, sans motif aucun je suis de nouveau séquestrée. Je m'ennuie bien de cet esclavage

Je voudrais bien être chez moi et bien fermer ma porte. Je ne sais pas si je pourrai réaliser ce rêve, être chez moi.

J'ai reçu dernièrement une lettre de Jessie Elborne. Elle m'annonce qu'elle viendra avec son mari vers la fin d'Avril ! À dire vrai c'est plutôt sur toi que je comptais ! Ils sont bien aimables mais que peuvent-ils pour moi ! Je crains qu'ils ne soient assez de tous leurs soucis ! Enfin c'est un bon sentiment qu'ils me montrent. Dans tous mes parents il n'y a pas un seul qui en fasse autant.

Je n'ai pas de nouvelles de tes enfants. Bien des amitiés à toi et à ta famille.

Ve.

Il paraît déjà que quelques années avant mon départ de Paris, les esquisses que je faisais à Villeneuve filaient chez lui à mesure (par quel miracle ? Dieu seul le sait) J'en ai retrouvé chez lui éditées en bronze et signées d'autres artistes : c'est réellement trop fort !... Et me condamner à la prison perpétuelle pour que je ne réclame pas ! Tout cela au fond sort du cerveau diabolique de Rodin. Il n'avait qu'une idée c'est que lui, étant mort, je prenne mon essor comme artiste et que je devienne plus que lui : il fallait qu'il arrive à me tenir dans ses griffes après sa mort comme pendant sa vie. Il fallait

JOINT CHRONOLOGY

CAMILLE CLAUDEL		AUGUSTE RODIN

1840

NOVEMBER 12. Birth of Auguste Rodin, Paris.

1864

DECEMBER 8. Birth of Camille Claudel, Fère-en-Tardenois.

Rodin meets Rose Beuret, who bears him a son and lives with him until the end of his life.

1876

AUTUMN. Louis-Prosper Claudel moves to Nogent-sur-Seine with his family. Camille meets the sculptor Alfred Boucher, who becomes her first teacher.

1877

Rodin exhibits *The Age of Bronze* in Brussels and Paris.

1880

The state acquires the plaster of *The Age of Bronze* and commissions a bronze.

AUGUST. The ministry of fine arts commissions *The Gates of Hell*. Rodin is allocated a studio in the Dépôt des Marbres in rue de l'Université.

1881

Camille moves to Paris with her mother, sister Louise and brother Paul. She attends lessons at Académie Colarossi. Alfred Boucher supervises her work.

1882

FEBRUARY–MAY. A certain "Camille" appears in Rodin's entourage.

Rodin agrees to teach Boucher's pupils.

Rodin does probably the first sculpted portrait of Camille, *Camille with Short Hair*.

1883

BEFORE MAY 1883. Camille rents a studio at 117 rue Notre-Dame-des-Champs, which she shares with other female artists.

Camille exhibits for the first time at the Salon des Artistes Français. In the catalogue, she is listed as a pupil of Rodin, Alfred Boucher and Paul Dubois.

At the end of the year, best wishes to
"Mademoiselle Claudel" become frequent in letters to Rodin,
suggesting that his intimate relationship with his pupil
was common knowledge.

1884

Camille joins Rodin's studio as an assistant. She remains until 1892.

Deeply in love with his pupil, Rodin sculpts her face:
Mask of Camille Claudel, Camille Wearing a Bonnet.

1885

The town of Calais commissions a
Monument to The Burghers of Calais.

Rodin and Camille work together in harmony,
sharing his studio and models. Camille's works show
Rodin's influence: *Crouching Woman.*

1886

Relations between the two lovers grow stormy.
Jealous and irritated by the society life
that Rodin seems to enjoy, Camille
distances herself from him.

Rodin, profoundly affected by the
deterioration in his relationship with Camille,
neglects his sculpture: "That's it, I'm not
working anymore, evil divinity, and yet I love
you passionately." (Rodin to Camille Claudel)

APRIL. Camille visits Jessie Lipscomb at
Peterborough, in England. In August, she stays
with Florence Jeans on the Isle of Wight.
She returns to Paris in September.

MAY–JUNE. Rodin goes to England and
tries in vain to meet Camille.

Rodin exhibits three "studies of human
rut," including *I Am Beautiful,*
at the Galerie Georges Petit.

OCTOBER 12, the "contract." Rodin undertakes
to have no other pupil than Camille, to
protect her in artistic circles, and to marry her
after a trip to Italy or Chile. In exchange,
Camille agrees to let him visit her four times a month.

NOVEMBER. Camille works on *Sakuntala.*

1887

The relationship between Camille and her
English friend Jessie Lipscomb deteriorates.

She shared Camille's studio and acted as
intermediary between Rodin and Camille.

1888

Eager for independence, Camille moves to
113 boulevard d'Italie, into a studio rented by Rodin.

At the Salon des Artistes Français, Camille
receives an honorable mention for *Sakuntala*.

She begins the bust of *Auguste Rodin* and *The Waltz*.

1889

JULY. Camille and Rodin visit Touraine.

Rodin exhibits with Monet at the Galerie
Georges Petit, and is commissioned to sculpt
monuments to Claude Lorrain and Victor Hugo.

1890

MARCH. To be closer to Camille, Rodin rents
the Folie Payen at 68 boulevard d'Italie.

SUMMER. Camille stays at Château de l'Islette,
in Touraine. Rodin joins her there.

1891

The Société des Gens de Lettres commissions
a monument to Honoré de Balzac.

SUMMER. Camille and Rodin return to the
Château de l'Islette. Rodin begins work on *Balzac*.

1892

Rodin refuses to leave Rose Beuret.

Camille rents an apartment at 11 avenue de la
Bourdonnais and distances herself from Rodin.
She keeps the studio in boulevard d'Italie.

Professional and personal relations between Camille and
Rodin loosen. Rodin continues to help Camille financially.

Camille sends Rodin sarcastic drawings in which she depicts
him as subservient to an old and ugly Rose Beuret.

Even the most enthusiastic critics
emphasize Camille's debt to her teacher.
Some even describe her work as pastiche.

SUMMER. Camille stays on her own at
Château de l'Islette in Touraine, possibly
recovering from an abortion she had between
1890 and 1893. She begins *La Petite Châtelaine*.

1893

APRIL. Rodin and Rose Beuret move to Bellevue. At the end of
the year, he rents the Villa des Brillants at Meudon.

Camille exhibits *Clotho* and *The Waltz* at the
Salon of the Société Nationale des Beaux-Arts.

Camille works on the first version of *The Age of Maturity*.

Seeking to gain her artistic independence, Camille
explores new directions. She begins the "sketches
from nature," small sculptures inspired by everyday life.

1895

Camille exhibits *Les Causeuses* at the
Salon of the Société Nationale des Beaux-Arts.

JUNE. Camille and Rodin see each other again.
Rodin continues to help Camille socially and financially.

Haunted by Camille's face, Rodin sculpts a series of
allegorical portraits: *Thought*.

DECEMBER. Rodin buys Villa des Brillants at Meudon.

1896

Camille meets Mathias Morhardt, editor
of the newspaper *Le Temps*.

Camille meets countess Arthur de Maigret,
who is her principal patron until 1905.

Rodin exhibits four marbles, more or less inspired
by Camille, including *Triumphant Youth*, at the
Salon of the Société Nationale des Beaux-Arts.

SEPTEMBER. Camille asks Mathias Morhardt to
persuade Rodin to stop visiting her. so that she
cannot be accused of owing the success of her works to him.

1897

At the Salon of the Société Nationale des Beaux-Arts,
Camille exhibits *The Wave* and Rodin the study for the
Monument to Victor Hugo.

NOVEMBER. In a letter to Rodin, Camille
expresses her admiration for *Balzac*.

1893

MARCH. Mathias Morhardt publishes an important
article on Camille Claudel in *Mercure de France*.

Camille moves her home and studio to 63 rue de Turenne.

Camille Claudel's *Hamadryad* and *Deep Thought*
are exhibited at the Société Nationale des Beaux-Arts,
at the same time as Rodin's *Balzac*.

Balzac is ridiculed by the press and public.
The Société des Gens de Lettres rejects it.

1899

JANUARY. Camille moves to 19 quai de Bourbon,
where she lives and works as a recluse.

The plaster of *The Age of Maturity* is shown at the
Salon of the Société Nationale des Beaux-Arts. The
commission for the bronze is cancelled by the director
of fine arts, Henry Roujon. Camille blames Rodin for this.

1900

To coincide with the Exposition Universelle, Rodin organizes
a major exhibition of his works at the Pavillon de l'Alma.

1902

Rodin shows eighty-eight sculptures and
seventy-five drawings in Prague.

Rodin anonymously sends Camille a monthly allowance.

1904

Rodin shows sculptures, photographs and drawings in
Düsseldorf, Dresden, Leipzig and Weimar.

From 1904, the art dealer Eugène Blot produces
bronze editions of fifteen of Camille's sculptures.

1905

Camille shows the marble of *Vertumnus and
Pomona* at the Salon des Artistes Français.

Camille's correspondence shows her increasing paranoia
concerning Rodin: "M. Rodin (whom you know) has amused himself
by cutting off my provisions everywhere, having forced me to leave the
Salon de la Nationale due to the spiteful things he was doing to me . . .
I will be pursued all my life by this monster's revenge."
(Camille Claudel to Henry Lerolle)

Camille shows eleven bronzes and two
marbles at the Galerie Eugène Blot.

She completes her last original composition,
a portrait bust of her brother:
Paul Claudel Aged Thirty-Seven.

1906

The fine arts administration commissions
Wounded Niobid.

1907

Walking Man is shown at the Salon of the
Société Nationale des Beaux-Arts.

Rodin has an affair with the Duchess of Choiseul,
who dominates his life until 1912.

1908

Camille shows nine bronzes and a marble
at the Galerie Eugène Blot.

Rodin rents the ground floor of the Hôtel Biron,
of which he later becomes the sole tenant.

1909

When he visits his sister, Paul Claudel is devastated
by the change in her: "In Paris, Camille crazy. Wallpaper
pulled off in long shreds, armchair broken and torn,
horrible filthiness. She, enormous and dirty, incessantly
speaking in a metallic monotone."

1913

MARCH 10. Camille is committed to the asylum at Ville-Évrard.
Raking over her old obsessions, she accuses Rodin of having
had her committed so as to get his hands on her works.

JULY. The periodical *Art décoratif* devotes an
abundantly illustrated article to her, a reprint
of the article written by her brother Paul in 1905.

1914

Despite her family's opposition, Rodin continues to send
money to Camille: "I would like you to see to it that
Mademoiselle Claudel's lot is softened until she
gets out of this Gehenna." (Rodin to Mathias Morhardt)

Rodin exhibits in London and donates eighteen
sculptures to the Victoria and Albert Museum.

SEPTEMBER 9. Due to the war, Camille
is transferred to the asylum at
Montdevergues in the Vaucluse.

1916

Rodin donates his entire oeuvre and
collection to the state, which agrees to create
a Rodin museum in the Hôtel Biron.

1917

JANUARY 29. Rodin marries Rose Beuret.

FEBRUARY 16. Death of Rose Beuret.

NOVEMBER 17. Death of Rodin, aged seventy-seven.

1919

AUGUST 4. The Musée Rodin opens to the public.

1938

Camille worries about what will happen to her works,
but refuses to take up sculpture again: "In fact they
want to force me to do sculpture here, seeing that
they cannot, they are causing me all kinds of
problems. But that will not make me change
my mind, on the contrary . . . Your sister in exile."
(Camille to Paul Claudel)

1943

OCTOBER 19. Death of Camille Claudel,
aged seventy-eight, at Montdevergues.

II

STUDIES

CAMILLE CLAUDEL AND CLAUDE DEBUSSY:

A FRIENDSHIP   Jean-Michel Nectoux

A certain mystery shrouds Claude Debussy and Camille Claudel's relationship. Little is known about it other than the account by Robert Godet, a close friend of the musician and a fervent admirer of Camille.[1] Debussy met Camille in 1888–89, at Austin, the café on rue d'Amsterdam so dear to Baudelaire. We also know that they went together to listen to the Javanese musicians at the 1899 Exposition Universelle. Camille, then twenty-five, was two years younger than Debussy, and men were attracted by her strange beauty.

There was an impediment to a friendship with the composer. According to Jules Renard, "She hates music, and makes no bones about it."[2] Godet wrote more discreetly that Camille quickly got bored listening to music, perhaps because of the over-repetitive piano playing of her younger sister Louise, reputedly a good musician. Yet, if the upright piano in a photograph of the studio on rue Notre-Dame-des-Champs that Camille and Louise shared with English friends is anything to go by, this aversion could not have been that pronounced. Debussy, who came to play for her on their mutual friend Robert Godet's piano, managed to gradually open up the universe of music for her and also perhaps allay her fear of losing herself in its infinitesimal sonorities: "Camille Claudel not only approached it without distrust and showed an increasingly keen curiosity for it, but ended up listening to it with a reverence that was in no way resigned," Godet wrote. "And the time came when she could be heard to say as she led the pianist to the fireplace to warm his cold hands, 'No comment, Monsieur Debussy.'"[3]

These were the years when Camille's talent was blooming under Rodin's loving eyes. The sculptor, consumed by his passion for her, traversed periods of bliss and terrifying crises. Camille, who, in the album of a friend, replied to the question "Your chief characteristic" wrote "impulsiveness and fickleness" and chose "Lady Macbeth" as her favorite fictional character (cat. 191, p. 74), had her teacher at her mercy. She made him sign all kinds of promises (of marriage in particular), in order to be allowed to visit her once a week (cat. 186, pp. 88–89), and above all, played the game of absence with consummate art, staying for months on end in England while he moped in Paris. The sculptor's submission is there to be seen in his figure group *The Eternal Idol* (cat. 156, p. 80), in which

Fig. 79
PIERRE LOUŸS
Claude Debussy
May 1894
Photograph
Maison Claude Debussy,
Saint-Germain-en-Laye

the naked man, kneeling, hands behind his back like a prisoner, is kissing the body of the woman, who is gesturing to him with one hand while holding her other foot up in a pose of manifest indifference. *The Eternal Idol* is Rodin's reply to Camille's *Sakuntala* (cat. 47, p. 105), in which the couple (the man naked, kneeling, his arms around the woman abandoning herself to him) exudes profound tenderness. In Camille's unpredictability, there was a profound rift between her blossoming as a woman and her fierce will to be an independent artist, and she chose the latter with a determination all the greater because the critics never missed an opportunity to emphasize the (real) kinship of her style with Rodin's. It is hardly surprising, then, that the woman whose reply to the question "Your idea of misery" was "being the mother of many children" chose not to give birth to Rodin's baby. One also wonders if the woman who modeled so many beautiful male bodies preferred their forms when she had them at her mercy and could bring them to life with her hands out of clay, plaster and marble rather than from her own flesh.

In this psychological context, the idea of an affair with Debussy, suggested by some biographers, at a time when Camille's chief concern was to protect herself, if need be against herself, from Rodin's passion, seems to me not only highly improbable but inappropriate. Their friendship developed, certainly, in the early 1890s, when the Camille–Rodin couple was breaking up and finally separated, but one can hardly see the fragile Camille, early in 1891, facing up to breaking with Debussy at the very moment she was trying to come out of Rodin's suffocating shadow. The hypothesis that Camille and Debussy had an affair stems from a letter, one of Debussy's most somber and most moving, in which we feel all the pain of a passion that has suddenly come to an end: "I am still utterly lost; the sadly awaited end of the story I told you about; a banal end, with anecdotes, words that should never have been said, I noticed a bizarre transposition, which is that as her lips uttered those so very hard words, within myself I heard only the very uniquely adorable things they had said to me! And the wrong notes (real, alas!), clashing with those singing inside me, tore me apart, almost without my being able to understand."[4]

But this letter was to Robert Godet, whose "so humanely gentle" nature the composer greatly appreciated. A close friend of the would-be lovers, he often invited them to his home, "where she was already, and would be ever more so, most respectfully welcome," he wrote.[5] If Godet had been the obligatory and discreet witness of their hypothetical passion, Debussy (fig. 79, p. 308) would not have had to reveal it to him and even less had to refer to it as "the story I told you about." Furthermore, Godet himself published part of this letter for the first time in 1920, introducing it with this periphrasis full of meaning

Cat. 10

ANONYMOUS, after HOKUSAI
The Wave
Cover of the score of
Claude Debussy's *La Mer*,

1905
33 x 25 cm
Collection Jean-Michel
Nectoux, Paris

another version, reduced to about 40 cm and half veiled, with the woman wearing only a long, sumptuous skirt swirling and blooming into a train, that *The Waltz* was widely reproduced.

Debussy no doubt showed such enthusiasm for *The Waltz* that Camille gave him one, very probably one of the series produced around 1893. According to Godet,[15] it never left his study and was the only valuable work he possessed. His precious sculpture has never been identified, but it seems highly probable that it wasn't a bronze cast, as the catalogue raisonné by Rivière, Gaudichon and Ghanassia has presumed.[16] Since the composer, like Camille, was far too short of money to afford one, it is more likely to have been one of the edition of twelve "small version" plasters patinated by the artist and intended for her friends. It is interesting that Robert Godet and Frits Thaulow, both friends of the composer and the sculptress, were each given one.

The Waltz, "intoxicated, swirling and lost in the fabric of music, in the storm and whirlwind of the dance," in Paul Claudel's words,[17] is, with the late *Siren* (cat. 97, p. 265), one of the rare works by the artist with a musical subject. On a more profound level, Debussy must have admired the wonderfully free and inventive beauty of its lines, the rhythms of its curves and its perfect realization of the "divine arabesque" that he himself was trying to capture in *Two Arabesques*, two compositions for piano written at the time of his meetings with Camille. For Camille, the swirling flight of the skirt was a kind of signature, echoed in the whorls of *Fortune*, *The Age of Maturity*, *Deep Thought* and *Perseus*, in the undone hair of *La Petite Châtelaine*,

Clotho and *Les Causeuses*, and in the frozen roll of *The Nave*. These figures, among the greatest achievements of Art Nouveau sculpture, express an inner dénouement but are perhaps a sign of a soul whose form, having reached its utmost equilibrium, is about to unravel.

According to Robert Godet, Debussy saw in Camille Claudel's oeuvre "the most perfect monuments of lyricism that sculpture has ever produced" and admired in it "the genius of arriving at a style without owing a thing to the Academy"[18]—an important declaration given that this was the very ambition that the composer himself was obstinately pursuing. Their fully assumed marginality vis-à-vis academic traditions, their refusal to mix their art with any careerist or mercantile preoccupations, and their disgust with the established systems clearly brought the young Debussy and Camille Claudel together. They shared the same intransigence and pride. An excerpt from *Entretien avec M. Croche* comes to mind: "To remain unique . . . without a defect . . . For me, the enthusiasm of the milieu spoils an artist, so afraid I am of him then becoming the expression of that milieu."[19] This is surely why Debussy preferred Camille Claudel to Rodin, who was probably too showered with praise, too surrounded by worldly people for the liking of this modern-day Saint-Just.

WOMEN SCULPTORS IN
NINETEENTH-CENTURY FRANCE   Odile Ayral-Clause

Camille Claudel is one of the few nineteenth-century women sculptors known today. The question arises as to what extent she owes her posthumous popularity to the public's fascination for her dramatic fate rather than a genuine understanding of the importance of her work. To appreciate Camille Claudel's sculpture, one must examine the constraints which hampered all women at that time in the arts, as in other spheres, and the solutions that they sometimes found to solve them or get around them.[1]

For a long time defined by her role as procreator, a woman was supposed to find her raison d'être in marriage and the well-being of the family. All other activities were considered amateur. In a popular publication in 1838, Madame Necker de Saussure, while recognizing the advantages of an artistic education for a young woman, added that it should remain an "agreeable accessory" since "society, frivolous as it is, so much feels the necessity for moral equilibrium in a woman that she who distinguishes herself with a too special gift is badly looked upon."[2] She of course limited this "accessory" to drawing and painting, since sculpture, with its material exigencies, was inconceivable for a well-brought-up young woman.

Sculpture, unlike painting, cannot be practiced in the home. Not only is it hard, dirty work requiring a large studio, but it is also costly. Works created in clay or plaster, which are inexpensive but not very durable materials, need to be cast in bronze or transposed into marble, and these are very costly processes. Furthermore, live models, indispensable in the nineteenth century, were a sufficiently heavy expense to force young sculptors to content themselves with modeling busts of members of their family and friends while waiting for better days.

Before the nineteenth century, chroniclers recorded only a few isolated cases of women sculptors. The first one known was Sabina von Steinbach, who, as the daughter of a sculptor, could study with her father and work on the commissions he received. When he died in 1318, she finished and signed the figures they had begun together for the south portal of Strasbourg Cathedral, thereby leaving her name for posterity.[3] It was not until the sixteenth century that the first study of a woman sculptor was written, by Giorgio Vasari, on the Italian Properzia di Rossi, whose energy and

Fig. 80
ADÈLE D'AFFRY (MARCELLO)
Abyssinian Chief
1870
Marble
Musée d'Orsay, Paris

talent for carving stone with her "fine and white" hands often amazed those who watched her work. Her premature death ended a career that was certainly on a par with those of her male colleagues, yet she is regarded today as merely a curious phenomenon.[4]

Over the ensuing centuries, although a more tolerant climate sometimes enabled French painters such as Elisabeth Vigée-Lebrun and Adélaïde Labille-Guiard to gain surprising fame, this was not so for women sculptors, who continued to come up against incessant obstacles of all kinds, partly due to the very nature of sculpture, but above all due to the social context of the period in which they lived. The most serious impediment was the lack of access to appropriate education and training.

For men, the way was paved from the outset. At the École Nationale de Dessin et de Mathématiques in Paris, in a Parisian studio, or in one of the many provincial schools, they could prepare for the entry exam to the École des Beaux-Arts. Once they were admitted, not only did they receive an intensive artistic education, but they could also eventually enter the Prix de Rome competition, whose laureates were guaranteed honors and, above all, commissions. Men who, like Rodin, were not admitted to the École des Beaux-Arts could nevertheless perfect their technique and learn various facets of their craft by working in the studio of a famous sculptor.

Since this option was not open to women for most of the nineteenth century, access to proper artistic training was all the more critical. But women were not admitted to the École des Beaux-Arts until 1897, after an epic battle led by sculptor Hélène Bertaux. This explains why so many female artists came from an artistic milieu, where they could receive training difficult to find elsewhere. For the others, the École Gratuite de Dessin pour les Jeunes Filles, which opened first in Paris in 1803 and then spread to the provinces, provided the foundations of an education specializing in industrial skills—fabrics, wallpaper, lace, decorative objects—or teaching. These "female" activities, giving poor young women the possibility of earning a living, were perfectly accepted by a society that admired women's taste, patience and sensibility, but did not believe them at all capable of becoming true artists.[5] Furthermore, for the same reasons and also out of propriety, none of these schools allowed women access to live human models. The same was true in neighboring countries. In England, for example, although the Royal Academy opened its doors to women in 1860, they were not allowed to study the nude until 1903.[6] Yet a thorough knowledge of the nude was the absolute foundation of any serious artistic education.

So during the first half of the century, the only possibilities offered to women outside the École Gratuite de Dessin pour les Jeunes Filles were private lessons—expensive and hard to find—or drawing manuals. It was not until the Second Empire that artists' studios began admitting women. It is therefore hardly surprising to note how few women artists —painters or sculptors—there were during the first half of the century. In sculpture, only Marie d'Orléans and Félicie de Fauveau achieved a certain renown.

Although these women were of noble birth and their position facilitated access to the patronage that could ensure regular production of their works, their social obligations imposed other constraints. As Louis-Philippe's daughter, Marie d'Orléans received an education designed to make her an accomplished hostess. She never had access to the life model and had to content herself with creating sculptures inspired by literature or history. Her *Joan of Arc Praying* was greatly acclaimed at the 1837 Salon and later admired by Rodin.[7] Marie d'Orléans would unfortunately have no subsequent successes, as she died two years later at the age of twenty-six.

Unlike Marie d'Orléans, Félicie de Fauveau lived a long life and achieved great fame before being forgotten by the end of the century. Born in Florence in 1802, the daughter of aristocrats exiled after the Revolution, she became a sculptor after her father's death and managed to gain social acceptance by emphasizing her role as a courageous woman helping her family to survive. During her long career (she died in 1886), Félicie de Fauveau worked in clay, marble and all kinds of metals. She produced busts, monuments and tombs, and also a great many ornamental pieces inspired by the Middle Ages and Gothic art, then in vogue, making her one of the precursors of the Pre-Raphaelite movement. Her ornaments,

such as sword sheaths and handles and other small objects, were particularly popular with aristocrats pleased to commission from one of their own.

When she exhibited for the first time at the 1827 Salon, Félicie de Fauveau was personally awarded a gold medal by Charles X for a bas-relief of Queen Christina of Sweden and Monaldeschi.[8] When the 1830 revolution put Louis-Philippe on the throne, de Fauveau launched into a whirlwind of pro-legitimist activities, taking part in the revolt in the Vendée and joining the Duchess of Berry. This led to her imprisonment, then exile, but did not hamper her artistic activities. On the contrary, her new aura as a heroine indefatigably loyal to her cause enhanced her popularity and brought her new commissions. Her most admired sculptures are the *Monument to Dante Alighieri* (1830–36), which depicts the story of Paolo and Francesca, and the impressive tomb of Louise Favreau (1857), now in the church of Santa Croce in Florence.[9]

Félicie de Fauveau, like most of her contemporaries, knew how to adapt to the constraints of her time but did not attempt to go any further. The artist expressed all her passionate revolt in her political activities, but did not challenge the artistic constraints imposed on her. She exploited the Romantic taste for the Gothic period, she produced utilitarian objects, and she transcribed her political and moral values in her work by choosing appropriate subjects. Yet she remained a prisoner of what society expected of a woman in the artistic domain, which condemned her to sink into oblivion despite her huge success in the middle of the century.

The Second Empire brought a major liberalization of the arts. Napoleon III encouraged artists and Empress Eugénie supported female artists in particular. As a result, the number of women sculptors increased from a few isolated cases at the beginning of the century to around twenty during the Second Empire.[10] In 1864, the empress went personally to the studio of Rosa Bonheur to present her with the first Légion d'Honneur ever awarded to a woman. Furthermore, Count Nieuwerkerke, superintendent of fine arts and lover of Princess Mathilde, herself a painter and sculptor, had a very open-minded attitude toward women and attempted to acquire a number of works for the state. Their combined efforts and the impressive building projects undertaken in Paris during that period enabled a number of commissions to be awarded to women. Marie-Louise Lefèvre-Deumier modeled the portrait of the empress, then produced a large draped nude for the Louvre, while Noémie Rouvier-Constant, also known as Claude Vignon, was commissioned to do a bas-relief for the Fontaine Saint-Michel.[11] But the most interesting case of the period was Adèle d'Affry, Duchess Castiglione Colonna, also known under the name Marcello.

Born in 1836 in Fribourg in Switzerland, Adèle d'Affry benefited from the advantages of her social status. Her many relations and her friendship with Empress Eugénie facilitated both her access to the Salon and the sale of her sculptures. As a young widow, Adèle d'Affry was free to pursue a career, and her financial situation enabled her to take private lessons. Despite all this, Adèle d'Affry had to maintain a delicate balance between what was expected of her as a "great lady" and what she passionately wanted as an artist. Inasmuch as she was a duchess, critics—perhaps with a hint of jealousy—tended to consider her a dilettante and not the artist she truly was.

Adèle d'Affry hit on an ingenious way of resolving the delicate question of the study of anatomy, considered a rather scandalous activity for a lady of her class. With the help of the Marquis of Montcalm, an old school friend of the dean of the faculty of medicine, she got permission to attend anatomy classes, provided that she arrive before the eight o'clock class, change into men's clothing and leave at midday with the professor. For two years, despite an initial revulsion, "this charming young man" wielded a scalpel in the amphitheater like "his" male colleagues.[12]

After her marriage and then widowhood, Adèle d'Affry attended modeling lessons at the studio of the Swiss sculptor Heinrich Imhof, then endeavored to

Fig. 81

ADÈLE D'AFFRY (MARCELLO)
Pythia
1870
Bronze
Opéra de Paris,
installed in 1875

perfect her technique alone. In 1869, she went to Rome, where she met Jean-Baptiste Carpeaux, with whom she had a long friendship. In Rome she worked on two sculptures for the 1870 Salon, a bust of an *Abyssinian Chief* (fig. 80, p. 314) and the most famous and admired of her pieces today, *Pythia* (fig. 81), the priestess who proclaimed the oracles at the Temple of Apollo. For *Pythia*, Adèle d'Affry daringly decided to partly model for it herself. She had her back and shoulders molded in the pose she wanted for the priestess and also modeled her own hands, arms and naked breasts.[13] It was obviously a closely kept secret, but it was not the only daring aspect of the sculpture. She decided to depict Pythia as she would have appeared in the temple, intoxicated by the vapors rising from the depths, her face in a trance and her arms outstretched toward some obsessive vision.

At the Salon, some critics acknowledged the work's power and originality, while others, knowing full well that "Marcello" was in fact a high society lady, took offence at the sculpture's excessiveness and sensuality. The jury did not award it a medal—hardly surprising considering that for most of the nineteenth century, the rare medals awarded to women were usually honorable mentions and third places. Adèle d'Affry was none the worse for this, however, because Charles Garnier, already captivated by *Pythia* when he had seen it in Rome, requested that the state acquire it for the Paris Opéra. It was installed there in 1875, beneath the main staircase, where it can still be admired today.[14] *Pythia* was Adèle d'Affry's last great success. Suffering from tuberculosis, she turned to painting and died in 1879.

Fig. 81

Ironically, the arrival of the Third Republic complicated the situation of women. On one hand, access to artistic training became easier and enabled more women to become artists; on the other, bourgeois society was so conservative that the advantages won by women in art education were reflected neither in the Salons nor in medals and commissions.

A number of artists' studios had opened their doors to women during the Second Empire, but the

_Fig. 82

_Fig. 82
JESSIE LIPSCOMB
Daydreams
Terracotta
1886
Private collection

quality of teaching varied enormously from one studio to another. In 1868, Rodolph Julian founded an academy that was both a commercial enterprise and a serious art school. He accepted women as early as 1873 and offered them access to nude life models a few years later. The Académie Julian was an immediate success and artists began flocking from all over the world to study there. Yet the situation at Julian's was far from ideal, since women usually worked in separate studios and paid twice as much as men for identical lessons. Unlike men, who always had the possibility of studying free of charge at the École des Beaux-Arts if their lessons at the Académie Julian became too expensive for them, women had no choice.[15] In her *Journal*, Marie Bashkirtseff, a pupil of Julian, complained bitterly about the situation and denounced the way in which teachers, all men, treated their female pupils. "These men despise us," she wrote, "and only when they see a strong, even brutal treatment are they content, because that particular vice is extremely rare in women."[16]

Around that time, the Académie Colarossi, which Camille Claudel attended in 1881, began a rivalry with Julian's. Philippo Colarossi had decided to imitate the model established by Rodolph Julian, but more equitably. Men and women paid the same price in Colarossi's studios on the Right Bank and lessons were open to both sexes. As Colarossi was himself a sculptor, he gave special attention to sculpture. This explains why many French and foreign women sculptors chose to study at Colarossi's. Such seems to be the case with Camille Claudel's English studio partners, Amy Singer and Emily Fawcett. The third partner, Jessie Lipscomb, joined them later in their studio.

Having the support of liberal-minded fathers, Camille Claudel's friends could obtain in Paris what was hard to find in England, that is, a certain liberty of expression in their art and a non-puritan lifestyle. At South Kensington (now the Royal College of Art), they had studied the nude, but had not been able to perfect their technique any further. Having been awarded the Queen's Prize in 1882 and the National Silver Medal in 1883, Jessie Lipscomb could easily have entered the Royal Academy, had this institution not still refused women access to the live model.

So Lipscomb crossed the Channel to study in Paris, where she ended up as Rodin's pupil, then assistant, at the same time as Camille Claudel. Lipscomb limited herself mostly to busts (fig. 82). Unlike Camille Claudel, she did not attempt large sculptures and avoided imaginary and allegorical subjects, which possibly explains why her sculptures were never exhibited in France.

The sudden end to Jessie Lipscomb's career illustrates what often happened in female artists' careers in the nineteenth century. A serious quarrel with Camille Claudel suddenly deprived her of her Paris studio and above all Rodin's teaching and protection. Given that it would be difficult for her to pursue her artistic career without the protection of an important artist, she decided to marry her childhood sweetheart and to give up sculpture. Her studio partner, Amy Singer, did the same a few years later. For both, as with many women, marriage marked the end of their artistic careers. It is therefore hardly surprising that neither Félicie de Fauveau nor Rosa Bonheur got married and that Adèle d'Affry chose to remain a widow.

And yet, marrying a famous artist could facilitate access to the Salon, whose jury was entirely male, and encourage contacts with critics and patrons. Working under the protection of their respective husbands, Charlotte Besnard and Marie Cazin had long careers, Besnard opting for historically inspired subjects and Cazin for religious or symbolic ones. Both enjoyed modest but regular success and obtained silver medals in 1900. Marie Cazin also had the honor of being the first woman on the jury of the Société Nationale des Beaux-Arts.[17] Yet both women never left the shadows of their famous husbands.

Hélène Bertaux did not have this problem. On the contrary, her husband sacrificed his own career for hers and ever became her marble carver. Perhaps to thank him, but above all to emphasize her condition as wife and mother and efface her divorce from the artist Charles Allévit, Hélène Bertaux always presented herself as Madame Léon Bertaux. Born in 1825, the daughter of a sculptor, she used her considerable gifts as a diplomat to obtain what she wanted for herself and other women.

Bertaux soon realized that the Académies Julian and Colarossi, despite their undeniable positive aspects, were too expensive for too many women. In 1879, she opened the École de Sculpture pour les Femmes, where young women of modest means could study for an artistic career. Bertaux offered a wide variety of courses, some oriented toward the crafts and industry, others toward the academic sculpture popular at the Salon. Two years later, in an attempt to get around the difficulties encountered by women at the Salon, she founded the Union des Femmes Peintres et Sculpteurs, which enabled her to organize annual exhibitions for female artists.[18]

Convinced that there could be no equality in artistic education as long as women were barred from the École des Beaux-Arts, Hélène Bertaux began a long struggle with officials who would hear nothing of it. In 1889, when Bertaux and the painter Virginie Demont-Breton demanded a special studio for women, they were told it would be too expensive. But the same officials were indignant at the idea of women sharing a studio with men. For years Bertaux and Demont-Breton wrote endless letters, petitioned and sought interviews, until in 1897 their efforts were finally rewarded: women were admitted into the École des Beaux-Arts—but in separate studios. Three years later, they gained access to the life model and in 1903 they could enter the competition for the Prix de Rome.[19] The first woman to obtain it was sculptor Lucienne Heuvelmans in 1911.

This success was largely due to Bertaux's tenacity and her gifts as a diplomat. Neither revolutionary nor profoundly feminist, she merely wanted to obtain the same rights for women and men in artistic education. She was not concerned about freedom of expression. As a sculptor, she was very conservative and unquestioningly adopted the academic style encouraged by the ministry of fine arts and the École des Beaux-Arts,

a choice that ensured her considerable commercial success and fame during her lifetime and only the indifference of posterity. After her death, the state even refused to accept Léon Bertaux's donation of her remaining sculptures.[20]

Hélène Bertaux contrasted sharply with Camille Claudel, whom she seems never to have met. Claudel never showed up at the Union des Femmes Peintres et Sculpteurs and kept away from feminist organizations. She utterly rejected the idea, advocated by Bertaux, of a female art different from male art. She expected to exhibit at the same Salons as her male colleagues and with the same freedom of expression.

If one compares, as Claudine Mitchell has done, Bertaux's greatest success, Psyche Under the Influence of Mystery (fig. 83), and a nude by Claudel, one is immediately struck by Claudel's daring and originality.[21] Bertaux's Psyche is chaste, the "virgin who is no longer a child but not yet a woman,"[22] modest, thoughtful, smooth, white, alone, and devoid of all sexuality. Most of Camille's nudes, however, often couples, exude sexuality. The woman's breasts are accentuated, her stomach is rounded, her pose is voluptuous or dramatic and her flesh bears the marks of the artist's fingers.

No other woman dared, like Claudel, to openly defy the constraints imposed on her freedom of expression. Sarah Bernhardt, who took up sculpture, did a few strange figure groups—The Kiss of the Sea, for example, in which a girl is being strangled by a crab[23]—but her indifference to propriety came from her demimonde lifestyle. The great actress did not need the encouragement of the art world to sell her sculptures: her admirers bought them for reasons other than their artistic merit. Other women sculptors sought success within the limits imposed by the institutions of the time. As a result, they were often accused of lacking imagination, but were nevertheless complimented for their "female gentleness."

At the end of the century, the influx of women from all classes into sculpture gave it a new aura of respectability without yet inciting women to join the avant-garde. In 1905, according to a contemporary source, 231 women were sculpting in Paris.[24] Many had come to study at the Colarossi, but a few became Rodin's pupils. Out of a hundred of Rodin's pupils, more than a third were women.[25] One of them was the Scotswoman Ottilie McLaren, who first tried to take lessons with Camille Claudel, then became Rodin's pupil. Two years later, she returned to Scotland, married her fiancé and opened a sculpture school for women based on Rodin's methods. Her respectable career, built on an enlightened but excessively short training and on brief contacts with the avant-garde, took the conventional path followed by most women of her generation. As Siân Reynolds has pointed out, these women were liberated from the forces of exclusion that had crushed previous generations, but did not yet have the freedom of expression associated with

_Fig. 83

a solid professional training. This would at last become possible in the twentieth century.[26]

The history of women sculptors in the nineteenth century is that of the enormous restrictions that artistic and social institutions imposed on them, and of the solutions they found to practice their art all the same. Apart from Camille Claudel, they did not openly rebel against the aesthetic values dictated by institutions but chose, for the most part, to work in the conventional style which would win them acceptance and success. Yet these pioneers all played their part in the slow but sure erosion of obstacles in artistic education, freedom of expression and the respect of society. They opened the way for great twentieth-century women sculptors such as Barbara Hepworth, Louise Bourgeois and Niki de Saint Phalle. Their contribution to the history of sculpture should be evaluated in the light of this not inconsiderable aspect of their work.

CAMILLE CLAUDEL, "A WOMAN OF GENIUS"? Marie-Victoire Nantet

When nature creates a man of genius, she shakes her torch on his head and says: go forth and be unhappy![1]

—Diderot

Camille Claudel most certainly was "a woman of genius," or "a genius" as one says today, the shorter formulation giving the proposition more power, as well as occulting the mark of the female sex that for so long barred women from the artistic Olympus. *Camille Claudel. Le génie est comme un miroir* ("Camille Claudel. Genius is Like a Mirror") is the enigmatic title of the most recent book on the artist.[2] Who, consequently, would dare contest such a universally acclaimed genius, one who imposes herself by virtue of being unquestioned. And how could one question it without pettiness, given the suffering the artist went through?[3] Was Camille Claudel's genius paid dearer than its worth, in such a way that one cannot approach the subject other than via the modest historical route? When was the word first used? On whose initiative? In what context? With what success? These questions laden with other questions enable one to query the artist's uncontested genius without stirring up a sterile debate.

A YOUNG WOMAN AT THE SALON OR THE POSSIBILITY OF GENIUS

This study being directed by its outcome, that is, Camille Claudel's accession to the status of genius,

I will outline here only the lineaments of a figure, perceptible in the very first review of the artist's work, and this of course in the knowledge that this hollow figure will only take on a full existence in relation to the word genius called upon to fill it in.

From 1885—date of the first critical mentions of Camille Claudel—to 1892, her principal intermediary was Léon Gauchez, writing under the pen name of Paul Leroi. Gauchez, editor of the review *L'Art*, was a devoted friend of Rodin and consequently an attentive critic of the work of the aspiring young artist. When, in 1886, he published several charcoal drawings by Rodin's twenty-two-year-old protégée in *L'Art*, Paul Leroi honored her with a short biographical note and praised her works on view at the Salon and also at the studio. Summing up, he wrote, "Character promises to be Mlle Camille Claudel's principal quality,"[4] for whom, motivated by a "sacred fire" and fortified by a "feeling of her worth," he saw more than promising horizons opening up for her "rare aptitudes" emphasized by "virile drawing." Yet already looming was the risk the young woman fascinated by her Master was taking: of becoming his "reflection."[5]

Faithful to his initial view, Paul Leroi modified it in 1887, 1888, 1889 and 1892 in his reports on new works by Camille Claudel at the Salon. Successively, the bust *My Brother* (cat. 27, p. 123), *Sakuntala* (cat. 47, p. 105) and the busts of *Charles Lhermitte* (cat. 49, p. 120) and *Auguste Rodin* (cat. 56, p. 77) magnetized the few motifs destined to crown the "inspired young woman." To her character, passion, virility and pride he added a "surprising sureness," a quality which triumphed in *Sakuntala*: "It is truly prodigious that a woman so young should have been able to conceive and execute a group of this importance so successfully."[6] From prodigy to genius is a short step, one which Paul Leroi, carried away, might have taken on seeing the bust of *Auguste Rodin* so acclaimed by the critics in 1892, particularly by the highly perspicacious Gustave Geffroy.[7] But he did not take it. His warning of 1886 had not been heeded. He considered the work a pastiche of the Master, to whom the pupil has deliberately sacrificed the originality with which she is nevertheless richly endowed. In Paul Leroi's eyes, Camille Claudel would never get over this failure. From then on it was his criticism of an artist who had not found herself, due to either excessive or insufficient originality, that prevailed over his praise. But had he not withdrawn his support, which his short and intermittent observations would not have sufficed to give substance, for the young woman's prodigious talent? It was the critic's fault that he was a personality known beyond his circle and disposed of a style and a platform worthy of him.[8]

THE COMMON GROUND OF THE GENIUS

Having reached the moment when Camille Claudel would be publicly proclaimed a genius by Octave Mirbeau in 1895, brief mention should be made of the historical and cultural stage constructed by the sum of experiences and reflections on the subject, a stage on which Camille Claudel is about to make her entry, and who by doing so, very much despite herself, will bring about her partial reconfiguration, linked to the unexpected appearance of her female person on it.

A pretty good picture of this stage is given by Pierre Larousse's entry in his *Grand dictionnaire universel du xixᵉ siècle* published between 1866 and 1879—that is, during Camille Claudel's childhood and adolescence. His examination of "genius" from all angles over several pages, of its semantic classifications, historical perspectives and eternally topical dilemmas, enables one to reconstruct, as a backdrop to the particular case created by the genius attributed to Camille Claudel, the common ground of the prevailing thought on the subject. To the extent that one is somewhat ashamed to recall it. Let us therefore go with Pierre Larousse through some truths already hackneyed in the late nineteenth century.

Firstly, the conception of genius in the French tradition—one still valid today—can be traced back to Diderot. From him stems its new promotion, linked to its uncompromising originality. A promotion which has its reverse side. The inspiring Muse of Antiquity, to whom the inspired responded by complying with academic rules, was superseded by the outstanding power of the innate gift. The genius-monster had now been singled out, one who suffers commensurately from his hypersensitivity and his acute awareness of his situation as someone misunderstood. His mission may be superior, but it is one which nobody understands or helps him accomplish. Sorrow becomes the genius's lot and the ever-recurrent theme of a litany of confessions, poems and novels. The grand gesture of the sacrificed genius is pursued from work to work, all the more successfully because the tragic life of so many great artists gives it credibility. For the record, with Pierre Larousse, one should mention, following the unfortunate poet Tasso, held as an example by the Romantic generation of 1830, one or two of these suffering creators. Balzac, for instance, who took up the gauntlet by saying, "There is not a voice here in my favor. Everything is hostile. One has to resign oneself to this. They treat me like a man of genius. One should feel proud, I suppose."[9] Or Delacroix, who observed at his own expense, "Unhappiness is the lot of great men."[10]

Onto the Romantic stage of genius no female artist could overtly step as such, except in fiction, in the person of the poetess Corinne, heroine of the novel by Madame de Staël.[11] or as Camille de Maupin, whose admirer Calyste du Guénic says in Balzac's *Béatrix*, "Camille is an artist, she has genius, and leads one of those exceptional existences that cannot be judged like ordinary existences."[12] Whereas the living model for Camille de Maupin, the writer George Sand, the only woman suspected of being a genius by some of her entourage, draws the modest circle within which she chose to situate herself: "I have always found the word 'inspiration' very ambitious and only applying to geniuses of the first order. I would never dare use it for myself, without protesting a little against the pomposity of a term that finds its outcome only in incontestable success."[13]

In Pierre Larousse's eyes, the genius, rid of the existential straitjacket of his misfortune, shines with a triple fire, by his originality, his individuality and his exemplariness. Genius cannot be acquired or demonstrated and manifests itself by a power of inventiveness and amplitude of vision, signs of an unpredictable and headstrong personality. Such was the backdrop that the living actors on the stage of genius were ceaselessly reweaving, particularly in the last third of the nineteenth century, when critics were intent on discovering the genius of the future.[14] There was no shortage of geniuses, eligible by their great works accomplished in misery and amid general hostility (Gauguin, Cézanne, van Gogh), and "artists' novels," with their cortege of sad destinies, were being churned out in droves. Out of them all, one should mention Émile Zola's L'Œuvre, published in 1886, which hit artistic circles like a bolt out of the blue. The essential aspect of this major novel is the direction given to the figure of the genius by his incarnation as a failed painter, in whom some —Monet, Cézanne—rightly or wrongly saw themselves. When Camille Claudel began her career, the fictional genius had momentarily ended its own in the naturalist degradation of the heroic model inherited from Romanticism.[15]

GENIUS BY ASSOCIATION

The year 1893 was a dazzling one for Camille Claudel. She freed herself from Rodin, and her strong and new creativity revealed itself in her famous letter to her brother, in which she describes her sculptures from life that she was working on (cat. 202, p. 239). In March, Armand Dayot highlighted her emancipation in a sensitive portrait of an artist who has retired to her "solitary retreat on boulevard d'Italie," where she was "seeking in relentless feverish work the definitive formula of her dream"[16]—a dream which bloomed in May in the broad daylight of the Salon of the Société Nationale des Beaux-Arts, where The Waltz (cat. 64, pp. 112, 114–16) and Clotho (cat. 63, pp. 152, 154–55) were widely acclaimed. The two works, mysteriously paired by their exhibition together, fired the imaginations of Roger Marx, Gabriel Mourey, Frantz Jourdain and many others. She swept them into the domain of the romance or novel. One can thus conclude that these two sculptures so suited to translation into literature responded by their motifs and manner to the spirit of the time and its innermost fantasies. Yet an article in May 1893 rises above the others in its scope and talent. Its author was the writer, journalist and art critic Octave Mirbeau, a great friend of Rodin and famous for his humorous articles. It is not his very fin-de-siècle description of The Waltz and Clotho which interests us here, but his two opening paragraphs devoted to the artist herself. From the outset, Octave Mirbeau links Camille Claudel to her dual filiation, recalling that she is the pupil of Auguste Rodin and the sister of Paul Claudel.[17] In other words, she was living in the company of two creators of genius. For Octave Mirbeau, Rodin's genius, which he had often praised to the skies, went without saying. But he goes to great pains to describe for his ignorant readers his impressions on reading Tête d'or and La Ville, two dramas of "sometimes still confused, sometimes obscure genius but which illuminate with lightning clarity." And he concludes concerning their author, "I have written genius, and this is the only quality one can ascribe to their author." How come Mirbeau in 1893 grants the young author of *Tête d'or* and *La Ville* the genius which he did not yet accord his sister, sculptor of two works he also admired, *The Waltz* and *Clotho*, and for which he manifestly felt more affinities? A detour into the then emerging history of the genius attributed to Paul Claudel will perhaps shed light on this.

Paul Claudel, then posted in the United States, wrote to Octave Mirbeau on June 3, 1893, thanking him for his article, in which his name, hidden behind *Tête d'or* and *La Ville*,[18] was revealed for the first time. Claudel had indeed published his two plays in 1890 and 1893, at his own expense and anonymously. Yet by sending them to certain targeted friends and literary personalities, he revealed that he was their author, a mystery-perpetuating strategy that rapidly developed into an admiring rumor. Maurice Maeterlinck wrote to Claudel in December 1890 that he found genius in *Tête d'or*—"You have burst into my house like a horrible tempest!"—and he made it known in his circles.[19] Marcel Schwob, a fellow disciple and friend of Claudel, enthused in turn. And this enthusiasm swept through the small group of artists and writers—Léon Daudet, Camille Mauclair, Jules Renard—who, along with Camille and Paul Claudel, used to meet in Marcel Schwob's loft around 1892. "Claudel is considered a man of genius by us,"[20] the latter wrote in his *Journal*, and Claudel acknowledged this, not without pride, sixty years later in his *Mémoires improvisés*.[21] A sentiment echoed, it seems, by his sister, "who wrote to him incessantly: I am proud of you. People say I resemble you."[22] And it was a reciprocal price, as proven by the eulogistic conclusion of Claudel's letter to Mirbeau: "I am even more grateful to you for my sister than myself; she has an admirable quality of imagination."[23]

Their brother-and-sister-as-equals relationship, induced by their reciprocal admiration, exhibited itself very early on in the bust *My Brother*, the sister's portrayal of her sixteen-year-old brother. She then saw him as she aspired to be seen by him, through his proud gaze. Until the day when, shifting into fantasy, this figure in turn embodied, for Marcel Schwob and his friends the conqueror of the Caucasus, to whom Claudel *nolens volens* lent his features in the 1890s: "Claudel has the head of his book, a head of gold, features etched in coal."[24] Words which became even truer when carried away by his passion for the work, Marcel Schwob had the audacity to patinate his plaster of the bust gold,[25] an act materializing the fantasy and giving it an archaic power of persuasion. *Tête d'or* exists. He can be seen and touched.

By paying homage to her brother with this bust, Camille Claudel was unwittingly favoring in advance the orchestration of his genius that took place between 1890 and 1893, when the mystery shrouding the play's author brought about the exaltation of his image, which became identified with that of his eponymous hero. This was to the detriment no doubt of the genius of the bust itself, eclipsed by the reincarnation of the figure she had created[26] in the mythical self-portrait of Paul Claudel, alias Tête d'or. The scales however tipped in favor of the younger brother in the eyes of the small literary and artistic world in which brother and sister were received and applauded together. The elder Camille was seen as the (certainly very gifted) parent of this Tête d'or now destined for the limelight, of this very young prodigy, author and hero all in one, who combined an extraordinary verbal creativity with a desire to conquer and an intrepid manner. Paul Claudel's genius—to which Marcel Schwob had drawn Octave Mirbeau's attention in 1892, with the consent of the person concerned, by sending him Tête d'or[27]—could but flow, in 1893, from the pen of a famous critic who had always been fascinated by geniuses—even if the latter had expressed reservations concerning the young dramatist in his reply to Marcel Schwob,[28] reservations that he developed in criticisms in his article on Camille Claudel.

THE BIRTH OF A WOMAN OF GENIUS

In 1893, Camille Claudel saw herself assigned the following position by Octave Mirbeau: "Instructed by such a master (Rodin), and living in the intellectual intimacy of such a brother, it is hardly surprising that Mlle Camille Claudel, true to her family, is delivering us works whose inventiveness and power of execution surpass everything one could expect from a woman."[29] For Mirbeau, Camille Claudel had still not yet become a great artist in her own right. She owed her "very

high, very male art" to the two artists who had supported her. Here perhaps lies one of the reasons why the great critic had not yet accorded her genius. But the stage was changing more quickly than imagined. Paul Claudel left it shortly after 1893, having only just come on to it, Camille Mauclair reveals in his mémoires.[30] The writer, now abroad, was soon forgotten. His star had only shone for three years in the limited firmament of the Symbolists.

Camille Claudel's star, on the other hand, reached its zenith thanks to Octave Mirbeau in 1895. The critic, full of admiration for Les Causeuses, which was shown at the Salon of the Sociéte Nationale des Beaux-Arts (cat. 76, p. 238),[31] devoted an entire article to her. He was undoubtedly also fulfilling the expectations of Camille Claudel's entourage, who, as a letter from Rodin to Mirbeau attests, were concerned about her difficult financial situation: "For Mlle Claudel, who has the talent for the Champ-de-Mars, she is almost unappreciated. You have a project for her, you have made this known, despite the time of lies you have sacrificed yourself for her."[32] On the one hand the "unappreciated" artist, on the other the critic who "sacrifices himself"—this was the marriage of inconvenience at the root of the article. From the bottom of an empty garden, far from the exhibition halls, could be heard a dual moan. One, Mirbeau's, taking over from another, that of his fictional alter ego, the painter Kariste, in resonating all the components of Camille Claudel's drama before they let out a final "cry of pain"—She is unknown! Collectors are only interested in famous artists! The state ignores her! She does not live from her art! Despair has shattered her!

What misfortune, yes, but also what glory! In one fell swoop the artist reached her apotheosis, described here by Kariste: "Do you realize that we're in the presence of something unique here, a revolt of nature: a woman of genius?" To which Mirbeau replies: "Of genius, yes, my dear Kariste, but don't say this so loud. There are those whom this bothers and who would not forgive Mlle Claudel for being thus described." There, in two sentences, is the lot of the genius which Madame de Staël had already described in her time: "Genius in society's midst is a pain, an inner fever that should be treated as one would an illness if the rewards of glory did not sweeten the sorrows."[33] For Mirbeau, there was nothing new in this. Many artists had already sided with him under the Romantic label of genius, Rodin first of all, but also Monet and others, thirteen in all according to specialists on the writer.[34] Thirteen martyrs of creation, then, only one of them a woman. Mirbeau's well-known misogyny matters little as soon as it gives way here in the face of evidence of female genius. It is more important, however, to understand why it was *that* particular woman at *that* particular time—the very artist who for a long time had been exhibiting the "masterpieces" recalled by Kariste, "the *Waltz,* the *Fate,* the *Head of a Child,* the *Bust of Rodin.*"

One should first note the reserved interest Mirbeau showed in female artists of renown. Marie Bashkirtseff has "admirable instincts" but "in the end resorts to procedure."[35] Mary Cassatt, on the contrary, has craft.[36] Berthe Morisot is disturbing: "She seems to paint on her nerves."[37] Eva Gonzales is "simplicity, sincerity and serenity!"[38] He finds graces in each, which he counterbalances with a few criticisms. Even the young Marie Bashkirtseff's very moving death does not transform her into an icon. The homage he pays Camille Claudel in 1895 contrasts stridently with this. Mirbeau is giving us to understand the *coup de force* the artist represented. Her female genius was a revolution against the order of things. Through Camille Claudel's example, genius rekindled its transgressive origins, the hostile response from society in so many spheres being only a substitute. Hence the attention Mirbeau gave to the case of Camille Claudel. As a "revolt of nature," it realized the paradigm of all genius. And paradox deserved to be staged!

Certainly, but why was it that at that time the honor of doing so fell to Camille Claudel? The reply is manifold. It was firstly a question of opportunity. At the heart of the empty garden that Octave Mirbeau chose as a stage set lay *Les Causeuses,* which she exhibited for the first time at the Salon Besides "the absolute beauty" of this "admirable group," it seems that it was by their very whispering that *Les Causeuses* inaugurated the legend of genius of which Kariste and Mirbeau made themselves the megaphone. But it so happened that in 1895 the misfortune indissociable from the legend became a reality for Camille Claudel. The so very favorable situation of 1893 had suddenly been reversed. The artist was now more to be pitied, she was short of money, her brother and Rodin had distanced themselves from her, a press campaign had been mounted against her at Châteauroux . . . in short, she had crossed the threshold of misfortune, both in reality and in hearsay. Listen to Mirbeau: "With these ardent natures, in these seething souls, despair can plumb such depths that hope carries them to soaring heights. She is thinking of abandoning her art." Where did Mirbeau get this information? From the rumor then circulating, no doubt. True to her image, Camille was in the process of becoming a figure of fantasy. Mirbeau bestowed genius on the artist at the tragic time when she was supposedly about to give up creating. In which case her genius would continue to manifest itself solely in the stigmata of her exalted temperament. Thus defined by Octave Mirbeau in 1895,

Camille Claudel, under the inherited sign of misfortune, was the vehicle of a dual displacement of the tradition of genius, from masculine to feminine and from the work to the human being.

A Genius That Goes Without Saying

From 1895, the word "genius" went hand in hand with Camille Claudel, Mirbeau having been the first to have uttered it. The manner in which the artist is designated in the correspondence of those close to her and in art criticism confirms this hypothesis. Rodin, for example, wrote to his friend Gabriel Mourey in reply to his letter of May 13, 1895, "We have been friends now for over two years so do something for this woman of genius (and I measure my words) whom I love so much" (cat. 204). Never before had he referred to Camille as such, but rather as, depending on whom he was speaking to, "my dear headstrong one," "our darling queen" or "my pupil Camille Claudel who has talent." As Mirbeau's article had just been published, one can assume that the door was already open. From the moment the word "genius" had been used, it would be jumped on. The detonating role played by Mirbeau is confirmed by critics' references to his article. In his report on the June 1895 Salon, Charles Morice proclaimed, "Mlle Claudel has genius, says Octave Mirbeau."[39] But on two occasions, in 1896 and 1897, Mirbeau repeated this, as though having to hammer the point home. His "aesthetic combat" on behalf of genius now benefited Camille Claudel, who had been excluded by academic critics apparently because of preconceived ideas about her gender.[40] Her confirmed status as victim was a perfect illustration of a scenario already used by Rodin and Monet and which no longer suited them given their success.

An enthusiastic article on the artist's life and career by Henry de Braisne in 1897 enables one to gauge the support for Camille's genius at that time: by making her a member of their jury "[the sculptors of the Champ-de-Mars] were not put off by the word genius formerly used by great writers when describing a woman whose energetic and obsessive physiognomy nobody has yet defined."[41] Does this mean that Camille Claudel owed her admission to the Société Nationale des Beaux-Arts to writers? The more "literary" the criticism of the time was in its perception and modalities, the more it saw Camille Claudel as having genius. The more professional critics, on the other hands, such as Gustave Geffroy, refrained from using the word while nevertheless expressing their admiration for the artist. One should also note that, rather unexpectedly, Mathias Morhardt, in his famous article in *Mercure de France* in 1898, only uses it with regard to Camille Claudel in its prime sense of ability. The model at work in the story of her life is a warlike one. An upright and courageous artist making her way to the summit alone: "She is of the race of heroes."[42]

As time passed, Camille Claudel's genius became nuanced by the growing pathos linked to the artist's fall. This was Paul Claudel's view of his sister from 1905. "The poor girl is sick . . . For all her genius, life for her is full of so many trials, tribulations and weariness that its prolongation is not to be desired,"[43] he wrote to his friend Gabriel Frizeau. Paul Vibert, for his part,

demanded in 1914 that "the master Rodin's great pupil of genius M.lle Camille Claudel"[44] should be released from her asylum. Thus formulated, his demand bestows upon Camille Claudel that tragic aura that forces admiration, respect and pity. Much later, Mathias Morhardt, Eugène Blot and Léon Daudet recalled it in the same terms, their memory now conditioned by her sad end.

COMPETITION AMONG GENIUSES

In fin-de-siècle France, Camille was not the only artist on the road to genius. The trajectories of Gauguin, van Gogh and Cézanne crossed hers in the 1890s. The particular profile of each emerged. The first genius to be suddenly recognized was van Gogh's, in an article by Georges-Albert Aurier published in *Mercure de France* in January 1890 entitled "The Isolated Ones—Vincent van Gogh." For the critics, the painter was the image of prodigious excess. "He is a fanatic, the enemy of bourgeois sobriety and meticulousness, a kind of drunk giant . . . a terrible and panic-stricken genius."[45] In her study *La Gloire de Van Gogh*, Nathalie Heinich interprets Aurier's stance in the context of a pro-modernist combat, for which van Gogh was the "battle horse." It was he who had been assigned the role of prophetically embodying the new truth in art, and Julien Leclerc, in his article in *Mercure de France* in May 1890, draws the following conclusions: "There are ten pictures by van Gogh at the Indépendants which show his rare genius." Mirbeau goes further in March 1891, after the tragic death of a painter "in whom died a beautiful flame of genius."[46]

In contrast to the explosion, innocent of any personal strategy, of van Gogh's "neurotic" genius, there was Gauguin's calculated, staged progress toward genius through his quest for a new footing. The publicity given his forthcoming departure for Tahiti in April 1891 prompted Stéphane Mallarmé to write to Octave Mirbeau as early as January asking the great critic to "support this rare artist, whom . . . few tortures are spared in Paris."[47] Mirbeau complied with a long article published in *L'Écho de Paris* on February 16, 1891. His homage takes the form of a novelized biography, the first expression of a legend in which Gauguin is portrayed as painter, poet, apostle and demon![48] If the word "genius" is never actually used, it is nonetheless there and waiting on the horizon for this man "fleeing civilization, deliberately seeking oblivion and silence to better listen to the inner voices that are drowned out by the din of our passions and quarrels." Two years later, in 1893, Charles Morice takes melancholic stock in *Mercure de France* of all the fuss made over Gauguin: "Other critics, carried away by this (Mirbeau) and to appear *avant-garde*, have also proclaimed Gauguin's genius . . . and soon ran out of breath."[49] It was a means for Morice to single himself out as the only persevering and unhypo-

critical defender of the exiled genius who had recently returned to France.

There was also a legend afoot concerning the "misanthrope" Cézanne, fuelled by Gustave Geffroy, Emile Bernard, his dealer Ambroise Vollard and many others. Among the many anecdotes is this one by Bernard: "One evening, when I was telling him about Balzac's *Chef-d'œuvre inconnu* and about Freinhofer, the hero of the drama, he stood up at table and there before me, without a word, repeatedly tapping his chest with his index finger, accused himself of being the character in the novel."[50] In his quest for the absolute in painting, Cézanne saw himself as Balzac's portrayal of genius, as a painter driven to madness by the demands of his art. In doing so, in his clairvoyance, he leads the fictional hero to a realization of the failure that Balzac denied him. As a result of this quest for the absolute, Cézanne's refusal to delude himself about his oeuvre is perhaps the origin of his disturbing reputation as a difficult person.

What the geniuses of Camille Claudel, van Gogh, Cézanne and Gauguin have in common is that they were perceived and disseminated via scenarios-cum-legends that spotlighted the nature of their exceptionalness. Whether these artists did or did not, consciously or not, collaborate with the scenario depends. They also have in common their agreed misfortune, society's hostility toward them, the price of their pride, to be paid by their sacrifice. But each have their distinguishing traits. Van Gogh's genius is characterized by audacity and saintliness, Gauguin's by power and theatricality, Cézanne's by rigor and lucidity, and Camille Claudel's by defiance and pathos.

But how did Camille see herself? She talks little of herself in her letters and without undue consideration, but during her fits of paranoia, she emphasized her gifts as a great artist and Rodin and his consorts' total lack of talent—to the extent that her increasing exaltation in her genius can be seen as a measure of the progress of her pathology. As for the possible depictions of herself in her work, although a number of them admit their pain, none are direct depictions of genius and its poses.

To conclude, let us return to the question asked by Kariste in 1895: "Do you realize that we're in the presence of something unique here . . . a woman of genius?" The person he is speaking to, Mirbeau, certainly does know this because his intention is to declare it. His opinion is based on experience (he found the sculptures by Camille at the Salon admirable) and on the tragic notion he has of genius. In both her exceptional works and her painful life the artist responded to this dual expectation.

Was Camille Claudel "a woman of genius"? Yes, is our unanimous, heartfelt reply today. Her work moves us by what it confides. We apprehend *Sakuntala*, *La Petite Châtelaine*, *The Wave*, *The Age of Maturity*, *Deep Thought* and *Perseus* as the poignant story of a life, of which our own existences with their sufferings and failures are a modest echo. We are revolted by the fact that certain art historians could have contested Camille Claudel's genius. They claim that she did not renew the language of sculpture, that her work, with its frequently recycled motifs, is meager, uneven in quality—notably in the late anecdotal pieces (the *Fireplaces* series)—and academic (*Perseus*).

What a contrast to the daring, multiple and fecund oeuvre of Auguste Rodin or Paul Claudel. But must one for all that deprive Camille Claudel of her genius? One should rather trust Rodin and Claudel, who both paid tribute to her: "I showed where she would find gold; but the gold she found is all hers."[51] With Auguste Rodin, we discover the receptive aspect of Camille Claudel's genius, that of the artist with multiple antennae picking up the Rodinian, Symbolist or Art Nouveau ideas and methods then in the air. Yet, her brother tells us, a work by Camille Claudel "in the middle of the apartment is, simply by its form, like those curious rocks the Chinese collect, a kind of monument to inner thought, a snatch of a theme offered up to all dreams."[52] Receptivity is answered by interiority, in such a way that Camille Claudel's genius, born out of defiance and sensitive to pathos, is revealed by "the most 'animated' and most 'spiritual' art of the world."[53]

If "inner thought" really is the fire burning at the center of Camille Claudel's work, then could one not suppose that its secret light could radiate over the work of a lover and a brother? Kafka wrote, "The hollow which the work of genius has burned into our surroundings is a good place into which to put one's little light."[54]

NOTES

CLAUDEL: THE EARLY WORKS
(pp. 18–27)

[1] Letter from Camille Claudel to Paul Claudel, March 3, 1927. See CLAUDEL 2003, no. 280.

[2] CLAUDEL 1969, p. 13.

[3] See Xavier de Massary, "La famille Claudel à Villeneuve-sur-Fère," in RONDIN / NANTET 2003, pp. 69–87.

[4] CLAUDEL 1969, pp. 18–19.

[5] MORHARDT 1898, p. 710.

[6] Paul Claudel, "Ma sœur Camille," in MUSÉE RODIN 1951, p. 3. Paul Claudel confided to Henri Guillemin that Camille was "appallingly violent, with a furious genius for mockery" (GUILLEMIN 1968, p. 45). Again according to Paul: "In our frequent quarrels, I do not recall ever getting the upper hand; and anyway, if I happened to believe I had, a few well-applied scratches instantly reminded me of the true order of things." Published in Le Figaro littéraire, September 3, 1949, as quoted in GUILLEMIN 1968, p. 45.

[7] MORHARDT 1898, p. 711.

[8] MORHARDT 1898, p. 712.

[9] MORHARDT 1898, p. 711.

[10] CLAUDEL 1969, p. 19.

[11] MORHARDT 1898, p. 712.

[12] Since Boucher was in Italy in 1877–78, it is tempting to assume he would have met Camille Claudel in 1879, as Jacques Cassar did (CASSAR 2003, pp. 54–55). A plaster statuette currently in a private collection attests to this relationship. Signed and dedicated "To Camille Claudel in memory of A. Boucher," the work, depicting a young girl reading, is probably a portrait of Camille Claudel. (Reproduced in PINET / PARIS 2003, p. 20.)

[13] Quoted in ANTOINE 1988, p. 34.

[14] CLAUDEL 1969, p. 20.

[15] Quoted in ANTOINE 1988, p. 34.

[16] Paul Claudel's service record, which recently came to light, reveals that during his military service (1888) he was living at his father's in Compiègne. Anne Rivière, who alerted us to this fact, concludes from this that after the marriage of Louise Claudel on August 16, 1888, Madame Claudel and her son had probably joined Louis-Prosper in Compiègne.

[17] MORHARDT 1898, p. 713.

[18] Paul Claudel, "Ma sœur Camille," in MUSÉE RODIN 1951, p. 3.

[19] AYRAL-CLAUSE 2002, p. 27.

[20] Eugénie Plé told Paul Petit about this incident in 1931, quoted in ANTOINE 1988, p. 34.

[21] My thanks to Anne Rivière for this information.

[22] LEROI 1886, p. 65.

[23] Indeed, when he saw the David and Goliath figure group, Dubois is said to have asked Camille Claudel whether she had "taken lessons with Monsieur Rodin!" See MORHARDT 1898, p. 712.

[24] LEROI 1886, p. 65. Boucher won the Grand Prix du Salon with his figure group La Piété filiale in the summer of 1881.

[25] MORHARDT 1898, p. 716.

[26] As Ruth Butler emphasizes, the earliest document attesting to this trip is a letter from Boucher to Rodin from Florence dated September 12, 1882 (BUTLER 1993, p. 529 no. 3, chapter 15). The Musée Rodin Archives has a second letter from Boucher to Rodin from Florence dated January 14, 1883. Curiously, no mention at all is made in these two letters of either Camille Claudel or any other pupil that Boucher may have entrusted to Rodin before leaving for Italy. The tone of Boucher's letters to his "dear friend" Rodin amply illustrates their relatively close relationship. Although we know that Rodin also knew Paul Dubois, the scarce correspondence between the two sculptors and its content seem to indicate that their relationship was less close.

[27] Discussing Camille Claudel's teachers before she met Rodin, Odile Ayral-Clause writes that "she never claimed any of Colarossi's teachers as her masters. Instead, she named Alfred Boucher and Paul Dubois, although she does not appear to have studied with Dubois, who was director of the École des Beaux-Arts and Boucher's mentor" (AYRAL-CLAUSE 2002, p. 28). Ruth Butler is more prudent: "Dubois offered her enough critical advice that Camille saw fit to put his name on her roster of professors the first time she exhibited in the Salon" (BUTLER 1993, p. 180).

[28] Apart from the mention made in the 1883 Salon catalogue (and restated in the booklets of the Salons of 1888, 1903 and 1905), Alfred Boucher's name would never again resurface in Camille Claudel's career after his departure for Italy in late summer 1882. As regards Dubois, we know that Camille Claudel mentioned his name to a journalist in 1897 (see BRAISNE 1897). Much later, in December 1937, Paul Claudel also mentioned in his Journal "Camille and her first attempts at drawing and sculpture. The sculptor Boucher at Nogent-sur-Seine. Paul Dubois – Rodin –." See MUSÉE D'ORSAY 1988, p. 50.

[29] MORHARDT 1898, p. 715.

[30] CLAUDEL 1913, p. 6. Contrary to the caption, the work reproduced in L'Art décoratif is not a plaster but a terracotta.

[31] Taking into account the period of activity of the "Thiébaut Frères" company. See LEBON 2003, p. 247.

[32] CLAUDEL 1969, p. 14.

[33] This oil, whose whereabouts are today unknown, belonged to Mathias Morhardt when it was reproduced in L'Art décoratif in 1913 (CLAUDEL 1913, p. 10). Although Morhardt discusses this portrait at some length, he curiously finds no link between it and the Old Woman bust (see MORHARDT 1898, p. 725). No comparison has been attempted since.

[34] The connection between the two busts was first established in PARIS 1984, pp. 36–37.

[35] Morhardt mentions that the work was first exhibited at the 1882 Salon (MORHARDT 1898, p. 715), but it was not until the following year that Camille Claudel's name first appeared in the Salon catalogue. It is therefore highly probable that the journalist made a mistake, especially as the artist herself does not seem to have remembered the exact date of this event, which in a letter written in February 1892 she situates in 1884. Camille Claudel presented a plaster of her "old woman" at the Exposition des Arts Libéraux in 1892. One wonders whether Old Woman was not the "Alsatian Woman (bust, terracotta patinated silver), three-quarter life-size" she exhibited at the 1902 Salon, especially given that the latter piece was then already an old work (see RIVIÈRE / GAUDICHON / GHANASSIA 2001, p. 184, cat. 65). Similarly, should one still consider Old Woman to be the "Bust Old Woman" Eugène Blot exhibited in his gallery three years later and which he listed in the catalogue as an edition of "50 casts" (cat. 7), even though not one of the Blot casts of Old Woman has been found to this day? (In fact, rather confusingly, the only old cast of Old Woman to have been found bears the mark of the Fumière et Cie foundry, and was therefore cast between 1906 and 1926 [see supra, note 31], that is, in the middle of Blot's years of activity as Camille Claudel's dealer and publisher.) We at least know that Blot mentions an "Old Woman" to Jules Leblanc-Barbedienne in his letter dated December 17, 1936, when the former was selling to the latter "his reproduction rights for several pieces" by Camille Claudel (ANF). It was no doubt the same sculpture as the one presented in 1905. In the many commentaries on this exhibition, there is only one mention of the sculpture that intrigues us here in the numerous accounts of the event: "The Bust of an Old Woman, Abandon, The Waltz and Perseus are totally devoid of character" (DACIER 1905). Should one ascribe this lack of interest to the fact that critics had in front of them an old work that would have appeared pretty austere compared to Camille Claudel's mature works, which also included pieces as famous as The Implorer, Les Causeuses and The Wave? It seems legitimate and logical to suppose so.

Yet one has difficulty in understanding why in RIVIÈRE / GAUDICHON / GHANASSIA 2001 (cat. 45.4) the "Bust Old Woman" exhibited by Blot in 1905 is associated with the *Head of an Old Man from* The Age of Maturity *group*, only one Blot cast of which, marked "no. 1," has so far been identified, especially given that the latter composition was exhibited by Blot in 1908 (cat. 6) under the eminently explicit title "Bust. Old Man (study for no. 1)," "no. 1" being "Youth and the Age of Maturity." In fact, it is with the *Head of the Old Woman from* The Age of Maturity *group* that one might eventually be tempted to associate the "Bust Old Woman" exhibited in 1905. But one does so only with reluctance given that no bronze cast of this work has yet been located. Furthermore, if Blot owned the reproduction rights for this small work, he would not have failed to include it in the 1907 exhibition, in which, as mentioned above, not only the *Head of an Old Man from* The Age of Maturity *group* was exhibited, but also the group itself. A final consideration supports the association of the 1882 *Old Woman* and the "Bust Old Woman" exhibited by Blot in 1905. In his report on the exhibition, a journalist from *Studio* (ANONYMOUS 1906) writes that "in tiny pieces such as *The Bathers*, in busts and in the very beautiful couple in *The Waltz*, Camille Claudel shows us the full wealth of her admirable nature." Alongside "tiny pieces such as *The Bathers*," only some fifteen centimeters high, how could one believe that the only bust Blot exhibited in 1905 was the *Head of the Old Woman from* The Age of Maturity *group*, whose plaster version was only some 10 centimeters high?

36 Like RIVIÈRE / GAUDICHON / GHANASSIA 2001, p. 61, I am unable to attribute to Camille Claudel the *Buste d'homme* or *Bismarck* at the beginning of the PARIS 2000 catalogue raisonné, which is thought to be a fragment of a work dating from "c.1879–81" (p. 207). Neither does there seem to be any solid grounding for the premise by PARIS 2000 (p. 207, cat. 2) and RIVIÈRE / GAUDICHON / GHANASSIA 2001 (pp. 61–62, cat. 6) that the small plaster *Diana* reproduced

in their catalogues raisonnés dates from "1881" or "c.1881."

37 Contrary to RIVIÈRE / GAUDICHON / GHANASSIA 2001, p. 62 it is the bust *My Brother* or *Young Roman*, exhibited for the first time in 1887, to which Paul Leroi is referring when he discusses the "very remarkable bust of a *Young Man* sculpted by Camille Claudel" in his article on the 1886 Salon, and not the bust discussed here. The earliest reference to this work is in Joseph Beulay's *Catalogue du musée de Châteauroux*, published in 1910, in which the bust of *Paul Claudel as a Child* is listed under the title "Young Achilles," as a work by Camille Claudel, as "bust in bronze," and as a "gift of M. de Rothschild" (no. 499). Curiously to say the least. it is under the title "Young Roman" that the *Catalogue sommaire du musée de Châteauroux (musée Bertrand) et du Musée lapidaire* lists the same work in 1942 (cat. 104). When one discovers that this was a bronze 50 centimeters high exhibited at the Salon des Artistes Français in 1887 under the number 3779, one realizes that Henri Ratouis de Limay, author of the catalogue in question, is confusing two works: the Châteauroux bust of *Paul Claudel as a Child*, never exhibited during Camille Claudel's lifetime, with the *My Brother* or *Young Roman* bust whose bronze casts, donated by the Rothschild family, were then in four French museums: Avignon, Toulon, Toulouse and Tourcoing (see RIVIÈRE / GAUDICHON / GHANASSIA 2001, cat. 13.3). It is worth noting that the bronze in the Musée du Châteauroux was not in the *Camille Claudel* exhibition at the Musée Rodin in 1951, nor mentioned in the "Works by Camille Claudel unable to be included in this exhibition" section following the list of the forty exhibited pieces. The work was first shown in Paris in 1965, in the *Paul Claudel. Premières Œuvres 1886–1901* exhibition at the Bibliothèque Littéraire Jacques Doucet, under the title *Buste de Paul Claudel adolescent*, undated (BLJD 1965, p. 64, cat. 116). Gisèle Chovin uses the same erroneous Ratouis de Limay 1887 dating of the "Bust of Paul Claudel as a Child,"

shown in 1972 in her *Ernest Nivert 1871–1948* exhibition at the Musée Bertrand in Châteauroux (cat. 44).

38 This could explain certain "imperfections" pointed out by Reine-Marie Paris and which she considers "far more perceptible than in *La Vieille Hélène*, yet dating from the same period" (PARIS 2000, p. 209).

39 MORHARDT 1898, p. 715.

40 MORHARDT 1898, p. 715.

41 In his article in *L'Art décoratif*, Paul Claudel included a reproduction of the work with this caption: "Paul Claudel Aged Sixteen (1884)" (CLAUDEL 1913, p. 9). Very curiously, Morhardt includes this bust "with the rigid and sharp . . . profile of a Roman emperor" among the works sculpted by the artist before she entered Rodin's studio (MORHARDT 1898, p. 715).

42 In the catalogue at the end of his *Dossier Camille Claudel* published in 1937, six years after his death, the historian Jacques Cassar, equally interested in both Paul and Camille Claudel mentions, no doubt searching for the best interpretation of Morhardt's article. two busts sculpted by Camille Claudel in 1883: the first, the Châteauroux bust, entitled "Paul Claudel Aged Thirteen" or "Paul Claude as a Child," and the second, "Paul Claudel Aged Sixteen" or "My Brother" (CASSAR 2003, p. 504). From then on, authors understandably wanted to separate the execution dates of the two busts of Paul Claudel. In 1983, Anne Rivière dates the Châteauroux bust to 1882, entitling it "Paul Claudel (bust)" or "Roman Child" in the catalogue at the end of her work (RIVIERE 1983, p. 73), whereas the work is reproduced in the text itself as *Paul Claudel Aged Thirteen* (p. 11). The following year, Reine-Marie Paris, in her first "Catalogue de l'œuvre," lists the Châteauroux bronze as "YOUNG ROMAN. Paul Claudel Aged Thirteen," dating it to 1881 (PARIS 1984, p. 354). Also in 1984, Bruno Gaudichon opens the catalogue of the sculptures in the *Camille Claudel (1864–1943)* exhibition at the Musée Rodin and at the Musée Sainte-Croix in Poitiers with the *Bust of Paul Claudel Aged Thirteen*,

dating it to 1881 (one surely has to attribute the reference to "Paul Aged Eleven" in the commentary on the work to a typographical error, even if, by making the model two years younger, one is getting a little closer to what seems to be the truth) (PARIS / POITIERS 1984, p. 27). The same title and date are kept in the catalogue of the *Camille Claudel* exhibition at the Fondation Gianadda in Martigny and at the Musée Rodin in Paris in 1990–91 (MARTIGNY / PARIS 1990–91, pp. 141 and 145), and also in the two catalogues raisonnés of Camille Claudel's work (PARIS 2000, p. 209, cat. 3; RIVIÈRE / GAUDICHON / GHANASSIA 2001, pp. 62–63, cat. 7), and are now unhesitatingly adopted by all researchers.

43 RIVIÈRE / GAUDICHON / GHANASSIA 2001, p. 63.

44 RIVIÈRE / GAUDICHON / GHANASSIA 2001, p. 61.

45 MORHARDT 1898, p. 716. From the same period the journalist also mentions "various oil portraits among which one should note that of Mme Claudel," a work traditionally believed to have been destroyed by none other than the model herself, the artist's mother. See RIVIÈRE / GAUDICHON / GHANASSIA 2001, p. 200, cat. 95.

RODIN IN 1882:
ON THE ROAD TO SUCCESS
(pp. 28–35)

1 On this period, see MUSÉE RODIN 1997.

2 BARTLETT 1889, p. 263.

3 ANONYMOUS 1877.

4 Letter from Auguste Rodin to the president of the jury of the Exposition des Beaux-Arts [April 1877], AMR.

5 Letter from Auguste Rodin to Rose Beuret [after April 13, 1877]. See RODIN 1985, no. 21.

6 RILKE 1928, p. 27.

7 CLADEL 1936, p. 241.

8 CLADEL 1936, p. 119.

9 DUJARDIN-BEAUMETZ 1913, p. 65.

10 Ruth Butler, "Rodin and the Paris Salon," in WASHINGTON 1981, pp. 38–39.

11 CLADEL 1936, p. 133.

[12] DARGENTY 1883, p. 37.

[13] ANONYMOUS 1881, p. 266.

[14] FOURCAUD 1883, pp. 2–3.

[15] *Journal des Artistes*, April 11, 1883.

[16] *L'Art*, vol. 22, p. 124. The drawing is currently in the Fogg Art Museum, Cambridge, Massachusetts. See LYON / LONDON / NEW YORK 2003–4, cat. 113.

[17] BOURDELLE 1909, p. 376.

[18] DUJARDIN-BEAUMETZ 1913, p. 81.

[19] BERGERAT 1882.

[20] On the bust and the monument to Victor Hugo, see BESANÇON 2002.

IN RODIN'S STUDIO
(pp. 36–65)

[1] Concerning this commission, see LE NORMAND-ROMAIN 2002.

[2] Undated, except by the payment of 2,700 francs on October 14, 1880, ANF.

[3] THURAT 1882, p. 180.

[4] The date from which she had a studio in rue Notre-Dame-des-Champs is not precisely known.

[5] This is what one is led to believe in a letter from Alfred Boucher to Auguste Rodin dated September 12, 1882, in which he gives an account of his first impressions of Florence (AMR).

[6] Letter from Léon Lhermitte to Auguste Rodin, February 11, 1883 (AMR).

[7] BUTLER 1998, p. 110.

[8] Letter from Madeleine Jouvray to Auguste Rodin, December 29, 1883 (AMR). She presents herself as a pupil of Boucher and Rodin in the catalogues of the Salons in which she exhibited from 1889. She asked Rodin for his authorization on March 31, 1889, preferring to write to him rather than go and see him as, in her words, "I always leave disheartened after visiting you." On Jouvray, see ROUBAIX 2003, p. 228.

[9] "Miss Lipscomb should know that you will have the goodness to give her lessons as I wrote to her on receiving your last letter. She has no doubt gone to Mme Rey at 41 bis rue de la Fontaine, Auteuil, as she wrote that she has decided to stay where I did" (letter from Amy Singer to Auguste Rodin, October 5, 1885, AMR). This letter seems to indicate that Jessie Lipscomb arrived in Paris only at that date, which confirms the first dated exchange of correspondence with Rodin, a laconic note written on October 4, 1885 (private collection), which begins "Miss Lipscomb," a far cry from the "My dear pupil" he later used.

[10] See Odile Ayral-Clause, "Une partenaire anglaise: Jessie Lipscomb," in RIVIÈRE / GAUDICHON / GHANASSIA 2001, pp. 55–58.

[11] MORHARDT 1898, p. 713.

[12] MORHARDT 1898, p. 720.

[13] ANF.

[14] ANF.

[15] The invoice for the cast is dated June 15, 1889.

[16] Octave Mirbeau, "Le Salon (VI)," *La France*, June 7, 1886. See MIRBEAU 1993, 1, p. 294.

[17] On this affair, see Antoinette Le Normand-Romain, "Rodin et Victor Hugo," in BESANÇON 2002, pp. 31–41.

[18] Concerning the *Burghers of Calais* commission, see LE NORMAND-ROMAIN / HAUDIQUET 2001.

[19] They protested, "Seeing that now you absolutely cannot give us the lessons that you undertook to give us and that even when we come to your studio you do not have the time to advise us much, I am afraid that I must ask you for an explanation. Can we count on you to compensate us later for the sum we advanced for our lessons? Unfortunately, we are unable to pay for lessons which we have not received." Dated "Thursday, March 5," this letter from Emily Fawcett to Rodin (AMR) was written in 1885. Aware that he had spent little time on his pupils, Rodin undoubtedly decided to reimburse the sum they had advanced him. Indeed, the following autumn, John Singer, Amy's father, thanked Rodin for the "good instruction" he had given his daughter "and also for the money that you refused" (November 28, 1885, AMR).

[20] Council meeting, September 26, 1884.

[21] COQUIOT 1913, pp. 133–34.

[22] Note approved by the monument committee and given to Rodin in August 1885. See CALAIS / PARIS 1977, pp. 116–17.

[23] See Antoinette Le Normand-Romain, "Rodin et Victor Hugo," in BESANÇON 2002, p. 34 and cat. 35.

[24] BARTLETT 1889, May 25, p. 249.

[25] JACQUES 1883, p. 3.

[26] "It is truly superb. And so I got my little Christmas present and never a more pleasant one" (letter from Paul Paulin to Auguste Rodin, AMR). The card can be dated to late 1887 at the latest because of the address, since Paulin moved on April 5, 1888. My thanks to Stephan Wolohojian for the research on this *Eve* that he kindly did at the Art Institute of Chicago.

[27] GEFFROY 1886.

[28] GONCOURT 1956. April 17, 1886.

[29] Letter from Auguste Rodin to Omer Dewavrin, July 14, 1885 (Archives Municipales de Calais). See CALAIS / PARIS 1977, cat. 30, p. 53.

[30] On this exhibition, see MUSÉE RODIN 1989.

[31] BUTLER 1993, p. 225.

[32] See MUSÉE DU LUXEMBOURG 2001, cat. 43.

[33] See MUSÉE RODIN / MUSÉE DU LUXEMBOURG 2001, cat. 116.

[34] See Antoinette Le Normand-Romain, "Du brio au génie," in MUSÉE RODIN 1997, pp. 74–75.

[35] Truman Bartlett, *Notes*, quoted in ELSEN 1985, p. 62. These notes were the basis for a series of articles Bartlett published in 1899 in *The American Architect and Building News*.

[36] MORHARDT 1898, pp. 718–19.

[37] MORHARDT 1898, p. 722.

[38] CLAUDEL 1913, p. 15.

[39] See LYON 1998.

[40] These two busts are undoubtedly those mentioned by Rodin in a letter to Léon Gauchez on December 20(?), 1885: "Thank you for sending the 500 f. for Mademoiselle Claudel. You will be brought on her behalf a bronze bust which is finished; the other one will arrive soon (that makes 1,000 received)" (Staatsarchivs, Vienna).

[41] Charles-Adolphe Gruet, who usually marked his bronzes "Gruet Jne Fondeur," worked for Rodin at the very beginning of the decade only (he cast the *Saint John the Baptist* acquired by the state). It seems more plausible that Camille, following Rodin's example, would have opted for François Rudier, who worked for Rodin between 1883 and 1887, or Griffoul et Lorge, to whom Rodin entrusted a great many casts from 1887 to 1894 (including *Monument to Claude Lorrain*). It is worth noting, however, that François Rudier sometimes marked his casts (as he did *Danielli*, in the Musée Rodin). Griffoul et Lorge, on the other hand, began signing theirs only very late on.

[42] "Mademoiselle Claudel has finished her bust must go to be fired and her bronze is ready. She has received a thousand francs there remains a thousand francs. If you like what she has done it would be good to encourage her a little for her group. I will go and see you this evening at 5 o'clock and talk a little with you about London" (letter from Auguste Rodin to Léon Gauchez, Staatsarchivs, Vienna.) The reference to London situates this letter after Rodin returned to Paris in June 1886.

[43] Letter from Léon Gauchez to Auguste Rodin, June 30, 1888 (AMR).

[44] BARTLETT 1889, April 27, 1889, p. 199. It was probably the marble *Children's Games* exhibited at the Galerie Georges Petit in 1887 and donated to the Musée de Picardie in Amiens in 1889.

[45] A large number of her works entered museums from 1892 to 1902, thanks to him. Three busts of *Giganti* went to the Lille, Reims and Cherbourg museums in 1892, 1901 and 1902 respectively. The bust of *Charles Lhermitte* went to the Musée Ingres in Montauban in 1892, *The Psalm* to Abbeville in 1893, *La Petite Châtelaine*, in bronze, to Beaufort-en-Vallée in 1896, *My Brother* to Toulon in 1899 and Tourcoing in 1900, while Baroness Nathaniel donated her copy to the Musée Calvet in Avignon in 1897. The Bar-le-Duc museum received a drawing, *The Old Lady of the Pont Notre-Dame*, from Alphonse de Rothschild in 1901 and the museums of Châteauroux and

Draguignan the bust of *Paul Claudel as a Child* and *Fireside Dream* in 1903.

46. Letter from Léon Gauchez to Auguste Rodin, March 14, 1892 (AMR).

47. Letter from Auguste Rodin to Léon Gauchez, received September 30, 1894 (Staatsarchivs, Vienna). Rodin was clearly alluding to the few lines by Paul Leroi in *L'Art* (see LEROI 1894, p. 253), accompanied by a drawing by Camille Claudel.

48. LEROI 1894, p. 253.

CLAUDEL OR RODIN?
(pp. 66–67)

1. MORHARDT 1898, p. 721.

TÊTE-À-TÊTE
(pp. 68–79)

1. CASO / SANDERS 1977, cat. 59. This plaster undoubtedly came from Eugène Rudier.

2. See RODIN 1992, no. 130.

3. Around July 17, 1910. See RODIN 1987, no. 127.

4. See MUSÉE RODIN / MUSÉE DU LUXEMBOURG 2001, cat. 3.

5. Another copy is in the Soumaya Museum, Mexico City.

6. REVAL 1903, pp. 520–21.

7. Others described them as "a pale green evoking young forest shoots." See REVAL 1903, pp. 520–21.

8. Paul Claudel, "Ma sœur Camille," in MUSÉE RODIN 1951, pp. 3–4.

9. MORHARDT 1898, pp. 709–10.

10. DEBUSSY 1942, p. 42.

11. MORHARDT 1898, pp. 728–29.

12. World's Columbian Exposition, Chicago, 1893; Salon of the Société Nationale des Beaux-Arts, Paris, 1893, not in catalogue; Galerie Bing, Paris, 1896, no. 325; Salon of the Société Nationale des Beaux-Arts, Paris, 1897, not in catalogue; Brussels, Rotterdam, Amsterdam and the Hague, 1899, *Rodin*, no. 65 (66); Prague, 1902, *Rodin*, no. 6/154. It is however worth noting that in 1900 it was Falguière's

portrait of Rodin and not Camille's that was reproduced on the frontispiece of the *Rodin* exhibition catalogue.

13. *Auguste Rodin, The Psalm, Léon Lhermitte* and *La Petite Châtelaine*, as well as *My Brother*, Musée d'Ixelles, Brussels (dated "1895") and the bust of *Charles Lhermitte* still belonging to the model's heirs, bearing the inscription "Gruet Aîné fondeur." As for Captain Tissier's *The Implorer* (RIVIÈRE / GAUDICHON / GHANASSIA 2001, cat. 44.7, cast by "le maître Gruet" (letter from General Tissier to Paul Claudel, August 31, 1943; see PARIS 2000, p. 551), given its date (1899), it could only have been cast by Edmond-Paul Gruet ("E. Gruet Jeune"), Adolphe's brother, active from 1891 until his death in 1904. On the Gruets, see LEBON 2003, pp. 176–79.

14. Letter from Edmond Bigand-Kaire to Auguste Rodin [May? 1892] (AMR).

15. Letter from Camille Claudel to Edmond Bigand-Kaire, between April 20 and May 7, 1892. See CLAUDEL 2003, no. 57.

16. The sum Bigand-Kaire offered for *The Old Woman*.

17. Letter from Camille Claudel to Karl Boès [1898?]. See CLAUDEL 2003, no. 132.

18. Exhibition of the Loïe Fuller Collection, New York, National Arts Club. See BEAUSIRE 1988, pp. 241–42.

"CAMILLE, MY BELOVED, IN SPITE OF EVERYTHING"
(pp. 80–119)

1. Félix Bracquemond did an engraving of the work to illustrate the poem *Aristophanes* in the *Édition nationale* of Hugo's works (vol. 6, 1886). See MAISON DE VICTOR HUGO 2003, cat. 6–7.

2. LEROI 1886, p. 67.

3. See PARIS 2000, p. 522.

4. See PARIS 2000, p. 524.

5. Letter from Auguste Rodin to Rose Beuret [between May 29 and June 1, 1886]. See RODIN 1985, no. 72.

6. According to a note by Georges Grappe (AMR), this marble should be identified as the one auctioned at the Hôtel Drouot in Paris on May 22, 1909, no.

135, for 1,500 francs, under the title *Jeunesse*. At an unknown date, it was acquired by Dr. Faure, who bequeathed it and his entire collection to the Musée d'Aix-les-Bains. It was acquired by the Musée Rodin by exchange in 1948.

7. It is therefore possible that Eugenia Errazuriz was introduced to Rodin by Dr. Paulin, who, thanking him for *Eve* at the end of 1887, added, "My Brazilian client was enchanted by your second reply. A car accident having unfortunately obliged her to keep her arm in a sling for a month, she has gone to Rome. On her return we will come and visit if you do not mind" (AMR). In as much as we know of no "Brazilian woman" in Rodin's entourage at that time, should one surmise that Paulin might have confused two Latin American countries, especially since the Errazurizes lived in several countries?

8. According to their son. See MORLA 1928.

9. Camille having banished Jessie in July, the photograph is definitely early and must have been taken while William Elborne was in Paris in April.

10. Plaster S.2434, in *L'Art français*, February 4, 1888.

11. GEFFROY 1889, p. 304.

12. AYRAL-CLAUSE 2002, pp. 44, 54–55.

13. RIVIÈRE / GAUDICHON / GHANASSIA 2001, p. 101.

14. And next to her younger sister, Anna, as I myself thought, given the date when it was mentioned for the first time. See MUSÉE RODIN / MUSÉE DU LUXEMBOURG 2001, p. 212.

15. "I am happy that Madame your mother was pleased with my small group, very happy about the friendship that Monsieur Lipscomb shows in inviting me" (letter from Auguste Rodin to Jessie Lipscomb [late May 1886], in PARIS 2000, p. 522).

16. Letter from Camille Claudel to Florence Jeans [February 12, 1887]. See CLAUDEL 2003, no. 25.

17. Letter from Camille Claudel to Florence Jeans [April 16, 1887]. See CLAUDEL 2003, no. 27.

18. Letter from Camille Claudel to Florence Jeans [July 6, 1887]. See CLAUDEL 2003, no. 29.

19. Letter from Jessie Lipscomb to Auguste Rodin, September 15, 1887 (AMR).

20. See letter from Auguste Rodin to Léon Gauchez, after June 1886, suggesting that he "encourage her a little for her group" (Staatsarchivs, Vienna).

21. When he gave a dowry to Louise, who married Ferdinand de Massary on August 16, 1888. See GUILLEMIN 1968, note 3, p. 54.

22. 68 boulevard d'Italie, now on the corner of rue Corvisart and boulevard Auguste Blanqui.

23. See MUSÉE D'ORSAY 1995, cat. 4.

24. Letter from Camille Claudel to Florence Jeans, March 6, 1888. See CLAUDEL 2003, no. 40.

25. Camille Claudel, *Sakuntala*, charcoal drawing of the plaster in the 1888 Salon. See LEROI 1888, p. 213.

26. LEROI 1888, p. 212.

27. JOUVE 1895, pp. 111–18. The gift was accepted by the museum on October 6. The present whereabouts of the picture are unknown. Camille went to Châteauroux in November to see how the work had been installed (*Journal du département de l'Indre*, November 18, 1895).

28. "A brownish coating is applied to the entire piece. The application of this coating constitutes the patination, and this costs 100 francs. One can obtain the same result, I am told, with ten centimes' worth of black sugar and a bucket . . . But no, this had to be done using the Italian process of Danieli, a Florentine gentleman who writes long letters on very fragrant paper extolling the virtues of his incomparable pommade" (see ANONYMOUS 1895). J. Danielli, whose bust Rodin exhibited at the 1883 Salon (bronze, Musée Rodin, S.6669), undertook "Hardening, Metalization and Artistic Decorations of plaster, permanent processes," a field in which he achieved great success, because in 1892 his letter heading states, "Gold Medals and Diplomas of Honor. Outstanding merit. Member of the Jury, Paris 1885, 1886, 1888, Copenhagen 1888, Paris 1890, 1891, etc." Rodin used his expert services: the plaster of *Saint John the Baptist*

shown at the 1879 Salon had been "galvanized" by Danielli according to CLADEL 1936, p. 67.

29 Letter from Camille Claudel to Gustave Geffroy [late 1895]. See CLADEL 2003, no. 98.

30 "Sakuntala's abandonment and partial destruction are part of its history and one should not be afraid of exhibiting it in its present, very changed and incomplete state" (Bruno Gaudichon, "Table ronde: quelques expériences de remise en état des fonds de province," in ÉCOLE DU LOUVRE 1986, p. 129).

31 Letter from Lecreux to Auguste Rodin, June 1, 1888 (AMR).

32 MARGUERITTE 1896.

33 Date when the bronze in this exhibition was delivered to the collector Antoni Roux and, to my knowledge, the first time the group is mentioned.

34 See LYON / LONDON / NEW YORK 2003, cat. 119.

35 Paul Claudel, "Ma sœur Camille," in MUSÉE RODIN 1951, p. 5.

36 MIRBEAU 1893.

37 Letter from Camille Claudel to Florence Jeans [February 24, 1889]. See CLADEL 2003, no. 48.

38 Letter from Camille Claudel to the minister of fine arts [February 8, 1892]. See CLADEL 2003, no. 55.

39 "I have brought back from the country a group that you do not know and that I spent three days wrapping" (letter from Camille Claudel to Marcel Schwob, undated [autumn 1892], Nantes, Médiathèque Jacques-Demy).

40 According to Marcel Schwob, quoted by AYRAL-CLAUSE 2002, p. 104.

41 MORHARDT 1898, p. 734.

42 As stated in the Salon's catalogue.

43 Émile Verhaeren, "Le Salon de la Libre Esthétique. Les Sculpteurs," L'Art Moderne, April 1, 1894. See VERHAEREN 1997, p. 596.

44 Paul Claudel, "Ma sœur Camille," in MUSÉE RODIN 1951, p. 5.

45 Letter from Eugène Blot to Mathias Morhardt, September 21, 1935, quoted in PARIS 2000, p. 550. The copy Blot produced is slightly different, the floor

having been modified and lightened. There were two sizes, H. 46.4 and 23.5 cm.

45 MORHARDT 1898, p. 733.

CAMILLE CLAUDEL THE PORTRAITIST
(pp. 120–33)

1 VAN LENNEP 1993, pp. 21–135.

2 VAN LENNEP 1993, p. 84.

3 Plus some twenty works on paper and oils on canvas.

4 GEFFROY 1897.

5 The order worn on a chain by the count is in fact completely imaginary since it represents the Perseus that his mother had commissioned from Camille and the plaster of which was exhibited in 1899 at the Salon of the Société Nationale des Beaux-Arts. It evokes the order of Saint Michael, whose necklace shows the saint slaying the dragon.

6 See RIVIÈRE / GAUDICHON / GHANASSIA 2001, cat. 60.

7 VAN LENNEP 1993, p. 40.

8 See, among others, the bust of Young Woman with Closed Eyes in RIVIÈRE / GAUDICHON / GHANASSIA 2001, cat. 15.

9 See RIVIÈRE / GAUDICHON / GHANASSIA 2001, cat. 11.

10 The bust does not seem to have been finished.

11 On this subject, see MUSÉE D'ORSAY 1991. It is also worth noting that, like Camille Claudel, Lhermitte was born and raised in the Aisne. Camille sculpted his bust between 1892 and 1895.

12 MORHARDT 1898, p. 743; see also RIVIÈRE / GAUDICHON / GHANASSIA 2001, cat. 46.

13 See RIVIÈRE / GAUDICHON / GHANASSIA 2001, cat. 96.

14 See RIVIÈRE / GAUDICHON / GHANASSIA 2001, cat. 94.

15 See RIVIÈRE / GAUDICHON / GHANASSIA 2001, cat. 92.

16 MORHARDT 1898, pp. 724–25.

17 Letter from Camille Claudel to Henry Lerolle [spring 1905?]. See CLADEL 2003, no. 183.

18 MORHARDT 1898, p. 723, about the bust of Louise Claudel.

19 LEROI 1887, p. 231, about My Brother bust.

20 BRAISNE 1897.

21 MARX 1895, p. 119.

22 HAMEL 1889, p. 26.

23 Read the mixed opinions on some of Rodin's portraits by the models themselves, such as Anna de Noailles and Clemenceau.

THE STAYS AT L'ISLETTE
(pp. 134–51)

1 On this important commission, see MUSÉE RODIN 1998.

2 FARGES 1891.

3 RODIN 1914, pp. 21–22 and 37–39.

4 CLADEL 1936, p. 187.

5 Letter from Gustave Geffroy to Auguste Rodin, October 4, 1891 (AMR).

6 MUSÉE RODIN 1998, p. 130.

7 The receipt for this postal order is in the Musée Rodin Archives.

8 Letter from Camille Claudel to Edmond Bigand-Kaire [May–June 1892]. See CLADEL 2003, no. 57.

9 This detail and the presumed date for the sittings were confirmed by the model's daughter recalling a family journal no longer in existence which recorded everyday life at L'Islette at that time. The sixty-two sittings were noted by Morhardt. See MORHARDT 1898, p. 737.

10 Letter from Camille Claudel to Auguste Rodin [1892?]. See CLADEL 2003, no. 60.

11 Letter from Paul Claudel to Marie Romain-Rolland, December 27, 1939. See ANTOINE 1988, pp. 166–67.

12 Letter from Camille Claudel to the minister of fine arts [April 28, 1894]. See CLADEL 2003, no. 73.

13 Letter from Camille Claudel to Auguste Rodin [June 25, 1893]. See CLADEL 2003, no. 69.

14 CLADEL 1913, p. 27.

15 Letter from Camille Claudel to Paul Claudel [December 1893]. See CLADEL 2003, no. 71. The four works were exhibited in Brussels in 1894 under the

titles The Waltz (Siot-Decauville cast), no. 94; Contemplation, no. 95 (no doubt La Petite Châtelaine); The Psalm, no. 96; The First Step, no. 97 (probably Sakuntala).

16 HAMEL 1889, p. 26.

17 LEROI 1889, p. 262.

18 WYZEWA 1894, p. 34.

19 MORHARDT 1898, p. 737.

20 MORHARDT 1898, pp. 728–29.

21 MORHARDT 1898, p. 723.

22 MORHARDT 1898, p. 729.

23 MARX 1894, p. 309.

24 GEFFROY 1895 /2, p. 148.

25 Letter from Matthias Morhardt to Auguste Rodin [March 30, 1895] (AMR). The work appears again in the inventory after Morhardt's death. Its whereabouts have since been unknown.

26 MORHARDT 1898, p. 735.

27 Letter from Camille Claudel to Antoine Bourdelle [May 15, 1895]. See CLADEL 2003, no. 90.

28 MAILLARD 1896, p. 329.

29 GEFFROY 1896, p. 200.

30 MUSÉE RODIN 1998, cat. 30–32, pp. 279–81.

31 In this exhibition, Fontaine was present in force, notably with an impressive series of ornamental ironwork plaques designed by Alexandre Charpentier.

32 Quoted by Danièle Gutmann in Robert Wlérick (1882–1944), exhibition catalogue, Paris: Musée Rodin; Mont-de-Marsan: Musée Despiau-Wlérick, 1982, p. 26.

OSTEOLOGY OF OLD WOMEN
(pp. 152–67)

1 See MIRBEAU 1893.

2 RODIN 1911, p. 44.

3 GEFFROY 1894, p. 380.

4 SERTAT 1893.

5 RODIN 1911, p. 29.

6 RODIN 1911, pp. 46, 51.

7 GSELL 1922, p. 385.

8 GSELL 1935.

9 Musée Rodin, Ph. 2396.

10 GONCOURT 1989, July 3, 1889.

11 COQUIOT 1911, p. 168.

12 Two terracotta studies are listed (Musée Rodin and Musée d'Orsay): they are slightly different, yet they are perhaps not original casts but rather, as the traces of seams suggest, reworked stampings. See HÉRAN 2004.

13 WEISINGER 1987, pp. 323–24. Anne Pingeot, in MUSÉE D'ORSAY 1988, pp. 5–8.

14 PINGEOT 1996, p. 65.

15 From 1931 (no. 148), once he had established the connection with the left jamb of The Gates of Hell.

16 AMR.

17 At an undetermined date, Élie Delaunay reccomended a Joseph Caira whom he described as "a donatello" to Gustave Moreau. Around 1905, Paul Richer noted in his model book a Marie Caira "Italian woman, 22 years, 25 rue du Moulin-Vert. stout, wide pelvis, with no exaggerated localisation of fat, middle pelvis sloping." The Public Office confirms that there were several Cairas living in Paris at that time, at least one of which, Silvio Caira, who died in 1892 aged fifty, was a life model. My thanks to Xavier Demange, Marie-Cécile Forest, Catherine Mathon and Diane Tytgat for their help with this research. Around 1900, Bourdelle again sent "this beautiful model Rafaela Caïra" to Rodin, who noted her name and address on one of his visiting cards (AMR).

18 See NEWTON 1989, pp. 45–48.

19 LAWTON 1906, p. 121.

20 Letter from Auguste Rodin to Victor Peter, February 22, 1890 (AMR).

21 Golubkina Studio-Museum, Moscow. The present-day plaster is a reproduction of the original that Golubkina did not take to Moscow. My warmest thanks to Édouard Papet for having drawn my attention to this work.

22 The plaster was exhibited at the 1900 Exposition Universelle. My warmest thanks to Pascale Grémont for having pointed this bust out to me.

23 ANONYMOUS 1890, p. 161.

24 BERNIER 1967, p. 26.

25 Madame de Saint-Marceaux, Journal, October 15, 1897 (private collection). The Four Seasons, marble bas-reliefs, were destined for the dining-room of his Paris mansion. They were exhibited at the 1902 Salon and are now in the Musée des Beaux-Arts. Reims. See Antoinette Le Normand-Romain, "René de Saint-Marceaux (1845–1915)," in MUSÉE D'ORSAY 1992, cat. 80–83.

26 A copy signed "Jeanneney 1903 Sain Amand" was sold at the auction house at Moulins on November 2, 1998. My thanks to Sophie Weygand for having informed me of this.

27 See MUSÉE RODIN 1998, cat. 145–46.

28 Around 60 cm high according to MORHARDT 1898, p. 734.

29 MORHARDT 1898, p. 734.

30 See the letter from Camille Claudel to Karl Boës [July? 1899]. See CLAUDEL 2003, no. 142.

31 See the letter from Mathias Morhardt to Judith Cladel, December 7, 1929, in PARIS 2000, p. 408. On this affair, see the correspondence between Rodin. Morhardt and Bénédite, June–December 1905, in PARIS 2000, pp. 540–41.

32 FOURCAUD 1899, p. 250.

33 E.D.-G. 1889, pp. 451–52.

34 LEROI 1892, p. 18.

35 Board of directors of the Musée Rodin, January 29, 1955.

36 Letter from Camille Claudel to Maurice Guillemot [after May 28, 1899). See CLAUDEL 2003, no. 138. On May 28, 1899, L'Europe artiste, of which Guillemot was the editor, had alluded to the Rodin drawing and to its influence on Camille.

37 Letter from Mathias Morhardt to Judith Cladel, August 18, 1934. See RIVIÈRE / GAUDICHON / GHANASSIA 2001, p. 286.

THE AGE OF MATURITY OR FATE
(pp. 168–97)

1 Louis Aragon, Le Fou d'Elsa. Paris: Gallimard, 1963.

2 See ARNOUX 2001, p. 37.

3 Camille kept the studio until 1898. Rodin moved into the Clos-Payen at 68 boulevard d'Italie in May 1890 and lived there until August 1902.

4 BRAISNE 1897, p. 368.

5 GONCOURT 1989, p. 959.

6 PINET / PARIS 2003, pp. 70–71.

7 PINET / PARIS 2003, pp. 74–75.

8 The commission, dated July 25, 1895, was accepted by the artist a few days later

9 Letter from Auguste Rodin to Hélène Wahl [February 5, 1896]. See RODIN 1985, no. 243.

10 Yet, during his visit to her studio in boulevard d'Italie the following year, Henry de Braisne expressly noted that she was "not at all concerned about her appearance" and of a "plainness verging on absolute modesty." BRAISNE 1897.

11 LE NORMAND-ROMAIN 2003, p. 38.

12 AYRAL-CLAUSE 2002, p. 146.

13 AYRAL-CLAUSE 2002, p. 122.

14 LEROI 1894, p. 253.

15 MORHARDT 1898, p. 740.

16 Rodin's appreciation of The Vanished God would certainly have been more reserved had he known that it in fact belonged to the three-figure group of the first version of The Age of Maturity.

17 Baffled by the relative clumsiness of these drawings, Claudie Judrin, curator of Rodin's drawings at the Musée Rodin, seriously considered the possibility that they might be by Auguste Beuret, Rodin and Rose's illegitimate son. While echoing these questions, my colleague Jacques Vilain favored the attribution to Camille, basing this on graphological and psychological studies. He classified the awful caricatures Camille sent to Rodin as "breaking-up drawings."

18 PARIS 2000, p. 345.

19 PARIS 2000, p. 345.

20 Letter from Camille Claudel to the minister of fine arts [July 27, 1895]. See CLAUDEL 2003, no. 97.

21 Letter from Camille Claudel to the director of fine arts, October 14, 1898. See CLAUDEL 2003, no. 127.

22 Letter from Camille Claudel to Auguste Rodin [November? 1897]. See CLAUDEL 2003, no. 120.

23 Letter from Auguste Rodin to Camille Claudel, December 2, 1897. See CLAUDEL 2003, no. 121.

24 See CLAUDEL 2003, p. 150, note 2.

25 See RAMBOSSON 1899 /2.

26 GEFFROY 1900, p. 349.

27 MOUREY 1899, p. 5.

28 FONTAINAS 1899, p. 747.

29 MARX 1899, p. 560.

30 HAMEL 1899, p. 655.

31 SAUNIER 1899, p. 337.

32 FAGUS 1899.

33 BERNARD 1899.

34 ARNOUX 2001, p. 37.

35 PINGEOT 1982, p. 292.

36 Order for a bronze cast of The Age of Maturity, early June 1899 (ANF); note to the director of fine arts postponing the order, June 16, 1899 (ANF); note from the director of fine arts canceling the commission, June 24, 1899 (ANF); report by the undersecretary of state Dujardin-Beaumetz to the minister of public instruction and fine arts, August 13, 1907 (ANF). On this question, see ARNOUX 2001, p. 47.

37 On this question, see PARIS 2000, pp. 349–62.

38 Letters from Ottilie McLaren to William Wallace, April–July 1899 (National Library of Scotland, Edinburgh). See particularly the letters of May 10, 13, 21, 23 and 28. My thanks to Antoinette Le Normand-Romain for having communicated them to me.

39 REYNOLDS 2004, pp. 201–15.

40 Rodin "says he thinks poor miss Claudel has overworked and that she is really ill. That this mania against seeing any one is really an illness" (letter from Ottilie McLaren to William Wallace, May 28, 1899, National Library of Scotland, Edinburgh).

41 Liliane Colas, "Portraits de praticiens," in MUSÉE D'ORSAY 1988, p. 58.

42 PINGEOT 1982, pp. 292ff.

43 It should be borne in mind that Morhardt was a staunch defender of Dreyfus.

44 Letter from Camille Claudel to Captain Tissier [June 10, 1889]. See CLAUDEL 2003, no. 139.

45 For correspondence concerning the casting of the *Kneeling Woman*, see CLAUDEL 2003, nos. 137, 139, 140, 143, 144, 145 and 169.

46 The base was divided into two parts held together by tenons and the drapery was attached by two screws. See PINGEOT 1991, p. 33.

47 Letters from Camille Claudel to Captain Tissier [December 1901–January 1902] and [January 10?, 1902]. See CLAUDEL 2003, nos. 163 and 165.

48 Letter from Camille Claudel to Captain Tissier [March 16, 1902]. See CLAUDEL 2003, no. 169.

49 Letter from Camille Claudel to Captain Tissier [February 25, 1902]. See CLAUDEL 2003, no. 168.

50 Exhibit no. 2658, simply entitled "Age of Maturity, bronze group, belonging to Capt. T…"

51 MICHEL 1903.

52 COCHIN 1903; A.M. 1903; ROLLAND 1903.

53 MORICE 1903, p. 691.

54 Letter from Eugène Blot to the undersecretary of state, November 6, 1905 (ANF).

55 One of these casts was shown again in December 1908.

56 Louis Vauxcelles, "Introduction," in BLOT 1905.

57 Letter from Camille Claudel to the minister of fine arts [July 25, 1907]. See CLAUDEL 2003, no. 222.

58 Letter from Camille Claudel to Paul Claudel [1909?]. See CLAUDEL 2003, no. 232.

59 Report by the undersecretary of state, Dujardin-Beaumetz, to the ministry of public instruction and fine arts, August 13, 1907 (ANF); letter from the undersecretary of state for the fine arts to Camille Claudel, November 20, 1907. See CLAUDEL 2003, no. 229.

60 Letter from Camille Claudel to Captain Tissier [February 25, 1902]. See CLAUDEL 2003, no. 168.

61 Letter from Camille Claudel to Paul Claudel [1909?]. See CLAUDEL 2003, no. 232.

62 Concerning Philippe Berthelot, his friends, his career in the French foreign ministry and his love of literature, see MUSÉE D'ORSAY 1988, pp. 24–26.

63 Camille used this title as early as June 20, 1899 in a letter to Captain Tissier. See CLAUDEL 2003, no. 140.

64 DACIER 1905.

65 MONOD 1906.

66 VAUXCELLES 1905.

67 L.T. 1906.

68 KAHN 1905.

69 Letter from Eugène Blot to Camille Claudel, September 3, 1932. See CLAUDEL 2003, no. 295 (the letter has since disappeared).

70 When the inspector of fine arts Henry Havard visited her studio in February 1905, Camille "made known to him her wish to obtain a commission for a marble of bronze of her group *The Age of Maturity*, whose plaster she has kept." In a letter to Havard she mentions the "group *The Age of Maturity* or *Fatality*" [March 1905]. See CLAUDEL 2003, no. 182.

71 MORHARDT 1898; HAMEL 1899; FOURCAUD 1899; BENGESCO 1899; HAMEL / ALEXANDRE 1903; MICHEL 1903.

72 FOURCAUD 1899, p. 250.

73 Paul Claudel, "Ma sœur Camille," in MUSÉE RODIN 1951, pp. 10–11.

74 Paul Claudel, "Ma sœur Camille," in MUSÉE RODIN 1951, p. 11.

75 Letter from Matthais Morhardt to Auguste Rodin, June 5, 1914, and letter from Matthias Morhardt to Judith Cladel, December 7, 1929, in PARIS 2000, pp. 545–46 and 548.

76 Anne Rivière has suggested interpreting *The Age of Maturity* as a funerary and religious work, a kind of allegory of death, given the nature of its staging and the presence of an implorer recalling the praying figures on tombs. See Anne Rivière, "Portrait funéraire: *L'Âge mûr*," in MUSÉE D'ORSAY 1988, pp. 72–74.

77 CLAUDEL 2003, introduction.

78 ARNOUX 2001, pp. 47–48.

79 One obviously notes that the mature man, unlike Rodin, is beardless and that poor Rose, who embodies old age, has been exaggeratedly aged.

80 MORICE 1903, p. 69*.

81 This recourse to the chignon is not unusual in Camille Claudel's work. She used it in *The Waltz*, *Les Causeuses* and *Fireside Dream*. In *The Vanished God* (1894), however, the young woman has an unruly head of brass hair.

82 CLAUDEL 1913, p. 50.

83 The spread fingers of the man's right hand are a modest formal echo of the cape of the old woman deployed in the other direction.

84 The situation would be very different in November 1897, when Camille wrote to Rodin: "Old mother Courcelles has dared to ask me to pay 1000 francs for having left some plasters with her, at first I wanted to attack her then I got scared." See CLAUDEL 2003, no. 120.

85 My thanks to Rosine Lapresle-Tavera for having drawn my attention to this precise passage in a letter from Camille Claudel to Auguste Rodin [July 1891] concerning *The Age of Maturity*. See CLAUDEL 2003, no. 54.

86 Paul Claudel, "Ma sœur Camille," in MUSÉE RODIN 1951, p. 7.

87 See the March 24, 1925, June 15, 1930 and September 11–12, 1933 entries in Paul Claudel's *Journal* (BNF).

CAMILLE CLAUDEL:
VITRIOLIC CARICATURES
(pp. 198–201)

1 DELBEE 1982, pp. 302–3.

2 PARIS/POITIERS 1984, cat. 52–55.

BALZAC
(pp. 202–15)

1 See MUSÉE RODIN 1998.

2 CLADEL 1936, p. 46.

3 Roland Chollet, in MUSÉE RODIN 1998, p. 111.

4 CHINCHOLLE 1894, p. 3.

5 ANONYMOUS 1892.

6 Paris, archives of the Société des Gens de Lettres, committee of July 3, 1893.

7 Letter from Henry Houssaye to Auguste Rodin, March 15, 1898 (AMR).

8 Letter from Auguste Rodin to Henry Houssaye, March 17, 1898, Bibliothèque d'Art et d'Archéologie, Fondation Jacques Doucet, Paris.

9 ANONYMOUS 1898 /1.

10 CHINCHOLLE 1898.

11 LEROUX 1898.

12 Letter from Claude Monet to Auguste Rodin, June 30, 1898 (AMR).

13 He continues: "Rejected by the Gens de Lettres! That scares me more than the catastrophe in Martinique." Atuana, September 1902, in GAUGUIN 1951, pp. 48–49.

14 ANONYMOUS 1898 /2.

15 Quoted by Edouard Papet in TOULOUSE / BLÉRANCOURT 1999, p. 25.

16 ANONYMOUS 1898 /3.

17 Quoted by CLADEL 1936, p. 218.

18 AMR.

19 Steichen, quoted by Hélène Pinet in MUSÉE RODIN 1998, p. 200.

CAMILLE SUBLIMATED
(pp. 216–31)

1 CLADEL 1936, p. 229.

2 CLADEL 1936, pp. 233–34.

3 Notebook 42, sheet 83 recto and verso (AMR).

4 Paul de Musset, *Lui et Elle* (Paris: Charpentier, 1868), p. 127.

5 See MUSÉE RODIN / MUSÉE DU LUXEMBOURG 2001, cat. 3.

6 Plaster, Musée Rodin, S.1796.

7 Plaster, Musée Rodin, S.1775, *c.*1898; marbles, Musée Rodin, S.1199, *c.*1905–8. See LYON 1998, cat. 54, 57, 58.

8 RILKE 1928, pp. 197–98.

9 GRAUTOFF 1910, p. 36.

10 "M. Sulzberger attaches great importance to the master's handwritten note referring to the masterpiece in his possession, and I pray you to be good enough to address this letter to me" (letter from Edouard Ziegler to Auguste Rodin, October 22, 1913, AMR).

11 AMR.

12 Plasters, Musée Rodin, S.1708 and S.2488.

[13] Léonce Bénédite, handwritten inventory card (AMR).

[14] See Victor Peter's receipts (AMR).

[15] See MUSÉE RODIN / MUSÉE DU LUXEMBOURG 2001, cat. 72.

[16] Letter from Alexander Harrison to Auguste Rodin, March 8, 1901 (AMR).

[17] Letter from Alexander Harrison to Auguste Rodin, March 8, 1901 (AMR).

[18] Letter from John G. Johnson to Auguste Rodin, July 20, 1901 (AMR). My thanks to John Zarobell for having helped me decipher this particularly illegible letter.

[19] Part of Jules Mastbaum's fourth order, it was delivered on January 14, 1926. See TANCOCK 1976, cat. 108. It is listed as the "second proof," but is the only known one at present.

[20] T. Beauregard, The Daily News, February 23, 1906, quoted by Anne Pingeot in MUSÉE D'ORSAY 2001, cat. 62.

[21] Notes, AMR.

[22] Letter from Guillaume Mallet to Auguste Rodin, April 3, 1904 (AMR).

[23] See Emmanuel Ducamp, Le Bois des Moutiers, Paris: Flammarion, 1998, p. 82.

[24] Letter from Auguste Rodin to Guillaume Mallet, October 4, 1904. Archives of the Mallet family. My thanks to Emmanuel Ducamp for having communicated these documents to me.

[25] See BUTLER / LINDSAY 2000, pp. 376–81.

[26] See Janet M. Brooke, "Rodin et le Canada," in QUÉBEC 1998, p. 239.

[27] HANOTAUX 1912, pp. 4–5.

POETIC VARIATIONS ON AURORA
(pp. 232–35)

[1] In this letter to Antoine Bourdelle from her studio at 63 rue de Turenne, Camille writes, "I will go with pleasure to see your exhibition, which I am sure has many a surprise in store for me," yet, also clearly worried about meeting Rodin there, she asks him who "other people" exhibiting with him are, all of whom belonged to the society he told her about in the letter to which she is replying (AMB).

[2] In a previous letter, on May 10 [1895?], Camille Claudel wrote to Antoine Bourdelle, "I am very flattered by the admiration you have shown for my works; the approval of an artist like you is very precious for me." See CLAUDEL 2003, no. 90.

[3] In this draft of a letter, which may never have been sent, Antoine Bourdelle, comparing Camille Claudel's works to opened flowers and giving her encouragement, writes, "Mademoiselle, If my garden had roses, I would send you a blazing basket, but the few rosebushes I have still only have a few hesitant leaves. You whom I saw yesterday as pale as an aster, your roses will come out tomorrow and those roses have nothing to do with the garden variety. It is not solely your portrait of Rodin that I am congratulating you for, but for being the kindred spirit of other creatures of thought . . . it is the image of Rodin written by Rodin, a Rodin complicated by a woman" (draft of a letter from Antoine Bourdelle to Camille Claudel, undated, AMB).

[4] The type of paper on which the draft sonnet was written and certain graphological clues suggest that it was very probably written by Bourdelle in the late 1890s, which corresponds to the usual dating of Aurora and would, in my view, if we accept that the poem was contemporary with the bust it describes, confirm the hypothesis that the work could have been created around 1895.

[5] Letter from Auguste Rodin to Antoine Bourdelle, Fougères, July 18, 1907. Quoted by Edmond Campagnac in "Rodin and Bourdelle," from unpublished letters, in La Grande Revue, November 1929, p. 15.

[6] Antoine Bourdelle, "Le visage de Camille Claudel," 3, February 1926 (AMB).

[7] Antoine Bourdelle, "Visage de Camille Claudel," 2, February 1, 1926 (AMB).

[8] Antoine Bourdelle, "Visage de Camille Claudel," 2, February 1, 1926 (AMB).

[9] Antoine Bourdelle, "Mademoiselle Claudel," draft sonnet (AMB).

[10] Antoine Bourdelle, "Mademoiselle Claudel," draft sonnet (AMB).

[11] Paul Claudel. "Ma sœur Camille," in MUSÉE RODIN 1951, pp. 3–4.

[12] Antoine Bourdelle, "Melle Camille Claudel," 1, February 1926 (AMB).

[13] Antoine Bourdelle, "Le visage de Mademoiselle Claudel," 6, February 1926 (AMB).

[14] Antoine Bourdelle, "Camille Claudel," 7, February 1926 (AMB).

[15] Antoine Bourdelle, "Melle Claudel, à propos de son visage," 1, February 1926 (AMB).

[16] Antoine Bourdelle, "Le visage de Camille Claudel." 11th copy, February 1926 (AMB).

[17] Antoine Bourdelle, "Melle Claudel, à propos de son visage," 1, February 1926 (AMB).

[18] Antoine Bourdelle, "Camille Claudel, son visage," 10th version, February 1926 (AMB).

THE "SKETCHES FROM NATURE"
(pp. 236–49)

[1] MORHARDT 1898, p. 732.

[2] GEFFROY 1895 /1, p. 225.

[3] MIRBEAU 1895.

[4] MOURET 1895, for example.

[5] MORHARDT 1898, p. 744.

[6] Letter from William Sarment to Mathias Morhardt, October 3, 1896, quoted in PARIS 2000, p. 376.

[7] ALAIN-FOURNIER 1926, p. 66.

[8] MORHARDT 1898, p. 731.

[9] MORHARDT 1898, p. 747.

[10] MOURET 1895.

[11] Letter from William Sarment to Matthias Morhardt, October 3, 1896, quoted in PARIS 2000, p. 376.

[12] GEFFROY 1895 /3, p. 225.

[13] MAILLARD 1897, p. 315.

[14] MORHARDT 1898, p. 746.

[15] GEFFROY 1895 /3, p. 225.

[16] Paul Claudel, "Ma sœur Camille," in MUSÉE RODIN 1951, p. 12.

[17] Paul Claudel, Œuvres en prose, p. 44, quoted in CZYNSKI 1992, p. 53.

[18] SILVESTRE 1897.

[19] Martine Droit, "Camille Claudel et le marbre-onyx," in MARTIGNY / PARIS 1990–91, pp. 31–32.

[20] Letter from Camille Claudel to Mathias Morhardt [spring 1896?]. See CLAUDEL 2003, no. 103.

[21] Archives de la Ville de Paris, 2MI3/77 and 78.

[22] Letter from Eugène Blot to Gabriel Frizeau, quoted by RIVIÈRE / GAUDICHON / GHANASSIA 2001, p. 164.

[23] Letter from Camille Claudel to Eugène Blot [April? 1905]. See CLAUDEL 2003, no. 190.

[24] Paul Claudel, "Ma sœur Camille," in MUSÉE RODIN 1951, p. 11.

[25] See Anne Pingeot, "Archives d'un sculpteur, les livres de comptes," in DIJON 1994, pp. 118–19.

[26] My thanks to Antoinette Le Normand-Romain for having drawn my attention to this similarity.

[27] Emmanuelle Héran was the first to point out this similarity.

[28] Letter from Camille Claudel to Eugène Blot [April? 1905]. See CLAUDEL 2003, no. 191.

[29] Paul Claudel, "Ma sœur Camille," in MUSÉE RODIN 1951, p. 12.

[30] BOUTE 1995, p. 91.

[31] CLAUDEL 1913, p. 16.

[32] CLAUDEL 1950, p. 238.

[33] Letter from Camille Claudel to Auguste Rodin [March 30, 1896]. See CLAUDEL 2003, no. 105.

[34] MORHARDT 1898, p. 722.

[35] See MUSÉE RODIN / MUSÉE DU LUXEMBOURG 2001, cat. 163–65.

[36] MAILLARD 1897, p. 315.

[37] MORHARDT 1898, p. 743.

[38] Jacques Cassar and André Tissier, in RIVIÈRE / GAUDICHON / GHANASSIA 2001, p. 154.

[39] PARIS 2000, p. 302.

[40] BRAISNE 1897.

[41] Bruno Gaudichon, "Tu vois que ce n'est plus du tout du Rodin," in VIENNA 1996, p. 124.

[42] MORHARDT 1898, p. 745.

[43] Letter from Camille Claudel to

Maurice Guillemot [after May 28, 1899]. See CLAUDEL 2003, no. 138.

A PATRON: COUNTESS DE MAIGRET
(pp. 250–59)

[1] Letter from Camille Claudel to Gustave Geffroy [April 1905]. See CLAUDEL 2003, no. 186.

[2] Letter, unsent, from Camille Claudel to Henriette de Vertus [spring? 1913]. See CLAUDEL 2003, no. 249.

[3] Mathias Morhardt lived at 32 avenue Rapp.

[4] Letter from Mathias Morhardt to Auguste Rodin, October 5, 1897 (AMR).

[5] Letter from Maurice Pottecher to Gustave Geffroy, December 13, 1901 (AMR).

[6] On this work, see RIVIÈRE / GAUDICHON / GHANASSIA 2001, cat. 61.1. The marble was carved by François Pompon, as his ledger attests (see DION 1994, p. 118). It is noteworthy that the "stool" on which the woman is sitting originally replaced a chair with a broken back. Therefore, contrary to the hypothesis put forward in our catalogue raisonné, it cannot be a variation of the Draguignan marble. The same mistake is made in PARIS 2000, cat. 55.

[7] Letter from Maurice Pottecher to Gustave Geffroy, December 13, 1901 (AMR).

[8] "Pure and male like a Giambologna" (VAUXCELLES 1934, p. 391).

[9] MARCEL 1902, p. 133.

[10] BABIN 1902, p. 370.

[11] Paul Claudel, "Ma sœur Camille," in MUSÉE RODIN 1951, p. 12.

[12] See NANTET 2004 on this question.

[13] Paul Claudel, "Ma sœur Camille," in MUSÉE RODIN 1951, p. 12.

[14] The decorative aspect of these works and their various possible versions are suggested by the artist in letters to Eugène Blot: "You could, if you wanted to, have one of your Sirens made with a green onyx rock (recalling the sea); the flute in shiny metal" (Letter from Camille Claudel to Eugène Blot [April? 1905]; see CLAUDEL 2003, no. 190) and "A small fireplace less or more does not commit you to anything

(three times lucky), you will have my little cold one lying across the chimney for the modest sum of a hundred francs and I will finish it for you to my taste, it will be more beautiful for a nightlight" (letter from Camille Claudel to Eugène Blot [April? 1905]; see CLAUDEL 2003, no. 191).

[15] HAMEL 1902, p. 74.

[16] PARIS / LA CHAPELLE 1990, p. 197.

[17] Letter from Camille Claudel to Eugène Blot [1904?]. See CLAUDEL 2003, no. 191.

[18] See RIVIÈRE / GAUDICHON / GHANASSIA 2001, cat. 60.

[19] ADAM 1908, pp. 133–34. My thanks to M. Jacques Paul Dauriac for having indicated this bibliographic reference.

[20] RAMBOSSON 1899 /1, p. 282.

[21] Letter from Maurice Pottecher to Gustave Geffroy, December 13, 1901 (AMR).

[22] See Nicole Barbier in MARTIGNY / PARIS 1990–91, cat. 78; and PARIS 2000, cat. 59.

[23] See the reproduction in PARIS / POITIERS 1984, cat. 3.

[24] PARIS 2000, cat. 59.

[25] RIVIÈRE / GAUDICHON / GHANASSIA 2001, cat. 9.

[26] Letter from Camille Claudel to Henry Lerolle [spring 1905]. See CLAUDEL 2003, no. 183.

"TAKE THIS HELPING HAND I AM HOLDING OUT TO YOU"
(pp. 260–73)

[1] I have based my study of this question on the two catalogues raisonnés of the artist's work, PARIS 2000, RIVIÈRE / GAUDICHON / GHANASSIA 2001, and on MUSÉE D'ORSAY 1988 and CLAUDEL 2003. A great deal of complementary information came from the Musée d'Orsay's research department, both on Camille Claudel and on the foundries. On the latter, see MARTIN 1989 and LEBON 2003.

[2] On this subject, see CHEVILLOT 1992 and CHEVILLOT 1997.

[3] François-Louis Blot was born at Jouars-Pont-Chartrin (Seine-et-Oise) on February 6, 1828, the son of Jean

Louis Thomas Blot, who died at Vanves (Seine) on December 4, 1850, and Geneviève Françoise Gosselin, who was still alive in 1872. Blot père married Claire Leport, a dressmaker born in Lorient on January 7, 1835 and living in rue de Clichy, Paris, on October 8, 1857, in other words, five months after the birth of Louis Eugène Leport at 22 rue Saint-Roch and who later became Eugène Blot after François Louis officially acknowledged his paternity. It is worth noting, however, that the "father: ..." entry in the administrative form has been struck out (registry of births and death, Archives de la Ville de Paris).

[4] Concerning the firm's history, see LEBON 2003.

[5] BLOT 1934, p. 6.

[6] The rue des Enfants-Rouges had become part of rue des Archives. One can follow these extensions fairly precisely in the Calepin des propriétés bâties (Archives de la Ville de Paris, D1P4 379 (1852) and D1P4 40 (1862)), until Blot was declared the building's sole owner after its sale on March 23, 1874, for 290,000 F. Louis-Michel Drouard does not appear until 1860. The 1876 and 1900 rolls unfortunately contain nothing on no. 84. Mention is made of engraving and bronze-making workshops. Blot lived there in 1862, in an apartment with a kitchen, hall and four rooms with fireplaces and one without, giving onto the street and the courtyard, whose rent value was 1,000 F a month, which was quite expensive compared to the other apartments (the building originally had twenty-one tenants, mainly watchmakers, wood and ivory carvers and probably contract craftsmen—then a widespread practice). Drouard also lived there. Blot and Drouard formed a joint company for ten years on September 1, 1875.

[7] Eugène Blot married Alice Labourion, born November 22, 1861, in Paris and they had three children: Jacques (born May 8, 1885, died May 10, 1960), who became a painter and gallery owner; Claire Eugénie, born December 2, 1883, "wife of Moyse known as Themaulys"; and Denise Alice, born August 25, 1886, "wife of Kogan known as Semenoff" (Archives de la Ville

de Paris, D 33 U 3 / 1154; portrait of Jacques Blot in CHAVANNE et GAUDICHON 1988, p. 104). Galerie Eugène Blot, a limited company in which every member of the Blot family was a shareholder, was founded on December 15, 1928. It was liquidated on January 30, 1939 (Archives de la Ville de Paris, D 33 U 3 / 1154).

[8] For Antoinette Le Normand-Romain, who edited the catalogue of Rodin's bronzes (to be published in 2006), these editions remain unidentified to this day, yet Rodin, very demanding in this respect, followed transactions closely.

[9] BLOT 1934, p. 22.

[10] KAHN 1905, p. 1.

[11] BLOT 1906. The Carriès were all patinated plasters: no. 123, Evêque, sold for 490 F; no. 124, Louise Labbé, sold for 1,000 F; no. 125, Le Gentilhomme, sold for 410 F; no. 126, L'Enfant endormi, sold for 1,020 F.

[12] BLOT 1934, p. 23.

[13] BLOT 1934, p. 27.

[14] "I have to do so to cover the expenses of the shop on the boulevard where we are hardly selling, neither Rodin, Claudel, Constantin Meunier nor Maillol or the sculptures of Hoetger" (BLOT 1934, p. 30).

[15] BLOT 1934, p. 53; see also supra note 11.

[16] Letter from Eugène Blot to Camille Claudel, September 3, 1932. See CLAUDEL 2003, no. 295. He also talked about it to Morhardt: "And I have since taken many others, despite having never sold a single one for several years"; on The Waltz: "I am now publishing it in two sizes, but for the last five years [missing word] I have not sold a single one" (letter from Eugène Blot to Mathias Morhardt, September 21, 1935, typewritten copy, AMR). The incomplete nature of this transcription makes the text difficult to understand.

[17] Letter from Eugène Blot to Mathias Morhardt, 1935, typewritten copy (AMR).

[18] BLOT 1934, p. 51.

[19] BLOT 1934, p. 61. Only buyers of bronzes are mentioned here, and not of works in other materials, such as

the painter Thaulow (a bust of *Aurora*), which Blot bought back (Letter from Eugène Blot to Mathias Morhardt, September 21, 1936), and Philippe Berthelot, who owned a plaster of *Imploration* (letter from Eugène Blot to Mathias Morhardt, September 21, 1935).

20 See BLOT 1934, pp. 23–25.

21 Letter from Eugène Blot to Mathias Morhardt, 1935, typewritten copy (AMR).

22 The Barbedienne Collection in the Archives Nationales contains documents in which, under the photographs of the bronzes, there are numbers and annotations written mostly by Blot and by Barbedienne (*Abandon*, for example). These handwritten annotations indicate the number of casts planned and made. One can assume that it was either a published commercial catalogue or an internal catalogue.

23 See CHEVILLOT 1997.

24 Even if, in his letter to Mathias Morhardt, Eugène Blot gives *Fortune* as the very first purchase.

25 Letter from Camille Claudel to Captain Tissier, May 31, 1902. See CLAUDEL 2003, no. 173.

26 Letter from Camille Claudel to Captain Tissier [March 16, 1902]. See CLAUDEL 2003, no. 169.

27 Letter from Camille Claudel to Eugène Blot [autumn 1904?]. See CLAUDEL 2003, no. 176.

28 Letter from Camille Claudel to Gustave Geffroy [March–April 1905]. See CLAUDEL 2003, no. 185. Is the second title a slip? There could have been confusion with *Deep Thought* or *Perseus*, or an outright mistake, the two works perhaps in fact corresponding, as Blot always maintained, to *Fortune* and *The Implorer*. At any rate, we know of no letter to Blot or from Blot prior to 1904.

29 Without there necessarily having been a definitive sale at the date of the letter.

30 Letter from Camille Claudel to Eugène Blot [April? 1905]. See CLAUDEL 2003, no. 190.

31 Letter from Camille Claudel to Eugène Blot [autumn 1905]. See CLAUDEL 2003, no. 199.

32 Letter from Camille Claudel to Eugène Blot [October–November 1905]. See CLAUDEL 2003, no. 200.

33 Letter from Camille Claudel to Eugène Blot [1905?]. See CLAUDEL 2003, no. 201.

34 As we learn from a letter from Camille Claudel to Gustave Geffroy [March–April 1905]. See CLAUDEL 2003, no. 185.

35 BLOT 1905, cat. 10.

36 Letter from Camille Claudel to Captain Tissier [March 16, 1902]. See CLAUDEL 2003, no. 169.

37 Never clearly identified, but which I propose is *Giganti*.

38 BLOT 1905.

39 BLOT 1907, cat. 2.

40 BLOT 1907, cat. 1.

41 BLOT 1908, cat. 5.

42 See PARIS 2000, cat. 34; RIVIÈRE / GAUDICHON / GHANASSIA 2001, cat. 63. Auction May 1 and 6–7, 1907, Galerie Georges Petit, 8 rue de Sèze, no. 174, acquired by Blot for 930 francs.

43 Three casts of *Giganti* given to the museums; one cast of *The Psalm* given to the Musée d'Abbeville; one cast of *La Petite Châtelaine* given to the Musée de Beaufort-en-Vallée (incidentally, also in circulation were several plasters, marbles and another bronze); and *Aurora*, which is dedicated and appears in many respects to be another version of *La Petite Châtelaine*.

44 *La Vieille Hélène* was cast after 1905 by Fumière et Cie, which strengthens my conviction that it was not *Head of an Old Woman* (see the appendix, p. 273).

45 It should be noted that, for sculpture editions, throughout the nineteenth century the law constantly wavered between the principles of industrial property and artistic property. In the absence of an explicit agreement and depending on the period, possession of the model was tantamount to possession of the exploitation rights. See Catherine Chevillot, "Artistes et fondeurs au XIXe siècle," Paris: Musée du Louvre, Musée-Musées series, conference "Le bronze, l'édition originale et la reproduction," February 13, 2002.

46 Letter from Eugène Blot to Gustave Leblanc-Barbedienne, February 24, 1937 (ANF). The Barbedienne Collection, given to the Archives Nationales in 1955 after the company was liquidated, contains correspondence between Eugène Blot and Gustave Leblanc-Barbedienne, documents (pages with photographs and the number of casts of each work) clearly handed over by Blot in support of his letters and charts (which seem to have been drawn up by Barbedienne) detailing their state.

47 BLOT 1934, p. 23.

48 Letter from Barbedienne to Eugène Blot, May 27, 1937 (ANF).

49 Letter from Barbedienne to Eugène Blot August 31, 1937 (ANF).

50 Archives de la Ville de Paris; see *supra*, note 6.

51 It is difficult to know whether the facts recorded in the archives concern only the period contemporary with the sale to Barbedienne, or whether this had been a habit for Blot from the outset despite the indication on the stamps. It cannot at any rate have been Alexis, but Eugène who at that time used Alexis' mark.

52 Letter from Eugène Blot to Barbedienne, June 6, 1937 (ANF).

53 Letter from Eugène Blot to Barbedienne, December 17, 1936 (ANF).

54 BLOT 1934, p. 64.

55 The Réunion des Fabricants de Bronze became the Syndicat du Luminaire.

56 See VAUXCELLES.

57 "Articles for electricity" were one of Blot's specialties. His advertisement in the *Bottin du commerce* stayed the same. In 1901, it read "Blot (Eug.) Paris 1887 and 1889, two gold medals. Production of various artistic bronzes and casts. Pewter. Works for the Salons, objets d'art, furnishings and lighting, r. des Archives 84."

58 BLOT 1934, p. 27.

59 Letter from Eugène Blot to Barbedienne, December 22, 1937 (ANF).

60 Letter from Eugène Blot to Barbedienne, June 6, 1937 (ANF).

61 Letter from Camille Claudel to Gustave Geffroy [late March 1905]. See CLAUDEL 2003, no. 184.

62 Letter from Camille Claudel to Eugène Blot [autumn 1904?]. See CLAUDEL 2003, no. 176.

63 Letter from Camille Claudel to Eugène Blot [April 1905?]. See CLAUDEL 2003, no. 188.

64 Letter from Camille Claudel to Eugène Blot [December 1905]. See CLAUDEL 2003, no. 202.

65 Letter from Camille Claudel to Eugène Blot [November or December 1906]. See CLAUDEL 2003, no. 213.

66 KAHN 1905, p. 1.

67 Letter from Eugène Blot to Mathias Morhardt, 1935, typewritten copy (AMR).

68 Letter from Eugène Blot to Camille Claudel, September 3, 1932. See CLAUDEL 2003, no. 295.

69 And not *Thought*, as erroneously transcribed in the lists typed by Barbedienne; the comparison of the handwritten letters by Blot and of the lists is unequivocal on this subject. The letter does indeed indicate "Perseus 45 cm" ("Persée" in French) as "Thought 45 cm" ("Pensée" in French).

A *NIOBID* WOUNDED BY AN ARROW
(pp. 274–87)

1 REVAL 1903, p. 520.

2 Letter from Camille Claudel to Gustave Geffroy [April 4, 1905]. See CLAUDEL 2003, no. 187.

3 "According to your instructions, we will inform Mademoiselle Claudel that we are placing at her disposal . . . the sum of 200 francs, monthly, for two years" (letter from Joanny Peytel to Auguste Rodin, December 14, 1904, AMR).

4 Letter from Camille Claudel to Henry Lerolle [spring 1905]. See CLAUDEL 2003, no. 183.

5 MORHARDT 1898, p. 754.

6 VAUXCELLES 1905.

7 KAHN 1905.

8 HAMEL 1905, p. 650.

9 CLAUDEL 1913, p. 35.

10 Thanks to Rosine Lapresle-Tavera, who devoted several Saturdays to examining Camille's letters with us, for drawing my attention to this point.

11 Letter from Camille Claudel to Gustave Geffroy [March 1905]. See CLAUDEL 2003, no. 181.

12 Letter from Camille Claudel to Henry Lerolle [spring 1905]. See CLAUDEL 2003, no. 183.

13 Letter from Camille Claudel to Eugène Blot [April 1905]. See CLAUDEL 2003, no. 195.

14 Letter from Medardo Rosso to Jehan Rictus [1905–6]. See LISTA 1994, pp. 87–89.

15 Letter from Camille Claudel to Eugène Blot [April 1905]. See CLAUDEL 2003, no. 195.

16 Letter from Camille Claudel to the undersecretary of state for the fine arts [March 5, 1906]. See CLAUDEL 2003, no. 203.

17 Letter from Camille Claudel to the undersecretary of state for the fine arts [May 19, 1906]. See CLAUDEL 2003, no. 205.

18 Armand Dayot's report to the minister of fine arts, June 30, 1906 (ANF).

19 Allocated to the Bejaia Museum, Algeria, by ministerial order on April 11, 1910, where it still is.

20 MARSEILLE 1997.

21 Archives of Prince Eugene Waldemarsudde, Stockholm.

22 RILKE 1928, pp. 52–53.

23 MORHARDT 1898, pp. 719–20.

CAMILLE'S EXILE,
RODIN'S GLORY
(pp. 288–99)

1 The idea to do a bust of Paul Claudel came from Camille's old friend, the painter Henry Lerolle. The two artists exhibited together at the Salon of the Société Nationale des Beaux-Arts, of which Henry Lerolle was one of the founders. See PARIS 2000, p. 443.

2 Letter from Louis-Prosper Claudel to his son Paul [1904]. See "Louis-Prosper Claudel: lettres à son fils (1891–1912)," in CAHIERS CLAUDEL 1959, pp. 116–17.

3 Letter from Louis-Prosper Claudel to his son Paul [summer 1909], quoted in CLAUDEL 2003, p. 241, note 2.

4 Letter from Camille Claudel to Henriette Thierry [late 1912–early 1913?]. See CLAUDEL 2003, no. 237.

5 On this affair, see AYRAL-CLAUSE 2002, pp. 193–94.

6 BUTLER 1993, pp. 455–76.

7 BUTLER 1993, p. xii (Preface).

8 AYRAL-CLAUSE 2002.

9 LE NORMAND-ROMAIN 2003.

10 See "Testament" in RODIN 1911.

11 BUTLER 1993, p. x (Foreword).

12 Letter from Camille Claudel to Paul Claudel [March 3, 1927]. See CLAUDEL 2003, no. 280.

13 Recorded by his last secretary, Marcelle Martin. See TIREL 1923, p. 84.

14 RODIN 1911.

CAMILLE CLAUDEL AND
CLAUDE DEBUSSY:
A FRIENDSHIP (pp. 308–13)

1 Robert Godet, "Le lyrisme intime de Claude Debussy," La Revue musicale, I, no. 2 (December 1, 1920), special issue: "Debussy," pp. 167–90; "En marge de la marge," La Revue musicale, 7, no. 7 (May 1, 1926), special issue: "La Jeunesse de Claude Debussy," pp. 51–86; "Entretien préliminaire," in DEBUSSY 1942, pp. 1–86.

2 Journal, March 19, 1895, quoted by François Lesure in Claude Debussy, Paris: Fayard, 2003, p. 122.

3 DEBUSSY 1942, p. 41.

4 Claude Debussy: Correspondance 1884–1919, edited by François Lesure, Paris: Hermann, 1993, pp. 61–62.

5 DEBUSSY 1942, p. 41.

6 La Revue musicale 1920, p. 186. The italics are mine.

7 The expression certainly refers to the death of "the heroine" and not to Camille's madness, which had not yet manifested itself in 1893.

8 DEBUSSY 1942, p. 41.

9 In 1897, the Escudiers had acquired (then sold) the beautiful original plaster of The Wave (RIVIÈRE / GAUDICHON / GHANASSIA 2001, cat. 53.1) and still owned a marble of La Petite Châtelaine (RIVIÈRE / GAUDICHON / GHANASSIA 2001, cat. 35.7) and a bronze of the bust My Brother (RIVIÈRE / GAUDICHON / GHANASSIA 2001, cat. 13.3); Camille undoubtedly gave Godet plasters, which he himself patinated, of La Petite Châtelaine (RIVIÈRE / GAUDICHON / GHANASSIA 2001, cat. 35.1), Les Causeuses (RIVIÈRE / GAUDICHON / GHANASSIA 2001, cat. 41.4) and The Waltz (RIVIÈRE / GAUDICHON / GHANASSIA 2001, cat. 33.3); Thaulow owned marbles of Les Causeuses (RIVIÈRE / GAUDICHON / GHANASSIA 2001, cat. 41.3) and La Petite Châtelaine (RIVIÈRE / GAUDICHON / GHANASSIA 2001, cat. 35.6) (Thaulow auction, May 7, 1907), and plasters of The Waltz (RIVIÈRE / GAUDICHON / GHANASSIA 2001, cat. 33.3), La Petite Châtelaine (RIVIÈRE / GAUDICHON / GHANASSIA 2001, cat. 35.1) and Aurora (RIVIÈRE / GAUDICHON / GHANASSIA 2001, cat. 63.1). Various versions of these same works had been shown publicly at the Salons of the Société Nationale des Beaux-Arts (1892–1902), at Bing's gallery (1896–97) and at the Salon de la Libre Esthétique (1894).

10 Head of an Old Man Singing (RIVIÈRE / GAUDICHON / GHANASSIA 2001, cat. 43.3), Study for Hamadryad (RIVIÈRE / GAUDICHON / GHANASSIA 2001, cat. 50.6), Head of a Young Girl with a Chignon (RIVIÈRE / GAUDICHON / GHANASSIA 2001, cat. 70.2), and bust of Paul Claudel Aged Thirty-Seven (RIVIÈRE / GAUDICHON / GHANASSIA 2001, cat. 68.3), all works reproduced in CLAUDEL 1913.

11 This rare catalogue (passed on to me by Agnès Lamarre) gives its height as 33 cm, and excludes the marble of the same work belonging to H. Fontaine (H. 44 cm) and Aurora (H. 35 cm), a marble said to be in the artist's family in CLAUDEL 1913. This "Head of a Young Girl" could be the "marble II" version of La Petite Châtelaine indicated in 1913 as being in the Escudier Collection.

12 Letter from Camille Claudel to Henry Lerolle [spring 1905?] (SMAF). See CLAUDEL 2003, no. 183; unidentified picture.

13 Madame Ernest Chausson acquired a copy from Henry Lerolle, her brother-in-law. The bust is on the mantelpiece of her dining room in Paris in a photograph taken in 1920 (Julia archives).

14 DEBUSSY 1942, p. 44.

15 DEBUSSY 1942, p. 44.

16 RIVIÈRE / GAUDICHON / GHANASSIA 2001, p. 114.

17 CLAUDEL 1913, p. 35.

18 La Revue musicale 1926, pp. 71–72. These two phrases, which Godet puts in inverted commas, seem to be a transcript of Debussy's words.

19 Claude Debussy, Monsieur Croche et autres écrits, edited by François Lesure, Paris: Gallimard, 1987, p. 52; text dating from 1901.

WOMEN SCULPTORS IN
NINETEENTH-CENTURY FRANCE
(pp. 314–23)

1 In her famous article "Why Have There Been No Great Women Artists?" Linda Nochlin brilliantly explores the fundamental role played by social institutions in the artistic domain. See NOCHLIN 1989.

2 L'Éducation progressive ou Étude du cours de la vie, quoted in YELDHAM 1984, p. 41.

3 ELLET 1859.

4 Giorgio Vasari, The Lives of the Most Eminent Painters, Sculptors and Architects, quoted in HONIG 1978, p. 8.

5 YELDHAM 1984, pp. 40–44.

6 YELDHAM 1984, pp. 30–31.

7 TURNER 1996.

8 HONIG 1978, p. 56.

9 YELDHAM 1984, pp. 329–36.

10 EASTERDAY 1997, p. 179.

11 EASTERDAY 1997, pp. 202–10.

12 ALCANTRA 1961, p. 48.

13 ALCANTRA 1961, p. 135; see also PIERRE 2003.

14 GARNIER 2001, pp. 296–97.

15 BELLOC 1890, pp. 374–77.

16 BASHKIRTSEFF 1980, p. 396.

17 EASTERDAY 1997, p. 296.

18 LEPAGE 1911, p. 58.

19 LEPAGE 1911, pp. 123, 124, 170, 192.

20 EASTERDAY 1997, p. 323.

21 MITCHELL 1989, pp. 438–41.

22 LEPAGE 1911, p. 95.

23 EASTERDAY 1997, p. 322.

24 MITCHELL 1989, p. 419.

25 REYNOLDS 2004, p. 201.

26 REYNOLDS 2004, pp. 212–13.

CAMILLE CLAUDEL,
"A WOMAN OF GENIUS"?
(pp. 324–35)

1 Quoted by Pierre Larousse in the entry "Génie," *Grand dictionnaire universel du XIXᵉ siècle*, 1866–79, Slatkine edition, Geneva and Paris, 1892, vol. 8, part 2, p. 1156.

2 PINET / PARIS 2003. The complete quote, on the second title page, of the remark by Paul Claudel from which the title originated, made to Henri Mondor and published in the latter's book *Claudel plus intime*, 1960, sheds some light on the enigma: "Genius is like a mirror, one side of which receives light and the other side of which is rough and rusted."

3 See "I contemplate one after another all these works, each of which marks a stage in the horrible Calvary and whose clay was molded with the soul and with blood." In *Paul Claudel interroge le Cantique des cantiques*, CLAUDEL 2004, p. 90.

4 All quotes concerning contemporary criticism of Camille Claudel are taken from the excellent corpus compiled by Sophie Gauthier, as an appendix to her master's thesis. See GAUTHIER 2003.

5 LEROI 1886.

6 LEROI 1888, p. 212.

7 "Rodin's thoughtful and energetic head appears to have been sculpted strongly and delicately by Mlle Camille Claudel,

with the fine understanding of the great artist she had to bring to life" (GEFFROY 1893, p. 337).

8 Paul Leroi is not included, for example, in BOUILLON 1990.

9 Letter from Honoré Balzac to Eve Hanska, October 27, 1833, in *Lettres à madame Hanska, 1832–1844*. Paris: Robert Laffont, 1990, p. 72.

10 See "Génie," *Grand dictionnaire universel du XIXᵉ siècle*, p. 1156.

11 Madame de Staël, *Corinne ou l'Italie* (1807).

12 Honoré de Balzac, *Béatrix ou les amours forcés*, Paris: Classique Garnier, 1962, p. 64.

13 George Sand, *Histoire de ma vie, 1854–1855. Œuvres autobiographiques*, Paris: Gallimard, 1972, vol. 2, p. 163.

14 Anita Brookner, *The Genius of the Future, Diderot, Stendhal, Baudelaire, Zola, the Brothers Goncourt, Huysmans*, London and New York: Phaidon, 1971.

15 See Philippe Chardin, "Fins comparées de quelques artistes fictifs de la fin de siècle," in *Fins de siècle*, Toulouse: Presses du Mirail, 1989, pp. 231–39.

16 DAYOT 1893.

17 MIRBEAU 1893.

18 On this subject, see Jacques Petit, "Autour de la publication de 'Tête d'or,' lettres inédites de Paul Claudel, Maurice Maeterlinck, Marcel Schwob, Henri de Régnier, Octave Mirbeau, Charles-Henry Hirsch, Camille Mauclair, Jules Bois, Byvanck," in CAHIERS CLAUDEL 1959, pp. 135–70.

19 Letter from Maeterlinck to Mockel, December 21, 1890: "I have just received an incredible volume from Paris: *Tête d'or* by Paul Claudel . . . It is either the work of a madman or the most prodigious genius who ever existed" (Jacques Petit, "Autour de la publication de 'Tête d'or,'" in CAHIERS CLAUDEL 1959, p. 138).

20 RENARD 1965, March 13, 1895, p. 270.

21 Following Maeterlinck's letter on *Tête d'or* (see *supra*, note 19), Claudel wrote, "I have begun to believe myself something." See CLAUDEL 1959.

22 RENARD 1965, January 24, 1893, p. 149.

23 Catalogue Blaizot, February 1936, quoted in MIRBEAU 1993, p. 43, note 15.

24 RENARD 1965, November 14, 1892, p. 147.

25 Sylvain Goudemare recounts the story which he says Pierre Champion told him in *Marcel Schwob ou les Vies imaginaires*, Paris: Le Cherche midi éditeur, 2000.

26 She had already had the same misfortune with her bust of *Auguste Rodin* considered by some critics to be a self-portrait.

27 "Have you sent *Tête d'or* to Mirbeau? Would you mind if I wrote to him about it? I'm sure he does not know it. And as far as I can tell it will send him into raptures" (letter from Marcel Schwob to Paul Claudel, January 1892, quoted by Jacques Petit, "Autour de la publication de 'Tête d'or,'" in CAHIERS CLAUDEL 1959, p. 147).

28 The criticisms? Needless to say, I know the ones one can make. But they are blown away by the enormous force running through the tumultuous and beautiful work, *Tête d'or*" (letter from Octave Mirbeau to Marcel Schwob, March 6, 1892, quoted by Jacques Petit, "Autour de la publication de 'Tête d'or,'" in CAHIERS CLAUDEL 1959, p. 147).

29 MIRBEAU 1893.

30 Camille Mauclair, *Servitude et grandeur littéraires*, quoted by Jacques Petit, "Autour de la publication de 'Tête d'or,'" in CAHIERS CLAUDEL 1959, pp. 154.

31 MIRBEAU 1895.

32 Letter from Auguste Rodin to Octave Mirbeau, June 1895. See PARIS 2000, pp. 529–31.

33 See "Génie" in *Grand dictionnaire universel du XIXᵉ siècle*, p. 1156.

34 See Christian Limousin, "Mirbeau critique d'Art. De 'l'âge de l'hui et diluvienne' au règne de l'artiste de génie," in *Cahiers d'Octave Mirbeau* no. 1, 199-, pp. 1–41.

35 Octave Mirbeau, "L'Union des femmes peintres et sculpteurs," February 1885, in MIRBEAU 1993, p. 122.

36 Octave Mirbeau, "Exposition de peinture (1 rue Laffite)," May 1896, in MIRBEAU 1993, p. 276.

37 Octave Mirbeau, "Exposition de peinture (1 rue Laffite)," May 1896, in MIRBEAU 1993, p. 277.

38 Octave Mirbeau, "Éva Gonzales," January 17, 1885, in MIRBEAU 1993, p. 105.

39 MORICE 1895.

40 Octave Mirbeau, *Le Journal*, April 26, 1896 and April 25, 1897.

41 BRAISNE 1897.

42 MORHARDT 1898.

43 Letter from Paul Claudel to Gabriel Frizeau, November 15, 1905, in CLAUDEL 1952, p. 69.

44 Paul Vibert, "Le régime des aliénés et la loi de 1838" in *Le Grand National*, December 1914. See RIVIÈRE / GAUDICHON / GHANASSIA 2001, pp. 258–59.

45 Georges-Albert Aurier, "Les isolés – Vincent Van Gogh." See BOUILLON 1990, pp. 331–35.

46 Nathalie Heinich, *La Gloire de Van Gogh*, Paris: Éditions de Minuit, 1991. See also the articles quoted in the appendix under the title "Van Gogh et la critique d'art en France, 1888–1901."

47 Letter from Stéphane Mallarmé to Octave Mirbeau, January 5, 1891, in MALLARMÉ 1973, pp. 176–77.

48 Octave Mirbeau, "Paul Gauguin," *L'Écho de Paris*, February 16, 1891. See MIRBEAU 1993, pp. 418–22.

49 Charles Morice, "Paul Gauguin," *Mercure de France*, December 1893, pp. 289–300.

50 Emile Bernard, "Souvenirs sur Paul Cézanne," *Mercure de France*, October 1 and 16, 1907, articles reproduced in *Conversations avec Cézanne*, Paris: Macula, 1978, p. 65.

51 Auguste Rodin, quoted as the epigraph to MORHARDT 1898.

52 CLAUDEL 1913, p. 50.

53 CLAUDEL 1913, p. 35.

54 Kafka, *Diaries*, September 15, 1912.

III

LIST OF WORKS IN
THE EXHIBITION

READER'S NOTE

ORDER OF PRESENTATION

The pieces exhibited have been grouped into two main categories: 1) works and photographs; 2) archive documents.

The list of works and photographs lists works in alphabetical order by artist or photographer. Each artist's works are listed in chronological order, with datings around the same year listed by decreasing order of precision, i.e., "1900" followed by "1900?" followed by "c.1900." Works with identical dates are listed in alphabetical order by title. When a title is a person's name, the work is classified in alphabetical order by that person's surname: *Paul Claudel as a Child* (c.1885) thus precedes *Crouching Woman* (c.1885).

The list of archive documents lists documents in chronological order.

TITLE

When a work has several titles, the most widely used title is given.

When two titles, designated by the letters A and B, are listed under the same catalogue number, they refer to two copies of the same work or two closely related works, because the same works are not always exhibited in Quebec, Detroit and Martigny for conservation reasons.

DATE

The date which follows the title is that of the creation of the model. The date after the material is that of the work's execution in that material. When there are notable differences between the initial model and the version exhibited, the date of the creation of the model is mentioned in square brackets.

When no information enables a work's precise dating, the date is that of the first exhibition in which the work was included.

DIMENSIONS

The dimensions of works are given in centimeters in the following order: height, width and depth.

PROVENANCE

The original provenance of works is indicated when this information is instructive.

EXHIBITIONS

The "Exh." heading indicates, in an abbreviated form (see list of abbreviations at the end of the Reader's Note), the first exhibition of the work during the artist's lifetime. A second exhibition is sometimes mentioned if it took place shortly after the first exhibition.

When the cast in this exhibition corresponds exactly to the one in the first exhibition, the abbreviated mention of this exhibition is followed by no indications. When the material is identical but it is not the same piece, the identity of the piece presented in the first exhibition is indicated in brackets after the exhibition; when the material is identical, but it has not been possible to identify the piece shown in the first exhibition, it is listed as "unidentified." If the material is different, the nature of the material of the piece presented in the first exhibition is specified in brackets. If this material in unknown, the indication "undetermined cast" follows the exhibition.

CATALOGUES

The references listed under the "Cat." heading refer, in an abbreviated form (see list of abbreviations at the end of the Reader's Note), to the two catalogues raisonnés of Camille Claudel's works, to the inventory of Auguste Rodin's drawings, and to Camille Claudel and Auguste Rodin's correspondence.

ABBREVIATIONS

Exh.:

ALMA 1900 *Rodin* exhibition, Pavillon de l'Alma, Paris, June 1–November 27, 1900.

ANGERS 1889 *Exposition artistique de la Société des Amis des Arts*, Galerie Place Loraine, Angers, November 9, 1889–January 12, 890.

BLOT 1905 *Exposition d'œuvres de Camille Claudel et de Bernard Hoetger*, Galerie Eugène Blot, Paris, December 4–16, 1905.

BLOT 1908 *Exposition de Mesdames Camille Claudel, Gaston Devore, Jeanne Eliot, Alcide Lebeau-Hassenberg, Ann Osterlind (Mme. Edouard Sarradin)*, Galerie Eugène Blot, Paris, December 1–21, 1908.

BRUSSELS 1887 *Exposition générale des Beaux-Arts* or Brussels Salon, September–October 1887.

BRUSSELS 1894 *Salon de la Libre Esthétique de Bruxelles*, 1894.

BRUSSELS / ROTTERDAM / AMSTERDAM / THE HAGUE 1899 *Tentoonstelling van Beeldhouwwerken door A. Rodin [Exhibition of works by Auguste Rodin]*, La Maison d'Art, Brussels, Rotterdamsche Kunstkring, Rotterdam, Maatschappij "Arti & Amicitiae," Amsterdam, Haagsche Kunstkring, The Hague, May 8–November 5, 1899.

DRESDEN 1897 *International Kunst-Ausstellung*, National Palace of Exhibitions, Dresden, May 1–October 18, 1897.

DÜSSELDORF 1904 *International Exhibition of Fine Arts*, National Palace of the Arts, Düsseldorf, May 1–October 23, 1904.

LONDON 1899 *2nd International Exhibition of Art*, International Society of Sculptors, Painters and Engravers, Knightsbridge, London, c. May–July 1899.

LONDON 1914 *Exhibition of Contemporary French Decorative Art (1800–1885)*, Grosvenor House, London, July 1–21, 1914.

PARIS 1883 *Cercle des Arts Libéraux*, rue Vivienne, Paris, between February and March 1883.

PARIS 1886 *Ve Exposition Internationale de Peinture et de Sculpture*, Galerie Georges Petit, Paris, June 15–July 15, 1886.

PARIS 1887 *VIe Exposition Internationale*, Galerie Georges Petit, Paris, May–July 1887.

PARIS 1889 *Claude Monet – Auguste Rodin* exhibition, Galerie Georges Petit, Paris, June 21–August 1889.

PARIS 1900 *Exposition universelle de Paris*, 1900.

SA *Salon d'Automne*, Paris.

SAF *Salon of the Société des Artistes Français*, Paris.

SNBA *Salon of the Société Nationale des Beaux-Arts*, Paris.

STOCKHOLM 1897 *General Exhibition of Fine Arts and Industry*, Fine Arts Hall (Djurgaden), May 15–October 1, 1897.

CAT.:

CLAUDEL 2003 *Camille Claudel: Correspondance*, edited by Anne RIVIÈRE and Bruno GAUDICHON, Paris, Gallimard, 2003.

JUDRIN 1985 Claudie JUDRIN, *Inventaire des dessins*, vol. 3, Musée Rodin, Paris, 1985.

JUDRIN 1992 Claudie JUDRIN, *Inventaire des dessins*, vol. 5, Musée Rodin, Paris, 1992.

PARIS 2000 Reine-Marie PARIS, *Camille Claudel retrouvée: Catalogue raisonné*, Paris, Aittouarès, 2000.

RIVIÈRE/GAUDICHON/GHANASSIA 2001 Anne RIVIÈRE, Bruno GAUDICHON and Danielle GHANASSIA, *Camille Claudel: Catalogue raisonné*, Paris, Adam Biro, 2001.

RODIN 1985 *Correspondance de Rodin*, vol. 1: *1860–1899*, edited by Alain BEAUSIRE and Hélène PINET, Musée Rodin, Paris, 1985.

WORKS AND PHOTOGRAPHS (IN ALPHABETICAL ORDER BY ARTIST)

ANONYMOUS

Cat. 1
ANONYMOUS
Louise Claudel, Eyes Closed,
terracotta?,
by Camille Claudel
About 1886
Photograph, albumin print
9.2 x 5.6 cm
Musée Rodin (Ph.536), Paris,
Gift of Stephen Back, 1992
Formerly Florence Jeans
Collection

Cat. 2
ANONYMOUS
A) Sakuntala, *plaster model,*
by Camille Claudel
1888
Photograph, albumin print
15.6 x 10.2 cm
Musée Rodin (Ph.2218),
Paris
Donation Auguste Rodin,
1916

B) Sakuntala,
plaster model,
by Camille Claudel
1888
Photograph, albumin print
15.5 x 10.6 cm
Musée Rodin (Ph.2217),
Paris
Donation Auguste Rodin,
1916

Cat. 3
ANONYMOUS
Charles Lhermitte
About 1889
Photograph, aristotype
8.5 x 5.5 cm
Private collection, France

Cat. 4
ANONYMOUS
A) *Estager,*
"Conductor of Tours"
1891
Photograph, albumin print
14.4 x 11.2 cm
Musée Rodin (Ph.1216), Paris
Donation Auguste Rodin,
1916

B) *Estager,*
"Conductor of Tours"
1891
Photograph, albumin print
14.4 x 11.1 cm
Musée Rodin (Ph.1217), Paris
Donation Auguste Rodin,
1916

Cat. 5
ANONYMOUS
A) *Camille Claudel modeling*
the bust of Back, at Shanklin,
on the Isle of Wight
1893

Photograph, aristotype
10.9 x 8.3 cm
Musée Rodin (Ph.529), Paris
Gift of Stephen Back, 1992
Formerly Florence Jeans
Collection

B) *Camille Claudel modeling*
the bust of Back, at Shanklin,
on the Isle of Wight
1893
Photograph, aristotype
10.9 x 8.3 cm
Musée Rodin (Ph.530), Paris
Gift of Stephen Back, 1992
Formerly Florence Jeans
Collection

Cat. 6
ANONYMOUS
Auguste Rodin in front of
his atelier at the Dépôt
des Marbres, with Thought
in the background
About 1895
Photograph, albumin print
9.7 x 7.4 cm
Musée Rodin (Ph.21), Paris
Donation Auguste Rodin,
1916

Cat. 7
ANONYMOUS
The Farewell, *plaster model,*
first state, by Auguste Rodin
About 1898?
Judith CLADEL, *Auguste*
Rodin, l'œuvre et l'homme,
Brussels, Librairie Nationale
d'Art et d'Histoire G. van
Oest et Cⁱᵉ, 1908
36.5 x 28 cm
Private collection, France

Cat. 8
ANONYMOUS
Camille Claudel in her atelier
at 19 quai de Bourbon,
with the plaster of
Perseus and the Gorgon
About 1899
Photograph, gelatin silver print?
Approximately 17 x 12 cm
Bibliothèque Marguerite-
Durand, Paris
Gift of Mary Léopold Lacour,
about 1936?

Cat. 9
ANONYMOUS
A) *The Mask of Camille Claudel*
at the Rodin *exhibition,*
place de l'Alma, 1900
1900
Photograph, aristotype
6 x 4.5 cm
Musée Rodin (Ph.1964), Paris
Donation Auguste Rodin, 1916

B) *The* Mask of Camille
Claudel *at the* Rodin *exhibi-*
tion, place de l'Alma, 1900
1900
Photograph, aristotype
9.2 x 6 cm
Musée Rodin (Ph.2268), Paris
Donation Auguste Rodin, 1916

Cat. 10
ANONYMOUS, after HOKUSAI
The Wave

Cover of the score of
Claude Debussy's *La Mer,*
1905
33 x 25 cm
Jean-Michel Nectoux
Collection, Paris

Cat. 11
ANONYMOUS
The Thinker *in front*
of the Panthéon
1906
Photograph, gelatin
silver print
27.7 x 21.7 cm
Musée Rodin (Ph.2881), Paris
Donation Auguste Rodin,
1916

Cat. 12
ANONYMOUS
The park of the Hôtel Biron
About 1915
Photograph, gelatin
silver print
17 x 22.6 cm
Musée Rodin (Ph.1367), Paris
Donation Auguste Rodin,
1916

Cat. 13
ANONYMOUS
Auguste Rodin and Rose
Beuret in the garden of the
Villa des Brillants at
Meudon, March 25, 1916
1916
Photograph, gelatin
silver print
21.1 x 16.3 cm
Musée Rodin (Ph.1105), Paris
Donation Auguste Rodin,
1916

BERNÈS ET MAROUTEAU

Cat. 14

BERNÈS ET MAROUTEAU
Musée Rodin, Meudon.
The Master's Atelier
About 1917
Photograph, gelatin
silver print
21 x 29.2 cm
Musée Rodin (Ph.9001), Paris
Donation Auguste Rodin,
1916

ALFRED BOUCHER

(Bouy-sur-Orvin, France, 1850 –
Aix-les-Bains, France, 1934)

Cat. 15

ALFRED BOUCHER
My Mother
(Madame Julien Boucher)
1880
Bronze
55 x 28 x 28 cm
Signed in back, on neck and
right shoulder: *A. BOUCHER*
Musée Paul-Dubois –
Alfred-Boucher (NS 02.239),
Nogent-sur-Seine
Gift of Alfred Boucher, 1902
EXH.: SAF 1905, no. 2883

JACQUES-ERNEST BULLOZ

(Paris, France, 1858 – Paris,
France, 1942)

Cat. 16

JACQUES-ERNEST BULLOZ
Plasters by Auguste Rodin
in the Pavillon de l'Alma
reconstructed in Meudon
After 1903
Photograph, gelatin silver print

27.5 x 37 cm
Musée Rodin (Ph.966),
Paris
Donation Auguste Rodin,
1916

Cat. 17

JACQUES-ERNEST BULLOZ
The Farewell, marble,
by Auguste Rodin
After 1903–4
Photograph, carbon print
37.5 x 26.5 cm
Musée Rodin (Ph.3621), Paris
Donation Auguste Rodin,
1916

Cat. 18

JACQUES-ERNEST BULLOZ
France during execution,
plaster, by Auguste Rodin
After 1903–4
Photograph, gelatin
silver print
35.5 x 26.5 cm
Musée Rodin (Ph.970), Paris
Donation Auguste Rodin,
1916

CAMUS

Cat. 19

CAMUS
Paul Claudel
Between 1876 and 1879

Photograph, albumin print
10.5 x 6.5 cm
Private collection, France

CARAN D'ACHE
(EMMANUEL POIRÉ)

(Moscow, Russia, 1859 – Paris,
France, 1909)

Cat. 20

CARAN D'ACHE
(EMMANUEL POIRÉ)
Before the Statue.
Intellectual Effort
Psst...!, no. 17, May 28,
1898
40.3 x 28 cm
Alain Beausire Collection,
Paris

ÉTIENNE CARJAT

(Fareins, France, 1828 – Paris,
France, 1906)

Cat. 21

ÉTIENNE CARJAT
Camille Claudel
About 1886
Photograph, albumin print
16.5 x 10.5 cm
Private collection,
United Kingdom

Cat. 22

ÉTIENNE CARJAT
Auguste Rodin

About 1886
Photograph, albumin print
16.5 x 10.5 cm
Annotated at bottom:
hommage de ma vive
amitié/à mon/Elève Miss
Lipscomb/Rodin
Private collection,
United Kingdom

CÉSAR

Cat. 23

CÉSAR
A) *Camille Claudel*
1881
Photograph, albumin print
15.5 x 10.3 cm
Musée Rodin (Ph.527),
Paris
Gift of Stephen Back, 1992
Formerly Florence Jeans
Collection

B) *Camille Claudel*
1881
Photograph, albumin print
12.9 x 9.9 cm
Musée Rodin (Ph.1029),
Paris
Donation Auguste Rodin,
1916

Cat. 24

CÉSAR
Camille Claudel
About 1885
Photograph, albumin print
6 x 10.5 cm
Private collection,
France

PIERRE CHOUMOFF

(Grodno, western Russia, 1872 –
Lodz, Poland, 1936)

Cat. 25

PIERRE CHOUMOFF
A) *The funeral of*
Auguste Rodin at Meudon,
November 24, 1917
1917
Photograph, gelatin silver print
17.2 x 22.4 cm
Musée Rodin (Ph.1012), Paris
Donation Auguste Rodin,
1916

B) *The funeral of*
Auguste Rodin at Meudon,
November 24, 1917
1917
Photograph, gelatin silver print
17.2 x 22.5 cm
Musée Rodin (Ph.1008), Paris
Donation Auguste Rodin,
1916

CAMILLE CLAUDEL

(Fère-en-Tardenois, France, 1864 –
Montfavet, France, 1943)

Cat. 26

CAMILLE CLAUDEL
The Old Woman
1882
Bronze, cast by Fumière et
Cie, between 1906 and 1926
28 x 18 x 21 cm
Signed in back, to the left:
C. Claudel
Founder's mark in back, in a
circle: *FUMIÈRE ET CIE*
SUC^{RS}/THIEBAUT F^{RES}/PARIS
Private collection, France
EXH.: SAF 1885, no. 3497
(terracotta)
CAT.: PARIS 2000, no. 4;
RIVIÈRE/GAUDICHON/GHANASSIA
2001, no. 8.3

Cat. 27
___
CAMILLE CLAUDEL
My Brother (Paul Claudel)
1884
Bronze
51 x 44 x 25 cm
Signed on left shoulder:
Camille Claudel
Musée Calvet (T.511),
Avignon
Gift of [Baroness Nathaniel?]
de Rothschild, 1897
EXH.: SAF 1887, no. 3779
(probably this bronze)
CAT.: PARIS 2000, no. 9;
RIVIÈRE/GAUDICHON/GHANASSIA
2001, no. 13.3

Cat. 28
___
CAMILLE CLAUDEL
Giganti
1885
Bronze
30.6 x 30 x 26.5 cm
Signed on base:
Camille Claudel
Musée des Beaux-Arts
(901.27), Rheims
Gift of Baron Alphonse
de Rothschild, 1901
EXH.: SAF 1885, no. 3496
(unidentified bronze)
CAT.: PARIS 2000, no .16;
RIVIÈRE/GAUDICHON/GHANASSIA
2001, no. 19.3

Cat. 29
___
CAMILLE CLAUDEL
Mennie-Jean

354

1885
Charcoal with white chalk
highlights on ocher paper
48 x 37 cm
Signed and dated lower right:
*Camille Claudel/Gérardmer
Aout 29/85*
Annotated lower center:
mennie-jean
Musée Eugène-Boudin
(901.1.3), Honfleur
Gift of Baron Alphonse
de Rothschild, 1902
CAT.: PARIS 2000, no. 68;
RIVIÈRE/GAUDICHON/GHANASSIA
2001, no. 81

Cat. 30
___
CAMILLE CLAUDEL
Paul Claudel as a Child
About 1885
Bronze
40 x 36.5 x 22 cm
Signed in back, on left
shoulder: *C. Claudel*
Musée Bertrand (3391),
Châteauroux
Gift of Baron Alphonse
de Rothschild, 1903
CAT.: PARIS 2000, no. 3;
RIVIÈRE/GAUDICHON/GHANASSIA
2001, no. 7.2

Cat. 31
___
CAMILLE CLAUDEL
Crouching Woman
About 1885
Patinated plaster
37.8 x 24 x 37.3 cm
Private collection, France
CAT.: PARIS 2000, no. 6;
RIVIÈRE/GAUDICHON/GHANASSIA
2001, no. 14.1

Cat. 32
___
CAMILLE CLAUDEL
Crouching Woman, without
head or arms
[Complete figure: about
1885]
Found in 1913
Bronze, about 1913?
35 x 21 x 19 cm
Private collection, France
CAT.: PARIS 2000, no. 7;
RIVIÈRE/GAUDICHON/GHANASSIA
2001, no. 14.3

Cat. 33
___
CAMILLE CLAUDEL
*The Old Lady of the
Pont Notre-Dame*
About 1885
Charcoal on Canson paper
mounted on cardboard
60 x 48 cm
Musée Barrois (901.8.1),
Bar-le-Duc
Gift of Baron Alphonse
de Rothschild, 1901

Cat. 34
___
CAMILLE CLAUDEL
Louise Claudel
1886
Terracotta
49 x 22 x 25 cm
Palais des Beaux-Arts (Sc.80),
Lille
Gift of Léon Gauchez, 1892
CAT.: PARIS 2000, no. 11;
RIVIÈRE/GAUDICHON/GHANASSIA
2001, no. 20.4

Cat. 35
___
CAMILLE CLAUDEL
Louise Claudel
1886
Bronze
47 x 18 x 24 cm
Musée d'Art Roger-Quilliot
(894-327-2484),
Clermont-Ferrand
Gift of Baroness Nathaniel
de Rothschild, 1887 or 1888
EXH.: SAF 1886, no. 8674
CAT.: PARIS 2000, no. 11;
RIVIÈRE/GAUDICHON/GHANASSIA
2001, no. 20.3

Cat. 36
___
CAMILLE CLAUDEL
Jessie Lipscomb
1886
Charcoal with white chalk
highlights on paper
61 x 54.8 cm
Signed, dated and annotated
lower right: *Camille Claudel/
croquis d'après miss Lipscomb/
Peterborough 24 juin 86*
Private collection,
United Kingdom
CAT.: PARIS 2000, no. 70;
RIVIÈRE/GAUDICHON/GHANASSIA
2001, no. 88

Cat. 37
___
CAMILLE CLAUDEL
Study for Sakuntala?

1886?
or
Auguste RODIN
Study for The Kiss?
1880?
Terracotta
11 x 5.2 x 5.1 cm
Musée Rodin (S.6418), Paris
Donation Auguste Rodin, 1916

Cat. 38
___
CAMILLE CLAUDEL
Study for Sakuntala
1886?
Terracotta
15.5 x 12 x 11 cm
Private collection, France
CAT.: PARIS 2000, no. 21;
RIVIÈRE/GAUDICHON/GHANASSIA
2001, no. 23.2

Cat. 39
___
CAMILLE CLAUDEL
Study for Sakuntala?
1886?
or
AUGUSTE RODIN
Embracing Group
About 1880–86?
Terracotta
14.9 x 9.6 x 6.4 cm
Musée Rodin (S.235), Paris
Donation Auguste Rodin, 1916

Cat. 40
___
CAMILLE CLAUDEL
Study for Sakuntala

1886?
Terracotta
21 x 18 x 12 cm
Private collection, France
CAT.: PARIS 2000, no. 22;
RIVIÈRE/GAUDICHON/GHANASSIA
2001, no. 23.1

Cat. 41
CAMILLE CLAUDEL
The Young Girl with a Sheaf
1886?
Terracotta
60 x 21 x 21 cm
Signed on right side of the
support: *CAMILLE/CLAUDEL*
Musée Rodin (S.6738), Paris
National Treasure acquired
by the state for the Musée
National Auguste Rodin
through the patronage of
Natexis Banques Populaires
under the fiscal provisions of
the law of January 4, 2002,
concerning the Musées de
France, 2004
Formerly Léon Lhermitte
Collection
CAT.: PARIS 2000, no. 19;
RIVIÈRE/GAUDICHON/GHANASSIA
2001, no. 25.1

Cat. 42
CAMILLE CLAUDEL
Leaning Man
About 1886
Plaster
43.2 x 19 x 28 cm
Private collection, France
CAT.: PARIS 2000, no. 18;
RIVIÈRE/GAUDICHON/GHANASSIA
2001, no. 21.1

Cat. 43
CAMILLE CLAUDEL
Head of a Girl with a Chignon
About 1886
Bronze, edition by
Eugène Blot, 1908?
14.3 x 9.5 x 14.8 cm
Signed on the back: *Claudel*
Mark on back: *EUG.
BLOT/PARIS Nº 1*
Musée Rodin (S.6729), Paris
Purchase, 2003
EXH.: BLOT 1908, no. 7 or 8?
(unidentified bronze)
CAT.: PARIS 2000, no. 24;
RIVIÈRE/GAUDICHON/GHANASSIA
2001, no. 70.4

Cat. 44
CAMILLE CLAUDEL
Head of a Slave
About 1887?
Gray clay (unfired)
22 x 8.5 x 11.5 cm
Signed at base of neck,
at left: *Camille Claudel*
Private collection, France
CAT.: PARIS 2000, no. 14;
RIVIÈRE/GAUDICHON/GHANASSIA
2001, no. 18.1

Cat. 45
CAMILLE CLAUDEL
Head of a Slave
About 1887?
Patinated plaster
12.2 x 9.8 x 11.4 cm
Musée Rodin (S.4006), Paris
Donation Auguste Rodin,
1916?

Cat. 46
CAMILLE CLAUDEL
Head of a Slave
About 1887?
Bronze, cast by
Alexis Rudier, 1925?
12.7 x 9 x 10.8 cm
Signed on neck, at right:
A. Rodin
Founder's mark in back of
neck, at left: *Alexis Rudier/
Fondeur Paris*
Rodin Museum (F1929-7-77),
Philadelphia
Gift of Jules E. Mastbaum
CAT.: PARIS 2000, no. 14

Cat. 47
CAMILLE CLAUDEL
Sakuntala
1888
Patinated plaster, broken
190 x 110 x 60 cm
Signed and dated in front, on
plinth: *CAMILLE CLAUDEL/1888*
Musée Bertrand (518),
Châteauroux
Gift of Camille Claudel,
1895
EXH.: SAF 1888, no. 3930
CAT.: PARIS 2000, no. 23;
RIVIÈRE/GAUDICHON/GHANASSIA
2001, no. 23.4

Cat. 48
CAMILLE CLAUDEL
Ferdinand de Massary

1888?
Plaster
45 x 30 x 32 cm
Private collection, France
CAT.: PARIS 2000, no. 20;
RIVIÈRE/GAUDICHON/GHANASSIA
2001, no. 27.1

Cat. 49
CAMILLE CLAUDEL
Charles Lhermitte
1889
Bronze
32 x 30 x 20 cm
Musée Ingres (MEI 893.2),
Montauban
Gift of Baron Alphonse
de Rothschild, 1893
EXH.: SAF 1889, no. 4189
(bronze kept by the family)
CAT.: PARIS 2000, no. 26;
RIVIÈRE/GAUDICHON/GHANASSIA
2001, no. 30.2b

Cat. 50
CAMILLE CLAUDEL
The Psalm
1889
Bronze, cast by Adolphe
Gruet, between 1891
and 1893
47 x 32.5 x 31 cm
Signed on socle, at left:
Camille Claudel
Founder's mark on socle, in
back: *GRUET Ainé Fondeur*
Musée Boucher-de-Perthes
(A 108-A 144), Abbeville
Gift of Baron Alphonse
de Rothschild, 1893
EXH.: BRUSSELS 1894, no. 96
CAT.: PARIS 2000, no. 27;
RIVIÈRE/GAUDICHON/GHANASSIA
2001, no. 31.2

Cat. 51
CAMILLE CLAUDEL
Rodin Working
About 1890-92
Drypoint, about 1896
19.9 x 25.7 cm
Signed lower right: *Claudel*
Musée Rodin (G.7635), Paris
Donation Auguste Rodin,
1916
CAT.: PARIS 2000, no. 84;
RIVIÈRE/GAUDICHON/GHANASSIA
2001, no. 105

Cat. 52
CAMILLE CLAUDEL
1. *Rodin Looking at
    the Subject*
2. *Rodin Working*
Drypoint, about 1896
Léon MAILLARD, *Études sur
quelques artistes originaux:
Auguste Rodin, statuaire*,
Paris, Éditions Floury, 1899,
pp. 20-21
26.5 x 21.3 cm
Private collection, France
CAT.: PARIS 2000, nos. 85 and 84;
RIVIÈRE/GAUDICHON/GHANASSIA
2001, nos. 106 and 105

Cat. 53
CAMILLE CLAUDEL
Laughing Man
About 1891-92
Terracotta
20.6 x 9.3 x 11.5 cm
Musée Rodin (S.3903), Paris
Donation Auguste Rodin, 1916

Cat. 54
CAMILLE CLAUDEL
Laughing Man
About 1891–92?
Bronze, cast by
Alexis Rudier, 1925
12.5 x 9.3 x 11.7 cm
Signed on left side of neck:
A. Rodin
Founder's mark in back:
A. Rudier/Fondeur Paris
Musée Rodin (S.759), Paris
Cast executed for the
museum's collections in 1925

Cat. 55
Camille CLAUDEL
Man with Folded Arms
About 1891–92?
Terracotta
10 x 9.5 x 8 cm
Private collection, France
CAT.: PARIS 2000, no. 13;
RIVIÈRE/GAUDICHON/GHANASSIA
2001, no. 16

Cat. 56
CAMILLE CLAUDEL
Auguste Rodin
1892
Bronze, cast by
Adolphe Gruet, 1892
40.4 x 24.6 x 28 cm
Signed in back: *Camille Claudel*

356

Founder's mark in back:
Ad.Gruet fils aîné. Fondeur
Musée Rodin (S.1021), Paris
Gift of Eugène Rudier, 1950
EX-H.: SNBA 1892, no. 1482
CAT.: PARIS 2000, no. 25;
RIVIÈRE/GAUDICHON/GHANASSIA
2001, no. 22.5

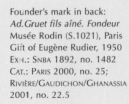

Cat. 57
CAMILLE CLAUDEL
Auguste Rodin
1892
Plaster coated with wax
42 x 26 x 30 cm
Signed in back: *Camille Claudel*
Musée Ziem (MZS 11),
Martigues
Gift of Louis Contencin
Formerly Edmond Bigand-
Kaire Collection
CAT.: PARIS 2000, no. 25;
RIVIÈRE/GAUDICHON/GHANASSIA
2001, no. 22.4

Cat. 58
CAMILLE CLAUDEL
Auguste Rodin
1892
Bronze, cast by François
Rudier, after 1898
40.7 x 25.7 x 28 cm
Signed in back:
Camille Claudel
Musée du Petit Palais
(PPS01268), Paris
Gift of Seligman, 1924
CAT.: PARIS 2000, no. 25;
RIVIÈRE/GAUDICHON/GHANASSIA
2001, no. 22.6

Cat. 59
CAMILLE CLAUDEL
The Collage
1892
Pen and black ink on verso
of circular letterhead of the
Palais du Champ-de-Mars,
Secrétariat, Société
Nationale des Beaux-Arts,
189[2], signed by secretary
general Hippolyte Durand-
Tahier
21 x 26.2 cm
Annotated in pen and black
ink upper center: *Le Collage/
Ah! ben vrai! ce que ça tient?*
Stamped: *Musée Rodin /
Bibliothèque / Livres
d'Auguste Rodin* lower left;
M. R. lower center
Annotated lower right: *1892?*
Stamped on verso: *Musée
Rodin / Bibliothèque / Livres
d'Auguste Rodin* lower
center; *M. R.* lower center
Musée Rodin (D.7634), Paris
Donation Auguste Rodin,
1916
CAT.: PARIS 2000, no. 80.4;
RIVIÈRE/GAUDICHON/GHANASSIA
2001, no. 102

Cat. 60
CAMILLE CLAUDEL
Le Réveil
Rodin and Rose embracing
1892?
Pen and black ink on cream
paper with notched upper
and left edge
17.8 x 26.7 cm
Annotated in pen and black
ink, lower right: *Le Réveil/
Douce remontrance/
par BEURET*

Stamped: *Musée Rodin /
Bibliothèque / Livres
d'Auguste Rodin* lower left;
M. R. lower right
Annotated lower right: *1892*
On verso: same subject
traced through with
some variants, pencil,
pen and black ink
Stamped: *Musée Rodin /
Bibliothèque / Livres
d'Auguste Rodin* lower left;
M. R. lower left
Musée Rodin (D.7631), Paris
Donation Auguste Rodin,
1916
CAT.: PARIS 2000, no. 80.1;
RIVIÈRE/GAUDICHON/GHANASSIA
2001, no. 100

Cat. 62
CAMILLE CLAUDEL
*Rodin in Chains and
Rose with a Broom*
1892?
Pen and brown ink wash
on cream laid paper
21 x 26.8 cm
Stamped: *Musée Rodin /
Bibliothèque / Livres
d'Auguste Rodin* lower
center, repeated lower right;
M. R. lower center
Musée Rodin (D.7633), Paris
Donation Auguste Rodin, 1916
CAT.: PARIS 2000, no. 80.3;
RIVIÈRE/GAUDICHON/GHANASSIA
2001, no. 101.2

Cat. 61
CAMILLE CLAUDEL
The Cellular System
Rodin in Chains and
Rose with a Broom
1892?
Pen and black ink wash on
cream paper with notched
upper and left edge
18.3 x 27.2 cm
Annotated in pen and
brown ink lower left:
Le système cellulaire
Stamped: *Musée Rodin /
Bibliothèque / Livres
d'Auguste Rodin* lower left,
repeated lower center;
M. R. lower center
On verso: same subject
traced through with
some variants, pencil,
pen and brown ink
Stamped: *Musée Rodin /
Bibliothèque / Livres
d'Auguste Rodin* lower left,
repeated lower center;
M. R. lower center
Musée Rodin (D.7632), Paris
Donation Auguste Rodin, 1916
CAT.: PARIS 2000, no. 80.2;
RIVIÈRE/GAUDICHON/GHANASSIA
2001, no. 101.1

Cat. 63
CAMILLE CLAUDEL
Clotho
1893
Plaster
90 x 49.5 x 43.5 cm
Musée Rodin (S.1379), Paris
Gift of Paul Claudel, 1952
EXH.: SNBA 1893, no. 38
CAT.: PARIS 2000, no. 32;
RIVIÈRE/GAUDICHON/GHANASSIA
2001, no. 37.3

Cat. 64
CAMILLE CLAUDEL
The Waltz, with drapery
partially covering the head
1893

Bronze, cast by
Siot-Decauville, 1893
96 x 87 x 56 cm
Signed on base, in front:
Camille Claudel
Founder's mark on base:
*CIRE PERDUE/SIOT-
DECAUVILLE/FOND^R*
Galleri Kaare Berntsen
Collection, Oslo
Formerly Paul Siot-
Decauville Collection
EXH.: SNBA 1893, no. 37
(plaster); BRUSSELS 1894, no. 94
CAT.: PARIS 2000, no. 28.1;
RIVIÈRE/GAUDICHON/GHANASSIA
2001, no. 33.2

Cat. 65
CAMILLE CLAUDEL
The Waltz
[1893]
Reduction with variants,
bronze, about 1895?
43.2 x 23 x 34.3 cm
Signed and titled on left side
of base: *Camille Claudel/
LA VALSE*
Musée Rodin (S.1013), Paris
Purchase, 1963
Formerly Joanny Peytel
Collection
CAT.: PARIS 2000, no. 28.5;
RIVIÈRE/GAUDICHON/GHANASSIA
2001, no. 33.4

Cat. 66
CAMILLE CLAUDEL
The Waltz
[1893]
Reduction with variants,

bronze, cast by Alexis
Rudier, after 1897
42 x 35 x 22 cm
Founder's mark: *Alexis
Rudier/Fondeur Paris*
Private collection, France
CAT.: PARIS 2000, no. 28.6;
RIVIÈRE/GAUDICHON/GHANASSIA
2001, no. 33.5

Cat. 67
CAMILLE CLAUDEL
The Waltz
[1893]
Reduction with variants,
bronze, edition by
Eugène Blot, early 1905
47 x 34 x 22 cm
Signed and numbered on base,
at left: *C. Claudel/17*
Mark: *EUG. BLOT/PARIS*
Musée Sainte-Croix
(953-11-67), Poitiers
Gift of André Brisson, 1953
EXH.: BLOT 1905, no. 10
(unidentified bronze)
CAT.: PARIS 2000, no. 28.7;
RIVIÈRE/GAUDICHON/GHANASSIA
2001, no. 33.7

Cat. 68
CAMILLE CLAUDEL
The Age of Maturity, first version
About 1893
Plaster
87 x 103.5 x 52.5 cm
Musée Rodin (S.1378), Paris
Gift of Paul Claudel, 1952
CAT.: PARIS 2000, no. 42;
RIVIÈRE/GAUDICHON/GHANASSIA
2001, no. 45.6

Cat. 69
CAMILLE CLAUDEL
*Head of the Old Woman from
The Age of Maturity group*
About 1893
Plaster
11 x 7.5 x 10 cm
Private collection, France
CAT.: PARIS 2000, no. 39;
RIVIÈRE/GAUDICHON/GHANASSIA
2001, no. 45.1

Cat. 70
CAMILLE CLAUDEL
*Head of the Old Man from
The Age of Maturity group*
About 1893
Bronze, cast by François Rudier,
1901 or 1902
18 x 9 x 9 cm
Signed on left shoulder:
Camille Claudel
Founder's mark on back:
F. Rudier fondeur Paris
Private collection, France
CAT.: PARIS 2000, no. 40;
RIVIÈRE/GAUDICHON/GHANASSIA
2001, no. 45.3

Cat. 71
CAMILLE CLAUDEL
La Petite Châtelaine, Mask
1894
Plaster
28 x 18 x 13 cm
Signed on the cut, at left:
C. Claudel
Private collection, France
CAT.: PARIS 2000, no. 33;
RIVIÈRE/GAUDICHON/GHANASSIA
2001, no. 35.2

Cat. 72
CAMILLE CLAUDEL
La Petite Châtelaine
1895
Bronze, cast by
Adolphe Gruet, 1895
33 x 28 x 22 cm
Signed on left shoulder:
C. Claudel
Founder's mark on back,
on right shoulder:
*A. GRUET.Aîné.Fondeur./PARIS
1895*
Musée Joseph-Denais (3294),
Beaufort-en-Vallée
Gift of Baron Alphonse
de Rothschild, 1896
EXH.: SNBA 1894, no. 36
(unidentified bronze)
CAT.: PARIS 2000, no. 33;
RIVIÈRE/GAUDICHON/GHANASSIA
2001, no. 35.4

Cat. 73
CAMILLE CLAUDEL
La Petite Châtelaine
1894
Marble, 1895
34.3 x 28.4 x 22 cm
Signed under base:
C. Claudel
Musée Rodin (S.1007), Paris
Purchase, 1968
Purchased by Joanny Peytel
from Camille Claudel in 1895
EXH.: SNBA 1895, no. 20
CAT.: PARIS 2000, no. 33;
RIVIÈRE/GAUDICHON/GHANASSIA
2001, no. 35.8

Cat. 74
CAMILLE CLAUDEL
*La Petite Châtelaine with
hair "tout à jour"*
[1894]
Marble, executed by
Camille Claudel, 1896
44 x 36 x 29 cm
Signed on plinth, at left:
Camille CLAUDEL
La Piscine – Musée d'Art et
d'Industrie André-Diligent
(996-5-1), Roubaix
Purchased by public
subscription in 1996
Purchased by Henri Fontaine
from Camille Claudel in 1896
EXH.: SNBA 1896, no. 24 bis
CAT.: PARIS 2000, no. 33;
RIVIÈRE/GAUDICHON/GHANASSIA
2001, no. 35.9

Cat. 75
CAMILLE CLAUDEL
*Head of an Old Blind
Man Singing*
About 1894?
Plaster
21 x 10 x 11.5 cm
Private collection, France
CAT.: PARIS 2000, no. 45;
RIVIÈRE/GAUDICHON/GHANASSIA
2001, no. 43.1

Cat. 76
CAMILLE CLAUDEL
Les Causeuses
1895
Plaster
40 x 40 x 40 cm
Signed on base, under
bench: *C. Claudel*
Musée Rodin (S.6291), Paris
Donation Auguste Rodin, 1916
EXH.: SNBA 1895, no. 23
(unidentified plaster)

357

CAT.: PARIS 2000, no. 43.5;
RIVIÈRE/GAUDICHON/GHANASSIA
2001, no. 41.4

Cat. 77

CAMILLE CLAUDEL
Les Causeuses
[1895]
Marble onyx and bronze, 1897
44.9 x 42.2 x 39 cm
Musée Rodin (S.1006), Paris
Purchase, 1963
Purchased by Joanny Peytel
from Camille Claudel in
1897 or 1898
EXH.: SNBA 1897, no. 25
CAT.: PARIS 2000, no. 43.4;
RIVIÈRE/GAUDICHON/GHANASSIA
2001, no. 41.7

Cat. 78

CAMILLE CLAUDEL
Léon Lhermitte
1895
Bronze, cast by
Adolphe Gruet
36 x 25 x 25 cm
Signed at base of neck, at
left: *Camille Claudel*
Founder's mark at base
of neck, in back:
A.GRUET.Aîné.Fondeur./PARIS
Private collection, France
EXH.: SNBA 1895, no. 21
CAT.: PARIS 2000, no. 44;
RIVIÈRE/GAUDICHON/GHANASSIA
2001, no. 32.2

Cat. 79

CAMILLE CLAUDEL
The Wave

358

1897
Marble onyx and bronze,
executed by Camille Claudel
and François Pompon,
1898–1903
62 x 56 x 50 cm
Musée Rodin (S.6659), Paris
Purchase, 1995
Paul Claudel Collection
before 1914
EXH.: SNBA 1897, no. 24
(plaster); BLOT 1905, no. 12
CAT.: PARIS 2000, no. 48;
RIVIÈRE/GAUDICHON/GHANASSIA
2001, no. 53.3

Cat. 80

CAMILLE CLAUDEL
Deep Thought
[1898]
Marble, 1900
23.5 x 23.3 x 31 cm
Signed on left corner of base:
C. Claudel
Musée Sainte-Croix
(2000-00-1), Poitiers
Purchase, 1996
Purchased by Joanny Peytel
from Camille Claudel in 1900
EXH.: SNBA 1898, no. 36
(unidentified bronze);
PARIS 1900, no. 139
CAT.: PARIS 2000, no. 53;
RIVIÈRE/GAUDICHON/GHANASSIA
2001, no. 57.3

Cat. 81

CAMILLE CLAUDEL
Deep Thought
1898
Master model, bronze, for
the edition by Eugène Blot,
about 1905?
23.5 x 21 x 27.5 cm
Signed on left corner of
base: *C. CLAUDEL*
Musée Sainte-Croix
(2000-00-2), Poitiers
Purchase, 1996

Cat. 82

CAMILLE CLAUDEL
The Age of Maturity
1899
Bronze, cast by Frédéric
Carvillani, after 1913
121 x 181.2 x 73 cm
Titled and signed on base:
L'ÂGE MÛR Camille Claudel
Founder's mark on base:
Cire perdue/CARVILLANI
Musée Rodin (S.1380), Paris
Gift of Paul Claudel, 1952
EXH.: SNBA 1899, no. 28
(plaster)
CAT.: PARIS 2000, no. 42;
RIVIÈRE/GAUDICHON/GHANASSIA
2001, no. 45.9

Cat. 83

CAMILLE CLAUDEL
The Implorer
1899
Bronze, edition by
Eugène Blot, early 1904
66.5 x 74.5 x 32.5 cm
Signed and numbered on
base: *C. Claudel/3*
Mark on plinth, in a triangle:
E /BLOT/PARIS
Private collection, France
EXH.: BLOT 1905, no. 1
(unidentified bronze)
CAT.: PARIS 2000, no. 41;
RIVIÈRE/GAUDICHON/GHANASSIA
2001, no. 44.8

Cat. 84

CAMILLE CLAUDEL
A) *The Implorer*
1899
Bronze, edition by
Eugène Blot, early 1904

28.4 x 30.3 x 16.5 cm
Signed on base, near left
knee: *C. Claudel*
Mark: *Eug. Blot Paris 14*
Musée Rodin (S.1377), Paris
Purchase, 1968
Formerly Joanny Peytel
Collection
EXH.: BLOT 1905, no. 2
(unidentified bronze)
CAT.: PARIS 2000, no. 41;
RIVIÈRE/GAUDICHON/GHANASSIA
2001, no. 44.9

B) *The Implorer*
1899
Bronze, edition by
Eugène Blot, early 1904
28.5 x 25.5 x 16 cm
Signed on base, near left
knee: *C. Claudel*
Mark: *EUG. BLOT/PARIS*
Fondation Pierre Gianadda,
Martigny
EXH.: BLOT 1905, no. 2
(unidentified bronze)
CAT.: PARIS 2000, no. 41;
RIVIÈRE/GAUDICHON/GHANASSIA
2001, no. 44.9

Cat. 85

CAMILLE CLAUDEL
*Count Christian de Maigret
Dressed as Henry II*
Marble, 1899
66 x 65 x 43 cm
Signed in back: *C. Claudel*
Inscribed on pedestal,
in a scroll: *Pro Christo
et contra inimicos ejus*
(motto of the Maigrets)
Private collection, France
Commissioned by
Countess Arthur de Maigret
from Camille Claudel
EXH.: SNBA 1899, no. 26
CAT.: PARIS 2000, no. 52;
RIVIÈRE/GAUDICHON/GHANASSIA
2001, no. 59

Cat. 86

CAMILLE CLAUDEL
Perseus and the Gorgon
[1899]
Marble, executed by
Camille Claudel and
François Pompon, 1902
196 x 111 x 99 cm
Titled and signed on socle,
in front: *Persée et la Gorgone/
Camille Claudel*
Assurances Générales
de France, Paris
Commissioned by
Countess Arthur de Maigret
from Camille Claudel
EXH.: SNBA 1899, no. 29
(plaster); SNBA 1902, no. 47
CAT.: PARIS 2000, no. 57;
RIVIÈRE/GAUDICHON/GHANASSIA
2001, no. 54.3

Cat. 87

CAMILLE CLAUDEL
Perseus and the Gorgon
About 1899
Bronze
51 x 30 x 25 cm
Signed on front: *C. Claudel*
Private collection, France
CAT.: PARIS 2000, no. 57;
RIVIÈRE/GAUDICHON/GHANASSIA
2001, no. 54.6

Cat. 88

CAMILLE CLAUDEL
Fireside Dream
[1900]
Marble and bronze,

edition by Eugène Blot,
early 1905?
22 x 29.5 x 24.5 cm
Signed on base, at left:
C. Claudel
Mark of Eugène Blot on base,
under the signature
Private collection, United States
CAT.: PARIS 2000, no. 55;
RIVIÈRE/GAUDICHON/GHANASSIA
2001, no. 61.4

Cat. 89

CAMILLE CLAUDEL
Aurora
1900?
Marble
35 x 29 x 30 cm
Signed in back, to the right:
C. Claudel
Private collection, France
Louise Claudel Collection
before 1919
CAT.: PARIS 2000, no. 34;
RIVIÈRE/GAUDICHON/GHANASSIA
2001, no. 63.2

Cat. 90

CAMILLE CLAUDEL
*Countess Arthur de Maigret,
née Marie Chandon de
Briailles*
Marble, 1902
78 x 48 x 47 cm
Signed on socle, at left:
Camille Claudel
Inscribed on pedestal:
*Pro Christo et contra inimicos
ejus* (motto of the Maigrets)
Private collection, France
Commissioned by Countess
Arthur de Maigret from
Camille Claudel
EXH.: SNBA 1902, no. 48
CAT.: PARIS 2000, no. 50;
RIVIÈRE/GAUDICHON/GHANASSIA
2001, no. 62

Cat. 91

CAMILLE CLAUDEL
*Countess Arthur de Maigret,
née Marie Chandon de Briailles*
1903
Charcoal with chalk and pastel
highlights on cream paper
66 x 53 cm
Annotated, dated and signed
lower right: *Souvenir de
Senlis 1903/C. Claudel*
Musée du Pays de
Château-Gontier (95601)
Bequest of the widow of
General Gérard
Formerly Countess Arthur
de Maigret Collection
CAT.: PARIS 2000, no. 87;
RIVIÈRE/GAUDICHON/GHANASSIA
2001, no. 107

Cat. 92

CAMILLE CLAUDEL
A) *Fortune*
Before 1904
Bronze, edition by
Eugène Blot, early 1905
48 x 35 x 17.5 cm
Signed on wheel: *C. CLAUDEL*
Mark on wheel, after signature:
EUG BLOT 9/PARIS
Musée Sainte-Croix
(953-11-68), Poitiers
Gift of André Brisson, 1953
EXH.: SA 1904, no. 1730
(unidentified bronze)
CAT.: PARIS 2000, no. 56;
RIVIÈRE/GAUDICHON/GHANASSIA
2001, no. 58.3

B) *Fortune*
Before 1904
Bronze, edition by Eugène
Blot, early 1905
47.8 x 35 x 17.5 cm
Signed on base: *C. CLAUDEL*

Cat. 93

CAMILLE CLAUDEL
Vertumnus and Pomona
Marble, carved by
Camille Claudel, 1905
92 x 80 x 42.5 cm
Signed on base, in back:
CAMILLE CLAUDEL
Titled on base, in front:
VERTUMNE ET POMONE
Musée Rodin (S.1293), Paris
Gift of Paul Claudel, 1952
Commissioned by Countess
Arthur de Maigret from
Camille Claudel
EXH.: SAF 1905, no. 2950
CAT.: PARIS 2000, no. 67;
RIVIÈRE/GAUDICHON/GHANASSIA
2001, no. 23.5

Cat. 94

CAMILLE CLAUDEL
A) *Abandon*
1905
Reduction of the marble,
bronze, edition by
Eugène Blot, early 1905
43 x 36 x 19 cm
Signed on base, in back:
C. CLAUDEL
Mark on base:
EUG. BLOT 9/PARIS
Musée Sainte-Croix

Mark on base:
EUG BLOT 8/PARIS
Fondation Pierre Gianadda,
Martigny
EXH.: SA 1904, no. 1730
(unidentified bronze)
CAT.: PARIS 2000, no. 56;
RIVIÈRE/GAUDICHON/GHANASSIA
2001, no. 58.3

(953-11-66), Poitiers
Gift of André Brisson, 1953
EXH.: BLOT 1905, no. 9
(unidentified bronze)
CAT.: PARIS 2000, no. 62;
RIVIÈRE/GAUDICHON/GHANASSIA
2001, no. 23.7

B) *Abandon*
1905
Reduction of the marble,
bronze, edition by
Eugène Blot, early 1905
42.3 x 36 x 19 cm
Signed on base, in back:
C. CLAUDEL
Mark on base:
EUG. BLOT II/PARIS
Fondation Pierre Gianadda,
Martigny
EXH.: BLOT 1905
(unidentified bronze)
CAT.: PARIS 2000, no. 62;
RIVIÈRE/GAUDICHON/GHANASSIA
2001, no. 23.7

Cat. 95

CAMILLE CLAUDEL
Abandon
1905
Reduction of the marble,
bronze, edition by
Eugène Blot, 1907
53 x 67 x 24 cm
Signed on plinth of base,
in front: *CAMILLE CLAUDEL*
Mark on pillar, in back:
EUG. BLOT/PARIS/8
Musée des Beaux-Arts
(2104), Cambrai
Purchased by the state
in 1907, on permanent
loan since 1932
EXH.: SA 1905, no. 350
(unidentified bronze)
CAT.: PARIS 2000, no. 62;
RIVIÈRE/GAUDICHON/GHANASSIA
2001, no. 23.6

Cat. 96

CAMILLE CLAUDEL
*Paul Claudel Aged
Thirty-Seven*
1905
Bronze, cast by P. Converset,
about 1912–13
48.2 x 52.5 x 31.5 cm
Signed below right shoulder:
Camille Claudel
Founder's mark:
P. CONVERSET/FONDEUR/PARIS
Musée Rodin (S.1218), Paris
Purchase, 1983
Formerly Maurice Denis
Collection
CAT.: PARIS 2000, no. 63;
RIVIÈRE/GAUDICHON/GHANASSIA
2001, no. 68.3

Cat. 97

CAMILLE CLAUDEL
The Siren
1905
Bronze, edition by
Eugène Blot, early 1905
53 x 27 x 24 cm
Private collection, Switzerland
CAT.: PARIS 2000, no. 60;
RIVIÈRE/GAUDICHON/GHANASSIA
2001, no. 64.2

Cat. 98

CAMILLE CLAUDEL
Wounded Niobid
1906
Bronze, cast through the
agency of Eugène Blot, 1907
90 x 50 x 51.5 cm

Titled and signed on back, on plinth: *NIOBIDE/C. Claudel* Mark on back, on plinth: *EUG BLOT/PARIS* Musée Sainte-Croix (D.985-1-1), Poitiers Commissioned by the state in 1906, on permanent loan since 1985 CAT.: PARIS 2000, no. 64; RIVIÈRE/GAUDICHON/GHANASSIA 2001, no. 24.2

ANTOINE DE COMBETTE

Cat. 99

ANTOINE DE COMBETTE *Auguste Rodin and Rose Beuret, October 8, 1915* 1915 Photograph, gelatin silver print 11 x 8.5 cm Musée Rodin (Ph.1621), Paris Donation Auguste Rodin, 1916

JULES DESBOIS

(Parçay-les-Pins, France, 1851 – Paris, France, 1935)

Cat. 100

JULES DESBOIS *Misery* About 1887–89 Terracotta 37.5 x 24.6 x 17.7 cm Signed below right foot, on left side: *J. Desbois* Inscribed on front, lower right: *LA MISÈRE* Musée Rodin (S.1150), Paris Gift of Mme. Eugène Rudier, 1954

Cat. 101

JULES DESBOIS and PAUL LOEWENGUT, known as JEANNENEY (Strasbourg, France, 1861 – Saint-Amand-en-Puisaye, Nièvre, 1920)? *Death Mask* Glazed stoneware, after 1900 31 x 22 x 13 cm Signed under chin: *J. Desbois* Conseil Général de Maine-et-Loire – on loan to the Musée Jules-Desbois, Parçay-les-Pins (PR D.001.2.3)

HENRY DUMONT

Cat. 102

HENRY DUMONT Young Roman, *by Camille Claudel* Paul LEROI, "Salon de 1887," *L'Art*, vol. 43, 1887, p. 233 43.2 x 31 cm Musée Rodin (8296), Paris

WILLIAM ELBORNE

(Grantham, England, 1858 – Peterborough, England, 1952)

Cat. 103

WILLIAM ELBORNE or JESSIE LIPSCOMB

(Grantham, England, 1861 – Peterborough, England, 1952) *Auguste Rodin at the Dépôt des Marbres, in front of* The Gates of Hell, *reflected in a mirror* 1887 Photograph, albumin print 16.5 x 12 cm Private collection, United Kingdom

Cat. 104

WILLIAM ELBORNE *Auguste Rodin in his atelier at 117 boulevard de Vaugirard, in front of a study of* Andrieu d'Andres, *with Jessie Lipscomb and Camille Claudel* 1887 Photograph, albumin print 12 x 16.5 cm Private collection, United Kingdom

Cat. 105

WILLIAM ELBORNE *Camille Claudel and Jessie Lipscomb in their atelier at 117 rue Notre-Dame-des-Champs* 1887 Photograph, gelatin silver print 15.2 x 9.8 cm Musée Rodin (Ph.1773), Paris Donation Auguste Rodin, 1916

Cat. 106

WILLIAM ELBORNE *Jessie Lipscomb, Camille and Louise Claudel in the atelier at 117 rue Notre-Dame-des-Champs* 1887 Photograph, albumin print 4.5 x 10.5 cm Private collection, United Kingdom

Cat. 107

WILLIAM ELBORNE *The Claudel family, Jessie Lipscomb, Ferdinand de Massary and his father, on the balcony of their apartment at 31 boulevard de Port-Royal* 1887 Photograph, albumin print 16.5 x 12 cm Private collection, United Kingdom

Cat. 108

WILLIAM ELBORNE *Camille Claudel at the Montdevergues public asylum at Montfavet* 1929 Photograph, gelatin silver print 8 x 5.5 cm Private collection, United Kingdom

D. FREULER

Cat. 109

D. FREULER Thought *covered in a veil, plaster, by Auguste Rodin* 1895? Photograph, salted paper print 24.2 x 17.6 cm Musée Rodin (Ph.1305), Paris Donation Auguste Rodin, 1916

ALBERT HARLINGUE

(Paris, France, 1879 – ?, 1963)

Cat. 110

ALBERT HARLINGUE *The park of the Hôtel Biron* About 1912 Photograph, gelatin silver print 17 x 12.5 cm Musée Rodin (Ph.1807), Paris Donation Auguste Rodin, 1916

MARCEL HUTIN

Cat. 111

MARCEL HUTIN *Inauguration of* The Thinker *in front of the Panthéon, April 21, 1906* 1906 Photograph, albumin print 11.7 x 16.6 cm Musée Rodin (Ph.754), Paris Donation Auguste Rodin, 1916

Auguste Léveillé

(Joué-du-Bois, France, 1840 – Paris, France, 1900)

Cat. 112

Auguste Léveillé
Auguste Rodin, by Camille Claudel
About 1896
Woodcut
50.5 x 32 cm
Signed in the print, lower left: *A. Leveille*
Signed in pencil below the print, lower right: *A. Leveille*
Musée Rodin (G.8328), Paris
Donation Auguste Rodin, 1916

Jean-François Limet

(Joinville-le-Pont, France, 1855 – Paris, France, 1941)

Cat. 113

Jean-François Limet
A) *Reception in honor of the presentation of the insignia of Commander of the Legion of Honor to Auguste Rodin, at Vélizy, June 30, 1903*
1903
Photograph, aristotype
17.4 x 23.5 cm
Musée Rodin (Ph.729), Paris
Donation Auguste Rodin, 1916

B) *Reception in honor of the presentation of the insignia of Commander of the Legion of Honor to Auguste Rodin, at Vélizy, June 30, 1903*
1903
Photograph, aristotype
18 x 24 cm
Musée Rodin (Ph.890), Paris
Donation Auguste Rodin, 1916

L. L.

Cat. 114

L. L.
Environs of Azay-le-Rideau. Château de l'Islette
Photomechanical postcard
Undated
9 x 13.8 cm
Musée Rodin (Ph.12615), Paris
Purchase, 1998

Neurdein Frères

(Étienne: Paris, France, 1832 – Paris, France, after 1915),
(Louis-Antonin: Paris, France, 1846 – Paris, France, after 1915)

Cat. 115

Neurdein Frères
A) *Environs of Azay-le-Rideau. Château de l'Islette*
Photomechanical postcard
Undated
9 x 13.9 cm
Musée Rodin (Ph.12613), Paris
Purchase, 1998

B) *Château de l'Islette (Indre-et-Loire). The Pond*
Photomechanical postcard
Undated
9 x 13.8 cm
Musée Rodin (Ph.12614), Paris
Purchase, 1998

François Pompon

(Saulieu, France, 1855 – Paris, France, 1933)

Cat. 116

François Pompon
A Good Old Woman

1883
Terracotta
24.5 x 10.2 x 16.5 cm
Musée des Beaux-Arts (3784 bis (1)), Dijon
Bequest of François Pompon, 1933

Auguste Rodin

(Paris, France, 1840 – Meudon, France, 1917)

Cat. 117

Auguste Rodin
Bellona
1879
Plaster
102 x 53 x 43 cm
Musée Rodin (S.756), Paris
Donation Auguste Rodin 1916

Cat. 118

Auguste Rodin
A) *Saint John the Baptist*
1880
Bronze, cast by Alexis Rudier, 1925
203 x 71.7 x 119.3 cm
Signed on base, between the feet: *A. Rodin*
Founder's mark on back of base, at left: *Alexis Rudier/Fondeur Paris*
Musée Rodin (S.999), Paris
Donation Auguste Rodin, 1916
Exh.: Saf 1880, no. 6640 (plaster); Saf 1881, no. 4253 (bronze, Musée d'Orsay, Paris)

E) *Saint John the Baptist*
1880
Bronze, cast by Alexis Rudier, 1926

200 x 53 x 98 cm
Signed on base, between the feet: *A. Rodin*
Founder's mark on back of base, at left: *Alexis Rudier/Fondeur Paris*
Rodin Museum (F.1929-7-48), Philadelphia
Gift of Jules E. Mastbaum

Cat. 119

Auguste Rodin
The Gates of Hell, third model
1880
Plaster
111.5 x 75 x 30 cm
Musée Rodin (S.1189), Paris
Donation Auguste Rodin, 1916

Cat. 120

Auguste Rodin
The Thinker on a fragment of a capital
About 1880–81
Plaster
87.5 x 59 x 42.6 cm
Musée Rodin (S.2521), Paris
Donation Auguste Rodin, 1916

Cat. 121

Auguste Rodin
Caryatid with a Stone
[About 1881–82]

Marble, executed by Bozzoni, 1883
50 x 26.7 x 30.5 cm
Museum of Fine Arts (17.3134), Boston
Gift of Julia Isham (Mrs. Henry Osborn Taylor), 1917
Purchased by Jules Bastien-Lepage from Rodin before 1887
Exh.: Paris 1883

Cat. 122

Auguste Rodin
The Crouching Woman
About 1881–82
Plaster
31.9 x 28.7 x 21.1 cm
Musée Rodin (S.2396), Paris
Donation Auguste Rodin, 1916
Exh.: Paris 1886 (unidentified plaster)

Cat. 123

Auguste Rodin
Ugolino and His Sons
About 1881–82
Bronze, cast by Griffoul and Lorge, 1889
41 x 61.5 x 41 cm
Signed on back of base: *Rodin*
Musée Rodin (S.1146), Paris
Purchase, 1924
Exh.: Saf 1883?; Brussels 1887, no. 689 (unidentified bronze)

Cat. 124

Auguste Rodin
Albert-Ernest Carrier-Belleuse
1882

361

Terracotta
48 x 45 x 34 cm
Musée Rodin (S.1981), Paris
Attributed to the Musée
Rodin by the Service de
Récupération Artistique in 1951
EXH.: SAF 1882, no. 4813
(unidentified terracotta)

Cat. 125
AUGUSTE RODIN
Jean-Paul Laurens
1882
Bronze, cast by
Alexis Rudier, 1930
58 x 37.1 x 33.1 cm
Signed at left on base,
in front: *A. Rodin*
Founder's mark in back:
Alexis Rudier/Fondeur Paris
Musée Rodin (S.981), Paris
Cast executed for the
museum's collections in 1930
EXH.: SAF 1882, no. 4812
(bronze, Musée des
Augustins, Toulouse)

Cat. 126
AUGUSTE RODIN
Camille with Short Hair
1882?
Plaster
27.5 x 21.5 x 21.5 cm
Musée Rodin (S.1776), Paris
Donation Auguste Rodin, 1916

Cat. 127
AUGUSTE RODIN
Jules Dalou
1883

362

Bronze, cast by Pierre
Bingen, 1889
47 x 42.5 x 23.5 cm
Signed in back, on left
shoulder: *A Rodin*
The Detroit Institute of Arts
(60.1)
Gift of Mr. and Mrs. Walter B.
Ford II
Formerly Joanny Peytel Collection
EXH.: SAF 1884, no. 3863 (plaster)

Cat. 128
AUGUSTE RODIN
Eve
[1833]
Marble, 1888
76.2 x 24.5 x 31.5 cm
The Art Institute of Chicago
(33.1304)
Gift of Martin A. Ryerson, 1933
Purchased by Paul Paulin
from Rodin in 1888
EXH.: PARIS 1883 (bronze)

Cat. 129
AUGUSTE RODIN
Eternal Spring
About 1884
Bronze, cast by
Alexis Rudier, 1926
64.5 x 58 x 44.5 cm
Signed on left side of base:
A. Rodin
Founder's mark in back:
Alexis Rudier/Fondeur Paris
Musée Rodin (S.989), Paris
Cast executed for the
museum's collections in 1926
EXH.: PARIS 1889, no. 18
or 19 (plaster)

Cat. 130
AUGUSTE RODIN
Awakening
About 1884
Bronze, cast by Léon
Perzinka, 1900
52.7 x 22.5 x 30.5 cm
Signed under the left leg:
A. Rodin
Founder's mark in back,
on edge of base:
L.Perzinka/fondeur/Versailles
Musée Rodin (S.488), Paris
Gift of Mme Eugène Rudier, 1954
EXH.: ALMA 1900, no. 160

Cat. 131
AUGUSTE RODIN
Mask of Camille Claudel
About 1884?
Plaster
22.8 x 17 x 16 cm
Musée Rodin (S.1763), Paris
Donation Auguste Rodin, 1916
EXH.: BRUSSELS / ROTTERDAM /
AMSTERDAM / THE HAGUE 1899
(unidentified plaster)

Cat. 132
AUGUSTE RODIN
Camille Wearing a Bonnet
About 1884?
Terracotta
25.7 x 15 x 17.7 cm
Musée Rodin (S.208), Paris
Donation Auguste Rodin, 1916

Cat. 133
AUGUSTE RODIN and JEAN CROS
(?, 1885 – Sèvres, France, 1932)
Camille Wearing a Bonnet
About 1884?
Glass paste, 1911
24.9 x 14.9 x 17.9 cm
Musée Rodin (S.463), Paris
Donation Auguste Rodin, 1916

Cat. 134
AUGUSTE RODIN
Camille Wearing a Bonnet
About 1884?
Bronze, cast by
Alexis Rudier, 1924
24.5 x 15.1 x 18.4 cm
Signed on base, at right:
A. Rodin
Founder's mark on base,
at right: *Alexis
Rudier/Fondeur Paris*
Musée des Beaux-Arts
(1951.72.1), Calais
Purchase, 1924
EXH.: LONDON, 1914, no. 93
(bronze, Victoria and Albert
Museum, London)

Cat. 135
AUGUSTE RODIN
Seated Old Woman
About 1884
Terracotta
43.2 x 18.6 x 32.2 cm
Musée Rodin (S.2411), Paris
Donation Auguste Rodin, 1916

Cat. 136
AUGUSTE RODIN
*Left Jamb, bottom section,
of The Gates of Hell*
About 1884–85
Patinated plaster
188.5 x 47 x 30 cm
Musée Rodin (S.5788), Paris
Donation Auguste Rodin,
1916

Cat. 137
AUGUSTE RODIN
*Sketch for the Head
of Jean de Fiennes?*
About 1885–86?
Terracotta
15.5 x 12.2 x 12.5 cm
Incised signature, on reverse:
RODIN
Musée Rodin (S.195), Paris
Donation Auguste Rodin, 1916

Cat. 138
AUGUSTE RODIN
*Mask Study for
Pierre de Wissant*
About 1885–86
Terracotta
27.4 x 20.5 x 11.5 cm
Musée Rodin (S.307), Paris
Donation Auguste Rodin,
1916

Cat. 139

AUGUSTE RODIN
*Study for the Head of
Pierre de Wissant*, type C
About 1885–86
Plaster
48 x 28.2 x 28.5 cm
Musée Rodin (S.438), Paris
Donation Auguste Rodin, 1916

Cat. 140

AUGUSTE RODIN
The Shade
Before 1886
Bronze, cast by
Alexis Rudier, 1949
96 x 44 x 37 cm
Signed on base, at
left of foot: *A. Rodin*
Founder's mark on back of base:
Alexis Rudier/Fondeur Paris
Musée des Beaux-Arts
(MO.37), Orléans
Purchase, 1954

Cat. 141

AUGUSTE RODIN
I Am Beautiful
1886
Bronze, cast by
Georges Rudier, 1969
69.4 x 36 x 36 cm
Signed in front, on rock:
A. Rodin
Inscribed in front: *Je suis
belle ô mortels comme un
rêve de pierre/Et mon sein
où chacun s'est meurtri tour*

*à tour/est fait pour inspirer
au poète un amour/Éternel
et muet ainsi que la matière*
Founder's mark in back:
Georges Rudier/Fondeur Paris
Musée Rodin (S.1151), Paris
Cast executed for the
museum's collections in 1969
EXH.: PARIS 1886 (plaster)

Cat. 142

AUGUSTE RODIN
The Cry
About 1886
Bronze, cast by
Georges Rudier, 1961
25.2 x 28.7 x 18.9 cm
Signed on left side of bust:
A. Rodin
Founder's mark in back,
at right: *Georges
Rudier/Fondeur Paris*
Musée Rodin (S.1126), Paris
Cast executed for the
museum's collections in 1961
EXH.: BRUSSELS / ROTTERDAM /
AMSTERDAM / THE HAGUE
1899, no. 2a/4 (plaster)

Cat. 143

AUGUSTE RODIN
Left Hand of Pierre de Wissant
About 1886
Terracotta
27 x 18.7 x 13 cm
Musée Rodin (S.96), Paris
Donation Auguste Rodin, 1916

Cat. 144

AUGUSTE RODIN
Head of Pierre de Wissant

About 1886–87
Plaster
36 x 24.5 x 27.5 cm
Musée Rodin (S.315), Paris
Donation Auguste Rodin, 1916

Cat. 145

AUGUSTE RODIN
Pierre de Wissant
1887
Bronze, cast by Fonderie
de Coubertin, 1948
214 x 106 x 118 cm
Signed in front, on base:
A. Rodin
Founder's mark on back
of base: shell surrounded by
the letters *FC*; near signature:
N° IV/IV
Musée Rodin (S.639), Paris
Cast executed for the
museum's collections in 1988
EXH.: PARIS 1887? (undeter-
mined copy); PARIS 1889,
no. 1 (monument, plaster)

Cat. 146

AUGUSTE RODIN
Avarice and Lust
About 1887
Plaster
22.5 x 53.5 x 46 cm
Musée Rodin (S.2152), Paris
Donation Auguste Rodin, 1916
EXH.: PARIS 1889, no. 24, 25,
26? (undetermined copy)

Cat. 147

AUGUSTE RODIN
Head of Avarice

About 1887
Plaster
15 x 10 x 10 cm
Private collection, France

Cat. 148

AUGUSTE RODIN
The Sirens
[About 1887]
Marble, executed by
Jean Escoula, 1889–92
44.5 x 45.7 x 27 cm
Signed on base, in back:
A. Rodin
The Montreal Museum
of Fine Arts (1958.1192)
Gift of the Huntley Redpath
Drummond family, 1958
Purchased by George
Alexander Drummond from
Rodin in 1891
EXH.: PARIS 1889, no. 29 (plaster)

Cat. 149

AUGUSTE RODIN
Galatea, model
for the marble
1887?
Plaster
39.5 x 27.7 x 22.3 cm
Musée Rodin (S.2434), Paris
Donation Auguste Rodin, 1916

Cat. 150

AUGUSTE RODIN
Galatea
[1887?]
Marble, before 1889
60.8 x 40.6 x 39.5 cm
Signed on the left side:

A. Rodin
Musée Rodin (S.1110), Paris
Bequest of Dr. Faure to the
city of Aix-les-Bains in 1942;
exchanged for bronzes in 1948
Purchased by Eugenia
Errazuriz before 1889
EXH.: PARIS 1889, no. 16

Cat. 151

AUGUSTE RODIN
Meditation
About 1887–88
Bronze, cast by
Alexis Rudier, before 1921
74.5 x 38 x 35 cm
Signed under left foot:
A. Rodin
Founder's mark on back
of base: *Alexis
Rudier/Fondeur Paris*
Musée Rodin (S.40), Paris
Gift of Léon Bérard, 1924

Cat. 152

AUGUSTE RODIN
*Sketch for the Head of She
Who Was Once the Helmet-
Maker's Beautiful Wife*
Before 1889
Terracotta
3.3 x 2.7 x 3.4 cm
Musée Rodin (S.6435), Paris
Donation Auguste Rodin, 1916

Cat. 153

AUGUSTE RODIN
She Who Was Once the

Helmet-Maker's Beautiful Wife
1889
Bronze, 1891
50 x 30 x 26.5 cm
Signed on socle, at right:
A. Rodin
Musée Rodin (S.1148), Paris
Purchased by the state in 1891,
on permanent loan since 1919
EXH.: ANGERS 1889 (bronze
from the Burrell Collection,
Glasgow)

Cat. 154

AUGUSTE RODIN
Danaid
1889
Bronze, cast by E. Godard, no. 11
35 x 60 x 49 cm
Signed in back: *A. Rodin*
Fondation Pierre Gianadda
(3426), Martigny
EXH.: PARIS 1889, no. 15
(marble from the Ateneumin
Taide Museo, Helsinski)

Cat. 155

AUGUSTE RODIN
*Façade of the Château de
l'Islette, Cheillé (Indre-et-Loire)*
1890 or 1891
Pen and brown ink on
watermarked cream paper
18.2 x 23 cm
Verso: three silhouettes of
dancers, pen and brown ink
Musée Rodin (D.3503), Paris
Donation Auguste Rodin, 1916
CAT.: JUDRIN 1985, no. 3503

Cat. 156

AUGUSTE RODIN
The Eternal Idol

Before 1891
Bronze, 1891
17 x 14 x 7 cm
Musée Rodin (S.39), Paris
Purchase, 1927
Purchase by Antoni Roux
from Rodin, 1891

Cat. 157

AUGUSTE RODIN
Sketch for the Head of Balzac
About 1891
Terracotta
23.9 x 9.6 x 14.4 cm
Musée Rodin (S.3900), Paris
Donation Auguste Rodin,
1916

Cat. 158

AUGUSTE RODIN
Balzac, mask study known as
"The Conductor of Tours"
1891
Plaster
24 x 21 x 17 cm
Musée Rodin (S.610), Paris
Donation Auguste Rodin, 1916

Cat. 159

AUGUSTE RODIN
Balzac, study for
Smiling Mask
1891
Terracotta
28.9 x 15.5 x 14.5 cm
Signed on the cut, below
left ear: *A. Rodin*
Musée Rodin (S.1769), Paris
Donation Auguste Rodin, 1916

Cat. 160

AUGUSTE RODIN
Balzac in Monk's Habit
About 1893
Bronze, cast by Georges Rudier
108 x 50 x 37 cm
Signed in front: *A. Rodin*
Fondation Pierre Gianadda
(3676), Martigny

Cat. 161

AUGUSTE RODIN
The Inner Voice or
Meditation
About 1894
Plaster
54 x 18 x 16 cm
Musée Rodin (S.680), Paris
Donation Rodin, 1916

Cat. 162

AUGUSTE RODIN
Thought
1895
Marble, executed by
Victor Peter
74.2 x 43.5 x 46.1 cm
Signed on left side of block:
A. Rodin
Musée d'Orsay (S.1003),
Paris
Gift of Mme. Durand to the
Musée du Luxembourg, 1902
Purchased by M. Durand
from Rodin in 1896
EXPO.: SNBA 1895, no. 100

Cat. 163

AUGUSTE RODIN
Thought
[1895]
Marble, executed by
Raynaud et Durand,
1900–1
76.2 x 43.4 x 46.1 cm
Signed on base, at right:
A. Rodin
Rodin Museum (1148),
Philadelphia
Purchased by John G.
Johnson from Rodin in 1901

Cat. 164

AUGUSTE RODIN
Triumphant Youth or *Fate
and the Convalescent*
About 1895
Plaster
50.5 x 46.7 x 33 cm
Musée Rodin (S.2240), Paris
Donation Auguste Rodin, 1916
EXH.: SNBA 1896, no. 116
(marble)

Cat. 165

AUGUSTE RODIN
*Assemblage: Mask of
Camille Claudel and Left
Hand of Pierre de Wissant*
About 1895?
Plaster
32.1 x 26.5 x 27.7 cm
Musée Rodin (S.349),
Paris
Donation Auguste Rodin,
1916

Cat. 166

AUGUSTE RODIN
Aurora
About 1895–97
Marble
56 x 58 x 50 cm
Musée Rodin (S.1019), Paris
Donation Auguste Rodin, 1916

Cat. 167

AUGUSTE RODIN
The Inner Voice or
Meditation, large model
1896
Bronze, cast by Fonderie
de Coubertin, 1981
146 x 75.5 x 55 cm
Signed on base, beside
right foot: *A. Rodin*
Founder's mark in back:
shell surrounded by
the letters *FC n° 0/*
Musée Rodin (S.792), Paris
Cast executed for the
museum's collections in 1981
EXH.: SNBA 1897, no. 125
(plaster presented with the
Monument to Victor Hugo);
DRESDEN 1897, no. 1166
(plaster); STOCKHOLM,
1897, no. 1698 (plaster,
whereabouts unknown)

Cat. 168

AUGUSTE RODIN
Brother and Sister
Before 1897
Bronze, cast by
Alexis Rudier, 1916
38.3 x 18 x 20.5 cm

Signed in front of base,
at left: *A. Rodin*
Founder's mark on back
of base: *Alexis Rudier
Fondeur Paris*
Musée Rodin (S.975), Paris
Donation Auguste Rodin, 1916

Cat. 169

AUGUSTE RODIN
Balzac
1898
Patinated plaster
277.5 x 116.2 x 125.5 cm
Musée Rodin (S.3151), Paris
Donation Auguste Rodin, 1916
EXH.: SNBA 1898, no. 150
(unidentified plaster)

Cat. 170

AUGUSTE RODIN
The Farewell, second state
About 1898?
Plaster
38.8 x 45.2 x 30.6 cm
Musée Rodin (S.1795), Paris
Donation Auguste Rodin, 1916

Cat. 171

AUGUSTE RODIN
Meditation with Arms
After 1900
Bronze, cast by Fonderie
de Coubertin, 1982
158 x 78 x 66 cm
Signed in back: *A. Rodin*

Founder's mark in back:
shell surrounded by the
letters *FC n° 11*
Fondation Pierre Gianadda
(3631), Martigny
Purchase, 1982

Cat. 172

AUGUSTE RODIN
Minerva in a Helmet
About 1902–3?
Plaster
49.8 x 50.1 x 36 cm
Musée Rodin (S.1482), Paris
Donation Auguste Rodin, 1916

Cat. 173

AUGUSTE RODIN
Study for France
About 1902–3
Bronze, cast by Alexis
Rudier, before 1916?
49.8 x 46.3 x 36.5 cm
Signed on left shoulder:
A. Rodin
Founder's mark in back,
at right: *Alexis Rudier
/Fondeur Paris*
Musée Rodin (S.1017), Paris
Donation Auguste Rodin, 1916

Cat. 174

AUGUSTE RODIN
France Turned Leftwards
About 1904
Bronze, cast by
Alexis Rudier, 1927
57 x 43 x 29 cm
Signed at base of left
shoulder: *A. Rodin*

Musée Rodin (S.490), Paris
Gift of Mme. Eugène
Rudier, 1957
EXH.: DÜSSELDORF 1904,
no. 1739 (plaster turned
to the right)

Cat. 175

AUGUSTE RODIN
The Farewell
Marble, executed by
Jean-Marie Mengue, 1906–7
50.8 x 49.5 x 42 cm
Signed on right side,
lower center: *A. Rodin*
Chrysler Museum of Art
(77.447), Norfolk, Virginia
Gift of the Max J. Sulzberger
family, 1960
Purchased by Max J. Sulzberger
from Rodin in 1913

Cat. 176

AUGUSTE RODIN
The Convalescent
Marble, begun by Jean-Marie
Mengue, 1906–7?;
completed by Émile
Matruchot, about 1914
48.5 x 71 x 56 cm
Musée Rodin (S.1016), Paris,
Donation Auguste Rodin, 1916

Cat. 177

AUGUSTE RODIN
*Duchess of Choiseul,
née Claire Coudert*
Marble, executed by
Victor Peter, 1911
49 x 50.3 x 31.9 cm
Musée Rodin (S.1040), Paris
Donation Auguste Rodin, 1916

Cat. 178
AUGUSTE RODIN
Address book
Undated
30.1 x 20.4 cm
Musée Rodin, Paris
Donation Auguste Rodin, 1916

Cat. 179
AUGUSTE RODIN
Notebook no. 54
1882
Inside front cover with
sketch for *The Gates of Hell*
and fol. 1 recto
29 x 19.2 cm
Musée Rodin (D.7106), Paris
Donation Auguste Rodin, 1916
CAT.: JUDRIN 1992, no. 7106

Cat. 180
*Letter from Léon Lhermitte
to Auguste Rodin*
Dated March 9, 1883
1 sheet, 20.8 x 26.4 cm
Musée Rodin (Ms.255), Paris
Donation Auguste Rodin,
1916

Cat. 181
SOCIÉTÉ DES ARTISTES FRANÇAIS
*Explication des ouvrages de
peinture, sculpture, architecture, gravure et lithographie
des artistes vivants exposés
au Palais des Champs-Élysées
le 1er mai 1883*, Paris, E.
Bernard et Cie, 1883.
17 x 10.2 cm
Musée national des beaux-arts
du Québec, Quebec City

Cat. 182
*Letter from Auguste Rodin
to Camille Claudel*
[Before May 1886?]
1 sheet, 21 x 27 cm

Musée Rodin (L.1451), Paris
Donation Auguste Rodin, 1916
CAT.: CLAUDEL 2003, no. 18

Cat. 183
*Letter from Camille Claudel
to Auguste Rodin*
[May–June 1886?]
1 sheet, 17.5 x 11.5 cm
Musée Rodin (Ms.369), Paris
Donation Auguste Rodin, 1916
CAT.: CLAUDEL 2003, no. 3

Cat. 184
*Letter from Camille Claudel
to Auguste Rodin*
[August 1886]
1 sheet, 15.4 x 22 cm
Musée Rodin (Ms.370), Paris
Donation Auguste Rodin, 1916
CAT.: CLAUDEL 2003, no. 11

Cat. 185
*Telegram from Auguste Rodin
to Jessie Lipscomb*
[Summer 1886]
1 sheet, 15 x 11.5 cm
Private collection,
United Kingdom

Cat. 186
*Contract between
Auguste Rodin and
Camille Claudel*
Dated October 12, 1886
1 sheet, 18.1 x 22.5 cm
Musée Rodin (L.1452), Paris
CAT.: CLAUDEL 2003, no. 19

Cat. 187
*Letter from Camille Claudel
to Florence Jeans*
Postmarked November 8,
1886
1 sheet, 17.6 x 22 cm
Musée Rodin (Ms.371), Paris
Gift of Stephen Back, 1992
CAT.: CLAUDEL 2003, no. 20

Cat. 188
*Letter from Jessie Lipscomb
to Auguste Rodin*
Dated March 15, 1887
1 sheet, 21 x 27 cm
Musée Rodin (Ms.249), Paris
Donation Auguste Rodin, 1916

Cat. 189
*Letter from Camille Claudel
to Florence Jeans*
Postmarked April 16, 1887
3 sheets, 17.7 x 11.3 cm (2);
17.8 x 11.4 cm (1)
Musée Rodin (Ms.360), Paris
Gift of Stephen Back, 1992
CAT.: CLAUDEL 2003, no. 27

Cat. 190
*Lease between Monsieur
Lecoursonnois and Auguste
Rodin for 113 boulevard
d'Italie*
Dated December 5, 1887
1 sheet, 25 x 17.9 cm
Musée Rodin (Ms.251), Paris
Donation Auguste Rodin, 1916

Cat. 191
*Confessions: An Album to
Record Opinions, Thoughts,
Feelings, Ideas, Peculiarities,
Impressions, Characteristics
of Friends, & c...*
Confession of Camille

Claudel dated May 16, 1888
38.2 x 23.2 cm
Musée Rodin (Ms.368), Paris
Gift of Stephen Back, 1992
CAT.: CLAUDEL 2003, no. 43

Cat. 192
*Letter from Camille Claudel
to Florence Jeans*
[with 5 fashion engravings
and a fabric sample]
Postmarked April 19, 1889
1 sheet, 17.8 x 22.8 cm
Musée Rodin (Ms.361), Paris
Gift of Stephen Back, 1992
CAT.: CLAUDEL 2003, no. 49

Cat. 193
*Letter from Camille Claudel
to Auguste Rodin*
[July 1891?]
1 sheet, 17.5 x 22 cm
Musée Rodin (Ms.362), Paris
Donation Auguste Rodin, 1916
CAT.: CLAUDEL 2003, no. 54

Cat. 194
*Letter from Camille Claudel
to Madame Léon Lhermitte*
[1891]
1 sheet, 17 x 25 cm
Private collection, France

Cat. 195
ARMAND DAYOT
*Report to the ministre
de l'Instruction publique,
des Cultes et des Beaux-Arts
on The Waltz by
Camille Claudel*
Dated March 20, 1892
2 sheets, 31 x 21 cm
Archives Nationales
de France (F21 4299), Paris

Cat. 196
*Letter from Auguste Rodin
to Armand Dayot*
Postmarked March 21, 1892
1 sheet, 14.8 x 9 cm
Musée Rodin (L.944), Paris
Purchase, 1932
CAT.: RODIN 1985, no. 180

Cat. 197
*Letter from Louise Claudel
to her daughter Camille
Claudel (recto)
Letter from Camille Claudel
to Auguste Rodin (verso)*
[May–June 1892?]
1 sheet, 17.6 x 22.6 cm
Musée Rodin (Ms.364), Paris
Donation Auguste Rodin, 1916
CAT.: CLAUDEL 2003, nos. 58–59

Cat. 198
ADOLPHE GRUET
*Invoice made out to Auguste
Rodin for the casting of his
bust by Camille Claudel*
Dated October 8, 1892
1 sheet, 18.4 x 20.9 cm
Musée Rodin (Ms.257), Paris
Donation Auguste Rodin, 1916

Cat. 199
*Letter from Camille Claudel to
the directeur des Beaux-Arts*
Dated December 21, 1892
1 sheet, 18 x 11.5 cm
Archives Nationales de
France (F21 4299), Paris
CAT.: CLAUDEL 2003, no. 63

Cat. 200

ARMAND DAYOT
*Report to the ministre
de l'Instruction publique et
des Beaux-Arts on* The Waltz
by Camille Claudel
Dated January 5, 1893
2 sheets, 31 x 21 cm
Archives Nationales de
France (F²¹ 4299), Paris

Cat. 201

*Letter from Paul Siot-
Decauville to Auguste Rodin*
Dated August 11, 1893
1 sheet, 19.5 x 25.2 cm
Musée Rodin (Ms.250), Paris
Donation Auguste Rodin, 1916

Cat. 202

*Letter from Camille Claudel
to Paul Claudel*
[Late 1893 or early 1894]
2 sheets, 17.5 x 22 cm
Société des Manuscrits des
Assureurs Français, Paris
CAT.: CLAUDEL 2003, no. 71

Cat. 203

*Letter from Camille Claudel
to Gustave Geffroy*
[April 1895]
1 sheet, 15 x 23 cm
Musée Rodin (Ms.366), Paris
Purchase, 1998
CAT.: CLAUDEL 2003, no. 84

Cat. 204

*Letter from Auguste Rodin
to Gabriel Mourey*
[Shortly before May 13,
1895?]
1 sheet, 17.7 x 22.7 cm
Musée Rodin (L.323), Paris
Purchase, 1931
CAT.: RODIN 1985, no. 229

Cat. 205

Letter from Auguste Rodin

---

to Octave Mirbeau
[May 1895?]
1 sheet. 8.4 x 12.6 cm
Musée Rodin (L.1560), Paris
Gift of Musée national des
beaux-arts du Québec, 2003

Cat. 206

*Letter from Auguste Rodin
to Camille Claudel*
[May 1895?]
1 sheet, 13.5 x 24.9 cm
Musée Rodin (L.1454), Paris
CAT.: CLAUDEL 2003, no. 93

Cat. 207

*Letter from Camille Claudel
to Antoine Bourdelle*
[May–June 1895]
1 sheet, 26.9 x 17.3 cm
Musée Bourdelle
(MS 00007), Paris
Bequest of Rhodia Dufet-
Bourdelle, 2002
CAT.: CLAUDEL 2003, no. 91

Cat. 208

*Letter from Camille Claudel
to Antoine Bourdelle*
[May–June 1895]
1 sheet, 26.8 x 17.3 cm
Musée Bourdelle,
(MS 00008), Paris
Bequest of Rhodia
Dufet-Bourdelle, 2002
CAT.: CLAUDEL 2003, no. 92

Cat. 209

*Letter from Auguste Rodin
to Camille Claudel*
[June 1895?]
1 sheet, 18 x 23 cm
Musée Rodin (L.1453), Paris
CAT.: CLAUDEL 2003, no. 95

Cat. 210

ARMAND SILVESTRE
Report to the ministre de

---

*l'Instruction publique et des
Beaux-Arts on* The Age of
Maturity *by Camille Claudel*
Dated February 1896
1 sheet, 31 x 21 cm
Archives Nationales de
France (F²¹ 2162), Paris

Cat. 211

*Letter from Camille Claudel
to Mathias Morhardt*
[March? 1896]
1 sheet, 21 x 13.5 cm
Société des Manuscrits des
Assureurs Français, Paris
CAT.: CLAUDEL 2003, no. 104

Cat. 212

*Telegram from Camille
Claudel to Auguste Rodin*
Postmarked April 25, 1896
1 sheet, 13.1 x 11 cm
Musée Rodin (Ms.363), Paris
Donation Auguste Rodin, 1916
CAT.: CLAUDEL 2003, no. 107

Cat. 213

*Letter from Camille Claudel
to Mathias Morhardt*
[September 1896?]
1 sheet, 21.5 x 50 cm
Société des Manuscrits des
Assureurs Français, Paris
CAT.: CLAUDEL 2003, no. 108

Cat. 214

*Letter from Henri Le Bossé
to Auguste Rodin*
Dated November 17, 1897
1 sheet, 8.8 x 11.5 cm
Musée Rodin (Ms.252), Paris
Donation Auguste Rodin,
1916

Cat. 215

*Letter from Camille Claudel
to Auguste Rodin*
[Between November 17 and
December 2, 1897]
2 sheets, 17.5 x 22.1 cm
Musée Rodin (Ms.365), Paris
Donation Auguste Rodin,
1916
CAT.: CLAUDEL 2003, no. 120

Cat 216

*Letter from Auguste Rodin
to Camille Claudel*
Dated December 2, 1897
Manuscript copy by Rodin's
secretary, René Chéruy
2 sheets, 17.7 x 22.1 cm
Musée Rodin (L.1394), Paris
Donation Auguste Rodin,
1916
CAT.: CLAUDEL 2003, no. 121

Cat. 217

ARMAND SILVESTRE
*Report to the ministre
de l'Instruction publique
et des Beaux-Arts on*
The Age of Maturity
by Camille Claudel
Dated November 1, 1898
1 sheet, 31 x 21 cm
Archives Nationales de
France (F²¹ 2162), Paris

Cat. 218

*Letter from Camille Claudel
to the directeur des
Beaux-Arts*
Stamped December 26,
1898
1 sheet, 15 x 23 cm
Archives Nationales de
France (F²¹ 2162), Paris
CAT.: CLAUDEL 2003, no. 13

Cat. 219

ANTOINE BOURDELLE
1. *Mademoiselle
   Camille Claudel*
[About 1898?]
1 sheet, 15.5 x 22.7
Musée Bourdelle
(MS 00010), Paris
2. *Mademoiselle
   Camille Claudel*
[About 1898?]
2 sheets, 11 x 17.3 cm
Musée Bourdelle
(MS 00013), Paris

3. *The Face of
   Camille Claudel* III
February 1926
1 sheet, 21.1 x 27.1 cm
Musée Bourdelle
(MS 00011), Paris
4. *The Face of
   Camille Claudel* IV
February 1926
1 sheet, 21.1 x 27.1 cm
Musée Bourdelle
(MS 00012), Paris
Bequest of Rhodia
Dufet-Bourdelle, 2002

Cat. 220

*Letter from Camille Claudel
to Gustave Geffroy*
[1901]
1 sheet, 14.9 x 22.6 cm
Musée Rodin (Ms.372), Paris
Purchase, 1998
CAT.: CLAUDEL 2003, no. 160

Cat. 221

FRANÇOIS POMPON
Ledger
Vol. 1 (July 1884–August 2,
1908)
Fol. 75 verso, April 14,
1901–April 11, 1902
32 x 13.8 cm

Musée d'Orsay, Paris
Gift of Jeanne and Anne
Demeurisse through the
Société des Amis du Musée
d'Orsay, 1989

_Cat. 222
*Letter from Joanny Peytel
to Auguste Rodin*
Dated January 23, 1902
1 sheet, 21.1 x 26.5 cm
Musée Rodin (Ms.253), Paris
Donation Auguste Rodin, 1916

_Cat. 223
*Letter from Camille Claudel
to Joanny Peytel*
[May 1902]
1 sheet, 15.7 x 23 cm
Musée Rodin (Ms.367), Paris
Donation Auguste Rodin, 1916
CAT.: CLAUDEL 2003, no. 172

_Cat. 224
*Letter from Joanny Peytel
to Auguste Rodin*
Dated March 4, 1903
1 sheet, 27.4 x 21.2 cm
Musée Rodin (Ms.254), Paris
Donation Auguste Rodin, 1916

_Cat. 225
GALERIE EUG. BLOT
*Exposition d'œuvres
de Camille Claudel
et Bernard Hoetger,
du 4 au 16 décembre
1905*
Catalogue
21.2 x 15 cm
Bibliothèque Nationale
de France, Paris

_Cat. 226
*Letter from Eugène Blot to
the sous-secrétaire d'État
des Beaux-Arts*
Dated March 8, 1906

368

1 sheet, 27 x 21.5 cm
Archives Nationales de
France (F²¹ 4189), Paris

_Cat. 227
MINISTERE DE L'INSTRUCTION
PUBLIQUE, DES BEAUX-ARTS
ET DES CULTES
*Purchase order for the
Wounded Niobid (plaster)
of Camille Claudel*
Dated April 26, 1906
1 sheet, 31 x 21 cm
Archives Nationales de
France (F²¹ 4189), Paris

_Cat. 228
*Letter from Camille Claudel
to the sous-secrétaire d'État
des Beaux-Arts*
Stamped May 30, 1906
1 sheet, 15 x 11.3 cm
Archives Nationales
de France (F²¹ 4189), Paris
CAT.: CLAUDEL 2003, no. 207

_Cat. 229
MINISTERE DE L'INSTRUCTION
PUBLIQUE, DES BEAUX-ARTS
ET DES CULTES
*Order to pay an account on
the cost of Wounded Niobid
(plaster) by Camille Claudel*
Dated July 9, 1906
1 sheet, 32 x 21.5 cm
Archives Nationales de
France (F²¹ 4189), Paris

_Cat. 230
*Letter from Camille Claudel
to the sous-secrétaire d'État
des Beaux-Arts*
Stamped October 6, 1906
1 sheet, 15 x 11.5 cm
Archives Nationales de
France (F²¹ 4189), Paris
CAT.: CLAUDEL 2003, no. 210

_Cat. 231
MINISTERE DE L'INSTRUCTION
PUBLIQUE, DES BEAUX-ARTS
ET DES CULTES

*Purchase order for the
Wounded Niobid (bronze)
by Camille Claudel*
Dated February 15, 1907
1 sheet, 31 x 21 cm
Archives Nationales de
France (F²¹ 4189), Paris
CAT.: CLAUDEL 2003, no. 215

_Cat. 232
*Letter from Camille Claudel
to the sous-secrétaire d'État
des Beaux-Arts*
Stamped April 4, 1907
2 sheets, 16.5 x 12.3 cm
Archives Nationales de
France (F²¹ 4189), Paris
CAT.: CLAUDEL 2003, no. 217

_Cat. 233
GALERIE EUG. BLOT
*Invoice for the purchase
by the state of Abandon
(bronze) by Camille Claudel*
Dated June 20, 1907
1 sheet, 27.5 x 21.4 cm
Archives Nationales de
France (F²¹ 4189), Paris

_Cat. 234
*Letter from Camille Claudel
to the ministre des
Beaux-Arts*
Stamped July 25, 1907
2 sheets, 29.5 x 21 cm
Archives Nationales de
France (F²¹ 4189), Paris
CAT.: CLAUDEL 2003, no. 222

_Cat. 235
*Letter from Camille Claudel
to the sous-secrétaire d'État
des Beaux-Arts*
Stamped September 19,
1907
1 sheet, 32 x 21 cm
Archives Nationales de
France (F²¹ 4189), Paris
CAT.: CLAUDEL 2003, no. 223

_Cat. 236
EUGÈNE MORAND
*Report to the sous-secrétaire
d'État des Beaux-Arts on the
Wounded Niobid (bronze)
by Camille Claudel*
Stamped October 15, 1907
1 sheet, 31 x 21 cm
Archives Nationales de
France (F²¹ 4189), Paris

_Cat. 237
GALERIE EUG. BLOT
*Exposition de sculptures
nouvelles de Camille Claudel
et de peintures par Manguin,
Marquet, Puy, du 24 octobre
au 10 novembre 1907*
Catalogue
13.6 x 10.7 cm
Bibliothèque Marguerite-
Durand, Paris

_Cat. 238
ARMAND DAYOT
*Report to the ministre de
l'Instruction publique, des
Beaux-Arts et des Cultes
on the Wounded Niobid
(bronze) by Camille Claudel*
Dated December 15, 1907
1 sheet, 31 x 21 cm
Archives Nationales de
France (F²¹ 4189), Paris

_Cat. 239
SOUS-SECRÉTAIRE D'ÉTAT
DES BEAUX-ARTS
*Memo to Camille Claudel
about the delivery of the
Wounded Niobid (bronze)
to Dépôt des Marbres*
Dated December?, 1907
1 sheet, 27 x 21.5 cm
Archives Nationales de
France (F²¹ 4189), Paris

_Cat. 240
EUGÈNE MORAND
Memo about registering

*the Wounded Niobid
(bronze) by Camille Claudel
on the Inventory*
Dated December 20, 1907
1 sheet, 21.5 x 13.5 cm
Archives Nationales de
France (F²¹ 4189), Paris

_Cat. 241
PAUL CLAUDEL
Journal
Vol. 2
Fol.75, September 5, 1909
36 x 43 cm
Bibliothèque Nationale
de France, Paris

_Cat. 242
*Letter from Camille Claudel
to Paul Claudel*
[1909?]
3 sheets
Société des Manuscrits des
Assureurs Français, Paris
CAT.: CLAUDEL 2003, no. 232

_Cat. 243
AUGUSTE RODIN
*L'Art: Entretiens réunis
par Paul Gsell, Paris,
Grasset, 1911*
24 x 19 cm
Musée Rodin (362), Paris

_Cat. 244
PAUL CLAUDEL
*"Camille Claudel, statuaire,"
L'Art décoratif, no. 193
(July 1913)*
29 x 21 cm
Musée Jean-de-La Fontaine,
Château-Thierry

_Cat. 245
*Letter from Auguste Rodin
to Mathias Morhardt*
Dated May 28, 1914
1 sheet
Bibliothèque Nationale
de France, Paris

Cat. 246

*Letter from Mathias Morhardt
to Auguste Rodin*
Dated June 5, 1914
1 sheet, 21.2 x 26.9 cm
Musée Rodin (Ms.256), Paris
Donation Auguste Rodin, 1916

Cat. 247

*Letter from Auguste Rodin
to Mathias Morhardt*
Dated June 9, 1914
1 sheet
Société des Manuscrits des
Assureurs Français, Paris

Cat. 248

*Letter from Camille Claudel
to Paul Claudel*
Dated March 3, 1930
2 sheets, 17.5 x 22.5 cm
Société des Manuscrits des
Assureurs Français, Paris
CAT.: CLAUDEL 2003, no. 289

Cat. 249

EUGÈNE BLOT
*Reminiscence of Eugène Blot
about his meeting with
Camille Claudel,* for Jules
Leblanc-Barbedienne
Dated December 17, 1936
2 sheets, 27 x 21.2 cm
Archives Nationales de
France (368 AP3), Paris

Cat. 250

GALERIE EUG. BLOT
The Implorer by C. Claudel,

edition record (no. 1465)
*illustrated with a
photograph by Larger*
Undated
28 x 18.7 cm
Archives Nationales de
France (368 AP3), Paris

Cat. 251

GALERIE EUG. BLOT
*Fortune, by C. Claudel,
edition record (no. 1752)
illustrated by a
photograph by Larger*
Undated
28 x 18.7 cm
Archives Nationales de
France (368 AP3), Paris

Cat. 252

GALERIE EUG. BLOT
*Fireside Group by
C. Claudel, edition record
(no. 1778) illustrated with
a photograph by Larger*
Undated
28 x 18.7 cm
Archives Nationales de
France (368 AP3), Paris

Cat. 253

GALERIE EUG. BLOT
*Intimacy by C. Claudel,
edition record (no. 1788)
illustrated with a
photograph by Larger*
Undated

28 x 18.7 cm
Archives Nationales de
France (368 AP3), Paris

Cat. 254

GALERIE EUG. BLOT
*Perseus by C. Claudel,
edition record illustrated
with a photograph by Larger*
Undated
15.9 x 10.2 cm
Archives Nationales de
France (368 AP3), Paris

Cat. 255

GALERIE EUG. BLOT
*Bust Aurora by C. Claudel,
edition record (no. 1864)
illustrated with a
photograph by Larger?*
Undated
28 x 18.7 cm
Archives Nationales de
France (368 AP3), Paris

Cat. 256

GALERIE EUG. BLOT
*Group Abandon by
C. Claudel, edition record
(no. 1784) illustrated with
a photograph by Larger*
Undated
28 x 18.7 cm
Archives Nationales de
France (368 AP3), Paris

Cat. 257

GALERIE EUG. BLOT
*Group The Waltz by
C. Claudel, edition record
(no. 1860) illustrated with
a photograph by Larger*
Undated
28 x 18.7 cm
Archives Nationales de
France (368 AP3), Paris

Cat. 258

GALERIE EUG. BLOT
*Siren by C. Claudel, edition
record (no. 1792) illustrated
with a photograph by Larger?*
Undated
28 x 18.7 cm
Archives Nationales de
France (368 AP3), Paris

Cat. 259

*Contract of transfer of the
rights of manufacture for
various models by the sculptors
Camille Claudel, Jules Jouant
and Hoetger, from Eugène Blot
to Jules Leblanc-Barbedienne*
Dated October 14, 1937
2 sheets, 24.8 x 17.5 cm
Archives Nationales de
France (368 AP3), Paris

Cat. 260

*List of models turned over
by Eugène Blot to maison*

Barbedienne in 1937
and 1938
1937–38
1 sheet, 27 x 20.8 cm
Archives Nationales de
France (368 AP3), Paris

Cat. 261

A) *Information provided by
Monsieur Blot Sr. on some of
the works from his edition,
for the firm of Barbedienne*
Undated
1 sheet, 27 x 20.8 cm
Archives Nationales de
France (368 AP3), Paris

B) *Information provided by
Monsieur Blot Sr. on some of
the works from his edition,
for the firm of Barbedienne*
Undated
1 sheet, 27 x 20.8 cm
Archives Nationales de
France (368 AP3), Paris

Cat. 262

PAUL CLAUDEL
Journal
Vol. 9 (1943–49)
Fol. 110 verso and 111
recto, September–October
1943
43 x 26.5 cm
Société des Manuscrits des
Assureurs Français, Paris

CAMILLE CLAUDEL AND RODIN: SELECTED LETTERS

My cruel friend,
My poor head is really sick and
I can no longer get up in the morning. This evening I
wandered [hours] without finding you, our places,
how sweet death would be to me and how long my
agony is. Why did you wait so long
for me at the studio? What has happened to you?
What pain I had in store for me. I have
moments of anemia in which I suffer less,
but today, the implacable pain
is still there. Camille my beloved in spite of everything,
in spite of the madness that will be
your doing if this goes on. Why
don't you believe me? I'll give up my
Salon. sculpture; if I could go
anywhere, to a country where I would forget, but
there isn't one. There are moments when frankly
I think I will forget you. But in an
instant I feel your terrible power.
Take pity, wicked one. I am at the end of my tether.
I can no longer go a day without seeing you.
Otherwise horrible madness.
That's it, I am no longer working, harmful deity,
and yet I love you passionately.
My Camille, I assure you there is no other
woman, that my entire soul
belongs to you.
I can't convince you and my reasons
are powerless. You don't believe I'm suffering,
you doubt that I weep.
I haven't laughed,
haven't sung in a long time,
everything is insipid,
nothing interests me. I am already dead
and no longer understand the trouble

I took over things
I am now indifferent to.
Let me see you
everyday, that would be a good deed
and perhaps something better will happen to me,
because you alone can save me
with your generosity.
I am trying not to let my mind succumb to this hideous
and slow illness, my passionate and
so pure love for you.
Take pity on me my darling and you yourself will be
rewarded.
Rodin
I kiss your hands my friend,
you who have given me such passionate delights,
with you my soul exists
so powerfully, and in its passion,
respect for you is always foremost.
The respect I have for your character,
for you my Camille is a
cause of my violent passion.
Don't treat me pitilessly,
I am asking so little of you.
Do not threaten me and let yourself see
that your so very gentle hand marks your
bounty for me and sometimes
leave it there so that I can kiss it in my
transports.
I don't regret a thing. Neither the
dénouement which I find dismal,
my life would have fallen into an
abyss. But my soul has had
its flowering, a late one, alas. I
had to meet you and
everything took on an unknown new life,

my dull existence went up
in a bonfire of joy. Thank you because
I owe you all that,
this piece of heaven that
I've had in my life.
Leave your dear hands on
my face, so that my flesh can be
happy that my heart is feeling
your divine love flowing over me
again. The exhilaration
of my life when I'm with you.
With you, when I
think I still have this happiness
I pity myself. And in my cowardice,
I believe I'm over being unhappy,
that I've reached the end. No, as long as
there is still a faint hope, the slightest,
I have to take advantage of it during
the night, the night afterwards.
Your hand Camille, not the one which is
withdrawn, no happiness in touching it if
it is not proof of a little of
your tenderness.
Ah, divine beauty, flower that
talks, and which loves, intelligent flower,
my darling. My love, on my knees before you
I embrace your beautiful body.
R

HSL from Auguste Rodin to Camille Claudel,
[before May 1886?]
AMR, L.1451 (cat. 182, pp. 82–83)

In future from today
October 12, 1886 I will have for my
Pupil only Mlle Camille Claudel and will
protect her alone by every means
at my disposal by my
friends who will be hers above all by my

influential friends
I will not accept other pupils in order
that there should not
by chance be rival talents although I do not suppose
that one often meets artists as naturally
gifted
At the exhibition I will do what I can
for sales, the newspapers
I will no longer under any pretext go to see Mme . . . . .
to whom I will no longer teach sculpture
After the exhibition in the month of May we
will leave for Italy and stay there for at least
6 months communally in an indissoluble relationship
after which Mlle Camille will become my wife.
I will be very happy to offer
a figurine in marble if Mlle Camille cares
to accept it within 4 to 5 months.
Between now and the month of May I will have
no other woman, and if I do, all the conditions
are dissolved.
If my commission from Chile is confirmed
we will go to Chile
instead of Italy
I will take none of the women models
I have known
There will be a photograph taken Chez
Carjat in the costume Mlle Claudel
wore wore to the Academy [when she was dressed]
for town, and perhaps one in evening dress
Mlle Camille will stay in Paris until May
Melle Camille undertakes to receive me
in her studio 4 times
a month until the month of May
Rodin

HSL from Auguste Rodin to Camille Claudel,
October 12, 1886
AMR, L.1452 (cat. 186, pp. 88–89)

Monsieur Rodin
as I have nothing
to do I am writing to you again.
You cannot
imagine how
good the weather is at l'Islette.
I ate today
in the middle room
(the one used as a greenhouse) where one
can see the garden on both
sides. Madame Courcelles
suggested to me (without me
saying anything) that if
you so wish
you can eat there
from time to time and
even always (I think
she really wants to do this) and it's
so beautiful there!
I went for a walk in
the park, everything has been mown,
hay, corn, barley, one
can go everywhere
it's lovely. If
you are sweet enough to keep
your promise it will
be heaven for us.
You can have any room
you want to
work in. The old woman
will be on her knees before us, I
think.
She told me that I [. . .]
bathe in
the river, where her daughter and
the maid go bathing
without danger.
With your permission,
I will do so as

it's a great pleasure
and it will spare me going to
the hot baths at
Azay. It would be so kind of you to buy me a
small bathing costume,
dark blue with white trimmings,
in two pieces,
blouse and trousers (medium
size) at the Louvre or
au bon marché (in serge)
or in Tours!
I sleep completely naked
to make myself believe
you are there but
when I wake it
is not the same thing.
With love
Camille
Above all do not be unfaithful to me
anymore!

HSL FROM CAMILLE CLAUDEL TO AUGUSTE RODIN,
[JULY 1891?]
AMR, MS.362 (CAT. 193, PP. 138–39)

My sovereign friend
I am still sick and yet
if am to heal, I will, because
the opening at which I saw you
was for me the beginning
of a consolation that will restore me
to health! My very dear friend
how kind you were how your
intelligence pleases me, all . . .
have got something new . . .
nor copy in your soul, which I
feel is so beautiful; with what pain I
am stricken, and how great my fault has been;

but I feel that in seeing you
there was a destiny I
could not flee.
Ah my divine friend. You will be happy
be patient, one has to pay for everything in this world.
I was paid for my work, I'm paying for my
faults and my continuing pain is a striking example
of justice.
Thaulow came to see me. He said
that your small figures are admirable . . .
saw perhaps breakages but he must . . .
disdain. At any rate, you [know your]
group will be accepted. Morhardt . . .
too. And people are still talking
about you, with constant references to what
you are doing, to you!
You have the gift of reigning over
everyone.
I send you my respectful
admiration   Your Rodin
Fulfilled and glad of your benevolence

HSL FROM AUGUSTE RODIN TO CAMILLE CLAUDEL
[MAY 1895?]
AMR, MS.362 (CAT. 206, PP. 172–73)

Dear Mademoiselle
I will do for Mr. Fenaille
what you desire will bring him
to your door as he is coming to see
me opposite.
As regards the minister
exceptionally he is coming to get me
at the studio Monday
to come and see you, and
I think for your interest and
out of politeness that
I should come with him, so that neither he nor I

should feel ill at ease,
besides there's a
whole plan I
want to see succeed and I
need the freedom to bring to see you
either now or later
M. Leygues M. Poincaré
M. Bourgeois.
In this way I will achieve
some kind of a result.
It will be the last step toward
your glory and position.
It is strictly in your interest,
so that you don't lose your
future.
M. Leygues spoke very
highly of you to M. Bourgeois
who was at my house yesterday of
your Waltz.
As for me I will
see you only when strictly
necessary the sight of you
terrifies me and would perhaps pitch me
into the greatest of suffering destiny has
killed me and I seek for nothing more, to lighten
my error was what I wanted, despite being ill
I did what I could and I have every hope of seeing
my efforts rewarded with a Commission
which would be your consecration in the eyes of the
world
and which would keep your collector friends.
I am unhappy about your plight as you can imagine.
I am not coming for myself, I have
to accompany
M. Leygues Morhardt having replied favorably
and I have committed myself.
Also, it wouldn't be right for me just
to accompany M. Fenaille to your door,
that would be perhaps frowned on

by these messieurs. If this only made me look ridiculous
then it matters little.
So make this sacrifice for your
future and soon you will be strong
and will no longer need a servant.

I send you my best wishes
not for your glory already achieved
but for the security that
your thoughts and work
should be assured
Your very devoted servant
Rodin

Hope only day by day
and if the delays are long
don't lose confidence as it's
the last effort and your position will be
so good like mine later
but happier as
you deserve.

HSL FROM AUGUSTE RODIN TO CAMILLE CLAUDEL
[JUNE 1895?]
AMR, L.1453 (CAT. 209, P. 174)

Monsieur Rodin.
You have had
Le Bossé ask me
my opinion on your statue
of Balzac: I find it
very great and very
beautiful and the best of
all your studies of the same
subject. Especially the very accentuated
effect of the head,
which contrasts with the

simplicity of the drapery
and is so well found and
striking. I also love
the idea of
the billowing sleeves,
which well convey Balzac's
negligent nature. In short, I
think you should
expect great success with it,
above all with true
connoisseurs, who could
find no comparison
between this statue and all
those which have until now
decorated the city of
Paris.
I will take this opportunity to
tell you a little about my
affairs. Morhardt recently
got Mercure de France
to commission me 10 busts of you
in bronze which will
sell for 300F each through
the newspaper: out of which I will
get 280F which [. . . ?] pay the foundry
[. . . ?] as well as do the
chaser's work that is
get rid of the seams and
engrave a caduceus. I
accepted this commission
knowing full well the work it
entailed but it takes me a day just
to engrave the caduceus and 5 to
6 days to satisfactorily remove the seams: I
beg you to tell Morhardt
that I cannot go on with
these busts, I haven't got
1000F to pay out of my own pocket
just so that afterwards

I can be accused of being wasteful
and commissions
like this are more
to make people
believe [. . . ?] they have than
to really help them.
You did well
to stop Morhardt from
publishing the article he
wrote on me
it was destined to bring anger
and revenge on me of which I
certainly have no need.
You are perhaps wrong in
believing in the Morhardts' total goodwill
toward me they pretend rather
but I think
that in fact not all their
clan looks favorably on him procuring
me commissions,
promoting me etc it would be
better if all
Morhardt's efforts went to
the benefit of Raymond
Vernet etc who are of the same
race and religion and whose wives
are close friends of
Mme Morhardt. You
must well know
what utter hatred
all these women have for me
as soon as they see me,
until I have gone
back into my
shell again they use
every weapon; and
what's more as soon as a
generous man tries
to get me out of difficulty

there is his wife
holding his arm and
preventing him. As well
it seems likely that I will never
reap the benefits of my
efforts and be tainted
by slander
and nasty suspicions.
What I am telling you is
absolutely secret and
so that you can get clear picture
of the situation.
I have been ill for
a while, hence my delay
in writing. Old
mother Courcelles has managed
to get me to pay 1000F
for having left some
plasters there, at first
I wanted to take her to court
then I thought better of it.
If you can find a way
to ask her for your
Dante saying that
you merely
forgot it there, this
would really please me.
My best regards
C Claudel

HSL FROM CAMILLE CLAUDEL TO AUGUSTE RODIN
[BETWEEN NOVEMBER 17 AND DECEMBER 2, 1897]
AMR, MS.365 (CAT. 215, PP. 206–7)

BIBLIOGRAPHY

This bibliography includes only publications cited in the essays.
The entries are preceded by their abbreviated forms, which are arranged in alphabetical order.
Some references, of less direct relevance to the main subject of the catalogue, are not
abbreviated and are cited in full in the notes to the essays. They are not included here.

ADAM 1908
ADAM, Paul. *Dix ans d'art français.*
Paris: Albert Méricant, 1908?

ALAIN-FOURNIER 1926
ALAIN-FOURNIER, Henri, and Jacques
RIVIÈRE. *Correspondance 1886–1925.*
vol. 2: *1905–1914.*
Paris: Gallimard, 1926.

ALCANTARA 1961
ALCANTARA, Comtesse d'. *Marcello:
Adèle d'Affry, duchesse Castiglione
Colonna.* Geneva: Éditions
Générales SA, 1961.

A. M. 1903
A. M. Untitled article.
La Petite Gironde (June 7, 1903).

ANONYMOUS 1877
Untitled article. *L'Étoile belge*
(January 29, 1877).

ANONYMOUS 1881
"La sculpture au Salon de Bruxelles."
L'Art moderne (October 23, 1881): 266.

ANONYMOUS 1890
"Au Champ de Mars." *L'Art moderne*
(May 25, 1890): 161.

ANONYMOUS 1892
"Prochaines statues. Chez Rodin."
L'Éclair (March 8, 1892).

ANONYMOUS 1895
"Lettre d'un bourgeois grincheux."
Journal du Centre
(November 21, 1895).

ANONYMOUS 1898 /1
"Œuvre achevée. M. Rodin et
la statue de Balzac." *L'Éclair*
(April 10, 1898).

ANONYMOUS 1898 /2
"Le Balzac de Rodin." *Le Progrès
de la Somme* (May 5, 1898).

ANONYMOUS 1898 /3
"La statue de Balzac." *Le Public*
(May 14, 1898).

ANONYMOUS 1906
Untitled article. *Le Studio*
(February 5, 1906).

ANTOINE 1988
ANTOINE, Gérald. *Paul Claudel
ou l'Enfer du génie.* Paris:
Robert Laffont, 1988.

ARNOUX 2001
ARNOUX, Danielle. *Camille Claudel:
l'ironique sacrifice.* Paris: Epel, 2001.

AYRAL-CLAUSE 2002
AYRAL-CLAUSE, Odile. *Camille
Claudel: A Life.* New York:
Harry N. Abrams, 2002.

BABIN 1902
BABIN, Gustave. "Les Salons de 1902."
La Revue de l'art ancien et moderne,
vol. 11 (January–June 1902).

BARTLETT 1889
BARTLETT, Truman H. "Auguste Rodin,
Sculptor." *The American Architect
and Building News* (April 27, 1889,
May 25, 1889 and June 1, 1889).

BASHKIRTSEFF 1980
BASHKIRTSEFF, Marie. *Journal.*
Paris: Mazarine, 1980.

BEAUSIRE 1988
BEAUSIRE, Alain. *Quand Rodin exposait.*
Paris: Musée Rodin, 1988.

BELLOC 1890
BELLOC, Marie Adelaïde. "Lady Artists
in Paris." *Murray's Magazine*
(September 1890): 374–77.

BENGESCO 1899
BENGESCO, M. "La sculpture au Salon
1899." *L'Œuvre d'art* (June 1, 1899).

BERGERAT 1882
BERGERAT, Émile. Untitled article.
Le Voltaire (May 31, 1882).

BERNARD 1899
BERNARD, Jean. "Le Salon de Paris,
5e visite." *L'Indépendance belge*
(June 2, 1899).

BERNE 1985
KUNSTMUSEUM BERN / MUSÉE DES
BEAUX-ARTS DE BERNE. *Camille Claudel
– Auguste Rodin. Dialogues d'artistes:
résonances.* Exh. cat., curator:
Sandor Kuthy. Fribourg:
Office du Livre, 1985.

BERNIER 1967
BERNIER, Rosamonde. "Henry Moore
parle de Rodin." *L'Œil*
(November 1967): 26.

BESANÇON 2002
MUSÉE DES BEAUX-ARTS ET
D'ARCHÉOLOGIE DE BESANÇON.
Victor Hugo vu par Rodin. Exh. cat.,
curators: Antoinette Le Normand-
Romain and Frédérique Thomas-Maurin.
Paris: Somogy Éditions d'Art, 2002.

BLJD 1965
BIBLIOTHÈQUE LITTÉRAIRE JACQUES
DOUCET. *Paul Claudel: premières
œuvres, 1886–1901.* Exh. cat., curator:
François Chapon. Paris: Bibliothèque
Littéraire Jacques Doucet, 1965.

BLOT 1905
*Exposition d'œuvres de Camille
Claudel et de Bernard Hoetger.*
Catalogue of the exhibition at the
Galerie Eugène Blot in Paris,
December 4–16, 1905.

BLOT 1906
Collection Eugène Blot: catalogue des tableaux, aquarelles, pastels et dessins. Paris, Hôtel Drouot, May 10, 1906.

BLOT 1907
Exposition de sculptures nouvelles par Camille Claudel et de peintures par Manguin, Marquet, Puy. Catalogue of the exhibition at the Galerie Eugène Blot in Paris, October 24–November 10, 1907.

BLOT 1908
Exposition de Mesdames Camille Claudel, Gaston Devore, Jeanne Eliot, Alcide Lebeau-Hassenberg, Ann Osterlind (Mme Edouard Sarradin). Catalogue of the exhibition at the Galerie Eugène Blot in Paris, December 1–24, 1908.

BLOT 1934
BLOT, Eugène. Histoire d'une collection de tableaux modernes: 50 ans de peinture (de 1882 à 1932). Paris: Éditions d'Art, 1934.

BOUILLON 1990
La Promenade du critique influent: anthologie de la critique d'art en France 1850–1900. Texts edited and presented by Jean-Paul Bouillon et al. Paris: Hazan, 1990.

BOURDELLE 1909
BOURDELLE, Antoine. "Rodin et la sculpture." Revue des études franco-russes (September 1909): 369–85.

BOUTÉ 1995
BOUTÉ, Gérard. Camille Claudel: le miroir et la nuit. Essai sur l'art

de Camille Claudel. Paris: Éditions de l'Amateur et Éditions des Catalogues Raisonnés. 1995.

BRAISNE 1897
BRAISNE, Henry de. Untitled article. Revue idéaliste 19 (October 1, 1897). Reprinted in: Jacques Cassar. Dossier Camille Claudel. Paris: Archimbaud et Maisonneuve & Larose, 2003, appendix 6.

BUTLER 1993
BUTLER, Ruth. Rodin: The Shape of Genius. London: Yale University Press, 1993.

BUTLER / LINDSAY 2000
BUTLER, Ruth, and Suzanne Glover LINDSAY. European Sculpture of the Nineteenth Century: The Collections of the National Gallery of Art Systematic Catalogue. Washington, D.C.: National Gallery of Art, 2000.

CAHIERS CLAUDEL 1959
Cahiers Paul Claudel, no. 1. Paris: Gallimard, 1959.

CALAIS / PARIS 1977
MUSÉE DES BEAUX-ARTS, CALAIS and MUSÉE RODIN. Auguste Rodin: le Monument des bourgeois de Calais (1884–1895) dans les collections du musée Rodin et du musée des Beaux-Arts de Calais. Exh. cat., curators: Claudie Judrin, Monique Laurent and Dominique Viéville. Calais: Musée des Beaux-Arts and Paris: Musée Rodin, 1977.

CASO / SANDERS 1977
CASO, Jacques de, and Patricia SANDERS. Rodin's Sculpture: A Critical

Study of the Spreckels Collection at the California Palace of the Legion of Honor. San Francisco: Fine Arts Museum. 1977.

CASSAR 2003
CASSAR, Jacques. Dossier Camille Claudel. Paris: Archimbaud et Maisonneuve & Larose. 2003.

CHAMPIER 1902
CHAMPIER, Victor. Les Industries d'art à l'Exposition universelle de 1900. Paris: Bureaux de la "Revue des arts décoratifs," 1902.

CHAVANNE and GAUDICHON 1988
CHAVANNE, Blandine, and Bruno GAUDICHON. Catalogue raisonné des peintures des XIXe et XXe siècles (artistes nés après 1774), dans les collections du musée de la Ville de Poitiers et de la Société des Antiquaires de l'Ouest. Poitiers: Musée de la Ville de Poitiers et de la Société des Antiquaires de l'Ouest, 1988.

CHEVILLOT 1992
CHEVILLOT, Catherine. "Les stands industriels d'édition de sculpture à l'Exposition universelle de 1889: l'exemple de Barbedienne." Revue de l'art 95 (1992): 61–67.

CHEVILLOT 1997
CHEVILLOT, Catherine. "Sculptures en fonte de fer," in La Métallurgie de la Haute-Marne: du Moyen Âge au XXe siècle. Châlons-sur-Marne: Inventaire Général des Monuments et des Richesses Artistiques de la France et Association pour la Valorisation des

Atouts Culturels de Champagne-Ardenne, 1997, 206–21.

CHINCHOLLE 1894
CHINCHOLLE, Charles. "Balzac et Rodin." Le Figaro (November 25, 1894): 3.

CHINCHOLLE 1898
CHINCHOLLE, Charles. "La vente de la statue de Balzac." Le Figaro (May 12, 1898).

CLADEL 1908
CLADEL, Judith. Auguste Rodin, l'œuvre et l'homme. Brussels: Librairie Nationale d'Art et d'Histoire. G. van Oest et Cie, 1980.

CLADEL 1936
CLADEL, Judith. Rodin: sa vie glorieuse, sa vie inconnue. Paris: Grasset, 1936.

CLAUDEL 1913
CLAUDEL, Paul. "Camille Claudel, statuaire." L'Art décoratif 193 (July 1913): 5–50.

CLAUDEL 1950
CLAUDEL, Paul. "La Rose et le Rosaire," in Œuvres complètes. Vol. 21. Paris: Gallimard, 1950.

CLAUDEL 1952
CLAUDEL, Paul. Correspondance Paul Claudel, Francis Jammes et Gabriel Frizeau, 1897–1938. Paris: Gallimard, 1952.

CLAUDEL 1969
CLAUDEL, Paul. Mémoires improvisés: quarante et un entretiens avec Jean Amrouche. Paris: Gallimard, 1969.

CLAUDEL 2003
Camille Claudel: correspondance.
Edited by Anne Rivière and Bruno
Gaudichon. Paris: Gallimard, 2003.

CLAUDEL 2004
CLAUDEL, Paul. *Le Poëte et la Bible*,
vol. 2: *1945–1955*. Paris: Gallimard,
2004.

COCHIN 1903
COCHIN, Henry. "Quelques réflexions
sur les Salons: 2ᵉ et dernier article."
Gazette des Beaux-Arts
(2nd semester, 1903): 20–52.

COQUIOT 1911
COQUIOT, Gustave. "Jules Desbois."
L'Art et les artistes (July 1911): 161–68.

COQUIOT 1913
COQUIOT, Gustave. *Le Vrai Rodin.*
Paris: Éditions Jules Tallandier, 1913.

CZYNSKI 1992
CZYNSKI, Konrad. "Paul Claudel's
Singular Dept to Camille: The
Discovery of Japan." *Claudel Studies*,
vol. 19, nos. 1–2 (Dallas: University
of Dallas, 1992): 50–56.

DACIER 1905
DACIER, Émile. Untitled article.
Bulletin de l'art ancien et moderne
(December 9, 1905).

DARGENTY 1883
DARGENTY, G. "Le Salon national."
L'Art 35 (1883): 26–40.

DAYOT 1893
DAYOT, Armand. "La vie artistique.
Portraits d'artistes." *Le Figaro
illustré* (March 1893).

DEBUSSY 1942
DEBUSSY, Claude. *Lettres à deux amis:
78 lettres inédites à Robert Godet
et Georges Jean Aubry.*
Paris: José Corti, 1942.

DELBÉE 1982
DELBÉE, Anne. *Une femme.* Paris:
Presses de la Renaissance, 1982.

DELCLAUX 2003
DELCLAUX, Marie-Pierre. *Rodin.
Éclats de vie.* Paris: Éditions du
Musée Rodin, 2003.

DIJON 1994
MUSÉE DES BEAUX-ARTS DE DIJON.
François Pompon, 1855–1933.
Exh. cat., curator: Anne Pingeot.
Paris: Gallimard and Electa/Réunion
des Musées Nationaux, 1994.

DUJARDIN-BEAUMETZ 1913
DUJARDIN-BEAUMETZ, Henri-Charles-
Étienne. *Entretiens avec Rodin.*
Paris: Paul Dupont, 1913.

EASTERDAY 1997
EASTERDAY, Anastasia Louise.
"Charting a Course in an Intractable
Profession: Women Sculptors
in Nineteenth-Century France."
Ph.D. thesis, University of
California (L.A.), 1997.

ÉCOLE DU LOUVRE 1986
*La Sculpture du XIXᵉ siècle:
une mémoire retrouvée. Les Fonds
de sculpture.* Rencontres de
l'École du Louvre. Paris:
La Documentation Française, 1986.

E. D.-G. 1889
E. D.-G. "L'exposition artistique

d'Angers." *L'Artiste*
(December 1889): 446–53.

ELLET 1859
ELLET, E. F. *Women Artists.* London:
Richard Bentley, 1859.

ELSEN 1985
ELSEN, Albert E. *The Gates of Hell
by Auguste Rodin.* Stanford: Stanford
University Press, 1985.

FAGUS 1899
FAGUS, [Félicien]. Untitled article.
La Revue blanche (May 15, 1899).

FARGES 1891
FARGES, A. B. de. "La statue de
Balzac. L'opinion des deux artistes."
La France (July 15, 1891).

FONTAINAS 1899
FONTAINAS, André. "Les Salons
de 1899." *Mercure de France*
(June 1899): 747.

FOURCAUD 1883
FOURCAUD, Louis de. "Exposition
nationale des Beaux-Arts.
Notes critiques." *Le Gaulois*
(September 16, 1883): 2–3.

FOURCAUD 1899
FOURCAUD, Louis de. "Les Arts
décoratifs au Salon de 1899:
la sculpture à la S.N.B.A." *Revue des
arts décoratifs* 19 (1899): 247–57.

GARNIER 2001
GARNIER, Charles. *Le Nouvel Opéra.*
Paris: Éditions du Linteau, 2001.

GAUGUIN 1951
GAUGUIN, Paul. *Racontars de rapin.*
Paris: Éditions Falaize, 1951.

GAUTHIER 2003
GAUTHIER, Sophie. "Les images de
Camille Claudel dans le discours
critique de son époque."
Master's thesis, Université de Reims
Champagne-Ardenne, 2003.

GEFFROY 1886
GEFFROY, Gustave. "Chronique: Rodin."
La Justice (July 11, 1886).

GEFFROY 1889
GEFFROY, Gustave. "Le statuaire
Rodin." *Les Lettres et les Arts*
(September 1889): 289–304.

GEFFROY 1893
GEFFROY, Gustave. "Salons de 1892
au Champ-de-Mars: la sculpture et
les objets d'art." *La Vie artistique*,
2nd series (1893): 337–46.

GEFFROY 1894
GEFFROY, Gustave. "Salons de 1893
au Champ-de-Mars: la sculpture et
les objets d'art." *La Vie artistique*,
3rd series (1894): 300–86.

GEFFROY 1895 /1
GEFFROY, Gustave. "L'art aux Salons."
La Revue de Paris (May 1895): 225.

GEFFROY 1895 /2
GEFFROY, Gustave. "Salon de 1894."
La Vie artistique, 4th series (1895):
85–203.

GEFFROY 1895 /3
GEFFROY, Gustave. "Salon de 1895.
La sculpture au Champ-de-Mars."
La Vie artistique, 4th series (1895).

GEFFROY 1896
GEFFROY, Gustave. "Salon de 1896 au

Champ-de-Mars. VII. La sculpture."
La Vie artistique, 5th series (1896): 200.

GEFFROY 1897
GEFFROY, Gustave. "Salon de 1897 au
Champ-de-Mars. III. La sculpture."
La Vie artistique, 5th series (1897): 365.

GEFFROY 1900
GEFFROY, Gustave. "Sculpture."
La Vie artistique, 6th series (1900).

GONCOURT 1989
GONCOURT, Edmond and Jules de.
Journal: mémoires de la vie littéraire,
vol. 3: *1887–1896*.
Paris: Robert Laffont, 1989.

GRAUTOFF 1910
GRAUTOFF, Otto. "Auguste Rodin."
Die Kunst für Alle
(October 15, 1910): 25–46.

GSELL 1922
GSELL, Paul. "Un poète de la chair:
le sculpteur Jules Desbois."
*La Renaissance de l'art français et
des industries de luxe* (1922): 382–89.

GSELL 1935
GSELL, Paul. "Le grand sculpteur
Jules Desbois est mort hier."
Comœdia, 1935.

GUILLEMIN 1968
GUILLEMIN, Henri. *Le "Converti"
Paul Claudel*. Paris: Gallimard, 1968.

HAMEL 1889
HAMEL, Maurice. "Salon de 1889. III.
La sculpture." *Gazette des
Beaux-Arts* 2 (1889): 20–27.

HAMEL 1899
HAMEL, Maurice. "Les Salons de 1899."

La Revue de Paris (June 1, 1899):
655–56.

HAMEL 1902
HAMEL, Maurice. *Le Salon de 1902*.
Paris: Goupil et Cⁱᵉ, 1902.

HAMEL 1905
HAMEL, Maurice. "Les Salons
de 1905." *La Revue de Paris*
(June 1, 1905).

HAMEL / ALEXANDRE 1903
HAMEL, Maurice, and Arsène
ALEXANDRE. *Salons de 1903*.
Paris: Manzi, Joyant & Cⁱᵉ, 1903.

HANOTAUX 1912
HANOTAUX, Gabriel. "Pour un grand
Français." *Les Annales politiques
et littéraires* (May 19, 1912): 4–5.

HÉRAN 2004
HÉRAN, Emmanuelle. "Jules Desbois:
La Misère." 48|14 *La Revue
du musée d'Orsay* 19
(autumn 2004): 44–46.

HONIG 1978
HONIG, Elsa. *Women and Art*.
Montclair and London: Allanheld
and Schram, 1978.

JACQUES 1883
JACQUES, Edmond. "Beaux-Arts.
Exposition des Arts libéraux."
L'Intransigeant (March 7, 1883).

JOUVE 1895
JOUVE, Lucien. "Don fait au musée:
Sakountala, groupe en plâtre patiné
par Camille Claudel." *Bulletin
du musée de Châteauroux* 118
(1895): 111–18.

KAHN 1905
KAHN, Gustave. "Au jour le jour.
Les éditions Blot." *Le Siècle*
(December 29, 1905).

LAWTON 1906
LAWTON, Frederick. *The Life
and Works of Auguste Rodin*.
London: T. Fisher Unwin, 1906.

LEBON 2003
LEBON, Élisabeth. *Dictionnaire des
fondeurs de bronze d'art, France
1890–1950*. Perth (Australia):
Marjon Editions, 2003.

LE NORMAND-ROMAIN 1999
LE NORMAND-ROMAIN, Antoinette.
Rodin: The Gates of Hell. Paris:
Musée Rodin, 1999.

LE NORMAND-ROMAIN 2003
LE NORMAND-ROMAIN, Antoinette.
*Camille Claudel & Rodin: Time Will
Heal Everything*. Paris: Musée Rodin,
2003.

LE NORMAND-ROMAIN
/ HAUDIQUET 2001
LE NORMAND-ROMAIN, Antoinette,
and Annette HAUDIQUET.
Rodin. The Burghers of Calais.
Paris: Musée Rodin, 2001.

LEPAGE 1911
LEPAGE, Édouard. *Une page
de l'histoire de l'art au
dix-neuvième siècle*.
Paris: 1911.

LEROI 1886
LEROI, Paul. "Salon de 1886 (fin)."
L'Art 41 (1886): 64–80.

LEROI 1887
LEROI, Paul. "Salon de 1887 (fin)."
L'Art 43 (1887): 231–42.

LEROI 1888
LEROI, Paul. "Salon de 1888:
la sculpture." *L'Art* 44
(1888): 209–18.

LEROI 1889
LEROI, Paul. "Salon de 1889:
la sculpture." *L'Art* 46
(1889): 259–69.

LEROI 1892
LEROI, Paul. "Salon de 1892."
L'Art 53 (1892): 14–18, 35–37.

LEROI 1894
LEROI, Paul. "Salon de 1894:
à propos de M. Auguste Rodin."
L'Art, 2nd series, vol. 3
(1894): 250–53.

LEROUX 1898
LEROUX, Gaston.
"À Paris: le vernissage."
Le Matin (May 1, 1898).

LISTA 1994
*Medardo Rosso: la sculpture
impressionniste*. Texts and chronology
established by Giovanni Lista.
Paris: L'Échoppe, 1994.

L. T. 1906
L. T. "Les expositions: deux sculpteurs."
Psyché (April 1906): 103–6.

LYON 1998
MUSÉE DES BEAUX-ARTS DE LYON.
*Les Métamorphoses de Mme F.:
Auguste Rodin, Maurice Fenaille
et Lyon*. Exh. cat., curators:
Antoinette Le Normand-Romain

and Claudie Judrin. *Bulletin des musées et monuments lyonnais* 2–3 (Lyon: Association des Amis du Musée des Beaux-Arts, 1998).

LYON / LONDON / NEW YORK 2003
MUSÉE DES BEAUX-ARTS DE LYON, NATIONAL GALLERY, LONDON and METROPOLITAN MUSEUM OF ART, NEW YORK. *Ingres, Burne-Jones, Whistler, Renoir . . . La Collection Grenville L. Winthrop: chefs-d'œuvre du Fogg Art Museum, Université de Harvard*. Exh. cat., curator: Stephan Wolohojian. Paris: Réunion des Musées Nationaux, 2003.

MAILLARD 1896
MAILLARD, Léon. "Le Salon du Champ-de-Mars." *La Plume* 170 (May 15, 1896).

MAILLARD 1897
MAILLARD, Léon. "Le Salon du Champ-de-Mars." *La Plume* 194 (May 15, 1897): 314–20.

MAILLARD 1899
MAILLARD, Léon. *Études sur quelques artistes originaux: Auguste Rodin statuaire*. Paris: Éditions Floury, 1899.

MAISON DE VICTOR HUGO 2003
MAISON DE VICTOR HUGO. *D'ombre et de marbre: Hugo face à Rodin*. Exh. cat., curator: Danielle Molinari. Paris: Somogy Éditions d'Art, 2003.

MALLARMÉ 1973
MALLARMÉ, Stéphane. *Correspondance*, vol. 4: *1890–1891*. Paris: Gallimard, 1973.

MARCEL 1902
MARCEL, Henry. "Les Salons de 1902." *Gazette des Beaux-Arts* 2 (1902): 123–41.

MARGUERITTE 1896
MARGUERITTE, Paul. Untitled article. *L'Écho de Paris* (May 21, 1896).

MARSEILLE 1997
MUSÉE DES BEAUX-ARTS DE MARSEILLE. *Rodin: La Voix intérieure*. Exh. cat., curators: Luc Georget and Antoinette Le Normand-Romain. Marseille: Musées de Marseille, 1997.

MARTIGNY / PARIS 1990–91
FONDATION PIERRE GIANADDA. *Camille Claudel*. Exh. cat., curator: Nicole Barbier. Martigny (Switzerland): Fondation Pierre Gianadda, 1990. / MUSÉE RODIN. *Camille Claudel*. Exh. cat., curator: Nicole Barbier. Paris: Musée Rodin, 1991.

MARTIN 1989
MARTIN, Pierre-François. "1888–1910: renaissance de la fonte à cire perdue pour les statuettes de bronze." D.E.A. dissertation, Université de Paris IV Sorbonne, 1989.

MARX 1894
MARX, Roger. "Beaux-Arts. L'art aux deux Salons: expositions de Paris en 1894," in *L'Encyclopédie*, supplement to *La Revue encyclopédique Larousse* 87 (July 15, 1894).

MARX 1895
MARX, Roger. "Les Salons de 1895: 4e et dernier article." *Gazette des Beaux-Arts* (August 1, 1895): 105–22.

MARX 1899
MARX, Roger. "Les Salons de 1899." *La Revue encyclopédique* (July 15, 1899): 560.

MICHEL 1903
MICHEL, André. "Promenades aux Salons." *Feuilleton du Journal des débats* (May 12, 1903).

MIRBEAU 1893
MIRBEAU, Octave. "Ceux du Champ-de-Mars. La sculpture." *Le Journal* (May 12, 1893).

MIRBEAU 1895
MIRBEAU, Octave. "Çà et là." *Le Journal* (May 12, 1895).

MIRBEAU 1993
MIRBEAU, Octave. *Combats esthétiques*. 2 Vols. Edition presented, annotated and established by Pierre Michel and Jean-Franços Nivet. Paris: Nouvelles Éditions Séguier, 1993.

MITCHELL 1989
MITCHELL, Claudine. "Intellectuality and Sexuality: Camille Claudel, the Fin de Siècle Sculptress." *Art History*, vol. 12, no. 4 (December 1989): 419–47.

MONOD 1906
MONOD, François. "L'exposition de Mlle Claudel et de Bernard Hoetger." *Art et Décoration* (January 1906).

MORHARDT 1898
MORHARDT, Mathias. "Mlle Camille Claudel." *Mercure de France* (March 1898): 709–55.

MORICE 1895
MORICE, Charles. *L'Idée libre* 6 (June 1895).

MORICE 1903
MORICE, Charles. "Les Salons de la Société nationale et des Artistes français." *Mercure de France* (June 1903): 666–92.

MORLA 1928
MORLA, Carlos. "Devant le buste de ma mère." Chile. *Revue du Chili* (July 1928).

MOUREY 1895
MOUREY, Gabriel. "Le Salon. Champ-de-Mars." *Le Nouveau Monde* (May 4, 1895).

MOUREY 1899
MOUREY, Gabriel. "L'art en 1899. Deuxième partie: les Salons de Paris." *Le Studio*, vol. 17, no. 75 (June 15, 1899): 3–6.

MUSÉE D'ORSAY 1988
MUSÉE D'ORSAY. *"L'Âge mûr" de Camille Claudel*. Exh. cat., curator: Anne Pingeot. Paris: Réunion des Musées Nationaux, 1988.

MUSÉE D'ORSAY 1991
MUSÉE D'ORSAY. *Léon Lhermitte et La Paye des moissonneurs*. Exh. cat., curator: Monique Le Pelley Fonteny. Paris: Réunion des Musées Nationaux, 1991.

MUSÉE D'ORSAY 1992
MUSÉE D'ORSAY. *Une famille d'artistes en 1900: les Saint-Marceaux*. Exh. cat., curators: Jean-Michel Nectoux, Antoinette Le Normand-Romain and Véronique Alemany-Dessaint. Paris: Réunion des Musées Nationaux, 1992.

MUSÉE D'ORSAY 1995
MUSÉE D'ORSAY. Le Baiser de Rodin.
Exh. cat., curator: Antoinette
Le Normand-Romain. Paris: Réunion
des Musées Nationaux, 1995.

MUSÉE D'ORSAY 2001
MUSÉE D'ORSAY. Italies, 1880–1910:
l'art italien à l'épreuve de la modernité.
Exh. cat., curators: Gianna Piantoni
and Anne Pingeot. Paris: Réunion
des Musées Nationaux, 2001.

MUSÉE RODIN 1951
MUSÉE RODIN. Camille Claudel
(décembre 1864 – octobre 1943).
Exh. cat., curator: Cécile
Goldscheider. Paris: Musée Rodin, 1951.

MUSÉE RODIN 1989
MUSÉE RODIN. Claude Monet –
Auguste Rodin. Centenaire de l'expo-
sition de 1889. Exh. cat., curator:
Jacques Vilain. Paris: Musée Rodin, 1989.

MUSÉE RODIN 1997
MUSÉE RODIN. Vers L'Âge d'airain:
Rodin en Belgique. Exh. cat., curator:
Antoinette Le Normand-Romain.
Paris, Musée Rodin, 1997.

MUSÉE RODIN 1998
MUSÉE RODIN. 1898: le Balzac
de Rodin. Exh. cat., curator:
Antoinette Le Normand-Romain.
Paris: Musée Rodin, 1998.

MUSÉE RODIN / MUSÉE DU
LUXEMBOURG 2001
MUSÉE RODIN. Rodin en 1900:
l'exposition de l'Alma. Exh. cat.,
curator: Antoinette Le Normand-
Romain. Paris: Réunion des
Musées Nationaux, 2001.

NANTET 2004
NANTET, Marie-Victoire. "Camille
Claudel médusée," in De Claudel
à Malraux. Mélanges offerts
à Michel Autrand. Besançon: Presses
Universitaires de Franche-Comté, 2004.

NEWTON 1989
NEWTON, Joy. "Rodin's Celle qui fut
la Belle Heaulmière and Mirbeau's
L'Octogénaire: A Note." Gazette des
Beaux-Arts (January 1989): 45–48.

NOCHLIN 1989
NOCHLIN, Linda. "Why Have There
Been No Great Women Artists?"
in Women, Art and Power
and Other Essays. New York:
Harper and Row, 1989.

PARIS 1984
PARIS, Reine-Marie et al.
Camille Claudel 1864–1943.
Paris: Gallimard, 1984.

PARIS 2000
PARIS, Reine-Marie. Camille Claudel
re-trouvée: catalogue raisonné.
Paris: Éditions Aittouarès, 2000.

PARIS / LA CHAPELLE 1990
PARIS, Reine-Marie, and Arnaud de
LA CHAPELLE. L'Œuvre de Camille
Claudel: catalogue raisonné.
Paris: Adam Biro-Arhis, 1990.

PARIS / POITIERS 1984
MUSÉE RODIN and MUSÉE SAINTE-CROIX.
Camille Claudel (1864–1943).
Exh. cat., curators: Monique Laurent
and Bruno Gaudichon.
Paris: Musée Rodin and Poitiers:
Musée Sainte-Croix, 1984.

PIERRE 2003
PIERRE, Caterina Y. "A New Formula
for High Art: The Genesis and
Reception of Marcello's Pythia."
Nineteenth-Century Art Worldwide
(autumn 2003).

PINET / PARIS 2003
PINET, Hélène, and Reine-Marie PARIS.
Camille Claudel. Le génie est comme
un miroir. Paris: Gallimard, 2003.

PINGEOT 1982
PINGEOT, Anne. "Le chef-d'œuvre
de Camille Claudel: L'Âge mûr."
Revue du Louvre et des Musées de
France, vol. 31 no. 4 (1982): 287–95.

PINGEOT 1991
PINGEOT, Anne. "L'Âge mûr de
Camille Claudel." Voir et apprendre
à voir (Paris: Musée d'Orsay and
La Documentation Française. 1991):
19–37.

PINGEOT 1996
PINGEOT, Anne. "L'Hiver de Rodin."
Revue du Louvre et des Musées
de France, vol. 44, no. 4 (1996).

QUÉBEC 1998
MUSÉE DU QUÉBEC. Rodin à Québec.
Exh. cat., curators: John R. Porter
and Yves Lacasse. Quebec:
Musée du Québec, 1998.

RAMBOSSON 1899 /1
RAMBOSSON. Yvanhoë. "Le Salon de
1899 – Sculpture." La Plume 243
(June 1, 1899).

RAMBOSSON 1899 /2
RAMBOSSON, Yvanhoë. Untitled article.
L'art décoratif (June 1899).

RENARD 1965
RENARD, Jules. Journal (1887–1910).
Paris: Gallimard, 1965.

REVAL 1903
REVAL, Gabrielle. "Les artistes femmes
au Salon de 1903." Fémina 35
(May 1, 1903): 520–21.

REYNOLDS 2004
REYNOLDS, Siân. "Art Education in the
Rodin Circle and Women's Relation
to the Avant-garde: The Case of
Ottilie McLaren," in Claudine
Mitchell, ed., Rodin: The Zola
of Sculpture (Burlington: Ashgate,
2004): 201–15.

RILKE 1928
RILKE, Rainer Maria. Auguste Rodin.
Paris: Éditions Émile-Paul Frères,
1928.

RIVIÈRE 1983
RIVIÈRE, Anne. L'Interdite:
Camille Claudel 1864–1943.
Paris: Tierce, 1983.

RIVIÈRE / GAUDICHON / GHANASSIA 2001
RIVIÈRE, Anne, Bruno GAUDICHON and
Danielle GHANASSIA. Camille Claudel:
catalogue raisonné. Paris: Société
Nouvelle Adam Biro, 2001.

RODIN 1911
RODIN, Auguste. L'Art. Interviews
collected by Paul Gsell.
Paris: Grasset, 1911.

RODIN 1914
RODIN, Auguste. Les Cathédrales
de France. Paris: Librairie
Armand Colin, 1914.

RODIN 1985
BEAUSIRE, Alain, and Hélène PINET. *Correspondance de Rodin*, vol. 1: *1860–1899*. Paris, Musée Rodin, 1985.

RODIN 1987
BEAUSIRE, Alain, and Florence CADOUOT. *Correspondance de Rodin*, vol. 3: *1908–1912*. Paris: Musée Rodin, 1987.

RODIN 1992
BEAUSIRE, Alain, Florence CADOUOT and Frédérique VINCENT. *Correspondance de Rodin*, vol. 4: *1913–1917*. Paris: Musée Rodin, 1992.

ROLLAND 1903
ROLLAND, Romain. Untitled article. *La Revue de Paris* (June 1, 1903).

RONDIN / NANTET 2003
RONDIN, Madeleine, and Marie-Victoire NANTET, eds. *Origine d'une œuvre, mémoire d'un pays: Camille et Paul Claudel*. Amiens: Académie d'Amiens, 2003.

ROUBAIX 2003
LA PISCINE – MUSÉE D'ART ET D'INDUSTRIE ANDRÉ-DILIGENT. *Des amitiés modernes. De Matisse à Rodin: Carolus-Duran et la Société nationale des beaux-arts, 1890–1905*. Exh. cat., curators: Bruno Gaudichon, Dominique Lobstein, Anne Rivière and Emmanuelle Héran. Paris: Somogy Éditions d'Art, 2003.

SAUNIER 1899
SAUNIER, Charles. "Salon de 1899: la sculpture." *La Revue populaire des Beaux-Arts* (June 3, 1899): 337–40.

SERTAT 1893
SERTAT, Raoul. "Revue artistique du Salon du Champ-de-Mars." *La Revue encyclopédique Larousse*, 1893.

SILVESTRE 1897
SILVESTRE, Armand. *La Sculpture aux Salons de 1897*. Paris: E. Bernard et Cⁱᵉ, 1897.

TANCOCK 1976
TANCOCK, John L. *The Sculpture of Auguste Rodin: The Collection of the Rodin Museum, Philadelphia*. Philadelphia: Philadelphia Museum of Art, 1976.

THOMAS 1901
THOMAS, Albert. "Petits bronzes d'art." *L'Art décoratif* 29 (February 1901): 180–89.

THURAT 1882
THURAT, Henri. "Galerie des sculpteurs célèbres. École française: Auguste Rodin." *L'Art populaire* (April 30, 1882).

TIREL 1923
TIREL, Marcelle. *Rodin intime ou l'Envers d'une gloire*. Paris: Éditions du Monde Nouveau, 1923.

TOULOUSE / BLÉRANCOURT 1999
MUSÉE DES AUGUSTINS and MUSÉE NATIONAL DE LA COOPÉRATION FRANCO-AMÉRICAINE. *Augustus Saint-Gaudens, 1848–1907: un maître de la sculpture américaine*. Exh. cat., curators: Catherine Gaich and Anne Dopffer. Paris: Somogy Éditions d'Art, 1999.

TURNER 1996
TURNER, Jane, ed. *The Dictionary of Art*. 34 vols. London: Macmillan and New York, Grove, 1996.

VAN LENNEP 1993
VAN LENNEP, Jacques. *Les Bustes de l'Académie royale de Belgique. Histoire et catalogue raisonné*, preceded by an essay, "Le Portrait sculpté depuis la Renaissance." Brussels: Classe des Beaux-Arts, Académie Royale de Belgique, 1993.

VAUXCELLES
VAUXCELLES, Louis. "Une visite à la Galerie Eugène Blot." *Tourismes* (n.d.).

VAUXCELLES 1905
VAUXCELLES, Louis. "Exposition Camille Claudel et Bernard Hoetger." *Le Gil Blas* (December 4, 1905).

VAUXCELLES 1934
VAUXCELLES, Louis. "Les arts: rétrospective Camille Claudel." *Le Monde illustré* (May 12, 1934): 391.

VERHAEREN 1997
VERHAEREN, Émile. *Écrits sur l'art*, vol. 1: *1881–1892*. Brussels: Éditions Labor, 1997.

VIENNA 1996
PALAIS HARRACH DU KUNSTHISTORISCHEN MUSEUM. *Auguste Rodin, Eros et Passion*. Exh. cat. Milan: Skira, 1996.

WASHINGTON 1981
NATIONAL GALLERY OF ART, WASHINGTON. *Rodin Rediscovered*. Exh. cat., curators: Ruth Butler, Albert E. Elsen and Kirk Varnedoe. Boston: New York Graphic Society, 1981.

WASHINGTON 1988
NATIONAL MUSEUM OF WOMEN IN THE ARTS. *Camille Claudel*. Exh. cat., curator: Reine-Marie Paris. Washington: National Museum of Women in the Arts, 1988.

WIESINGER 1987
WIESINGER, Véronique. "Jules Desbois (1851–1935), sculpteur de talent ou imitateur de Rodin?" *Bulletin de la Société de l'histoire de l'art français* (1987): 315–30.

WYZEWA 1894
WYZEWA, T. de. "Le Salon de 1894: 2ᵉ et dernier article." *Gazette des Beaux-Arts* (1894): 25–42.

YELDHAM 1984
YELDHAM, Charlotte. *Women Artists in Nineteenth-Century France and England*. 2 vols. New York and London: Garland, 1984.

PHOTO CREDITS

ADAGP / ART RESOURCE, NY: CAT. 31, 44 – JANNIN, FRANÇOIS: FIG. 35

ATELIER PHOTOGRAPHIQUE DU CENTRE HISTORIQUE DES ARCHIVES NATIONALES, PARIS: CAT. 199, 231, 233, 238, 250, 251, 252, 253, 254, 255, 256, 257, 258, 260

BIBLIOTHÈQUE MARGUERITE-DURAND, PARIS: FIG. 72

BIBLIOTHÈQUE NATIONALE DE FRANCE, PARIS: CAT. 225; FIG. 83

BILDARCHIV PREUSSISCHER KULTURBESITZ / ART RESOURCE, NY, KLAUS GÖKEN: FIG. 31

CALAN, JEAN DE: CAT. 32, 66, 70, 71, 78, 85, 87, 90

CHRYSLER MUSEUM OF ART, NORFOLK: CAT. 175

CLARK, DAVID: CAT. 36

CONSERVATION DÉPARTEMENTALE DES MUSÉES DE MAINE-ET-LOIRE / ROUSSEAU, B.: CAT. 72; FIG. 38

DWYER, GARY: CAT. 21, 22, 103, 106, 107, 108; FIG. 33, 82

ÉCOLE NATIONALE SUPÉRIEURE DES BEAUX-ARTS DE PARIS: FIG. 7

FONDATION PIERRE GIANADDA, MARTIGNY: CAT. 154, 160, 171

INSTITUTO PORTUGUÊS DE MUSEUS: FIG. 42

KAARE BERNTSEN GALLERY, OSLO: CAT. 64

KUNSTHAUS, ZÜRICH: FIG. 65

LA PISCINE – MUSÉE D'ART ET D'INDUSTRIE ANDRÉ DILIGENT, ROUBAIX / LOUBRY, ARNAUD: CAT. 74; FIG. 29

L'IMAGE PRO: CAT. 30, 47

MAISON CLAUDE DEBUSSY: FIG. 79

MAK, VIENNA / MAYER, GEORG: FIG. 47

MONTREAL MUSEUM OF FINE ARTS: CAT. 148

MUSÉE BOUCHER-DE-PERTHES, ABBEVILLE: CAT. 50

MUSÉE BOURDELLE, PARIS: CAT. 219; FIG. 13

MUSÉE CALVET, AVIGNON: CAT. 27

MUSÉE D'ART ROGER-QUILLIOT, CLERMONT-FERRAND / BAYLE: CAT. 35

MUSÉE DES BEAUX-ARTS DE CALAIS / KLEINEFENN, F.: CAT. 134

MUSÉE DES BEAUX-ARTS DE CAMBRAI / MAERTENS, HUGO: CAT. 95

MUSÉE DES BEAUX-ARTS DE DIJON / JAY, FRANÇOIS: CAT. 116

MUSÉE DES BEAUX-ARTS DE LYON / FRANCHELLA, ALAIN: FIG. 57

MUSÉE DES BEAUX-ARTS D'ORLÉANS: CAT. 140

MUSÉE DES BEAUX-ARTS DE REIMS / DEVLEESCHAUWER, C.: CAT. 28; FIG. 43

MUSÉE D'ORSAY, PARIS: CAT. 221; FIG. 36, 62, 64, 67, 71, 84

MUSÉE EUGÈNE-BOUDIN, HONFLEUR: CAT. 29

MUSÉE INGRES, MONTAUBAN / ROUMAGNAC: CAT. 49

MUSÉE JULES-DESBOIS, PARÇAY-LES-PINS / ROUSSEAU, BRUNO: CAT. 101

MUSÉE RODIN, PARIS: CAT. 1, 2 B, 3, 4 A, 5 A, 6, 9 A, 13, 14, 17, 18, 23 A, 25 A, 52, 84 A, 104, 105, 109, 110, 111, 113 A, 114, 115 B, 117, 136, 164, 194: FIG. 5, 8, 9, 17, 19, 20, 21, 23, 25, 51
– ADAGP / HATALA, BÉATRICE: CAT. 133 – HEMERG, ERIK AND PETRA: CAT. 93 – JARRET, BRUNO: CAT. 167 – RZEPKA, ADAM: CAT. 37, 39, 43, 45, 53, 54, 56, 63, 65, 68, 73, 76, 77, 79, 86, 96, 100, 119, 126, 130, 131, 135, 137, 141, 149, 152, 157, 158, 161, 168, 170, 174 – BARAJA, CHRISTIAN: CAT. 41, 82, 122, 177; FIG. 4, 12
– BARAJA, CHRISTIAN OR HESMERG, ERICK AND PETRA: CAT. 16 – CALAN, JEAN DE: CAT. 112, 156, 179, 183, 184, 186, 187, 193, 205, 206, 209, 212, 215, 216; FIG. 24, 52, 63, 74 – MUSÉE RODIN / HATALA, BÉATRICE: CAT. 145, 146, 150, 155, 166, 173, 176; FIG. 40, 56
– MANOUKIAN, JÉRÔME: CAT. 7, 10, 20, 51, 59, 60, 61, 62, 102, 182; FIG. 6, 14, 18, 26, 27, 28, 39, 59, 68 – MANOUKIAN, JÉRÔME OR CALAN, JEAN DE: CAT. 91, 197, 198
– RZEPKA, ADAM: CAT. 120, 123, 124, 125, 129, 132, 138, 139, 142, 143, 144, 151, 153, 159, 169, 172; FIG. 11, 30, 41, 49, 50, 53, 54, 55, 66, 75, 78

MUSÉES DE POITIERS / VIGNAUD, CH.: CAT. 67, 80, 81, 92 A, 94 A, 98

MUSEUM OF FINE ARTS, BOSTON: CAT. 121

PALAIS DES BEAUX-ARTS DE LILLE / LEWANDOSKI, HERVÉ: CAT. 34 – BERNARD, PHILIPPE: FIG. 22

PMVP / PIERRAIN: CAT. 58

RÉUNION DES MUSÉES NATIONAUX, ART RESOURCE, NY: FIG. 10, 16, 37, 81 – OJEDA, R.G.: CAT. 162 – LAGIEWSKI: FIG. 80 – LEWANDOSKI, H.: FIG. 44 – OLLIVIER, THIERRY: FIG. 48

RODIN MUSEUM, PHILADELPHIA: CAT. 88 – ROSENTHAL, LYNN: CAT. 46 – WEISS, MURRAY: CAT. 118 B – WOOD, GRAYDON: CAT. 163

ROMAIN, ANTOINETTE: FIG. 58

RZEPKA, ADAM: FIG. 15

SCHAEFER, ANNE: CAT. 57, 97, 244; FIG. INTRO., 1, 2, 3, 32, 34, 45, 46, 60, 70, 73, 76, 77

SEBERT, PH.: CAT. 26, 38, 40, 42, 48, 55, 69, 75, 89, 147

SOCIÉTÉ DES AMIS DE LA BIBLIOTHÈQUE FORNEY, PARIS: CAT. 8

SOCIÉTÉ DES MANUSCRITS DES ASSUREURS FRANÇAIS, PARIS: CAT. 202, 213, 247, 248, 262

SOCIÉTÉ PAUL CLAUDEL, PARIS: CAT. 19, 24; FIG. 69

STUDIO DU GENETEIL: CAT. 91

STUDIO VILLAIN: CAT. 33

STUDIO VOGEL, TROYES: CAT. 15

THE ART INSTITUTE OF CHICAGO / HASHIMOTO, ROBERT: CAT. 128

THE DETROIT INSTITUTE OF ARTS: CAT. 127

THE NATIONAL MUSEUM OF ART OF ROMANIA, BUCHAREST / RZEPKA, ADAM: FIG. 61